MEREDITH AND THE NOVEL

Also by Neil Roberts

GEORGE ELIOT: Her Beliefs and Her Art
THE LOVER, THE DREAMER AND THE WORLD: The Poetry of
Peter Redgrove
TED HUGHES: A Critical Study (*with Terry Gifford*)

Meredith and the Novel

Neil Roberts
Senior Lecturer in English
University of Sheffield

First published in Great Britain 1997 by
MACMILLAN PRESS LTD
Houndmills, Basingstoke, Hampshire RG21 6XS and London
Companies and representatives throughout the world

A catalogue record for this book is available from the British Library.

ISBN 0–333–67594–0

 First published in the United States of America 1997 by
ST. MARTIN'S PRESS, INC.,
Scholarly and Reference Division,
175 Fifth Avenue, New York, N.Y. 10010

ISBN 0–312–16535–8

Library of Congress Cataloging-in-Publication Data
Roberts, Neil.
Meredith and the novel / Neil Roberts.
p. cm.
Includes bibliographical references (p.   ) and index.
ISBN 0–312–16535–8 (cloth)
1. Meredith, George, 1828–1909—Criticism and interpretation.
2. Fiction—Authorship.   I. Title.
PR5014.R63   1997
823'.8—dc20   96–32087
                                                                         CIP

© Neil Roberts 1997

All rights reserved. No reproduction, copy or transmission of this publication may be made without written permission.

No paragraph of this publication may be reproduced, copied or transmitted save with written permission or in accordance with the provisions of the Copyright, Designs and Patents Act 1988, or under the terms of any licence permitting limited copying issued by the Copyright Licensing Agency, 90 Tottenham Court Road, London W1P 9HE.

Any person who does any unauthorised act in relation to this publication may be liable to criminal prosecution and civil claims for damages.

The author has asserted his rights to be identified as the author of this work in accordance with the Copyright, Designs and Patents Act 1988.

This book is printed on paper suitable for recycling and made from fully managed and sustained forest sources.

10 9 8 7 6 5 4 3 2 1
06 05 04 03 02 01 00 99 98 97

Printed in Great Britain by
The Ipswich Book Company Ltd
Ipswich, Suffolk

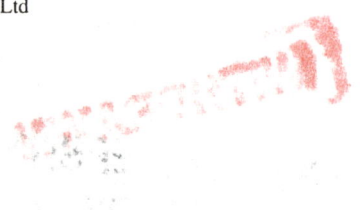

To the Memory of Jim McCabe, Teacher

Contents

List of Abbreviations		viii
Introduction		1
1	*The Ordeal of Richard Feverel*	13
2	The Novels of the 1860s	47
3	*The Adventures of Harry Richmond*	89
4	*Beauchamp's Career*	111
5	*The Egoist*	150
6	*The Tragic Comedians*	187
7	*Diana of the Crossways*	205
8	The Final Phase	230
Notes		254
Bibliography		276
Index		282

List of Abbreviations

AM:	The Amazing Marriage
BC:	Beauchamp's Career
DC:	Diana of the Crossways
E:	The Egoist
EH:	Evan Harrington
HR:	The Adventures of Harry Richmond
'IC':	'Essay on the Idea of Comedy and of the Uses of the Comic Spirit'
LOHA:	Lord Ormont and His Aminta
OOC:	One of Our Conquerors
ORF:	The Ordeal of Richard Feverel
RF:	Rhoda Fleming
SB:	Sandra Belloni
TC:	The Tragic Comedians
V:	Vittoria

Introduction

There has always been an element of provocation, scandal and unfinished business about Meredith's reputation. His earliest reviewers could not cope with the stylistic variation and genre-breaking formal innovation of a novel such as *The Ordeal of Richard Feverel*. At the height of his popularity, in the early 1890s, Oscar Wilde wrote that 'His style is chaos illumined by flashes of lightning. As a writer he has mastered everything except language; as a novelist he can do everything, except tell a story: as an artist he is everything except articulate.'[1] When his reputation was in decline, in the 1930s, Virginia Woolf offered an assessment that might have established him as a precursor of modernism, asserting that he was 'at great pains to destroy the conventional form of the novel. ... And what is done so deliberately is done with a purpose.... to prepare the way for a new and an original sense of the human scene.'[2] In the period of most intense recent critical attention, the early 1970s, one of his best modern critics, David Howard, described him as the 'most irritating novelist of nineteenth century', adding that 'if we ignore that capacity to irritate we are inventing a safe Meredith to argue about'.[3]

Allowing for the seductions of paradox, Wilde's description is a perceptive way into the often irritating but profoundly original world of Meredith's novelistic art. The irritation and the originality are the obverse and reverse sides of the sense of the *new* in art. What is, if not unique, then certainly highly unusual among major Victorian novelists, is that this sense of the new is still felt by readers encountering Meredith today. As Gillian Beer has said, he is 'a writer whom individuals discover with excitement for themselves'.[4] This excitement is like that of reading new work. The question of his place among his peers is complicated by the fact that the Brontës, Dickens, George Eliot, Hardy, James are, for the present at least, known quantities: Meredith is the unknown quantity that changes one's sense of the possibilities of the novel in the way that important new work does.

Consider Wilde's description in the light of Mikhail Bakhtin's account of the real life of language:

> any concrete discourse (utterance) finds the object at which it was directed already as it were overlain with qualifications, open to dispute, charged with value, already enveloped in an obscuring mist – or, on the contrary, by the 'light' of alien words that have already been spoken about it. It is entangled, shot through with shared thoughts, points of view, alien value judgements and accents. The word, directed toward its object, enters a dialogically agitated and tension-filled environment of alien words, value judgements and accents, weaves in and out of complex interrelationships, merges with some, recoils from others, intersects with yet a third group.[5]

This is one of Bakhtin's many highly metaphorical descriptions of what he calls heteroglossia, the many-voiced, already-uttered, already-intended, ideologically crowded character of language as it really exists in society, which cannot be adequately understood on the Saussurean model of a system of *langue* from which individuals produce the individual speech-acts of *parole* by a free process of combination.[6]

The fundamental idea of Bakhtin's poetics of the novel (or what Gary Morson and Caryl Emerson call 'prosaics')[7] is that '[the novelist] welcomes the heteroglossia and language diversity of the literary and extraliterary language into his own work not only not weakening them but even intensifying them'.[8] The novel, in other words, embraces a conflict-ridden linguistic diversity that may resemble Wilde's 'chaos'.[9] It is true that Bakhtin's novelist 'compels [words] to serve his own new intentions, to serve a second master',[10] but this mastery is of a peculiar kind. It is unlike Bakhtin's conception of the mastery of the poet who achieves a 'tension-filled unity of language' by 'stripping all aspects of language of the intentions and accents of other people, destroying all traces of social heteroglossia and diversity of language',[11] or of what he calls the 'monologic' author who *combines in his person a direct and fully competent ideological power to mean* with *individuality*, in such a way that *they do not weaken one another*'.[12]

The idea of Meredith as a self-conscious stylist whose prose is marked by idiosyncratic mannerisms that are everywhere present like a signature is misleading and invariably results in denigration.[13] There *are* certain distinctively Meredithian stylistic characteristics, which are well summarized by Margaret Conrow:

> It is generally non-periodic and deliberately abrupt in rhythm, made complex by isolated and sometimes incompatible images, by a lack of connectives and an emphasis on abstract and startling nouns. It is more particularly characterised by a peculiar use of articles, either omitted where one would expect to find them or substituted for the personal pronoun; by a great fondness for prepositions, either in an adverbial function or in a prepositional phrase, often used in preference to a verbal noun or verbal adjective, and particularly in strings of prepositional phrases; and by a tendency to use adjectives as nouns and occasionally to use transitive verbs intransitively.[14]

These could however be seen as evidence of an unstable relation to language, of an author who is not, in the most obvious sense, 'master' of it. Where Meredith *is* self-conscious about style, and *does* show mastery, is not in imposing his own stylistic personality on the text but in registering and organizing what Bakhtin calls the 'languages of heteroglossia'. He is less a stylist than a stylizer. This is abundantly evident in his first published fiction, *The Shaving of Shagpat*, a sustained pastiche of such intensity that, in the first edition, Meredith or his publisher thought it necessary to include a note anticipating that it 'may read like a translation' and 'an avowal that it springs from no Eastern source, and is in every respect an original Work'.[15] However, this is a work whose achievement is the *tour de force* of sustaining a single artificial style. Except as a remarkable linguistic trace of the mid-Victorian fascination with the Orient its stylization does not lead beyond itself. It is a huge artistic step from this kind of virtuoso performance to *The Ordeal of Richard Feverel* (*ORF*), in which Meredith is able by the finest subtleties of imitation and accentuation to represent and enter into dialogue with – or set in dialogue with each other – the numerous voices of the ideological environment with which the novel engages. This has often been noticed by modern critics: the 'artificial rhetorics'[16] analysed by Jacob Korg, the 'projected inner rhetoric'[17] of Donald Stone or the 'imagistic area between the character and the narrator's consciousness'[18] of Gillian Beer. Bakhtinian theory enables us to see this not just as a highly developed narratorial technique (anticipating such great modernists as

Joyce, Lawrence, Woolf and Mansfield) but as one of the keys to Meredith's representation and critique of (or dialogue with) various aspects of contemporary ideology.

Wilde's second paradox was that as a novelist Meredith could do everything except tell a story. Forster unpacked this paradox well in *Aspects of the Novel* (which unfortunately in other respects merely reflected and reinforced his generation's incomprehension of Meredith):

> A Meredithian plot is not a temple to the tragic or even to the comic Muse, but rather resembles a series of kiosks most artfully placed among wooded slopes, which his people reach by their own impetus, and from which they emerge with altered aspect. Incident springs out of character, and having occurred it alters that character.[19]

Richard Stang's study of the theory of the Victorian novel suggests that the early Victorians tended to think of plot and character separately, and of plot as a mechanical contrivance,[20] and Gillian Beer says that 'Conventional plot is, in [Meredith's] view, an invitation to conservatism.'[21] In the Victorian period 'conventional plot' above all means revelation, where plot hinges on what has always been the case, and resolution is a matter of coming to terms with this. Consider for example the importance of the hidden parentage motif in novels such as *Oliver Twist, Bleak House, Daniel Deronda* and *The Mayor of Casterbridge*, or such revelations as Bulstrode's past in *Middlemarch* or the identity of Pip's benefactor. Meredith never relies on devices such as this. His use of the hidden parentage motif in *Harry Richmond* typically subverts the conventional plot, since the truth about Richmond Roy's parentage is never explained: it is his obsession, not the fact, that is important. In *One of Our Conquerors*, the only novel in which the pre-diegetic past casts a shadow, the truth about Victor's marriage is in the open as far as the reader is concerned – there is no melodrama of the kind that infects even George Eliot when she uses the revelation plot – and it is Victor's present actions that determine his fate, not the already-decided past.

Plot is a function of genre and genres are, as Morson and Emerson say, 'the residue of past behaviour' which 'provide a specific field for future activity'. This activity is however not a mere 'repetition of a pattern.... [B]eginning with the given, something different must be created'.[22] This new activity is not an easy matter, any more than the struggle of discourse that is Bakhtin's central theme (of which, indeed, it is an aspect). It is of course an ideological matter – for example, as Allon White says, 'it is impossible to dissociate the formal difficulties of Meredith's work from the "feminist" content'.[23] Critics such as Kate Millett, Patricia Stubbs and Carolyn Williams have raised objections to the concluding marriages of Meredith's heroines, arguing that his commitment to feminism, genuine though it is, is compromised by such a plot resolution. This may seem to be a captious criticism, since (at least in the cases most at issue, *The Egoist* and *Diana of the Crossways*) Meredith takes pains to provide his heroine with an enlightened and devoted partner who has proved his worth, and the alternatives are celibacy or social ostracism. The real weakness of this line of criticism, however, is its failure to notice how aware Meredith is of the issue, and how it is written into his treatment of the marriage plot. However Meredith may have been, personally, committed to heterosexual fulfilment with marriage as its only realistic vehicle, he was aware of how the marriage plot is already written, countless times, in texts in which there is no question of any other kind of fulfilment for the heroine, and that it thus inevitably brings a conservative drag to any novel that uses it.

Exactly how this awareness is written into *The Egoist* and *Diana of the Crossways* is discussed at length in my chapters on those novels. My concern here is to make the general point that, when 'plot' is present as a discrete element in Meredith's novels it is typically *represented*, just as the language of which it is composed is represented – and for Bakhtin dialogism exists at the level of genre as well as the word.[24] Generic models – often competing models within a text, such as the novel of education and New Comedy in *Richard Feverel*, Romance and *Bildungsroman* in *Harry Richmond*, Molièrean comedy and the Richardsonian novel in *The Egoist* – are not taken for granted, but exposed to the reader's scrutiny, and to questioning. In *Diana of the Crossways* not merely a genre but the source story itself – a malicious rumour about Caroline Norton – is brought into question.

The stylistic features that Bakhtin claims are characteristic of the novel – what he variously calls double-voiced, dialogized or hybridized discourse; the deployment of a socially accented multiplicity of registers that he terms 'heteroglossia'; the 'polyphonic' organization of discourses that eliminates the dominance of the authorial voice;[25] the mixing and subversion of genres – are indeed so characteristic of the novel since the mid-nineteenth century that the 'application' of Bakhtinian theory can easily be a mechanical and pointless exercise. Few admirers of Meredith would hesitate to agree that he is, in these stylistic and formal respects, a Bakhtinian novelist par excellence: that dialogism in its many forms is exceptionally prominent in and crucial to his work. Such an argument, however, runs the danger of diminishing the importance of Bakhtin's ideas: of reducing a great sociocultural theory to a description of the performance of certain privileged texts.

Much of the analysis that follows will, inevitably, focus on Meredith's 'performance', on matters of style and form. But the illumination that the study of Bakhtin brings to the works of Meredith – the vital connection, even, that exists between the two writers – is not and cannot be confined to such matters. As Bakhtin/Voloshinov writes in *Marxism and the Philosophy of Language*, 'A word in the mouth of a particular individual person is a product of the living interaction of social forces.'[26] This fact is manifested in Meredith's novels at a variety of levels which, in their interaction, generate the peculiar energy and life of the texts.

At the level of the individual character's 'word', language in Meredith is highly differentiated and, in the case of his most important characters, constitutes a 'discourse' that can function in the novel independently of the particular character it is attached to, and enter into dialogue with other such discourses. This is a phenomenon that Bakhtin calls 'character zone'. Such discourse is typically a locus of significant 'social forces'. In *Beauchamp's Career* (*BC*) Cecilia Halkett's father tells her that '"Women must not be judging things out of their sphere," with the familiar accent on "women" which proves their inferiority' (*BC*, 32, 365). Such a 'word' frequently inscribes a 'social force' into a character's discourse in a way that is not in itself particularly remarkable. The word, with its accent, however, passes into the consciousness of his daughter who is unable to advise the man she loves at a crisis in his life because 'she was one of the artificial creatures called women (with the accent)' (*BC*, 32, 366).

'"Women" (with the accent)' is a simple but nonetheless powerful example of social forces acting coercively through language in the concrete context of a father–daughter relationship. Note that Meredith does not need to describe the 'accent': such pointing to something too familiar to need description, in the world surrounding the text, is typical of his novels' immersion in that world. Another example is the narrator's comment on Bella Mount's life-story: 'A woman's history, you know: certain chapters expunged' (*ORF*, 38, 443). At a much more elaborate level the discourse both of the narrator and of the characters may be an 'image' of a recognizable style, author or even specific text. So, the remarkable passage of free indirect discourse explaining Cecilia's inability to act, from which I have quoted, is a close imitation of a particular passage from Mill's 'The Subjection of Women'. Mill's analysis of women's internalization of their oppression, translated into the inner discourse of a potentially rebellious Tory heiress afflicted by the sound of ' "women" (with the accent)' in her father's mouth, becomes *dramatized*, and the liberal discourse, placed here and in this intimate relation to hostile social forces, rather than attributed to a didactic narrator, is immeasurably enriched. (See Chapter 4, pp. 123–5, for more detailed discussion of these passages.)

Meredith's reputation has suffered from the prestige of his great rival Henry James, which has given widespread currency to James's remark that in Meredith 'the artist was nothing to the good citizen and the liberalised bourgeois'.[27] This study by contrast is committed to the contention that in Meredith the artist was nothing *without* the good citizen and liberalized bourgeois. Certainly Meredith was as conscious as James of the demands of art and the dangers of subduing art to polemic: see for example the letter in which he lampooned Frederick Maxse's suggestion that he write 'one volume novels on Questions of the Day'[28] (discussed in Chapter 4). In his case, however, this consciousness had to grapple with an equally developed social commitment. If Meredith seems, in literary history, a stranded writer, passages such as Cecilia's inner discourse suggest that this might be because he was the precursor of a modernism that never happened in this country – a liberal, socially committed modernism.

For Bakhtin the essence of the stylistics of the novel is the presentation of the image of a language. Meredith not only does this with his immense array of imitations, stylizations, parodies and character zones, but also constantly makes it a theme. His characters constantly quote each other and reflect on the style as well as the substance of each other's utterances. This is the main function of the numerous 'interpolated genres' in Meredith's novels. The aphorisms of Sir Austin Feverel and Mrs Mountstuart Jenkinson, the letters of Beauchamp and Shrapnel, the conversation and novels of Diana Warwick, Colney Durance's satire and Gower Woodseer's journal are not only cited by the narrator but also commented on and criticized by the characters. In many cases, most notably in *Beauchamp's Career* where the social control of discourse is a central theme, the original text is not cited directly but disappears in its reaccentuation – usually hostile – in the words of another.

The relation of Meredith's novels to 'the agitated and tension-filled environment of alien words' is not merely one of representation. In 1859 *The Ordeal of Richard Feverel* was banned by Mudie's circulating library – the most important channel for the dissemination of fiction – and its generic unorthodoxy condemned by critics. For at least the next decade Meredith struggled unsuccessfully to reconcile his artistic priorities with various formulae for popular success. It was not until 1885, with the publication of *Diana of the Crossways*, that he was granted widespread recognition, and by this time the habit of considering himself an unappreciated writer was too ingrained to shed. For the whole of the period in question Meredith, unlike James, had no unearned income and a family to support. For many years he had to supplement his literary income by reading manuscripts for Chapman and Hall, mercenary journalism (for the Tory *Ipswich Journal* – a curious instance of 'double-voiced discourse') and even reading aloud to an old lady. From the vain attempts to imitate currently popular modes in early novels such as *Evan Harrington* (*EH*) and *Rhoda Fleming* to the arguably defiant indulgence in unrestrained obscurity in the late *One of Our Conquerors*, his work is scored through with an at best uneasy and at worst inimical relation to the reading public. L.G. Hergenhan, who made a study of the reception of Meredith's early novels, argued that he was 'the first major novelist to find himself more or less permanently cut off from the general reading public', the first example of what Q.D. Leavis called the 'highbrow novelist, who, unlike the merely serious novelists of the past...set out to develop the possibilities of his medium for ends outside the understanding of the ordinary reader'.[29] The context of this phenomenon has been ably explored by Peter Keating.[30] David Howard goes so far as to argue that in *Rhoda Fleming*, where Meredith was trying to write a popular novel to be published by a popular publisher, the thematic preoccupation with money echoes the novel's actual place in the world.[31] It follows that the generic dialogism of such novels, in which a popular vein often seems to be simultaneously intended and subverted, and the dialogues between mutually antagonistic narrators, most explicit in *Sandra Belloni* and *The Amazing Marriage*, are not mere options, epiphenomena in the aesthetic sphere, but aspects of the books' real existence in society.

This kind of relationship to the potential answering word Bakhtin theorizes as 'hidden polemic' or 'sideward glance'. This is one of the most original ways in which Bakhtin explores the permeation of discourse by the words of others – here extending to words not yet spoken. Discussing Dostoevsky's early novel *Poor Folk* he observes that 'The word "kitchen" bursts into Devushkin's speech from out of the other's potential speech.'[32] Similarly, in *One of Our Conquerors* (*OOC*), the word 'punctilio', once heard in the mouth of a hostile workman, bursts into the speech of Victor Radnor, as if to forestall its use by a friend (*OOC*, 3, 24). In such episodes Meredith is dramatizing a fundamental quality of his own relation to the language of others: compare the narrator's outburst in *Sandra Belloni* (*SB*), 'I need not be told what odium frowns on such a pretention to excess of cleverness' (*SB*, 13, 110–11), which reacts to the word of a reviewer of an earlier book and anticipates its use again by critics of *this* book (see Chapter 2, p. 262, n. 34). This is only a small-scale and explicit instance of a relationship to the 'answering word' that everywhere shapes Meredith's style and the generic form of his novels.

To this I should add a comment on the author's real existence in society. Like most great English novelists Meredith was lower middle class, the son of a tailor. Like many writers with such a social formation he is accused of being, and perhaps was, a snob. Even as a young boy he was facetiously known as 'Gentleman Georgy'.[33] But real or apparent snobbery may be a manifestation of intense awareness of linguistic and other codes on the part of a person of insecure or borderline status in a stratified society. Such a person *lives* heteroglossia, perhaps more than any other, and it is relevant to Bakhtin's theory of the novel that so many English novelists of this period had this kind of social formation.

Equally important is the unorthodox and miscellaneous nature of Meredith's education. He received his most significant schooling in Germany at a school run by Moravian Brethren. One consequence of this is that among his contemporaries he is matched only by George Eliot in his awareness of European culture. Judith Wilt argues that the 'spasmodic' and in part 'autodidactic' nature of his education fostered a style that Bakhtin would have called heteroglot:

> mixing concepts from nineteenth-century science, philosophy, religion, politics and even street-lore with fragments of French and German literature, Celtic locutions and Latin epigram.... [H]e hopped among the mixed contents of his mind with a facility and audacity at times equally irritating to the man in the street and the graduate of Oxford.[34]

I have tried to show that 'the living interaction of social forces' in Meredith's personal formation fostered a peculiar sensitivity to heteroglossia; that the social forces operating on his novels through their real existence in the world had a profound effect on their style and form; that the social control of discourse – the ideological field that the novels literally enter – is one of their central themes; and that an acutely critical consciousness of discourse, from generic form to the single word uttered 'with the accent' results in an art of stylization that is always responsible and, at its best, a brilliant orchestration of the 'interaction of social forces' at all these levels.

I want to conclude this introduction with some further and miscellaneous comments on my use of Bakhtin. It will already be evident that I make frequent use of the word 'discourse'. The translators of *The Dialogic Imagination* use this word to translate the Russian *slovo*, which can also be translated as 'word'. The simplicity of 'word' is seductive, but its frequent use in English to signify more than a single lexical item would be an affectation. Emerson and Holquist gloss Bakhtin's *slovo* in several ways but conclude that 'it is more often than not his more diffuse way of insisting on the primacy of speech, utterance, all *in praesentia* aspects of language'.[35] In other words, it has a crucial role in his polemic against the primacy of *langue* in Saussurean linguistics. It is in this spirit that I use the word, but I have at times succumbed to the need for variety and used 'language' in the same sense: it would be artificial to write as if this word always meant the same as the French *langue*.

Conversely, readers of this study will notice that I make very sparing reference to one of Bakhtin's most influential concepts, carnival, or to the book in which he announced it, *Rabelais and His World*. A number of commentators have questioned Bakhtin's utopian idealization of carnival, his blindness to its uglier aspects, such as anti-semitism, and his indiscriminate praise of Rabelais. My own unease with this aspect of Bakhtin's work is epitomized by the opening of Chapter 3 of *Rabelais and His World*, concerning Pantagruel's visit to the island of the Catchpoles, and his relish for passages such as the following:

> They laid on so heartily that blood spurted from his mouth, nose, ears and eyes. Catchpole was beaten to a pulp; his shoulders dislocated; his head, neck, back and breast pounded into mincemeat.[36]

Bakhtin describes passages like this as 'gay thrashings and abuse'.[37] This squeamishness on my part should not however be taken as a refutation of those critics who have seen connections between Meredith's comedy and the carnivalesque.[38] Nor does my scepticism about the carnivalesque extend to the profound and influential writing about the body in Chapters 5 and 6 of *Rabelais and His World*, to which I make reference in my chapter on *Diana of the Crossways*.[39]

Another term which is central to my analysis is 'intertextuality'. This term was coined by Julia Kristeva in her essay 'Word, Dialogue and Novel', which played an important role in the introduction of Bakhtin to Western readers: 'any text is constructed as a mosaic of quotations; any text is the absorption and transformation of another. The notion of *intertextuality* replaces that of intersubjectivity, and poetic language is read as at least *double*.'[40] However, the opposition posited here reads Bakhtin as a French post-structuralist. Its resonance can be detected in Barthes's essay 'From Work to Text':

> The intertextual in which every text is held, it itself being the text-between of another text, is not to be confused with some origin of the text...; the citations which go to make up a text are anonymous, untraceable, and yet *already read*: they are quotations without inverted commas,[41]

in which can also be heard an echo of Bakhtin's phrase, 'intonational quotation marks'. Both Kristeva's opposition of intertextuality and intersubjectivity, and Barthes's assertion that the citations that make up a text are 'anonymous, untraceable', seem to me alien to Bakhtin. In the late essay 'The Problem of the Text' he writes explicitly of 'the meeting of two texts – of the ready-made and the reactive text being created – and, consequently, the meeting of two subjects and two authors'.[42] Much as Bakhtin may insist on the discursive character of subjectivity – as Bakhtin/Voloshinov writes, *'the inner psyche is not analyzable as a thing but can only be understood and interpreted as a sign'*[43] – this does not entail the cancellation of one term by the other. Bakhtinian intertextuality is defined in his assertion that 'The authentic environment of an utterance, the environment in which it lives and takes shape, is dialogized heteroglossia, anonymous and social as language, but simultaneously concrete, filled with specific content and accented as an individual utterance',[44] and my use of the word should be understood in the light of this definition. Barthes stops short of the second part of the definition. His 'intertextual' is an undifferentiated, *Bouvard et Pécuchet*-like *langue* of received ideas. This would be incompatible with Bakhtin's central contention about Dostoevsky, that 'His form-shaping worldview does not know an *impersonal truth*, and in his works there are no detached, impersonal verities.'[45]

1
The Ordeal of Richard Feverel

The Ordeal of Richard Feverel has attracted more critical commentary than any other novel by Meredith; it is, with *The Egoist* (E), one of the two novels that have continued to be read by more than a small band of enthusiasts. Yet it has caused more consternation to readers than any other of Meredith's works. There was, for contemporary reviewers, the issue of 'some of the most unflinching sketches of immorality that the pen of a modern Englishman has ventured to draw',[1] and the resulting suspicion that the author's 'mind is not of the purest',[2] with the disastrous consequence that, in Meredith's own words, 'I have offended Mudie and the British Matron. He will not, or haply, dare not put me in his advertised catalogue.'[3]

The banning by Mudie is more pertinent to Meredith's subsequent development than to *Feverel* itself. Of more interest to modern readers of this novel, because more persistent, are the generic challenges that it presents. Samuel Lucas, a sympathetic critic who defended Meredith against accusations of 'impurity', thought the whole of the novel after the marriage of Richard and Lucy a 'faulty remnant', and the conclusion a 'catastrophe in defiance of poetical justice'.[4] The most perceptive of Meredith's early critics, Justin McCarthy, in a retrospective essay of 1864, wrote of the catastrophe that 'the course of the story does not lead us to expect anything of the kind, while its whole construction does lead us to expect a harmonious and dramatic conclusion' and that for this reason the novel 'assuredly forfeits some of its legitimate influence'.[5]

J.B. Priestley repeats the complaint after Meredith's death, in respect both of this novel and of *Beauchamp's Career*: 'It mars the tale...because it is out of key, like a splash of black or crimson oil paint in a water-colour';[6] and it returns with renewed force in the 1960s, with all the dogmatic authority of the New Criticism. The classic instance is John W. Morris's essay, characteristically titled 'Inherent Principles of Order in *Richard Feverel*', which asserts that because the eponymous inherent principles – 'generic archetype (New Comedy), harmony of parts...and the metaphoric base of the language' – do not 'finally determine the form, the book fails to realize its artistic potential'.[7]

The best critics of the novel have been those who have recognized that some other criterion than order, harmony and a narrowly conceived unity is necessary to explain the distinctive arousal that *Richard Feverel* is capable of creating in its readers. At their head stands Virginia Woolf, and her often cited recognition that Meredith was 'at great pains to destroy the conventional form of the novel.... And what is done so deliberately is done with a purpose...to prepare the way for a new and an original sense of the human scene'.[8] Gillian Beer remarks that Morris's approach is 'to flatten and resolve precisely what is energetic and equivocal in Meredith's handling of plot', and that 'Meredith is not just repeating well-known literary forms...; he invokes them as emblems, as possible but limited ways of looking at his world.... He counterpoints literary patterns against life.'[9] Sven-Johan Spånberg, in an excellent and infrequently cited intertextual study of the novel, writes that Meredith 'uses similarities only to set off differences and to emphasise that his novel is utterly unlike anything the reading public had come to expect', and that the novel is 'based on a consistent repudiation of genre and convention'.[10] Such critics also recognize the dialogic character of Meredith's style: Beer writes that 'a multitude of points of view are presented, values shift, and the narrator's relationship to his characters is devious and inconstant'[11] – a perception developed by Jacob Korg in one of the best essays published on the novel:

> There is no single narrative voice, no single impression to be conveyed by it, no sense of a consistent world view or authorial personality. Instead we encounter a procession of occasionally recurrent artificial styles staging a performance that anticipates Joyce's *Ulysses*....Its first function is that of embodying the various states of mind represented in the novel in parodistic style laced with irony so subtle that it often escapes detection.[12]

All of these critics, especially Korg, anticipate a Bakhtinian approach, and more recently Donald D. Stone, in the most substantial discussion of Meredith and Bakhtin to date, has remarked that 'Like Pushkin's *Eugene Onegin*...*Richard Feverel* might be called "an encyclopedia of the styles and languages of the epoch".[13]

The novel opens by describing the publication and reception of 'The Pilgrim's Scrip', a 'selection of original aphorisms' by the father of the eponymous hero, Sir Austin Feverel. The provenance of these aphorisms, and their citational character, will be discussed later. What is immediately apparent to readers of the novel is that the first example given, 'I expect that Woman will be the last thing civilized by Man', is presented as Bakhtin would say 'on display',[14] as 'an example of his ideas of the sex', by an ironically distanced narrator; in the first edition several more aphorisms were presented in this way,[15] but the two other extracts cited in the revised text are presented as confirmations of points made by the narrator, with no such distance. This ambivalent method of citation continues throughout the novel, epitomizing the unstable relationship between narrator and character.

The first narrator's discourse that we hear is a detached, ironic voice that many readers take for the unmediated voice of Meredith as author, since it recurs frequently:

There was a half-sigh floating through his pages for those days of intellectual coxcombry, when ideas come to us affecting the embraces of virgins, and swear to us they are ours alone, and no one else have they ever visited: and we believe them. (1, 1)

Even a reader familiar with the Bakhtinian concept of character zones could be excused for not recognizing that the tone of this is at least partly that of a character who has not yet been introduced. A character zone is 'the field of action for a character's voice, encroaching in one way or another upon the author's voice', a 'sphere that extends – and often quite far – beyond the boundaries of the direct discourse allotted to him'.[16] It is not until seven pages later (three chapters in the first edition) that we are introduced to Adrian Harley, Richard's cousin and tutor who 'had no intimates except Gibbon and Horace, and the society of these fine aristocrats of literature helped him to accept humanity as it had been, and was; a supreme ironic procession, with laughter of Gods in the background' (1, 8). The narrator is able to turn irony on Adrian, and objectify him, as with the comment that he 'had mastered his philosophy at the early age of one-and-twenty. Many would be glad to say the same at that age twice-told: they carry in their breasts a burden with which Adrian's was not loaded' (1, 9). Frank D. Curtin has commented that Adrian 'writes and talks like Meredith, and yet he remains in character'.[17] He represents 'the limits of Meredith's comedy'. Thus he can frequently combine with the voice of the Meredithian narrator who, however, knows and can speak beyond those limits.[18]

The summarized narration of Sir Austin's marital catastrophe, which in the revised edition follows almost immediately, is in another voice:

> The outline of the baronet's story was by no means new. He had a wife, and he had a friend. His marriage was for love; his wife was a beauty; his friend was a sort of poet. His wife had his whole heart, and his friend all his confidence....
>
> A languishing, inexperienced woman, whose husband in mental and in moral stature is more than the ordinary height above her, and who, now that her first romantic admiration of his lofty bearing has worn off, and her fretful little refinements of taste and sentiment are not instinctively responded to, is thrown into no wholesome household collision with a fluent man, fluent in prose and rhyme. (1, 2–3; my ellipsis)

Again, this is not unmediated authorial narration or even that of an impersonal narrator securely outside the diegesis. There is a shadow of stylization over both paragraphs. The account begins with a defensive-dismissive assertion of the familiarity of the story, a gesture towards an implied Barthesian *endoxa* about wives and friends, so much a received idea that it does not need to be stated. This sense of not needing to state the obvious is continued in the following sentences, each one of which trails, as it were, a row of dots leading to the unstated conclusion, implied by the combination of laconic gruffness and rocking-horse antithesis. This sense of the 'obvious' is a defence against investigation into the *particular* reasons for Sir Austin's marital catastrophe.

The stylization in the second paragraph is quite different, but congruent. Here we have a long sentence, which conceals beneath a superficial periodic control a telling inconsistency of tone. In the opening phrase, 'a languishing, inexperienced woman', the second adjective might just confer a sympathetic accent on the first, to carry the reader over the personal insult and misogynistic undertow of 'whose husband in mental and moral stature...'. The reader might thus be able to entertain the idea that 'now that her first romantic admiration of his lofty bearing has worn off' reflects as much on him as on her, only to be rebuffed by the sneer of 'her fretful little refinements of taste and sentiment'. The sentence attempts to recover its poise with the sonorous litotes, 'thrown into no wholesome household collision', but it is likely to sound merely pompous, and reinforce any unfavourable impression the reader has formed.[19]

Both paragraphs voice a haughty repulsion of sympathetic and/or critical interest on the part of the addressee. If one imagines them spoken, one has to attribute the intention of stunning any incipient reply. This is not at all the voice of a reader-friendly narrator. There is only one possible subject of such an utterance: the injured cuckold himself; and, indeed, the extensive portrayal of Sir Austin throughout the novel is of a man who deforms his passions into simulacra of principles, repels sympathy, and affects a stoical superiority, with tragic consequences for those who are closest to him. In fact these characteristics of Sir Austin, encoded as it were in his character zone, are almost immediately portrayed in action, when an unlucky nursemaid surprises him weeping over his baby son:

> One night she was strangely aroused by a sound of sobbing. The baronet stood beside the cot in his long black coat and travelling cap. His fingers shaded a lamp, and reddened against the fitful darkness that ever and anon went leaping up the wall. She could hardly believe her senses to see the austere gentleman, dead silent, dropping tear upon tear before her eyes. She lay stone-still in a trance of terror and mournfulness, mechanically counting the tears as they fell, one by one. The hidden face, the fall and flash of those heavy drops in the light of the lamp he held, the upright, awful figure, agitated at regular intervals like a piece of clockwork by the low murderous catch of his breath: it was so piteous to her poor human nature that her heart began wildly palpitating. Involuntarily the poor girl cried out to him, 'Oh, sir!' and fell a-weeping. Sir Austin turned the lamp on her pillow, and harshly bade her go to sleep, striding from the room forthwith. He dismissed her with a purse the next day. (1, 4–5)

Even here we do not have a monologic authorial discourse. Polly does not become a 'character' until much later in the novel, but it is not difficult to detect traces of her voice in the simpler, more naive style of, for example, the fourth sentence quoted. However, unlike the previous example, there is no dialogic *angle*: the narrator is wholly sympathetic to Polly, sees through and feels with her, there is no irony or objectification in his borrowing of her speech (unusual for lower-class speech in Meredith). One might even say that his speech is chastened by hers. As Bakhtin says of Dostoevsky, 'even *agreement* retains its *dialogic* character, that is, it never leads to a *merging* of voices and truths in a single *impersonal* truth, as occurs in the monologic world'.[20]

At this point in our analysis it will be helpful to pause and consider *why* Meredith wrote the novel like this. Korg, Beer and many others have recognized that Meredith at least anticipated some of the main developments of the modernist novel. He did this in a book published in the same year as *Adam Bede*, a major advance in English realism, but not within hearing distance of modernism – he overleaped realism before it had consummated itself in Eliot's later work. As Spånberg has said, Meredith was not trying to write 'a novel with a purpose'.[21] Throughout his career he strove for ways to articulate what Bakhtin called 'unfinalizability'. Allon White theorized this fairly evident empirical observation as follows: 'He is witness to a "legitimation crisis" in which the traditional, easily assumed mantle of single author/ity would no longer quite fit', and this is partly 'a result of a rapid transformation in the relationship between reader and writer and, correlatively, a destabilized conception of what constitutes one's public and private self'.[22]

How did Meredith experience this crisis? The date of *Richard Feverel*, its thematic content, and the suddenness of its emergence against the background of Meredith's earlier work combine to suggest, as White goes on to show, that it was experienced overwhelmingly through the breakdown of his first marriage. As a married man whose wife had left him for his friend, and borne that friend's child, he was experiencing the most painful kind of 'legitimation crisis', involving the most practical 'destabilized conception of what constitutes one's public and private self'. And all this, of course, concerned an institution that was at the heart of Victorian ideology. There is little reliable biographical evidence about the marriage, though the openly speculative approach of Diane Johnson's *Lesser Lives* is provocative. We can however say with some assurance that Meredith behaved, *and continued to behave after the publication of the novel,* in a way distressingly like Sir Austin, maintaining a haughty reticence, refusing to see his wife when she was dying, and even alleging that she was mad. Moreover his relations with his son, after a few years, became distant and difficult. In the novel Sir Austin's disillusioned admirer Lady Blandish reads in his notebook, 'There is no more grievous sight, as there is no greater perversion, than a wise man at the mercy of his feelings', and reflects, 'He must have written it...when he had himself for an example – strange man that he is!' (44, 537) It is hard to believe that the application to himself can have escaped Meredith.

It is conversely only too easy to believe that when he wrote the novel the 'mantle of single author/ity would no longer quite fit' the writer whose patriarchal 'mantle' had been so rudely snatched away. We have seen that the authorial narrator combines with Sir Austin, the character whose experience, and possibly personality, most closely matches Meredith's at the time of writing. At the same time this character is fiercely satirized and ruthlessly exposed. The temptation of ironic detachment, or the affectation of it, is also both courted by the narrative voice and objectified in the character of Adrian. It has been suggested by Phyllis Bartlett that the ironic portrayal of Richard's 'chivalric' attitude to women is a repudiation of Meredith's earlier attitude to women in general and to Mary in particular.[23] However this may be, Bartlett conclusively showed that Meredith attributed his own early poetry not only to Richard but also to Sir Austin's false friend Diaper Sandoe: an intertextual relationship that complicates the apparently self-indulgent contempt with which Sandoe is portrayed. Bakhtin says of Dostoevsky, 'the genuine life of the personality takes place at the point of non-coincidence between a man and himself'.[24] For Bakhtin this is a universal truth: for the author of *Richard Feverel*, both as man and as author, it has a very particular application.

Gary Morson and Caryl Emerson, in their study of Bakhtin, comment that his own examples of 'hybrid discourse' in the novel are relatively simple, and argue that this is because 'The most complicated examples of hybridized discourse develop and accumulate over the course of a novel, and unless the critic discusses the particular character zones *as* they are being established, their presence in later passages is likely to be invisible.'[25] We have seen simple instances of the 'character zones' of Sir Austin and Adrian. Now let us examine some slightly more complex examples. Here are the two in dialogue, in Adrian's free indirect discourse, on the occasion of his gleeful announcement of Richard's marriage to members of the family:

> The women were the crowning joy of his contemplative mind. He had reserved them for his final discharge. Dear demonstrative creatures! Dyspepsia would not weaken their poignant outcries, or self-interest check their fainting fits [unlike the male relatives]. On the generic woman one could calculate. Well might THE PILGRIM'S SCRIP say of her that, 'She is always at Nature's breast'; not intending it as a compliment. Each woman is Eve throughout the ages; whereas the PILGRIM would have us believe that the Adam in men has become warier, if no wiser; and weak as he is, has learnt a lesson from time. Probably the Pilgrim's meaning may be taken to be, that Man grows, and Woman does not. (32, 328)

This is a dialogue between two variants of cynicism. However, the dialogue is not explicit, and may not be heard if the reader does not register the *voices* at work. There is an obvious difference of style between Adrian's flippant, dandyish delight in the 'dear demonstrative creatures' and Sir Austin's aphoristic gravity. But this is the expression of a more profound difference. Sir Austin's misogyny entails, as we have seen, a fixed belief in the superiority of men. This is registered here in 'the PILGRIM would have us believe that the Adam in men has become warier, if no wiser'. Adrian is equally misogynistic, and his ironic detachment does not detach him from some of the crassest clichés of his period. However, as we have seen, his cynicism is universal, and his citation of Sir Austin's belief in Man's progress entails an implicit reservation, or even dissent, which only a prior knowledge of his 'voice' can fully alert the reader to.

In the first phase of the novel, which the narrator follows Adrian in calling 'The Bakewell Comedy', concerning Richard's juvenile exploit of setting fire to a neighbouring farmer's hayrick, we hear Adrian's voice reflecting on Sir Austin's custom of watching over the members of his household, especially his son, at night:

> A monomaniac at large, watching over sane people in slumber! thinks Adrian Harley, as he hears Sir Austin's footfall, and truly that was a strange object to see. – Where is the fortress that has

not one weak gate? where the man who is sound at each particular angle? Ay, meditates the recumbent cynic, more or less mad is not every mother's son? Favourable circumstances – good air, good company, two or three good rules rigidly adhered to – keep the world out of Bedlam. But, let the world fly into a passion, and is not Bedlam the safest abode for it? (4, 32)

Most of this could be put in quotation marks (and, in fact, was in the first edition), but their absence reinforces the 'choric' character of, at least, the opening observation. It is noteworthy that Lady Blandish, a much more sympathetic and 'reliable' character than Adrian, does not pronounce Sir Austin 'mad and wicked' until Chapter 38, the chapter in which Bella Mount's seduction puts the seal on the egotistical folly of Sir Austin's treatment of Richard. Lady Blandish's judgement, however, has been clouded by attachments – by the 'burden' from which Adrian is free. After this opening observation there is a looseness about Adrian's thoughts and about the narrator's relation to them – as if he too is 'recumbent' – which might smack of irresponsibility if it were not for the strikingly contrasting passage that follows a few pages later:

[Sir Austin] was half disposed to arrest the two conspirators [Richard and Ripton] on the spot, and make them confess, and absolve themselves; but it seemed to him better to keep an unseen eye over his son: Sir Austin's old system prevailed.

Adrian characterized this system well, in saying that Sir Austin wished to be Providence to his son.

If immeasurable love were perfect wisdom, one human being might almost impersonate Providence to another. Alas! love, divine as it is, can do no more than lighten the house it inhabits – must take its shape, sometimes intensify its narrowness – can spiritualize, but not expel, the old lifelong lodgers above-stairs and below.

Sir Austin decided to continue quiescent. (4, 35–36)

Here Meredith draws on Adrian for an observation that is, as we shall see, at the heart of the novel, of its generic and intertextual dialogism. It relates to the later ironic remark that Sir Austin is not Prospero, and to two of the most significant putative generic models, *Emile* and *Wilhelm Meister*. Here, however, in contrast to the previous example, the elaboration of the observation is in a style markedly different from Adrian's character zone. The heartfelt earnestness of the ensuing paragraph is in fact so unlike Adrian that, despite the approval just expressed, it could almost be voiced as a rebuke to him. Such a possibility, however, is available only to a reader who can hear Adrian's voice at this point, for whom it echoes as an incongruous contrast to the tones we are actually hearing. We might think that here, if it is possible at all in this novel, we have 'direct authorial' discourse. But the final sentence of the extract, a brief sentence isolated in a paragraph of its own, links Sir Austin to the foregoing passage in a peculiar way. The implication is that his decision is consequent upon the thoughts that have just been expressed: as if, while we can not perhaps imagine him to have spoken them, he has heard them, as if they were voiced *for* if not *by* him.

'Character zones' are most easily recognizable in the free indirect or direct discourse of the character in question. Such effects can be described in terms of conventional narratology.[26] Of more interest to dialogical analysis is the occurrence of a character zone in the narrator's discourse, without the grammatical markers of free indirect discourse, and even remote from any direct reference to the character concerned. Such are the examples that I have discussed from Chapter 1 of *Richard Feverel*. Most difficult to detect, and probably quite unusual, would be the occurrence of one character's 'zone' in *another character's* free indirect discourse. Such, however, is the following example, which occurs in the chapter of Richard's seduction by Bella Mount:

> Though this lady never expressed an idea, Richard was not mistaken in her cleverness. She could make evenings pass gaily, and one was not the fellow to the other. She could make you forget she was a woman, and then bring the fact startlingly home to you. She could read men with one quiver of her half-closed eye-lashes. She could catch the coming mood in a man, and fit herself to it. What does a woman want with ideas, who can do thus much? Keenness of perception, conformity, delicacy of handling, these be all the qualities necessary to parasites. (38, 442–3)

Most of this passage is in a style peculiar to Richard's relations with Bella – which enters the novel only when those relations begin. It is an example of Meredith's ability to register the 'psychic sexual sphere' which, according to Peter Cominos, was virtually 'non-existent' to the Victorians.[27] It is markedly different from the frank idyllic sexuality of Richard's relations with Lucy. It is perhaps not until the final word, 'parasites', that one becomes aware of another voice in the passage, but once one becomes aware of it, it re-accents at least the last two sentences, so that they sound like a quotation from the 'Pilgrim's Scrip'. The word 'be' rather than 'are' in the final sentence gives it an archaic formality more suitable to a self-conscious aphorism than to the free-running interior discourse of the foregoing passage. The whole of Richard's 'psychic sexual sphere' with Bella becomes coloured by Sir Austin's misogyny. And this happens at a peculiarly double-edged moment, when Richard is paradoxically both flouting and confirming his father's system – the paradox deriving from Sir Austin's own perversity. He has brought his son up to be above all sexually pure, and there can be no doubt that he is about to commit an act of impurity – adultery with a courtesan. However, in his father's eyes Richard has already breached the system by marrying Lucy; Richard is in this dangerous situation with Bella because of an unholy and unconscious alliance between his father's pride, keeping him waiting in London, and Lord Mountfalcon's machination, setting Bella on to seduce him. There is a perverse satisfaction available to Sir Austin in Richard's rebellion coming to this. Moreover, we see that Richard's inheritance of his father's misogyny has caused him not only to underestimate Lucy (which is well documented) but also to patronize Bella: the combination of the two is fatal to him.

When Lady Blandish warns Richard about his association with Bella she says, 'Have you forgotten you have a wife?' to which Richard answers, 'Do you think I love any one but Lucy? poor little thing!' (38, 437) 'To have his wife and the world thrown at his face, was unendurable to Richard. ... Charming Sir Julius [Bella dressed as a man], always gay, always honest, dispersed his black moods' (38, 438). This deceptive impression of honesty is a dialogic gift for adapting her speech and moving among the various stereotypes by which men will inevitably see her. It casts a shadow on Lucy, who has no such gift:

> She told him of her history when this soft horizon of repentance seemed to throw heaven's twilight across it. A woman's history, you know: certain chapters expunged. It was dark enough to Richard. (38, 443)

The image of 'heaven's twilight' beautifully conveys the way the face-saving obscurity of Bella's narrative seems virtuous to the sheltered Richard. The passage has a strong orientation towards a masculine addressee who is expected to fill in the expunged chapters from his own experience, and understand the limits of what can be said. The final sentence excludes Richard from this masculine company that understands without being told. The following dialogue comes soon after:

> 'You had some affection for him? He was the first?'
> She chose to admit that. 'Yes. And the first who talks of love to a girl must be a fool if he doesn't blind her'.
> 'That makes what is called first love nonsense'.
> 'Isn't it?'
> He repelled the insinuation. 'Because I know it is not, Bella'.
> Nevertheless she had opened a wider view of the world to him, and a colder. He thought poorly of girls. A woman – a sensible, brave, beautiful woman seemed, on comparison, infinitely nobler than those weak creatures.
> She was best in her character of lovely rebel accusing foul injustice. 'What am I to do? You tell me to be different. How can I? What am I to do? Will virtuous people let me earn my bread? I could not get a housemaid's place!... Do you expect me to bury myself alive? Why, man, I have blood: I can't become a stone. You say I am honest, and I will be. Then let me tell you that I have been used to luxuries, and I can't do without them.' (38, 444)

Bella does not conform to the stereotype of the fallen woman, but nor does she conform to the alternative stereotype by which Richard judges her here, to contrast with the equally inaccurate stereotype of Lucy. To break the charm that Bella has over Richard – and perhaps over the reader – the narrator has recourse to Adrian's character zone:

> His casus belli, accurately worded, would have read curiously. Because the world refused to lure the lady to virtue with the offer of a housemaid's place, our knight threw down his challenge. But the lady had scornfully rebutted this prospect of a return to chastity. Then the form of the challenge must be: Because the world declined to support the lady in luxury for nothing! But what did that mean? In other words: she was to

receive the devil's wages without rendering him her services. (ibid., p. 445)

The rather arch irony of, in particular, the first two sentences, is precisely the tone of Adrian, or the tone that the narrator shares with Adrian. In other words it is a voice whose disillusion is grounded in cynicism and misogyny. To identify it thus is to place it as a voice in dialogue with Bella's, and with Richard's in response to Bella, and not as a finalizing authorial comment.

Meredith's dialogic style does not work only with 'character zones'. The other voice that combines with or supplants the narrator's may be the stylization or parody of another author (for example there are a number of pastiches of Carlyle in this novel, as in several of Meredith's). More characteristic in this novel is the stylization of genre: the text constantly alludes to other kinds of generic treatment that might be given to this material. For example, when Farmer Blaize's rick has been burned and Richard's accomplice, the ploughman Tom Bakewell, is in prison, the 'Juvenile Stratagems' of Richard and his friend Ripton to help him to escape are narrated in this manner:

> 'There's only one chance', said Richard, coming to a dead halt, and folding his arms resolutely.
> His comrade inquired with the utmost eagerness what that chance might be?
> Richard fixed his eyes on a flint, and replied: 'We must rescue that fellow from jail'.
> Ripton gazed at his leader, and fell back with astonishment. 'My dear Ricky! but how are we to do it?'
> Richard, still perusing his flint, replied: 'We must manage to get a file in to him and a rope. It can be done, I tell you. I don't care what I pay. I don't care what I do. He must be got out'.
> 'Bother that old Blaize!' exclaimed Ripton, taking off his cap to wipe his frenzied forehead, and brought down his friend's reproof.
> 'Never mind old Blaize now. Talk about letting it out! Look at you. I'm ashamed of you. You talk about Robin Hood and King Richard! Why, you haven't an atom of courage'. (6, 43)

This is the style of a boy's adventure story. If it does not take Richard entirely at his own valuation, there is merely the slightest accent, in phrases such as 'folding his arms resolutely', of an indulgent irony, hinting that these 'Juvenile Stratagems' may be absurd and will come to nothing, but Richard is a grand lad for attempting them, and they promise well for his future. At this point in the novel it is likely that most readers will respond in this way. But this style, like the whole of the 'Bakewell Comedy' episode, is deceptive. Richard got into this scrape because, in the first place, he absconded from his birthday celebrations in a sulk about being medically examined (his state of mind is much more fully portrayed in the original text); then he behaved with intolerable arrogance to Farmer Blaize, who understandably if brutally flogged him; and finally Richard disgracefully involved a sacked ploughman in his 'gentleman's' revenge. His heroic stratagems are motivated by a wish to do anything rather than confess and humble himself before the farmer. The situation is resolved in a shifty and obscure way, but Richard's preference for heroic gestures to facing his responsibilities foreshadows the conclusion, when he shatters the promised comedic resolution by fighting a duel.

In the following chapter we see Richard being counselled by another grown-up cousin, Austin Wentworth. Austin is one of a recognizable class of Meredith characters whom Richard C. Stevenson has enlighteningly compared to the *raisonneurs* in Molière's comedies, characters like Philinte in *Le Misanthrope* who 'dramatize a moderate and sane point of view in contrast to the antics of men of deformed reason'.[28] Others include Merthyr Powys (*SB* and *Vittoria* (*V*)), Vernon Whitford (*E*), Dartrey Fenellan (*OOC*) and Matthew Weyburn (*LOHA*). Such characters usually play a restrained role in the novels (one of the reasons for the failure of *Lord Ormont and His Aminta* (*LOHA*) is that Meredith makes the *raisonneur* the hero – as Stevenson comments, these characters tend to be predictable and a little dull). They are often educators and most of them have unfortunate marital histories. As reasonable man Austin contrasts with his namesake, and as earnest devotee of 'Parson Brawnley' (Charles Kingsley) he contrasts with Richard's appointed tutor, Adrian. Austin married a housemaid whom he had seduced, and from whom he subsequently separated, and the original text makes it clear that this quixotically honourable action (which contrasts with the clandestine philandering of Adrian) is the reason why Richard's education was not entrusted to him:

Very different for young Richard would it have been had Austin taken his right place in the Baronet's favour: but Austin had offended against the Baronet's main crotchet: who said, in answer to Lady Blandish, that, to ally oneself randomly was to be guilty of a crime before Heaven greater than the offence it sought to extinguish.[29]

In Chapter 7 we see Austin persuading Richard to make a clean breast to Blaize:

> 'I never met a coward myself', Austin continued. 'I have heard of one or two. One let an innocent man die for him'.
> 'How base!' exclaimed the boy.
> 'Yes, it was bad', Austin acquiesced.
> 'Bad! Richard scorned the poor contempt. How I would have spurned him! He was a coward!'
> 'I believe he pleaded the feelings of his family in his excuse, and tried every means to get the man off. I have read also in the confessions of a celebrated philosopher, that in his youth he committed some act of pilfering, and accused a young servant-girl of his own theft, who was condemned and dismissed for it, pardoning her guilty accuser'.
> 'What a coward!' shouted Richard. 'And he confessed it publicly?'
> 'You may read it yourself'.
> 'He actually wrote it down, and printed it?'
> 'You have the book in your father's library. Would you have done so much?'
> Richard faltered. No! he admitted that he never could have told people.
> 'Then who is to call that man a coward?' said Austin. (7, 53–4)

The generic dialogism of this passage is more subtle than in the previous example. It has to do with its exemplary quality. One way in which things would have been 'different for young Richard' if Austin had been his tutor is that we would have had a conventional *Erziehungsroman*, or novel of education, instead of the genre-breaking, uncategorizable fiction that Meredith actually wrote. Austin's counselling of Richard about the fire is an episode from such a novel, from a 'pattern' book on the making of a gentleman. It is probably a coincidence that the philosopher mentioned here is

Rousseau, author of the most celebrated *Erziehungsroman*, *Emile*, which as we shall see is one of the most important intertextual presences in *Richard Feverel*.

But the most obvious example of generic stylization is the pastoral love-idyll framing the meeting and early love of Richard and Lucy, especially in the chapters 'Ferdinand and Miranda' and 'A Diversion Played on a Penny-Whistle'. The stylization is immediately obvious, particularly in the later chapter:

> Away with Systems! Away with a corrupt World! Let us breathe the air of the Enchanted Island.
>
> Golden lie the meadows: golden run the streams; red gold is on the pine-stems. The sun is coming down to earth, and walks the fields and the waters....
>
> The plumes of the woodland are alight; and beyond them, over the open, 'tis a race with the long-thrown shadows; a race across the heaths and up the hills, till, at the farthest bourne of mounted eastern cloud, the heralds of the sun lay rosy fingers and rest.
>
> Sweet are the shy recesses of the woodland. The ray treads softly there. A film athwart the pathway quivers many-hued against purple shade fragrant with warm pines, deep moss-beds, feathery ferns. The little brown squirrel drops tail, and leaps; the inmost bird is startled to a chance tuneless note. From silence into silence things move. (19, 153)

The stylization is plainly evident in the exclamations, inversions, archaisms and poeticisms (later in the chapter Richard and Lucy speak in blank verse). It is however combined with elements of unselfconscious Meredithian nature-writing, especially in the last paragraph quoted. This makes it difficult to regard the stylized language as parodic. For stylization to exist, according to Bakhtin, two linguistic consciousnesses must be present: the stylizer and the stylized.[30] However, a passage such as the one quoted *could* be unconscious or 'monologic' imitation. We infer the presence of the stylizing consciousness from the context of 'dialogized heteroglossia' in the novel as a whole. Even in the 'Ferdinand and Miranda' chapter, where the stylization is less marked, the idyll is shadowed by a detachment, if not irony, deriving from the way the narrative has led up to it: Richard has just had a conversation with a neighbouring boy, Ralph Morton, about girls' names, through which he discovers that his cousin Clare is 'a very charming creature'. At the moment of his meeting Lucy he is actually thinking about Clare in these terms:

> Clare Doria Forey – oh, perfect melody! Sliding with the tide, he heard it fluting in the bosom of the hills.
> When nature has made us ripe for love, it seldom occurs that the Fates are behindhand in furnishing a temple for the flame. (14, 118)

Obviously, if Clare had happened to be on the island, Richard would have fallen in love with her.[31]

The titles 'Ferdinand and Miranda', with its allusion to the enchanted island (sustained through the chapter), and 'A Diversion' are obvious framing devices, as are the pastoral exclamations at the beginning of the latter. The idyll is thus barricaded against the alien discourses that constitute novelistic language. 'The utterly conventional simplicity of life in the bosom of nature is opposed to social conventions, complexity and the disjunctions of everyday private life; life here is abstracted into a love that is completely sublimated.'[32] The idyll in both chapters is haunted by portents: in the former, by the pointed remark that 'Sir Austin was not Prospero' (*ORF*, Chapter 15, p. 119); in the latter by a comparison of Richard and Lucy to 'darkling nightingales', with incongruous Keatsian associations of death. Moreover, the nightingales are substituted by a nightjar which 'spins his dark monotony': the nightjar is traditionally a bird of ill-omen, associated with owls and ravens according to *OED*, and the image of 'spinning', though derived from the sound it makes, is suggestive of the Fates – the image is repeated in the last sentence of the chapter.

Perhaps the harshest 'objectification' of the style of these chapters is supplied retrospectively by the contrast with the narration of Richard and Lucy's wedding, which in places uncannily foreshadows the late Hardy:

> At an altar stand two fair young creatures, ready with their oaths. They are asked to fix all time to the moment, and they do so. If there is hesitation at the immense undertaking, it is but maidenly. She conceives as little mental doubt of the sanity of the act as he. Over them hangs a cool young curate in his raiment of

office. Behind are two apparently lucid people, distinguished from each other by sex and age. (29, 299–300)

So far we have looked at the representation of genre by *stylization*, perceptible in small extracted portions of the text. These genres are not exactly repudiated, or even parodied (Austin's dialogue with Richard is certainly not a parody), but by being represented they are deprived of the 'finalizing' power that they would have in, for example, an actual boy's adventure story, *Erziehungsroman* or love-idyll. Since genre always has an ideological character, this is not a narrowly formalistic matter. The charmingly absurd heroism of the boy-gentleman shows promise of a great man; the boy rigorously educated by these or those principles will grow up a paragon; love thrives best in seclusion from the corrupt world: these are generically coded ideological discourses more or less active in Meredith's world which play a significant part in the 'dialogized heteroglossia' of the novel.

Genre is even more significantly represented at the structural level. Here the two most important generic influences, about which much has been written, are the *Bildungsroman* (overlapping with the *Erziehungsroman*) and the 'New Comedy' of lovers triumphing over tyrannical elders, deriving from Menander, Terence and Plautus. According to Bakhtin, genre is determined by what he calls 'chronotope' or 'the intrinsic connectedness of temporal and spatial relationships that are artistically expressed in literature'.[33] To illustrate this with a simple example, Greek Romance takes place in what Bakhtin calls 'adventure time': namely, a time which is abstracted from the biographical flow of the hero's life and has no consequences. An unlimited series of adventures may occur in this time, typically between betrothal and marriage, or marriage and its consummation, after which the hero and heroine resume their lives as if nothing had happened. The space of such tales Bakhtin describes as an 'abstract-alien' world.[34] The adventures need space, but any space will do, an adventure that occurs in one place could equally occur in another, place names are merely formal markers and adventures are interchangeable. What links time and space in such a world is above all chance: not being, shall we say, Caesar in the Forum at the time the conspirators have decided to murder him, but the adventure hero in the place (which could be any place) at the time (which could be any time) when the band of robbers is also there. One of Bakhtin's chief interests is the development of the relations between time and space in the novel, from these simple and abstract beginnings to the *Bildungsroman* in which there is not merely a changing hero in a concrete world, but a hero who 'emerges *along with the world* and he reflects the historical emergence of the world itself'.[35]

An important aspect of Bakhtin's theory of chronotopes is their potentially dialogic character. 'Within the limits of a single work and within the total literary output of a single author we may notice a number of different chronotopes and complex interactions among them.... The general characteristic of these interactions is that they are *dialogical* (in the broadest use of the word).'[36] The relevance of this to *Richard Feverel* should already be obvious.

The relation of *Richard Feverel* to the *Bildungsroman* tradition has been the topic of much critical commentary. Susanne Howe discussed the novel in her study of the English influence of *Wilhelm Meister*;[37] J.H. Buckley has a chapter on Meredith in his book on the *Bildungsroman* in England;[38] Sven-Johan Spånberg's intertextual study focuses primarily on *Emile* and *Wilhelm Meister*; and more recently Nikki Lee Manos has asked whether the novel is a *Bildungsroman* or anti-*Bildungsroman*.[39]

Of these discussions Spånberg's is both the most extensive and the most illuminating, especially of the relationship between *Richard Feverel* and *Emile*. *Emile* is a generically peculiar work which presents itself as (and has been widely influential as) an educational treatise. For much of its course the narrative elements have a merely exemplary function, and it could be argued that they do not make *Emile* a novel any more than the exemplary episodes in a work such as *Being and Nothingness* make it a collection of short stories. However, the fictional element becomes dominant in the final Book, dealing with Emile's courtship and marriage. Spånberg rightly calls the conclusion a 'Utopian fantasy',[40] and the emotional investment in this of Jean-Jacques, as both author and character, justifies the reader in considering the work as, at least, something other than a scientific treatise.

Spånberg points out a number of thematic parallels between *Emile* and *Richard Feverel*, most importantly the obsessive preoccupation of the systems in both works with sexual development, and the significant relationship between this and current 'scientific' thinking on the topic.[41]

Most relevant to my argument, however, is the relationship between author and character in *Emile*. Spånberg points out that

Rousseau as author (and, since the work begins as a treatise, it is artificial to think of him as a *narrator*) 'casts himself as the tutor of Emile.... He thus becomes an active participant in the events of the story, and as the work progresses, it becomes increasingly difficult to keep the two personae of the author apart.'[42] Bakhtin, in his early essay 'Author and Hero in Aesthetic Activity', represents the relationship between author and hero as one of 'transgredience'. This means that the author's consciousness

> *encompasses* the consciousness and world of a hero.... The author not only sees and knows everything seen and known by each hero... but he also sees and knows *more* than they do; moreover, he sees and knows something that is in principle inaccessible to them.[43]

For this reason

> the author must be situated on the boundary of the world he is bringing into being as the active creator of this world, for his intrusion into that world destroys its aesthetic stability.[44]

This intrusion of the author into the world he is bringing into being is precisely the most striking characteristic of *Emile*, considered as a work of narrative fiction. This is not merely a naive response to the fact that the tutor is referred to in the first person and called Jean-Jacques. In 'Author and Hero' Bakhtin writes that, in autobiographical writing, the author 'must become another in relation to himself, must look at himself through the eyes of another'.[45] This is what makes it possible, even in the most nakedly autobiographical of narratives, to speak of the author, or narrator, as distinct from the character. But this does not happen in *Emile*. Instead, the author's privilege of transgredience is conferred upon the tutor. There is nothing about Emile that the tutor does not know. As Spånberg remarks, he refers to Emile as his 'oeuvre'. Events are narrated which at first appear to have occurred spontaneously, but which Jean-Jacques then admits to having manipulated. This device is most striking in the final Book, when Jean-Jacques invents a character called Sophie, describes her to Emile as the model of an ideal wife, and then takes his pupil on a roundabout tour which ends up, as if by accident, in their taking shelter in the house where Sophie lives: a kind of Möbius strip of diegetic levels. The tutor intrudes upon Emile in ways that are justifiable only on the grounds that he is in fact Emile's author. At the outset he states that 'towards the end I never lose sight of him for a moment, until, *whatever he may say*, he needs me no longer'.[46] Towards the end, when Emile is already a young adult, Rousseau writes, 'So long as I could not get the mastery over his will, I retained my control over his person; I never left him for a moment', and he counsels other tutors to:

> watch carefully over the young man; he can protect himself from all other foes, but it is for you to protect him against himself. Never leave him night or day, *or at least share his room*; never let him go to bed till he is sleepy, and let him rise as soon as he wakes.[47]

The reason for this is Rousseau's horror of masturbation, which is so great that he thinks even unchastity preferable. The phrase I have italicized implies that the ideal would be for the tutor to share his pupil's bed to prevent him from masturbating. In the final pages, Jean-Jacques delivers a lengthy lecture on sexual manners to Emile and Sophie between the wedding-ceremony and wedding-night, knows that the marriage is consummated on the first night but that Sophie denies Emile access to her bed on the second night, and delivers another lecture to Sophie about this.

The projection of authorial transgredience on to the level of the story also occurs in the definitive *Bildungsroman*, *Wilhelm Meister's Apprenticeship*, and accounts for most readers' extreme disappointment with its conclusion. *Wilhelm Meister* appears to be a story of the hero's free and unpredictable development, but he turns out to have been watched over and guided by a masonic-style organization called the Tower. Goethe does not, like Rousseau, naively put *himself* into the story as transgredient character, but the result is that the reader feels defrauded: as Spånberg says, Wilhelm's 'freedom of choice and action was...never as absolute as he and the reader were led to believe'.[48]

Spånberg speaks of 'sinister elements in the relations between tutor and pupil in *Emile*',[49] and most readers would agree. Moreover, Spånberg adds, 'and between father and son in *The Ordeal of Richard Feverel*', and it is this parallel that interests us.[50] I have already quoted Adrian's description of Sir Austin as a 'monomaniac at large' (a description that also fits Rousseau's tutor), apropos of his habit of listening at bedroom doors; also Adrian's remark that Sir Austin 'wished to be a Providence to his son'. This last comment is cited by the narrator while Sir Austin is observing, unnoticed, Richard and Ripton's excited conversation about the burning of Farmer Blaize's rick. He keeps his knowledge a secret because 'it allowed him to act, and in a measure to feel, like Providence; enabled him to observe and provide for the movements of creatures in the dark' (5, 38–9). Providence is the ultimate transgredience, and if the most obvious gloss on Sir Austin's behaviour here is that he wishes to be God to his son, it would be equally appropriate to say that he wishes to act as his author, much as Jean-Jacques is the author of Emile. This gives an added twist to the ominous comment, in the 'Ferdinand and Miranda' chapter, that 'Sir Austin was not Prospero' (15, p. 122). Prospero is the most author-like of characters, and many readers and audiences of *The Tempest* find him, too, sinister, because of not only his treatment of Caliban, but also his transgredient relationship to Ferdinand and Miranda, which reduces them to ciphers. However one may judge Prospero, his transgredience is genuine and, in his terms at least, successful. The irony for Sir Austin is that this episode of the fire is perhaps the only moment at which he enjoys a genuinely transgredient relationship to his son; however, even this is merely snooping (he habitually spies on Richard) and he persists throughout the novel in behaving as if he were Richard's author – see for example his mind-boggling question to Ripton's father:

> do you establish yourself in a radiating centre of intuition: do you base your watchfulness on so thorough an acquaintance with his character, so perfect a knowledge of the instrument, that all its movements – even the eccentric ones – are anticipated by you, and provided for? (16, 133)

The point of stressing that Sir Austin's wished-for transgredience is that of an *author* (rather than God) is that if *The Ordeal of Richard Feverel* is not an *Erziehungsroman* or *Bildungsroman*, it is because it represents one, and the author of it is not Meredith but Sir Austin. As Emile becomes what his author-tutor plots him to become so Richard does *not* become what his father plots him to become, but the plot is no less that of an *Erziehungsroman*. Sir Austin even gives titles to the chapters:

'What can this be?' the Baronet meditated, and referred to his Note-Book... wherein the Youth's progressionary phases were mapped out in sections, from Simple Boyhood to the Blossoming Season, The Magnetic Age, The Period of Probation, from which, successfully passed through, he was to emerge into a Manhood worthy of Paradise.[51]

(Meredith uses two of these as chapter-titles for *his* novel, where they are, of course, in 'intonational quotation marks'.)[52]

Later, when Sir Austin keeps Richard waiting in London, subject to the temptations to which he eventually falls, he is behaving as if this story, which Richard has torn up by marrying Lucy, were still being written. Richard is 19, therefore it is the Period of Probation. Such a probation for a married man has, however, considerably more dangers than for a young bachelor.

But what, in all this, of the real author, and *his* transgredience? I have already cited and expanded upon Allon White's assertion that Meredith was a writer whom 'the mantle of single author/ity would no longer quite fit'. The provenance and function of 'The Pilgrim's Scrip' (and of the poems attributed to the youthful Richard and Diaper Sandoe) illustrate this.

Late in life Meredith is reported to have dissociated himself from these aphorisms, saying that 'he had written all the aphorisms of his Austin Feverel straight off. "I am not responsible for them, they are Sir Austin Feverel's – only one came to me."'[53] However, Meredith's hand had perhaps been forced by the last episode in the convoluted history of the Scrip's 'authorship' when, in 1888, his American publishers brought out a volume titled *The Pilgrim's Scrip: or, Wit and Wisdom of George Meredith*. He wrote moderately to the compiler of this volume, 'I speak honestly in saying I could wish you were more worthily engaged. Over here I have not encouraged the collecting of extracts from my books.' His moderation is perhaps explained by his statement that 'I would not, were it in my power, impose obstacles to Messrs. Roberts' wishes, as they have behaved well to me.'[54] However, he must have been intensely irritated by such a crass attribution of the Scrip to himself, and it may have been some reference to this that caused him to make the opposite assertion. Fifteen years later, when yet another edition of the Scrip was published in America, he wrote, 'It is hard on me that the Scrip should be laid to my charge. These aphorisms came in the run of the pen, as dramatizings of the mind of the System-maker. I would not have owned to half a dozen of them.'[55]

The truth, almost certainly, is that the Scrip is neither the 'wit and wisdom of George Meredith' nor the securely fictionalized utterances of a character in a novel. The extant manuscript aphorisms are in what Gillian Beer calls the Maroon Notebook, which 'seems to have been in use from about 1858 to late 1862'.[56] This is published as pp. 40–55 of *The Notebooks of George Meredith*. Here it is evident that he did not write them all 'straight off', but they are mixed in with other material, including aphorisms that Meredith was to use, as Gillian Beer points out, in *Beauchamp's Career* and *Diana of the Crossways*. Meredith continued 'to assign sayings to "Sir A. Fev." after the novel was published'.[57] His friend William Hardman recorded that in 1862 Meredith 'overhauled his notebooks and read me a mass of the aphorisms hereafter to be published in "The Pilgrim's Scrip*, by Sir Austin Feverel, edited by Adrian Harley"'.[58]

Beer concludes that 'In "The Pilgrim's Scrip" Meredith satirized his own private methods of recording experience but the "Scrip" is also shown to be wise.'[59] A better way of putting it might be that the aphorisms were from the start 'double-voiced', and that their use in *Richard Feverel* is at least partly *citational*. Its citational character was not evident to its first readers, but it is now – Meredith typically covered his tracks when drawing on his personal resources. Meredith also wrote aphorisms which deplore the habit of aphorism.[60] Dostoevsky, according to Bakhtin, found the classical and Enlightenment habit of 'thinking in separate rounded-off and self-sufficient thoughts which were purposely meant to stand independent of their context...particularly alien and antagonistic'. In his works there are no 'detached, impersonal verities', only 'integral and indivisible voice-ideas'.[61] So Meredith, the inveterate aphorist and satirist of aphorists, wrote to the compiler of *The Pilgrim's Scrip* that 'Many of the excerpts can hardly be intelligible without the context.'[62] They are *imitations* of 'detached, impersonal verities' which, in their context, are decidedly 'integral and indivisible voice-ideas'. In being also citations of himself, they are typical of the oblique character of Meredithian utterance, and of its abstention from 'single author/ity'.

The most overt sign of generic self-consciousness is the persistent and at times even heavy-handed reference to Richard as the Hero. This is implicit as early as the second chapter when Richard and

Ripton fight and the narrator remarks, 'The Gods favour one of two parties. Prince Turnus was a noble youth; but he had not Pallas at his elbow. Ripton was a capital boy; he had no science' (2, 13). This is not merely routine mock-heroic. Turnus lost because he was not the designated hero of the epic: he did not, like Aeneas, bear the heroic destiny. Similarly, Ripton is a 'boy without a Destiny' (12, 95). He is even, at the very first mention of him, 'a boy without a character' (1, 11). Even at this early point there is a hint of generic self-consciousness, since the introduction of Ripton follows a series of virtually Theophrastan 'characters' of Richard's relatives. In this novel, however, it is an advantage to be without character or Destiny. Ripton is the one who gets drunk, reads pornography and shames his father in front of a smug Sir Austin, but in the end he shows more devotion to Lucy than Richard does.

At this stage the story of which Richard is the Hero is the *Erziehungsroman* being 'written' by his father. The most straightforward instance of generic dialogism is the usurpation of this story by another. The story of Richard's education and harmonious development under the watchful eye of the transgredient author/mentor is usurped by a 'New Comedy', a story of erotically motivated rebellion of youth against age, in which the author/mentor becomes, in Northrop Frye's parlance, the 'blocking agent'. By the time Richard is facetiously referred to as the Hero in the title of Chapter 20, this is the kind of story he is the hero of. The chapter's full title is 'Celebrates the time-honoured treatment of a dragon by the hero'; the dragon is 'Heavy Benson', agent of the tyrannical father (though also a free-lance voyeur) and the only true believer in Sir Austin's misogynistic doctrine, whom Richard thrashes for spying on him and Lucy: a suitably 'New Comedy' exploit.

Three successive chapters leading up to the marriage refer in their titles to the hero or heroine. The story is referred to twice as a 'New Comedy' in Chapter 26, 'Rapid Development of the Hero', and the chapter that narrates the wedding ceremony has the famously convoluted title, 'In which the Last Act of a Comedy takes the Place of the First'. In this chapter, as shown above, the narrator adopts a scathingly ironic and ominous Hardyesque voice. In these chapters the ironic references to Hero and Heroine are so frequent and heavy-handed that they threaten to lose their dialogic quality and shrink to a fixed and mechanical mannerism. They are, however, part of a more general and not always so blatantly signalled subversion of conventional roles.

For example, Sir Austin as Mentor, Lord Mountfalcon as Villain (in the Victorian melodramatic mould) and Bella as Seductress all either contradict or modify the role that the story apparently allots to them.

The most important of these subversions however is Lucy's role as Heroine. The language of the novel so often proposes her as the conventional weak and submissive heroine that many readers have regarded her as such. Consider, for example, the commentary accompanying the dialogue on pp. 262–4 (Chapter 27), when Richard has just abducted her from the railway station: 'dutiful slave...pretty wisdom...shamed cheeks...trembled... shrank timidly...wise little speech' against Richard's 'mastery' and 'mighty eloquence'. It would be special pleading to claim that this language is, at this point, securely in 'intonational quotation marks' and carries no authorial weight. Later in the novel, however, such language is differently accented when we hear it in the mouth, for example, of Richard's friend Lady Judith Felle, a rather unsatisfactorily presented character but one who is associated with Richard's sentimental and dangerous knight-errant fantasies: 'you must learn to humour little women' (34, 373); we have already seen that Richard's own habit of thinking of Lucy as a 'poor little thing' reinforces his fascination with Mrs Mount, and when he calls her a 'little timid girl' Mrs Berry retorts, 'Oh, lor', how she must ha' deceived ye to make ye think that!' (37, 426)

At the present time in his personal and writing life, Meredith was not able to create a heroine who positively transcended the convention of the 'little woman', as he was later to do with Cecilia Halkett, Clara Middleton, Diana Warwick and, indeed, all his later heroines. He does, however, subvert the convention by suggesting that it is deceptive. For example, Richard's main reason for comparing Lucy unfavourably with Bella is her refusal to accompany him to London, which he attributes to her fear of meeting his father. In fact, she has been persuaded by Adrian that it would be unwise to go. This turns out to be disastrous advice, but only because of Sir Austin's perverse and manipulative delay in meeting his son, which Lucy could not possibly foresee. In fact, she shows considerable strength in resisting Richard's pressure to accompany him, and even accepting his unfavourable interpretation of her behaviour. The other significant subversion of the convention is the overt sexuality of her behaviour when Richard returns to Raynham at the end of the novel:

He had left her a girl: he beheld a woman – a blooming woman: for pale at first, no sooner did she see him than the colour was rich and deep on her face and neck and bosom half shown through the loose dressing-robe, and the sense of her exceeding beauty made his heart thump and his eyes swim.

'My darling!' each cried, and they clung together, and her mouth was fastened on his. (44, 545–6)

We have seen that, according to Bakhtin, it is 'the chronotope that defines genre', and he adds that 'in literature the primary category in the chronotope is time'.[63] If we were to compare the character of time in *Emile* and in *Wilhelm Meister*, we could say that in the former time is a threat, a cause of anxiety; the tutor must always be aware of the stage of the pupil's development, and control his experience accordingly; above all time brings the onset of sexuality which has to be vigilantly controlled. In *Wilhelm Meister*, on the other hand, time is on the hero's side, it is available to him, a medium in which he develops, his mistakes are not final; this is true of the reader's experience of most of the novel despite the eventual revelation about the role of the Tower. The same is true of place: Emile's location is always controlled, whereas Wilhelm travels (apparently) freely.

Time and place for Sir Austin (and therefore for his '*Erziehungsroman*') have the same character as for Rousseau. Most readers, however, are likely to take a more relaxed and positive view, which appears to be confirmed when Sir Austin's attempt to control time by planning Richard's marriage is subverted by the meeting of Richard and Lucy. What follows from this, however, is not a *Bildungsroman* on the lines of *Wilhelm Meister*. Spånberg perceptively points out that in the *Bildungsroman* the hero's first love (Marianne in *Wilhelm Meister*) is typically sacrificed, abandoned or outgrown, but that, while this *seems* to happen when Richard emerges from his illness apathetic, it turns out that the relationship was 'far more than a pastoral idyl or a youthful error' but 'one of the decisive events in the course of the action'.[64] Instead of a *Bildungsroman* we have, or appear to have, a 'New Comedy'. In this genre time has a different character again: it is to be *seized*. The hero and heroine have to create or take what slight chronotopic opportunities they can wrest from the control of the elders. Chance and/or contrived meetings are prominent among these. Thus, when Richard exploits Tom Blaize's confusion about railway stations to take possession of Lucy, he is perfectly acting out the role of a New Comedy hero.

The second characteristic of time in New Comedy is that it ceases to have any force once the hero and heroine triumph. It is an emphatically finalizing genre. The gloomy hints at the end of some of Shakespeare's comedies are of course signs of incipient subversion of the genre. Most readers probably experience some confusion when the New Comedy appears to be accomplished half way through *Richard Feverel*, and the 'Last Act of a Comedy Takes the Place of the First'. The time that remains to be filled looms disturbingly – what can happen now? – and the possibility of the novel not ending happily is (*pace* John W. Morris) already implicitly raised.

The character in the novel who takes the relaxed view of time is Adrian – for example, 'Time will extricate us, I presume, or what is the venerable signor good for?' (41, 501). This conforms to Adrian's 'recumbent' posture towards life. What the time that gapes after the consummation of the New Comedy shows, however, is that it *can* be threatening, though not in the way Sir Austin thinks. In Meredith the uncontrolled passage of time, especially when it involves separation, is invariably corrosive. We see this in *Rhoda Fleming*, *Vittoria* and *The Amazing Marriage*, as well as *Richard Feverel*.

We have moved into the territory of the 'novel of ordeal' whose simplest form, the Greek Romance, is according to Bakhtin a 'test of fidelity in love and the purity of the ideal hero and heroine', in which, however, 'The static, immutable nature of their characters and their abstract ideality preclude any emergence or development.'[65] This model, however, 'complicated...by all that has been created by the biographical novel and the *Bildungsroman*', becomes an important resource in the nineteenth-century novel.[66] The word 'ordeal' has several overlapping meanings in *Richard Feverel*. The original idea is Sir Austin's egotistical notion of the special ordeal of the men of his family in their necessary but dangerous relations with women. As the novel progresses, the idea accrues the more universal sense of the inevitable struggle in growing from childhood to adulthood – the other side, as it were, of *Bildung*. In the novel's second half, however, we discover that Richard's particular ordeal is the separation and temptation imposed on him by his father in his fanatical adherence to the System.

As we have seen, the all-important development of the hero in the *Bildungsroman* entails a tendency to regard other characters, particularly women, as instrumental and disposable. This tendency becomes even stronger when, in the post-Napoleonic period, the French realists develop a more ruthlessly egotistical kind of hero, such as Stendhal's Julien Sorel and Balzac's Eugène Rastignac.[67] Richard's story entails female victims too. First there is his cousin Clare, the victim of her mother's obsession with marrying her to Richard, Sir Austin's insistence on keeping his son away from girls during adolescence, which leads to her banishment from Raynham, and finally Richard's own egotism. Clare plays a suppressed role throughout the novel – 'She too was growing, but nobody cared how she grew' (12, 94); 'the poor mocked-at heart' (29, 299) – but she is eventually, shatteringly, given voice. When her heart is broken by Richard's marriage to Lucy she succumbs to marriage with an old admirer of her mother's, a decent but worn-out man. Her sexual apathy in this marriage is foreshadowed when, at the putting on of the ring, she 'spread out her fingers that the operation might be the more easily effected' (35, 387).

Immediately before the marriage Richard berates her for it, saying 'if I had done such a thing I would not live an hour after it', self-righteously adding, 'kiss me for the last time.... I'll never kiss you after it', upon which 'she threw her arms wildly round him, and kissed him convulsively, and clung to his lips, shutting her eyes, her face suffused with a burning red'. Meredith perhaps strains credulity when he adds that Richard 'left her, unaware of the meaning of those passionate kisses' (35, 384–5). However, the contrast between his callow and preening affectation and her helpless, spontaneous passion is the relevant context for Clare's eventual suicide and the brief but memorable usurpation of the narrative by her diary, in which she writes, 'Richard despises me. I cannot bear the touch of my fingers or the sight of my face.... Richard said he would die rather than endure it. I know he would. Why should I be afraid to do what he would do?' (40, 496) The most famous of the 'Pilgrim's Scrip' aphorisms is the definition of Sentimentalists as 'they who seek to enjoy without incurring the Immense Debtorship for a thing done' (24, 220). In this case the Debtorship for Richard's sentimentalism is incurred by Clare.

Clare's suicide occurs after Richard's seduction by Bella, and the onset of the self-loathing which convinces him that he can never return to Lucy. He travels on the continent with the quixotic sentimentalist Lady Judith Felle, 'preparatory to his undertaking the release of Italy from the subjugation of the Teuton' in Adrian's words (41, 501). His cousin Austin seeks him out and informs him that he has a son, and in the wake of this discovery he takes the celebrated walk through a thunderstorm in the forest, where he picks up a frightened leveret and 'Nature Speaks' to him through the medium of the leveret licking his hand, with the result that he has a vision of his wife and son, and 'a sense of purification so sweet he shuddered again and again' (42, 523).

This is a magnificently sustained and justly celebrated piece of writing. There is nothing parodic about it. Nevertheless it is dialogized by the context of the novel as a whole. It narrates the kind of quasi-religious, epiphanic experience that exerts an enormous pull on the destinies of novel-heroes. As in *Wilhelm Meister*, the experience centres on the belated discovery that he is a father. After this apparently redemptive episode, the shock of the ending is considerable.

But what would it mean for this episode to exert, as it seems it *must*, a decisive pull in the direction of a harmonious, comedic resolution? The chapter is titled 'Nature Speaks', and nature speaks to Richard voluminously, but most intimately through the associative link between the news that he is a father and the close contact with a young animal. What sort of a resolution would this be to a novel that is so fundamentally a critique of patriarchy in its purest form, the obsessive, exclusive and dynastic love of a father for his son, with its associated misogyny and other consequent emotional deformations in both?

The failure of this episode to generate the expected resolution may be made yet more explicable if we can accept as significant a marked similarity of parts of it to a comparable episode in Carlyle's *Sartor Resartus*. The 'Nature Speaks' chapter opens, in fact, with one of Meredith's many pastiches of Carlyle:

> Briareus reddening angrily over the sea – where is that vaporous Titan? And Hesper set in his rosy garland – why looks he so implacably sweet? It is that one has left that bright home to go forth and do cloudy work, and he has got a stain with which he dare not return. (42, 513)

This overt pastiche is not sustained throughout the chapter, and indeed it is most memorable and moving for the marked lack of mannerism of any kind in passages such as the following, which is not remotely reminiscent of Carlyle:

> He was next musing on a strange sensation he experienced. It ran up one arm with an indescribable thrill, but communicated nothing to his heart. It was purely physical, ceased for a time, and recommenced, till he had it all through his blood, wonderfully thrilling. He grew aware that the little thing he carried in his breast was licking his hand there. The small rough tongue going over and over the palm of his hand produced the strange sensation he felt. (42, 522)

However, it is between these extremes of unmannered writing and overt pastiche that the intertextual relationship is most striking. The second part of *Sartor Resartus* is a kind of condensed and fragmented *Bildungsroman*.[68] At a comparatively early stage of his spiritual development the hero, Diogenes Teufelsdröckh, has an epiphanic experience in the mountains:

> No trace of man now visible.... But sun-wards, lo you! how it towers sheer up, a world of Mountains, the diadem and centre of the mountain region! A hundred and a hundred savage peaks, in the last light of Day; all glowing, of gold and amethyst, like giant spirits of the wilderness; there in their silence, in their solitude, even as on the night when Noah's deluge first dried! Beautiful, nay solemn, was the sudden aspect to our Wanderer. He gazed over those stupendous masses with wonder, almost with longing desire; never till this hour had he known Nature, that she was One, that she was his Mother and divine. And as the ruddy glow was fading into clearness in the sky, and the Sun had now departed, a murmur of Eternity and Immensity, of Death and Life, stole through his soul; and he felt as if Death and Life were one, as if the Earth were not dead, as if the Spirit of the Earth had its throne in that splendour, and his own spirit were therewith holding communion.[69]

This epiphanic 'spell was broken' by the cruel coincidence of seeing his beloved and friend driving from their wedding. We next hear of Teufelsdröckh commenting sardonically on 'the epidemic, now endemical, of view-hunting'.[70]

The corresponding passage in *Richard Feverel* also has a mountain setting, but it is the thunderstorm that first inspires awe in Richard, and the leveret, followed by the sight of a statue of Virgin and Child, that completes the epiphany:

> Up started the whole forest in violet fire. He saw the country at the foot of the hills to the bounding Rhine gleam, quiver, extinguished. Then there were pauses; and the lightning seemed as the eye of heaven, and the thunder as the tongue of heaven, each alternately addressing him; filling him with awful rapture. Alone there – sole human creature among the grandeurs and mysteries of storm – he felt the representative of his kind, and his spirit rose, and marched, and exulted, let it be glory, let it be ruin!....
> Vivid as lightning the Spirit of Life illumined him. He felt in his heart the cry of his child, his darling's touch.... And as they led him he had a sense of purification so sweet he shuddered again and again. (42, 521 and 523)

This is not pastiche. One could not even say, as in the case of Mill's 'Subjection of Women' in *Beauchamp's Career* (see Chapter 4, p. 123), that it is an 'image' of Carlyle's discourse. Some readers may go as far as to say that the connection with Carlyle is completely insignificant, because both passages are merely examples of Romantic nature-exaltation. But the Carlyle is not merely that. *Sartor Resartus* is a work that could with some exaggeration be said to inaugurate Victorian literature – particularly the Victorian quarrel-cum-fascination with Romanticism. The passage quoted is *already* an 'image' of a Romantic discourse, and Teufelsdröckh's remark about 'view-hunting' and subsequent descent into 'The Everlasting No' cast a Bakhtinian 'shadow of objectification' over it. Kerry McSweeney and Peter Sabor write, 'this momentary renewal proves a false dawn because it is bathed in the light of the ego as well as of the setting sun'.[71] Substituting lightning for the setting sun, the same could be said of Richard's epiphany.

Richard returns to England only to find, on his way home to his now mutually reconciled wife and father, a letter from Bella exposing the plot of Lord Mountfalcon to seduce Lucy.

> Richard folded up the letter silently.
> 'Jump into the cab', he said to Ripton.
> 'Anything the matter, Richard?'

'No'.

The driver received directions. Richard sat without speaking. His friend knew that face. He asked whether there was bad news in the letter. For answer, he had the lie circumstantial. He ventured to remark that they were going the wrong way.

'It's the right way', cried Richard, and his jaws were hard and square, and his eyes looked heavy and full. (43, 529)

Ripton 'knows that face' from the fourteenth birthday escapade and Richard's 'gentlemanly' resentment at being beaten by farmer Blaize:

'Where *are* you going to?' he inquired with a voice of the last time of asking, and halted resolutely.

Richard now broke his silence to reply, 'Anywhere'.

'Anywhere!' Ripton took up the moody word. 'But ain't you awfully hungry?' he gasped vehemently, in a way that showed the total emptiness of his stomach.

'No', was Richard's brief response. (2, 19)

Indeed, the title of this later chapter, 'Again the Magian Conflict', explicitly recalls the one in which Richard hatched his revenge against Blaize. In this respect, at least, Richard has not developed, and it would be sentimental to assume that the 'Nature Speaks' experience should have had this effect.

Bakhtin traced the ancestry of the novel less in the exclusively defined genres such as comedy, tragedy and epic than in what he called 'serio-comic' or 'carnivalistic' genres, and much of his work is devoted to realigning European literary history to rescue such genres from the marginal place traditionally allotted to them. He characterizes them as follows:

They reject the stylistic unity (or better, the single-styled nature) of the epic, the tragedy, high rhetoric, the lyric. Characteristic of these genres are a multi-toned narration, the mixing of high and low, serious and comic; they make wide use of inserted genres – letters, found manuscripts, retold dialogues, parodies on the high genres, paradoxically reinterpreted citations; in some of them we observe the mixing of prosaic and poetic speech, living dialects and jargons... are introduced, and various authorial masks make their appearance. Alongside the representing word there appears the *represented* word; in certain genres a leading role is played by the double-voiced word. And what appears here, as a result, is a radically new relationship to the word as the material of literature.[72]

This is almost precisely a description of *The Ordeal of Richard Feverel*. Among such genres Bakhtin pays particular attention to 'menippean satire' (of which the classic examples are the works of Lucian and Apuleius), in which:

> Scandals and eccentricities destroy the epic and tragic wholeness of the world, they make a breach in the stable, normal ('seemly') course of human affairs and events, they free human behaviour from the norms and motivations that predetermine it.[73]

Bakhtin polemically sees menippean satire as destroying the most privileged genres in the hierarchy, epic and tragedy, but it is equally possible to imagine a work in which 'scandals and eccentricities destroy the *comic* wholeness of the world'. *The Ordeal of Richard Feverel* is such a work. The 'norms and motivations' from which it frees the representation of human behaviour 'to prepare the way for a new and an original sense of the human scene' are, largely, generically determined ones. Typical 'scandals and eccentricities' in this novel include the way the 'boys' adventure' of the 'Bakewell Comedy' leaves a sour sense of the hero's character; the way he falls in love with one girl after meditating on the beauty of another girl's name; the hero's adultery when he is still in love with his young wife; and his perverse turning away from a happy ending in order to fight a duel. In these episodes, and many others, it can be seen that Richard's development is shaped by the continual offering and refusal of generic norms. As I have said earlier, genre is always a bearer of ideological meaning, and this is not a narrowly formalistic matter. Lucy, like Clare, is shockingly sacrificed at the end of the novel. However she is not, like Goethe's Marianne, sacrificed to the *Bildung* of the hero but to the contention that the deformations which the novel has analysed are too deep-rooted to be corrected by a thunderstorm, a leveret, or even the discovery that one is a father.

2

The Novels of the 1860s

The most significant review of *The Ordeal of Richard Feverel* was one that appeared, rather belatedly, in *The Times* on 14 October 1859. This was by Samuel Lucas, the editor of the new weekly magazine *Once a Week*, who had already agreed to serialize Meredith's next novel. In a clear attempt to counteract the damage done by the Mudie ban, Lucas asserted that the novel 'may be read by men and women with perfect impunity if they have no corrupt imaginations of their own to pervert the pure purpose of the author'.[1] However, although Lucas's review is generally laudatory, he strikes at the heart of the novel's originality by saying that Richard is 'untrue to his own nature' when he is seduced by Bella, that the conclusion is 'a catastrophe in defiance of poetical justice', and describes the whole of the story after Richard's marriage as 'the faulty remnant, which spoils an effective story by inconsequential proceedings on the part of both father and son'.[2] This was the judgement of the first and most important reader of Meredith's next novel.

Meredith made his first and only entry into the world of popular serial publication at an unusually dramatic time. Earlier in 1859 Dickens had broken with his publishers, Bradbury and Evans, because they refused to print a statement about his marriage breakdown. As a consequence the immensely popular weekly journal, *Household Words*, ceased publication, and Dickens independently published its successor, *All the Year Round*. *Once a Week* was Bradbury and Evans's response to this. The two journals were in effect in competition for the *Household Words* public, and the serial publication of novels was the chief ground of battle. Some of the most important novels of the time were published in the rival magazines. *All the Year Round* began with *A Tale of Two Cities* and followed with Wilkie Collins's *The Woman in White*; after a lapse with Charles Lever's *A Day's Ride*, which was unpopular and caused sales to drop, Dickens fought back with *Great Expectations*. *Evan Harrington*'s predecessor in *Once a Week* was Charles Reade's *The Cloister and the Hearth* (under the title *A Good Fight*), which was abruptly terminated because of a dispute, putting pressure on Meredith to begin publication sooner than he wished.

When *Evan Harrington* began publication it was running against *The Woman in White*, which John Sutherland has described as 'The pioneer sensation novel and one of the most popular and stylistically influential novels of the century.'[3] This fact was clearly uppermost in the minds of author and editor when Meredith began writing. In December 1859 Meredith wrote to Lucas:

> And please don't hurry for *emotion*. It will come. I have it. But – unless you have mysteries of the W[ilkie] Collins kind – interest, not to be false and evanescent, must kindle slowly, and ought to centre more in *character* – out of which incidents should grow.[4]

A few weeks later he writes, 'serial reading demands excitement enough to lead on, but, more and better, amusement of a quiet kind. The tension of the *W[oman] in W[hite]* is not exactly pleasant, though cleverly produced. One wearies of it.'[5]

Lucas appears also to have proposed Smollett as a model, for we find Meredith responding: 'I *do* want a dash of Smollett and I know it. But remember that *full* half the *incident* in Smollett trenches on amusing matter not permitted me by my public', and, 'Remember that in Smollett conduct is never *accounted* for. My principle is to show the events flowing from evident causes.'[6]

In these extracts from the letters we have seen Meredith upholding his 'principle' in the agitated context of competitive serial publication against one of the great Victorian best-sellers. Elsewhere, however, we see him, as Lionel Stevenson says, 'eager to co-operate with the editor at every turn'.[7]

For example, in the same letter in which he discusses Smollett, we find him rather pathetically promising a description of a cricket field:

> I will cut it in what pieces you please – especially the early part. But cricket fields are rather liked. I will attend to your suggestions if you will look over the number at once, and send them. The paragraph about 'eating and drinking' shall be cut out.... I ... will defer to my editor almost entirely.[8]

We have evidence here of a complex dialogic situation, which we may expect to see reflected in the novel. The reception of *Richard*

Feverel, including the Mudie ban, the dubiously sympathetic critique of Lucas, Lucas's role as editor, the demands of serial publication (with readers' responses coming in while the novel is still being written) and the immediate presence of competitor novels, constitute a powerful dialogic context. We have seen that Meredith was very aware of *The Woman in White* as a model for popular serial fiction, but there is no evidence that this directly influenced his practice in *Evan Harrington*.[9] Behind Wilkie Collins was a more powerful figure, and perhaps the most important in the context of *Evan Harrington*: Charles Dickens himself.

Meredith's recorded comments on Dickens are almost invariably unfavourable. When he was first approached about contributing to *Once a Week* he wrote, 'If it is of the character of *Household Words*, I am not suited to contribute. Facts on the broad grin, and the tricky style Dickens encouraged, I cannot properly do.'[10] A few years later he wrote to Swinburne that Robert Buchanan 'is always on the strain for pathos and would be a poetic Dickens'.[11] He could not even be gracious on the occasion of Dickens's death: 'Dickens gone! The *Spectator* says he beats Shakespeare at his best; and instances Mrs Gamp as superior to Juliet's nurse. This is a critical newspaper, you remember?'[12] Later in life he is reported by Edward Clodd as saying:

> Not much of Dickens will live, because it has so little correspondence to life. He was the incarnation of cockneydom, a caricaturist who aped the moralist; he should have kept to short stories. If his novels are read at all in the future, people will wonder what we saw in them, save some possible element of fun meaningless to them. The world will never let Mr Pickwick, who to me is full of the lumber of imbecility, share honours with Don Quixote.[13]

On the other hand an appreciative familiarity with Dickensian humour is evident in a series of locutions borrowed from Mrs Gamp and Mr Mantalini in letters to his friend William Hardman.[14] And, as we shall see in the next chapter, his response to Dickens in *Harry Richmond* tells a different story from his explicit comments.

Evan Harrington (subtitled in periodical form 'He Would Be A Gentleman') is an intelligent and entertaining, though uneven novel, which deserved to be more successful than it was, and might still be popular with people who read Victorian novels, or even as a television serialization. Like *The Ordeal of Richard Feverel* it has a profound autobiographical element and, indeed, the writer who was so touchy and secretive about his social origins seems almost reckless in the way he based this story of a socially aspiring tailor's family on his own – even using his grandfather's unusual name Melchizedek – and bringing into fictional proximity two elements that he must have been anxious to keep separate in life: those origins and his new familiarity with the aristocratic Duff Gordon family (the models for the Jocelyns in the novel).

Evan and his older sisters are the children of the 'Great Mel', a remarkable tailor who mixed with the aristocracy and was mistaken for a marquis, but left a burden of debt. The three daughters have risen by marriage, especially Louisa, who married a Portuguese Count, and although they admire their father intensely they deny him and their whole early lives. The novel opens with the return of Evan and Louisa from Portugal, after some unspecified disaster has befallen the Count, to be greeted with the news of their father's death and, for Evan, the insistence by his powerful and principled mother that he redeem the family honour by carrying on the business and repaying the debts. But Evan, under Louisa's influence, has himself developed a revulsion for his origins, and is moreover in love with the aristocratic Rose Jocelyn, whose comment on shopkeepers is 'I can't bear that class of people.... You can always tell them' (4, 38), and whose definition of a gentleman (to Evan) is 'Something you are, sir' (4, 45).

The novel's theme, then, is that most typical theme of the English novel, love and class, or love across the classes, with in this case the conflict between probity and social aspiration intensified by love. Evan and two of his sisters pay a prolonged visit to the Jocelyns' mansion, but only after he has drunkenly declared that he is the son of a tailor to a company that turns out to include Rose's brother and suitor. After much complication and speculation, the truth about the Harringtons' origin is established at Beckley Court, but by now Evan's demeanour has won the respect of Rose's family and their reluctant acceptance of him as her lover. However, Evan apparently ruins himself by taking upon himself a disgraceful action committed by his scheming sister Louisa, and leaves the house under a cloud. Eventually his fortunes are restored when the invalid young woman who inherits the Jocelyns' home, and is also in love with Evan, leaves everything to him, and he honourably makes it over to the Jocelyns.

For some reason the general contempt of the class who did not have to work for those who made a living in 'trade' was traditionally accentuated in the case of tailors. This contempt strikes not merely at the tailor's social status but at his very manhood. According to a proverb cited in the novel, it takes nine tailors to make a man (17, 214). Meredith was probably familiar with this passage in Rousseau's *Emile*:

> No lad ever wanted to be a tailor. It takes some art to attract a man to this woman's work. The same hand cannot hold the needle and the sword. If I were king I would only allow needlework and dressmaking to be done by women and cripples who are obliged to work at such trades. If eunuchs were required I think the Easterns were very foolish to make them on purpose. Why not take those provided by nature, that crowd of base persons without natural feeling?[15]

Speculating on the reasons for this peculiarly intensified form of snobbery, Natalie Cole Michta remarks that, while 'the posture of the tailor invites ridicule' (a matter of which Evan is painfully conscious), it is also true that 'the measuring and baring of a client's body when being outfitted makes him vulnerable as well'.[16] Moreover, as Swift and more recently Carlyle had brought home, the tailor held the key to the part played by appearance and concealment in upholding social distinctions.

As I have said, the novel is intelligent and entertaining. The portrayal of the encounters of the classes, and of class attitudes, is subtle and varied; Rose Jocelyn, Evan's beloved, though simpler than the later heroines, inaugurates the brave and independent Meredithian heroine. But the reader who comes to it from *The Ordeal of Richard Feverel* is likely to be most impressed by how comparatively conventional it is, stylistically and generically. More than any other novel of Meredith's, it lends itself to the kind of traditional appreciative commentary offered by a critic such as J.M.S. Tompkins.[17] Meredith does, of course, make use of character zones and parody, but these are not more marked than in the average Victorian novel, and do not constitute anything like the kind of ideological dialogue that we have seen in *Richard Feverel*. The parodistic elements are mostly confined to routine mock-heroic such as one might find in any novel of the period, and the function of character zone is also not distinctively Meredithian. In this example, the narrator adopts the voice of Evan's sister Louisa, exercising her considerable social skills to keep up a conversation at a grand picnic and silence a man who has been paid by her enemies to embarrass her:

> Have you an idea of the difficulty of keeping up the ball among a host of ill-assorted, stupid country people, who have no open topics, and can talk of nothing continuously but scandal of their neighbours, and who, moreover, feel they are not up to the people they are mixing with? (31, 404)

Louisa is snobbish, dishonest, unscrupulous and manipulative; she is also, as we shall see, the greatest artistic triumph of the novel; the narrator frequently, as here, betrays his sympathy and even admiration for her belief that, despite her birth, she is more than the equal of the aristocrats and country gentry among whom she has infiltrated herself. This, however, is the most routine and straightforward use of double-voiced discourse. The difference of this novel from *Richard Feverel* (and from Meredith's later great dialogic novels) is evident when the possibility of dialogic complication is in the air. Another sister of Evan's, the beautiful and pure-hearted Caroline, is married to a brutal army officer and, on her visit to Beckley Court, falls in love with a Duke, who presses her to become his mistress:

> This brother who might save her, to him she dared not speak. Did she wish to be saved? She only knew that to wound Evan's *sense of honour and the high and chivalrous veneration for her sex and pride in himself and those of his blood*, would be wicked and unpardonable, and that no earthly pleasure could drown it. Thinking this, with her hands joined in pale dejection, Caroline sat silent, and Evan left her to lay bare his heart to Rose. (25, 308, my italics)

The situation is in some ways comparable to the relationship between Richard Feverel and his cousin Clare: in both cases the hero has a moral authority over his female relative, but lacks the sensitivity to exercise it responsibly. The italicized portion of the passage is the kind of stylistically and ideologically marked discourse that is typically hybridized in Meredith. It has the stiffness and formality of an attitude too self-consciously struck, as likely to repel as to sustain the person in need of moral support. The thought of wounding Evan in this way might 'save' Caroline, but it also prevents her from confiding in him. And in any case, to be 'saved' is to return to the violent Major Strike. This is Caroline's character zone, but there is no reason to doubt that it is an accurate reading of Evan's self-image. What is the accent of the narrator? The fact that Evan, having unconsciously repelled his sister's confidence, goes on to lay bare his own heart suggests an irony. We need the context of the whole novel to decide this kind of thing, and although Evan is behaving egotistically here, his portrayal does not justify – as Richard Feverel's, Wilfrid Pole's, or even Harry Richmond's and Nevil Beauchamp's would – confidently attributing the ironic accent. The instance remains isolated. It is not caught up in what Bakhtin called 'the great dialogue of the novel'.[18]

The novel's generic conventionality is evident from my summary of the plot. Of all Meredith's novels it is the only one that straightforwardly conforms to the demands of comedy. The resolution saves Evan from choosing between probity and love, or social aspiration. Moreover, the resolution is effected by that most stereotypical of early Victorian plot devices, a legacy. On one occasion, when Evan falls from a horse and lies apparently lifeless, the narrator comments, 'But heroes don't die, you know' (20, 259). The archness, feebleness and irrelevance of this in comparison with the treatment of the Hero in *Richard Feverel* is revealing.

In the earlier part of the novel there are strong elements of a chronotopically more primitive kind of narrative, as Lionel Stevenson has pointed out.[19] As in Bakhtin's 'adventure time',[20] chance plays a major role in the turn of events when Evan sets out to walk from Lymport to London, with the intention of learning to be a tailor, and on the road meets Susan Wheedle, the sister of Rose's maid, who is pregnant by Rose's brother; he also meets an old schoolfriend, Jack Raikes; together they take Susan to an inn where Evan betrays his origins to a group of gentlemen who happen to include Rose's brother and suitor. The next day he attends a cricket match where he meets Rose and is invited to Beckley Court.

This part of the novel is full of motifs inherited by Dickens from Fielding and Smollett: roads, inns and coaches. As every critic of the novel has observed, there is also evidence of a conscious imitation of Dickens in certain of the overtly comic characters, particularly the Cogglesby brothers, lovably eccentric rich old men obviously inspired by the Cheerybles in *Nicholas Nickleby*, and Jack Raikes, who is modelled on early Dickens characters such as Dick Swiveller in *The Old Curiosity Shop*. Critics also universally agree that most of this comedy is dull and heavy-handed; in the case of Raikes, Meredith undoubtedly agreed himself, since he excised large portions concerning this character when he revised the novel.

By no means all of these conventional characteristics are to the novel's detriment. But, taken together, they do show a marked and consistent orientation towards the dialogic context that I sketched at the beginning of this chapter. In *Problems of Dostoevsky's Poetics* Bakhtin writes of speech which 'literally cringes in the presence or the anticipation of someone else's word, reply, objection'.[21] Something like this could be said of *Evan Harrington*. The laborious imitation of another author whom Meredith despised, or affected to despise, is the most extreme example of this phenomenon: this is the opposite of the sort of creative response to generic models that we saw in *Richard Feverel*. It is noteworthy, though not unusual for the time, that it is the early Dickens whom Meredith looks to: there is no sense, in his artistic response to him, that in the preceding decade, in works such as *Bleak House* and *Little Dorrit*, Dickens had invented a new kind of novel. And it is ironic that the novel Dickens next serialized in *All the Year Round*, *Great Expectations*, could easily have had the same subtitle as *Evan Harrington*, and was one of its author's greatest artistic triumphs.

There is, however, another, more positive sense in which *Evan Harrington* could be described as Dickensian, though it is unlikely that Meredith would have recognized it. Dickens's greatest comic characters are triumphs of language: the language of the Dickensian narrator, of course, but even more their own language. The great Dickensian characters are defined above all by their speech, and in many cases, such as Mrs Gamp and Mr Micawber, they are themselves conscious verbal artists, in control of the speech that defines them.[22] Meredith's borrowing of locutions from Mrs Gamp and Mr Mantalini suggests that he had some liking for this aspect of Dickens's art.

The Great Mel, the gentleman-tailor of Lympton and father of the novel's hero, dies in its first sentence. But, for the reader, he immediately comes to life as his fellow-tradesmen (and creditors) gather to talk about him. The language of the tradesmen is the standard vernacular of Victorian novels – 'coming the Marquis', 'there ain't many Marquises to match him' – but Kilne the publican is able extensively to reproduce the idiom of Mel himself: 'You know his way of talking.' In particular he repeats Mel's account of the occasion on which, in the company of gentlefolk, he renounced the snobbery that had made him relish the title 'Marquis':

' "When I was a younger man, I had the good taste to be fond of good society, and the bad taste to wish to appear different from what I was in it": that's Mel speaking; everybody was listening; so he goes on: "I was in the habit of going to Bath in the season, and *con*sorting with the gentlemen I met there on terms of equality; and for some reason that I am quite guiltless *of*," says Mel, "the hotel people gave out that I was a Marquis in disguise; and, upon my honour, ladies and gentlemen – I was young then, and a fool – I could not help imagining I looked the thing. At all events, I took upon myself to act the part, and with some success, and considerable gratification; for, in my opinion," says Mel, "no real Marquis ever enjoyed his title so much as I did. One day I was in my shop – No. 193, Main Street, Lymport – and a gentleman came in to order his outfit. I received his directions, when suddenly he started back, stared at me, and exclaimed: 'My dear Marquis! I trust you will pardon me for having addressed you with so much familiarity'. I recognized in him one of my Bath acquaintances. That circumstance, ladies and gentlemen, has been a lesson to me. Since that time I have never allowed a false impression with regard to my position to exist. I desire," says Mel, smiling, "to have my exact measure taken everywhere; and if the Michaelmas bird is to be associated with me, I am sure I have no objection; all I can say is, that I cannot justify it by letters patent of nobility."... Ah!' said Kilne, meditatively, 'I see him now, walking across the street in the moonlight, after he'd told me that. A fine figure of a man! and there ain't many Marquises to match him!' (1, 8–9)

This both is, and represents, an impressive achievement. Mel's speech is elegant but dignified. There is nothing of the 'coxcomb' about it. In asserting his true social status there is neither grovelling nor defiance. He gives the address of his shop, puns on taking measurements and gracefully plays with the standard joke about tailors and geese (a 'goose' is a tailor's smoothing-iron). The whole speech, in fact, is a response to a malicious jibe about geese, by George Uploft, one of the 'gentlemen' present. This remarkable speech, in which Mel displays the discursive skill which enabled him to 'pass' while renouncing the desire to do so, demonstrates his superiority not only to the George Uplofts and well-born oafs such as Harry Jocelyn and Ferdinand Laxley, but even to the genuinely civilized gentlefolk such as Lady Jocelyn: they inherit a style and a discourse; he has to invent one, that is not a mere imitation, still less a pretence, but a true social innovation, implicitly assuming equality with his company for the present, while acknowledging that their relations will change if one of them steps into his shop the next morning.

This is where we see Meredith's dialogic art in *Evan Harrington*. The speech is completely of its moment, shaped by the unique context of the tailor strangely yet somehow naturally commanding the admiring attention of gentlemen and ladies, from whom he will walk back to his shop at 193 Main Street. At the same time it is re-accented by Kilne the publican: we do not need to be told that the accents indicated by the italics are his and not Mel's.

This speech is proleptic, in relation to the central theme of the whole novel, and specifically in relation to the episode in which Evan deploys his command of the language and code of a gentleman to assert that he is not one:

> There was a disdainful smile on Evan's mouth, as he replied: 'I must first enlighten you. I have no pretensions to your blue blood, or yellow. If, sir, you will deign to challenge a man who is *not* the son of a gentleman, and consider the expression of his thorough contempt for your conduct sufficient to enable you to overlook that fact, you may dispose of me. My friend here has, it seems, reason to be proud of his connections. That you may not subsequently bring the charge against me of having led you to 'soil your hands' – as your friend there terms it – I, with all the willingness in the world to chastise you or him for your impertinence, must first give you a fair chance of escape, by telling you that my father was a tailor'. (12, 149)

Evan is a very young man, who has inherited a contradiction in his social formation, not, like his father, created an original hybrid.

Therefore it is not surprising that his speech lacks the ease of Mel's, or the maturity of realizing that Ferdinand Laxley, like George Uploft, is an unworthy opponent. In place of Mel's self-assurance there is egoistic self-assertion, and Evan's speech, unlike his father's, is a strained and defiant imitation of upper-class discourse, rather than his own invention. Like *Great Expectations*, Meredith's novel is a dramatization of the mid-Victorian struggle for possession of the ideological magic word, 'gentleman' – a struggle historically waged in, for example, the proliferation of public schools, the campaign for competitive entry to the Civil Service and the outcry, a few years before the publication of both novels, against aristocratic bungling in the conduct of the Crimean War. As Peter Bailey has written:

> There was a continuing radical animus against the aristocracy, exemplified in the campaign against the mismanagement of the Crimean War but, in general, hostility towards the old class enemy was diminishing. The guardians of the new morality... had no wish to ostracise their betters, but sought rather to use the new code as a discreet vehicle for advancing their own class by redefining the qualifications of a gentleman more in terms of conduct than heredity.[23]

Mel is not, of course, an ideal. He is financially irresponsible and a philanderer, dependent on and a trial to the very different strength of his wife. But he is a living spirit, almost the posthumous hero of the novel. Perhaps its most successful scene is a dinner at Beckley Court, focalized through Louisa, when, despite all her efforts to divert, the ghost of the Great Mel takes over the conversation. Just as the dull tradesman Kilne is gifted with the speech of Mel, so the dull squire George Uploft is transfigured by the tales of Mel into an entertaining raconteur. The episode is torment to Louisa and to Caroline (who eventually collapses), but to the reader it is testimony to the genius of their father.

As Lady Jocelyn says, 'The man's an Epic!' Margaret Tarratt compares him to Falstaff as 'the poet creator of his own image' and 'Carlyle's tailor/poet whose poetic creation is his own style of life and enduring reputation'.[24] Or, as I have suggested, the self-creating characters of Dickens.

A dead man cannot *quite* be the hero of a novel, but Mel's daughter Louisa can claim to be the heroine. Louisa is undoubtedly the artistic triumph of *Evan Harrington*. Her disgraceful behaviour – above all writing an anonymous letter and letting someone else take the blame – her ruthlessly snobbish attitudes and her affected language appear to identify her as the scapegoat of the family's social aspiration. She has neither her father's unaffected ease nor her brother's highly developed sense of honour. But she is also seen as a heroine of class conflict, a comic epitome of the lengthy and complex historical process in which the 'trading' middle class imitates, infiltrates, merges with, flatters, despises and usurps the landed aristocracy. She shows genuine courage in entering Beckley Court even when she knows that Evan has publicly declared his origins, and endless wit and resourcefulness in gaining time for Evan to win one of the available young women before the pretence becomes unsustainable. In a real sense she is the representative of Meredith himself – indeed, of the typical Victorian novelist – in her borderline status, and in the boldness and perceptiveness with which she enters, represents (in her letters to her sister, which have an important narrative function), and criticizes the world of the aristocratic country house. She thus exemplifies at a high level the profound historical dimension of Bakhtin's concept of the chronotope, being a developed instance of his category of the 'parvenu' who 'has not yet found a definite or fixed place in life, but who seeks personal success', a role which 'impels him to study personal life, uncover its hidden workings, spy and eavesdrop on its most intimate secrets'.[25]

This borderline status is of course most effectively portrayed in her own language. The narrator several times comments on shifts in her discursive style, of which a good example can be seen in one of her letters:

> Your note awaited me. No sooner my name announced, than servitors in yellow livery, with powder and buckles started before me, and bowing one presented it on a salver. A venerable butler – most impressive! led the way. In future, my dear, let it be *de Saldar de Sancorvo*. That is our title *by rights*, and it may as well be so in England. English *Countess* is certainly best. Always put the *de*....Silva has great reliance upon me. The farther he is from Lymport, my dear! – and imagine me, Harriet, driving through Fallowfield to Beckley Court! I gave one peep at Dubbins's, as I passed. The school still goes on. I saw three little girls skipping, and the old swing-pole. SEMINARY FOR

YOUNG LADIES as bright as ever! I should have liked to have kissed the children and given them bonbons and a holiday. (14, 176–7)

The letter opens with a *grande dame* manner, instructing her older sister as a junior partner in the same enterprise, and barely controlling and disguising her parvenu's excitement at being accepted at Beckley Court. When she speaks of her old school, her manner becomes more spontaneous and idiomatic. This contrast is more marked in her speech. To the diplomat's family who bring her and Evan back from Portugal she speaks in a manner that Lady Jocelyn is to describe as euphuistic, with vocabulary consciously learned from Johnson's dictionary:

I can trust with confidence that, if it is for Silva's interest, he will assuredly so dispose of his influence as to suit the desiderations of his family, and not in any way oppose his opinions to the powers that would willingly stoop to serve us! (4, 37)

This, which comes perilously close to the comically inflated speech of the footman Berry in *Richard Feverel*, who also learns words from Johnson, is cunningly combined with a foreign accent and unidiomatic speech patterns, exaggerating the importance of her Portuguese background, and placing her outside the English system of class-dialects:

My brother perhaps does not think of us foremost; but his argument I can distinguish. I can see, that were you openly to plead Silva's cause, you might bring yourself into odium, Mr Jocelyn; and heaven knows I would not that! (ibid., p. 43)

In private to Evan, by contrast, she speaks succinctly and unaffectedly:

Put your faith in an older head, Evan. It is your only chance of society in England. For your brother-in-law – I ask you, what sort of people will you meet at the Cogglesbys? (ibid., p. 40)

Louisa, then, is another Dickensian character in the positive sense I have defined. As Donald D. Stone says, suggestively comparing her with another commoner 'ennobled' by marriage, the Baroness

Eugenia in James's *The Europeans* (1878): 'the Countess seems more of an artist with words than a simple *poseuse*'.[26]

Despite the real merits of the novel, and despite the clear evidence of Meredith's conscious attempt to adapt his writing to popular serial readership, *Evan Harrington* was not a popular success, either as a serial or in three-volume form, though it did go into a second edition in 1866. It was 'sparsely' reviewed, though the reviews it did receive were 'in the main warmly appreciative'.[27] Meredith himself appears to have felt more hostile to it, at least immediately after finishing it, than to any of his other novels. He accused Rossetti of speaking 'too favourably of it' and went on to disparage the book more severely than any reviewer:

> I fell into slipshod, and had to scuffle on anyhow. The Countess, you see, has only one side of her character to the reader. The action was too quick, continuous: the space too short. It is a comedy, as I have said, and this should explain some of the shortcomings of the work. The writing is atrocious. It is quite destitute of the *lumen purpureum* which I like to give. How a work without colour, can please you at all, astonishes me. Raikes is abominably vulgar.... I am so disgusted that I can't even persuade myself to touch it up for the re-issue. The nausea is too strong. It must go forth much as it is. But for the question of money I would quash it altogether.[28]

This is excessive, and would perhaps be so for any case of simple artistic failure. There is a strong case for believing that Meredith's 'nausea' was brought on by the consciousness of having compromised, artistically 'cringed', to no avail.

His disgust at *Evan Harrington* is relevant to the peculiarities of his next novel, *Sandra Belloni* (originally published as *Emilia in England*). This book took him three years to write, and there is abundant evidence in the letters of the immense difficulty it gave him.[29] On at least one occasion he completely rewrote it, and there seems to have been some fundamental change in the conception. There are certain features which suggest that he was still aiming for the same popularity that *Evan Harrington* failed to achieve. At the same time there is the strongest evidence yet of a defiantly highbrow conception of novelistic art, and the accompanying polemic with his readers. The novel was eventually published, in 1864, by Chapman and Hall at Meredith's risk.

In plot and theme there are certain obvious parallels with *Evan Harrington*. Again the novel is about an upwardly mobile brother and three sisters; all of them are seeking advantageous marriages. Their position in society is more secure than that of the Harringtons: they are rich, their father is a city merchant, which is more socially acceptable than a tailor, and the story is set at a later date, when aristocratic prejudice against 'trade' is less pronounced. The Poles do not need literally to conceal their background, but they do not choose to parade it, are embarrassed when their father drops aitches, and mortified when their genteel existence is invaded by his old friend, the grotesquely vulgar Irishwoman, Mrs Chump: 'Her main offence was, that she revived for them so much of themselves that they had buried' (27, 272). The mode is predominantly comic, but it is a different kind of comedy from that of *Evan Harrington*. The portrayal of the Pole family is remorselessly ironic. This is especially so in the case of Wilfrid, who is structurally the hero of the novel, but functions as Meredith's most extensive and explicit analysis of 'sentimentalism', almost as if he were a scapegoat for his author's indulgence to Evan Harrington. It is moreover a kind of comedy that can encompass tragedy, at least the muted 'tragedy of sentiment', when one of the characters commits suicide; and, in marked contrast to its predecessor, it has no recognizable plot and the conclusion 'holds aloft no nuptial torch'.[30] The novel's relation to comedy is also skewed by the character of the eponymous heroine, Emilia Alessandra Belloni, a musical genius and enthusiastic Italian patriot, who is conceived in a mode of heroic and passionate simplicity, and is completely impervious to irony or ridicule. For most of the novel Emilia is in love with the shifty and selfish sentimentalist Wilfrid, and no reader can hope for their union.

From the start of the novel we are made aware of an overt and dominant, even tyrannical narrator's voice, whose characteristic tone is ironic and favourite theme sentimentalism. This narrator informs us in the first few pages that the Poles are sentimentalists. The following is a good example of his tone:

Nor let the philosopher venture hastily to despise them as pipers to dilettante life. Such persons come to us in the order of civilization. In their way they help to civilize us. Sentimentalists are a perfectly natural growth of a fat soil. Wealthy communities must engender them. (1, 6)

To describe this rather elusive tone it might help to invoke Bakhtin's idea of the 'word with a loophole':

> A loophole is the retention for oneself of the possibility for altering the ultimate, final meaning of one's own words. If a word retains such a loophole this must inevitably be reflected in its structure. This potential other meaning, that is, the loophole left open, accompanies the word like a shadow. Judged by its meaning alone, the word with a loophole should be an ultimate word and does present itself as such, but in fact it is only the penultimate word and places after itself only a conditional, not a final, period.[31]

Judging by the 'meaning alone', the denotative meaning, the passage from *Sandra Belloni* seems to be a confession of complicity with the 'sentimentalists', a confession that the contemptuous irony which is conveniently attributed to the 'philosopher' is not entirely earned, or not entirely honest. The 'loophole' is in certain phrases which might be construed as imparting a sneer to the whole passage. 'Such people' distances the Poles, reduces them to an exemplary function which is at odds with their prominence in the novel; 'In their way' is a standard marker of condescension, carrying the implication that this startling admission about the link between sentimentalism and civilization is little more than a patronizing sop; 'perfectly natural' is a polemical rejoinder to an implied reader who would pronounce the Poles *un*natural, but the ironic tone lets this other meaning in, does not unambiguously contradict it. As we shall see, this 'loophole' is of central thematic importance.

The most damning evidence of the Poles' sentimentalism is their own speech, which Meredith subjects to the most ruthlessly satirical analysis. In the second chapter they go to a wood in the moonlight, drawn by reports that a wonderful singer frequents it. They are accompanied by Mr Pericles, a wealthy Greek musical enthusiast and connoisseur, to whom the eldest sister says, 'Does there not seem a soul in the moonlight?':

> Arabella, after a rapturous glance at the rosy orb, put it to Mr Pericles, in subdued impressive tones. She had to repeat her phrase; Mr Pericles then echoing, with provoking monotony of tone, 'Sol?' – whereupon 'Soul!' was reiterated, somewhat sharply: and Mr Pericles, peering over the collar of the bear

[skin coat], with half an eye, continued the sentence, in the manner of one sent thereby farther from its meaning: – 'Ze moonlight?' Despairing and exasperated. Arabella commenced afresh: 'I said, there seems a *soul* in it'; and Mr Pericles assented bluntly: 'In ze light!' – which sounded so little satisfactory that Arabella explained, 'I mean the *aspect*'; and having said three times distinctly what she meant, in answer to a terrific glare from the unsubmerged whites of the eyes of Mr Pericles, this was his comment, almost roared forth:

'Sol! you say *so-whole* – in ze moonlight – Luna? Hein? Ze aspect is of Sol! – Yez'. (2, 8)

This is dialogic comedy, in which the absurd re-accenting of Arabella's 'sentimentalism' pinches its substance to nothing. The party finds Emilia, and listens to her singing. Their speech is then contrasted with hers:

'You feel that the place inspires you?' said Cornelia.

'I am obliged to come', she explained. 'The good old dame at the farm is ill, and she says that music all day is enough for her, and I must come here, or I should get no chance of playing at all at night'.

'But surely you feel an inspiration in the place, do you not?' Cornelia persisted.

She looked at this lady as if she had got a hard word given her to crack, and muttered: 'I feel it quite warm here. And I do begin to love the place'.

The stately Cornelia fell back a step. (2, 13)

This direct, unselfconscious utterance is Emilia's most distinctive characteristic throughout the novel. In contrast the other characters' language is full of 'loopholes' – even, in the Pole sisters' case, on principle. When her father gets into a difficulty between two rival working-class clubs Adela, referring to Emila's promise to sing to one of the clubs, says, 'You should have done as our darling here did, papa. . . . You should have hinted something that might be construed as a promise or not, as we please to read it' (9, 75). Emilia, of course, keeps her promise.

In a later scene Meredith provides an example that Bakhtin would surely have pounced on delightedly if he had known it. Wilfrid is 'sentimentally' in love with Emilia and she responds with straightforward passion. At the same time, and with his father's encouragement, he allows himself to become implicitly engaged to the aristocrat, Lady Charlotte Chillingworth. Partly to secure Wilfrid, and partly to 'cure' Emilia of her passion, Lady Charlotte arranges a scene with him that Emilia overhears. In the course of this scene she tries to make him say that he loves her. Eventually she succeeds, but for some time he resists, and this piece of dialogue occurs:

> 'Dear Wilfrid', she whispered, 'you think you are doubted. I want to be certain that you think you have met the right woman to help you, in me?'
> He passed through the loophole here indicated, and breathed.
> 'Yes, Charlotte, I am sure of that. If I could only be half as worthy! You are full of courage and unselfishness, and, I could swear, faithful as steel'. (36, 387)

We have already seen that Emilia's speech is simple and direct. Closer examination, however, reveals that it is not entirely unproblematic. In this passage she is telling Wilfrid about her family background:

> My mother was English. But I feel that I am much more Italian than English. How I long for Italy – like a thing underground! My father did something against the Austrians, when he was a young man. Would not I have done it? I am sure I would – I don't know what. Whenever I think of Italy, night or day, pant-pant goes my heart. The name of Italy is my nightingale: I feel that somebody lives that I love, and is ill-treated shamefully, crying out to me for help'. (6, 39)

This speech is plainly not idiomatic English. Like that of Louisa in *Evan Harrington*, it is 'foreign'. But, despite Emilia's passionate attachment to Italy, there is no evidence that she has ever been there. Indeed, as the half-English daughter of an Italian politically exiled because of something he did 'when he was a young man', it is highly unlikely. Emilia is a working-class English girl with an Italian father. Such a person would not speak as she does: her speech is not realistically motivated. It is as artificial as Louisa's, though here the artifice is the author's, not the character's. Every example of working-class speech in Meredith shows that it would have been impossible for him to make such a heroine as Emilia speak realistically. The foreignness of her speech allows it to be simple without the taint of 'commonness'; it allows figurative effects such as 'like a thing underground' and 'my nightingale', without seeming pretentious; it lends a kind of stately formality to expressions such as 'Would not I have done it?' Above all it places Emilia outside the whole system of social dialects, and even outside 'civilization'.[32]

Emilia is considered uncivilized by characters with very varying degrees of closeness to the narrator. For Wilfrid, whose character zone is so objectified that there is rarely any danger of mistaking it for authorial commentary, she is 'a little unformed girl, who had no care to conceal the fact that she was an animal, nor any notion of the necessity for doing so' (5, 36). The following dialogue is between Merthyr Powys, whose unselfish love for Emilia is the antithesis of Wilfrid's, and his half-sister Georgiana Ford:

'You will not give up this task you have imposed on yourself?' she said.
'To do what?'
She could have answered: 'To make this unsatisfactory creature love you'; but her words were, 'To civilize this little savage'.
Merthyr was bright in a moment: 'I don't give up till I see failure'. (47, 497)

These characters, whose names so strikingly resemble their author's, and of whom the man at least is one of a long line of Meredithian 'raisonneurs' (see Chapter 1, p. 26), are eventually conceded by the narrator to be 'A sentimental pair likewise... but these were sentimentalists who served an active deity, and not that arbitrary projection of a subtle selfishness which rules the fairer portion of our fat England' (48, 510).

This displacement of what has appeared to be the novel's central concept is remarkable, but we must recall that very early 'loophole' utterance of the narrator, in which he acknowledged that 'Such persons [as the sentimental Poles] come to us in the order of civilization.' Another acknowledgement has been made in one of the most dialogized passages of the novel:

Bear in mind that we are sentimentalists. The eye is our servant, not our master; and so are the senses generally. We are not bound to accept more than we choose from them. Thus we obtain delicacy; and thus, as you will perceive, our civilization, by the aid of the sentimentalists, has achieved an effective varnish. There, certainly, to the vulgar mind a tail is visible. The outrageous philosopher declares vehemently that no beast of the field or the forest would own such a tail. (His meaning is, that he discerns the sign of the animal slinking under the garb of the stately polished creature. I have all the difficulty in the world to keep him back and let me pursue my course.) These philosophers are a bad-mannered body. Either in opposition, or in the support of them, I maintain simply that the blinking sentimentalist helps to make civilization what it is, and civilization has a great deal of merit. (29, 290)

This passage is apropos of Adela Pole's belief that one should 'not see' things which conflict with one's ideal conception of life. Its opening appears to be double-voiced in a fairly unambiguous way: the narrator adopts an ironic and merely grammatical identity with the sentimentalists, to speak 'for' them in a plain and revealing way that they would never adopt themselves. Then, in the fourth sentence, he drops this grammatical fiction and consigns 'the sentimentalists' to the objectifying third person. The dialogism is then complicated however by the intrusion of the 'philosopher'.

Judith Wilt, whose chapter in *The Readable People of George Meredith* is one of the most substantial discussions of *Sandra Belloni*, sees the dialogue between the novelist and the philosopher as central to the novel, and akin to that between Dame Gossip and the novelist in *The Amazing Marriage*. The novelist is 'a sort of theatrical promoter-cum-Mudie's-librarian, alive to the difficulties of pleasing the mass audience', while the Philosopher's role is to 'harass the Novelist into stopping the action of the novel long enough to allow...some meditation on character, motive, development, and the implications of events'.[33] This is certainly a part of his role, and an example of Meredith's newly overt polemic with his readership,[34] but only towards the end of the novel. Whereas the dialogue in *The Amazing Marriage* is sustained, consistent and structurally organic, this one is fitful and uncertain. We have seen the philosopher's first mention in Chapter 1, where he is merely a rhetorical device. He reappears in Chapter 8 as the absurd proponent of a theory about the influence of hats on the personality: a parody of a nineteenth-century psychologist. Chapter 29 is the first occasion on which we seem to be asked to take him seriously, and here the dialogue is not between different conceptions of novelistic art, but between different attitudes to sentimentality. The philosopher is the ferocious and uncompromising scourge of sentimentalists; the narrator speaks, as before, with a loophole. 'These philosophers are a bad-mannered body' certainly permits, if not encourages, an ironic interpretation, while the rather mincing litotes of 'civilization has a great deal of merit' is full of nods, winks, 'sideward glances' and other shifty dialogic properties. In other words, he not only half-confesses his complicity with the sentimentalists, he speaks like one. Adela would surely approve of the way he 'hint[s] something that might be construed...as we please to read it'.

But we might have suspected this as early as the second chapter, when the same narrator who scoffs at Arabella's 'Does there not seem a soul in the moonlight?' writes of Emilia:

> Tell me, what opens heaven more flamingly to heart and mind, than the voice of a woman, pouring clear accordant notes in the blue night sky, that grows light blue to the moon? (2, 10)

I think we can see that *Sandra Belloni* is a novel full of dialogic potential. The narrator is unreliable, or at least incompletely candid. The two central concepts, sentimentality and civilization, are unstable. The narrator is both the scourge of sentimentalism and a sentimentalist himself. Eventually the concept that has dominated the novel seems to concede to the old familiar ethical category of selfishness, the difference between Wilfrid Pole and Merthyr Powys essentially the same as that between Arthur Donnithorne and Adam Bede. Emilia is seen as an 'animal' and 'savage' in contrast to the whole range of 'civilized' and 'sentimental' characters, yet she is a mistress of the civilized art of operatic music (and has a *trained* voice and accepts the need for further training: she is no warbler of woodnotes wild, despite the setting) whose singing the narrator celebrates in the language of a sentimentalist. At the heart of the novel is a serious and important trouble about civilization and, if not its discontents, at least the deformations that it exacts. For a consciously highbrow novelist exercising the civilized art of the Victorian novel this trouble is intrinsically undecidable: it demands dialogic treatment. And the novel has many dialogic features: as in all of Meredith's novels, discourse is constantly put under explicit scrutiny; we have seen examples of double-voiced discourse; the dialogue with the philosopher, in which the shifty narrator is answered by a 'principled' voice that is self-consciously turgid and deaf to its audience, is, however undeveloped, a forum in which the trouble becomes explicit.

There is, however, one sentimental feature of the novel which is not dialogized. I have already argued that Emilia's foreign idiom is not realistically motivated, and that it allows Meredith to place her outside the system of class dialects, and above all to have a heroine who is working-class but not, in her most important attribute, her speech, 'common'. This is surely 'seek[ing] to enjoy without incurring the Immense Debtorship for a thing done' (*ORF*, 24, 220) with a vengeance. Moreover, since Emilia is one of Meredith's most seductive characters, it is almost impossible to read the novel without complying with this sentimentalism.

It would be both ungenerous and inappropriate to the undecidable character of this fascinating novel to close discussion with a finalizing comment, and it is in any case somehow characteristic of the book that some of its most striking effects have slipped my argument. One of these has an ironic bearing on what I have just said.

The first phase of the relationship between Wilfrid and Emilia culminates in an enigmatic scene following the fiasco of her performance for the working-men's club, when the rival clubs fight and her harp is broken. Emilia is rescued by Wilfrid, who incurs a blow on the cheek, and Captain Gambier. This latter is a reputed ladykiller with whom Emilia ingenuously confesses to have had assignations in London, who has followed her into the country and escorted her to the club. His pursuit of her continues throughout most of the novel, without ever being resolved, and it is later suggested that his reputation is a malicious slander. On her walk from the club with Wilfrid, Emilia suggests sitting:

> on the fork of a dry log under flowering hawthorn. A pale shadowy blue centre of light among the clouds told where the moon was. Rain had ceased, and the refreshed earth smelt all of flowers, as if each breeze going by held a nosegay to their nostrils.
>
> Wilfrid was sensible of a sudden marked change in her. His blood was quicker than his brain in feeling it. Her voice now,

even in common speaking, had that vibrating richness which in her singing swept his nerves. (12, 103)

Their conversation turns on her relations with Gambier, and she tells Wilfrid that she has agreed to go to Italy with him. At this point:

Wilfrid jumped up.
'The smell of this tree's detestable', he said, glancing at the shadowing hawthorn.
   Emilia rose quietly, plucked a flower off the tree, and put it in her bosom. (12, 107)

This scene seems to be both psychological and emblematic. Wilfrid's awareness of a change in Emilia could be both a response to the 'refreshed earth' and the smell of flowers, and a response to *her* response to these. When she tells him about her relations with Gambier, he suddenly finds the smell of the tree 'detestable' and Emilia emblematically puts a flower 'in her bosom'. This is a fine if extremely indirect example of the 'psychic sexual sphere' (see Chapter 1, pp. 22–3) in Meredith. The scene culminates in a kiss which Emilia for a long time, and Wilfrid for a moment, considers an emotional commitment. The following morning Wilfrid suddenly leaves without seeing her, and the narrator makes an elaborate and self-conscious attempt to explain that this is because of his disfigured face and the memory that Emilia's 'hair was redolent of pipe-smoke' which combine shamingly to remind him of her low associations. The pipe-smoke in particular seems to preoccupy him:

Wilfrid was young, and under the dominion of his senses; which can be, if the sentimentalists will believe me, as tyrannous and misleading when super-refined as when ultra-bestial. He made a good stout effort to resist the pipe-smoke. Emilia's voice, her growing beauty, her simplicity, her peculiar charms of feature, were all conjured up to combat the dismal images suggested by that fatal, dragging-down smell. It was vain. Horrible pipe-smoke pervaded the memory of her. (13, 113)

This is very curious, since no mention was made, in the narrative of the previous evening, of Wilfrid's susceptibility to pipe-smoke, or that Emilia's hair smelt of it; whereas his susceptibility to *another* smell, that of hawthorn blossom, was very marked and explicit. Moreover, the context of his susceptibility to that smell was not Emilia's low associations but the enigma of her sexuality. The narrator chides Wilfrid for being perturbed about Emilia's relations with Gambier:

> Could her artist nature, of which he had heard perplexing talk, excuse her and make her heart absolutely guiltless (what he called 'innocent'), in trusting herself to any man's honour? I regret to say that the dainty adorers of the sex are even thus grossly suspicious of all women when their sentiment is ever so triflingly offended. (11, 93)

Nevertheless a reader may legitimately wonder whether Emilia's insouciance about her relations with Gambier comes from an ignorance incredible in a working-class girl brought up in London, or from indifference. The reader may conclude that Meredith's refusal to clarify this matter is to his credit, but it is hardly surprising that it should perturb a young Victorian gentleman, or that he should be unsettled by the 'sudden marked change in her' which might well be sexual arousal, especially since it occurs in the scent of the hawthorn tree, under which she has chosen to sit, whose flower she puts in her bosom, and whose heavy, overpowering perfume is traditionally associated with female sexuality.[35]

From Emilia's sexuality to the smell of pipe-smoke Meredith makes a devious metaphoric/metonymic chain which enables him to hint at 'matter not permitted me by my public' (see note 6), and at the same time links Wilfrid's class susceptibilities with his sexual super-refinement, as symptoms of sentimentalism. The irony is that the author's recourse to an artificial idiom for Emilia is another symptom of the same thing.

Meredith planned and began a sequel to *Emilia in England* but, he wrote early in 1864, 'I have an English novel, of the real story-telling order that must roll off soon and precede it.'[36] In October of that year he was speaking of it as a one-volume novel entitled *Rhoda Fleming – A Plain Story*, which he expected to have 'ripe and ready' for January, and as 'a right excellent story'.[37] Already in November, however, it had become "A plain Story' of 600 pages (2 vols)',[38] and in January he wrote revealingly and entertainingly, in Biblical burlesque style (his correspondent was a clergyman):

But, hear! the man went and got married: it was well for him: he bought linen, he bought plate, disbursed early and eke late: the fat end of his purse did set flowing towards his fireside, and the lean was to them that did accredit him. So. And meantime, in prospect of the needful, he put aside *Vittoria* (which contains points of grandeur and epical interest), to 'finish off' *Rhoda Fleming* in one volume, now swollen to two – and Oh, will it be three? – But this is my Dd. Dd. Dd. uncertain workmanship.[39]

He is now saying that he has put into Rhoda's history 'more work than she deserves', and a month later he 'do[es]n't at all know what to think of the work'.[40]

The phrase 'plain story' survives into the second paragraph of the text of the novel itself but few readers, from its first reviewers to its best modern critic, David Howard, have thought it accurate. J.C. Jeaffreson, the *Athenaeum* critic, said bluntly that Meredith 'at times renders it no easy task for the reader to catch his meaning' and 'lacks the story-teller's special power of holding the attention by an easy flow of thoughts'.[41] Howard gives a subtle critical account of this 'irritating' characteristic as 'peripheralism', and moves from:

> considering *Rhoda Fleming* as incompetent or reluctant popular fiction... towards regarding it as subversive fiction. Subversive technically, that is, undermining the norms of fiction – not simply the norms of popular fiction, but the norms of fiction itself – in particular its centralities of action and protagonist, its revelations and climaxes. And subversive socially.[42]

Evidently, then, *Rhoda Fleming* is, like *Sandra Belloni*, a work that changed its character during the course of composition, possibly despite the author's intention. In the absence of early drafts it is impossible to determine the character of the one-volume plain story that Meredith thought he was writing, but a plot-summary of the actual novel clearly reveals strong traces of a straightforward and traditional story which might be described as a dialogic presence. In the following summary the italicized passages represent episodes that are narrated indirectly and/or analeptically.

Rhoda and Dahlia Fleming are sisters who grow up on a Kentish farm. Dahlia goes to stay with her uncle in London and *is seduced there by Edward Blancove, the nephew of the local squire.* She writes to her family that she is married but, *after a tour on the continent, is half-abandoned by Edward in a London lodging-house*, where she evades the attempts of her father and sister to see her. Rhoda, a young woman of 'savage... virgin pride' (5, 40) and Hebraic rigidity, refuses against the evidence to believe that her sister has been seduced. Robert Eccles, a reformed drunkard who has come to work on the farm, falls in love with an unresponsive Rhoda, *and adopts direct and violent means to bring the seducer to account, assaulting the wrong man in the process and being assaulted himself*. Edward, *under the spell of another woman, is complicit in a callous plot to pay a brutal man called Sedgett to marry Dahlia. She at first submits to this, having been weakened by brain-fever*, but on her wedding day makes clear that she is still deeply in love with Edward. Edward repents and tries to forestall the wedding, but Rhoda, who insists on regarding Sedgett as a 'noble man' who will retrieve her sister's honour, exerts her will to force the marriage. Because Edward's cousin, to whom the pay-off money was entrusted, has squandered it, *Sedgett is not paid and deserts Dahlia after the ceremony*. This dissipates Rhoda's illusions but her father still persists in seeing Sedgett as a rightful husband, and champions him when he returns to claim Dahlia. In a tumultuous conclusion, news arrives that the marriage was bigamous, it is discovered that Dahlia has taken poison, she recovers, but her passion for Edward has been exhausted by her suffering.

In this story there is evidently a strong presence of a conventional seduction-plot. The strength of its presence can be seen in the way J.C. Jeaffreson summarized the story: 'it is not without labour that Dahlia is traced through sin to shame, through shame to brain-fever in a London hospital, and onwards to a condition of angelic penitence'.[43] Every key word in this summary is wrong: it represents the reimposition on the novel of precisely the ideological fable that Meredith, by his dialogic art, is attempting to subvert.

The most obvious form of this subversion is what Howard calls 'peripheralism'. On the first page Meredith offers a conventional metaphor of the story as a stream which 'runs from a home of flowers into regions where flowers are few and sickly, on to where the flowers which breathe sweet breath have been proved in mortal fire'. But the story is no more a free-flowing stream than that of any other Meredith novel. The space which a reader might expect to be occupied by such episodes as Dahlia's seduction and abandonment, or Robert's violent campaign, is taken up with the extensive adventures of the comic characters, Edward's cousin and Dahlia's uncle.

The conclusion is particularly subversive of any of the conventional variants of the seduction fable. A series of resolutions, alternatively tragic and comic, is offered and withdrawn: Edward arrives just in time to save her from marriage to Sedgett; he is forestalled by Rhoda and the dreadful marriage goes ahead; it turns out to be bigamous, employing a motif that had just enjoyed a period of intense and notorious fashion;[44] she attempts suicide before this news reaches her; she does not die after all; despite which, her heart left 'among the ashes' (48, 499), she passes the remaining seven years of her life in an extremely unconvincingly evoked transcendence: 'In truth, she sat above the clouds' (ibid.). As Howard says, 'Meredith seems set to destroy his gently tearful ending.'[45]

As in *Richard Feverel*, the style varies in a way that suggests generic instability, especially in the earlier part of the novel. The early chapters, establishing the rural background, seem emulative of the recent success of George Eliot's early novels. Words such as 'yeomanry' and 'damsels' seem to be planted to produce a pastoral effect. However, the narrator's discourse also includes phrases that are jarringly suggestive of petty-bourgeois social aspiration: 'they were, if I may adopt the eloquent modern manner of eulogy, strikingly above their class'; 'they remembered, and crooned over, till by degrees they adopted, the phrases and manner of speech of highly grammatical people' (1, 4). The whole story, in fact, could be seen as a baleful version of *Adam Bede*, with Dahlia as an unrepentant Hetty; Robert as a stalwart Adam who assaults the wrong man and has a dark side as a drunkard; Edward as an Arthur who is both more contemptible and more intelligent; and Rhoda an obverse of Dinah who represents the harshly punitive and antisexual aspects of Christianity. In striking contrast to George Eliot's early novels, the rural setting conveys no sense of community, even when Meredith makes laboured attempts to emulate the pub conversation of the famous 'Rainbow Inn' scene in *Silas Marner*. The farm and the neighbouring squire's house are isolated from any context other than the traditional diagrammatic juxtaposition of high-born youth and lowly damsel.

When, for the first and only time, the relationship of Dahlia and Edward is directly narrated, a new manner enters the novel: the portrayal of their mutually alienated existence in London lodgings is done with a bleak naturalism that anticipates the lodging-house scenes of Gissing, and the conventional melodrama of the fallen woman out of sorts with her lover is undercut by constant references to unappetizing food. This episode also includes some of the best examples of the subtly dialogic style that is fitfully employed throughout the novel – for example, 'Men are so considerately practical!...But women, when they choose to be unhappy, will not accept of practical consolations!' (11, 99) where the first sentence is accented with an irony that implies a female speaker (or audience), and the second has the accentuation of a male complaint.

Perhaps the most extreme example of this generic instability occurs when Rhoda first learns of Dahlia's sexual danger. Making a surprise visit to her sister in London, she arrives while Dahlia is out. When she returns, Rhoda feigns sleep and hears Dahlia soliloquizing thus:

> 'I came for my Bible....I promised mother – oh, my poor darling mother! And Dody lying in my bed! Who would have thought of such things? Perhaps heaven does look after us and interfere. What will become of me? Oh, you pretty innocent in your sleep! I lie for hours, and can't sleep....
>
> 'How flushed I am!...No; I'm pale, quite white. I've lost my strength. What can I do? How could I take mother's Bible, and run from my pretty one, who expects me, and dreams she'll wake with me beside her in the morning! I can't – I can't! If you love me, Edward, you won't wish it'. (5, 42–43)

As we shall see, it is not unusual for Meredith to make parodic use of popular fictional styles and devices, especially those of the sentimental melodrama that he hated, such as *East Lynne*. His most effective use of such parody, however, is clearly linked to the ironic representation of a character's consciousness, such as Willoughby's retributive fantasy in *The Egoist* and Dacier's proposal to Constance in *Diana of the Crossways*. In these instances the parody serves to link the corrupt consciousness of the character with a current and powerful ideological discourse. In the present instance the rhetoric cannot be taken seriously in the hands of a novelist such as Meredith, but because Dahlia, as the supposed subject of this discourse, is a completely inappropriate target for this kind of irony, the effect is merely one of gratuitous mockery of the kind of reader who *could* take it seriously, or crude rib-nudging of the more sophisticated reader.

Another example of the incongruous presence of a popular novelistic mode is in the portrayal of Nicodemus Sedgett, the man bribed to marry Dahlia, and Robert Eccles's old enemy. The narrator writes of this character in the following manner:

> the look was unmistakably savage, animal, and bad.... Sedgett turned his dull brown eyes on him, the thick and hateful flush of evil blood informing them with detestable malignity. (29, 305 and 308)

Later Robert wonders how Rhoda 'could have looked on Sedgett for an instant without reading his villainous nature' (39, 413). The portrayal of Sedgett is probably the occasion of the worst writing in the novel. For the Bakhtinian critic there is always a ready temptation to pass off such writing as parody or stylization. How, from a Bakhtinian point of view, can one say that a piece of writing is simply bad? Bakhtin warns of the danger that, for the inept reader, 'stylization will be taken for style, parody simply for a poor work of art'.[46] However, he himself places an important constraint in 'Discourse in the Novel':

> In order to be authentic and productive, parody must be precisely a parodic *stylization*, that is, it must re-create the parodied language as an authentic whole, giving it its due as a language possessing its own internal logic and one capable of revealing its own world inextricably bound up with the parodied language.[47]

This is the case with the examples of parody, pastiche or stylization that I have already analysed in *Richard Feverel*, most notably the pastiche idyll, the parodies of Carlyle both in that novel and in *Beauchamp's Career*, and of popular fiction in *The Egoist* and *Diana of the Crossways*. Such instances not only give the parodied discourse 'its due as a language possessing its own internal logic and one capable of revealing its own world' but also incorporate it into a dialogue with other discourses that is ideologically and artistically describable. Such things as Dahlia's soliloquy, however, and even more the 'Lombroso' style of characterization applied to Sedgett, are isolated and meaningless except as convulsive stabs against despised fictional modes. In the latter case, it is difficult to argue even this, since the given and self-evident evil character of Sedgett is essential to the plot.

Near the end of the novel Meredith makes a revealing metafictional comment: 'There is a sort of hero, and a sort of villain, to this story: they are but instruments. Hero and villain are combined in the person of Edward' (46, 482). It is tempting to read into this what happened to Meredith's 'plain story'. While it is inconceivable that he ever intended to write a conventional seduction story of the kind J.C. Jeaffreson imposed on *Rhoda Fleming*, he may well have believed that the subversion of such a story was achievable within a one-volume 'plain story' of 'the real story-telling order', and with a hero such as Robert Eccles. He may have discovered that such an intention betrayed him into collusion with fictional modes that carried an ideological burden incompatible with his purpose. It is certainly more than likely that the novelist who had just written at such length about Wilfrid Pole would find Edward Blancove a more rewarding focus of attention than Robert Eccles. Edward is an extension of Wilfrid: more intelligent, more reprehensible, and putatively more capable of development. It follows that he needs even more attention, but the persisting demands of the 'plain story' make that impossible. As the metafictional comment implies, the real, complex 'hero and villain' is usurped by the 'instruments', especially the 'hero' Robert, whose role is subverted by his constant errors and the author's refusal to narrate his dubiously heroic exploits, but who nevertheless dominates the central portion of the narrative. Edward is no more than a sketch illustrated by a few finely realized episodes, particularly his letters, the lodging-house scene and the passages between him and another promising but not fully developed character, the half-reluctant *femme fatale*, Margaret Lovell. Most damagingly of all, his change of heart towards Dahlia has to be taken on trust: the reader can respond neither with belief, nor with productive scepticism.

As David Howard says, 'All expectations are defeated, all norms of fiction, not simply of popular fiction, defied or made a mess of.'[48] Predictably, *Rhoda Fleming* was another popular failure.

As I have said, the desire to make quick money by writing what was to have been a popular one-volume novel interrupted work on the sequel to *Emilia in England*, which was originally to have been called *Emilia in Italy*. Begun in 1863 this novel, retitled *Vittoria*, was not published until 1866. Despite the interruption, Meredith was consistently enthusiastic about this novel, believed that he had achieved a popular vein of colourful action narrative, and expected it to be a success. In this expectation he was, yet again, to be disappointed.

Perhaps the most interesting of his numerous reports on the progress of the novel is a letter to Maxse, written after its resumption (and therefore after the completion and failure of *Rhoda Fleming*):

> Much of my strength lies in painting morbid emotion and exceptional positions; but my conscience will not let me so waste my time. Hitherto consequently I have done nothing of mark. But I shall, and *Vittoria* will be the first indication (if not fruit) of it. My love is for epical subjects – not for cobwebs in a putrid corner; though I know the fascination of unravelling them.[49]

He had used the word 'epical' in an earlier letter, when he contrasted *Vittoria* with *Rhoda Fleming* by saying that the former had 'points of grandeur and epical interest'.[50] However, in a retrospective letter to Swinburne, a fellow-enthusiast for the Italian national cause, he wrote that his 'object was not to write the Epic of the Revolt – for that the time is yet too new: but to represent the revolt itself, with the passions animating *both* sides, the revival of the fervid Italian blood; and the character of the people'.[51]

These statements, and especially the confession of self-division in the letter to Maxse, are of particular interest to the present study because of the significance that Bakhtin attributes to the difference between epic and novel. The world of epic, according to Bakhtin, is:

> the national heroic past: it is a world of 'beginnings' and 'peak times' in the national history, a world of fathers and of founders of families, a world of 'firsts' and 'bests'.... In its style, tone and manner of expression, epic discourse is infinitely far removed from the discourse of a contemporary about a contemporary addressed to contemporaries....
>
> It is possible, of course, to conceive even 'my time' as heroic, epic time, when it is seen as historically significant....
>
> We must not forget that 'absolute past' is not to be confused with time in our exact and limited sense of the word; it is rather a temporally valorized hierarchical category.[52]

Epic epitomizes the 'poetic' genres that, for Bakhtin, are monologic. In this essay the novel is characterized as a genre in which 'the subject of serious literary representation... is portrayed without any distance, on the level of contemporary reality, in a zone of direct and even crude contact':

> The novel comes into contact with the spontaneity of the inconclusive present... [and] the 'depicting' authorial language now lies on the same plane as the 'depicted' language of the hero, and may enter into dialogic relations and hybrid combinations with it.[53]

We must be cautious about positing too straightforward a connection between Bakhtin's theory of epic and Meredith's use of the word. However, the theory does provide a useful frame for a discussion of some notable features of *Vittoria*, and particularly some of the ways in which it differs from Meredith's other novels. The action of the novel is centred on the uprising in Milan in 1848. This is clearly a 'peak time' not only in Italian history, as an heroic if abortive episode of the Risorgimento, but also, since this was one of a series of popular revolts all over Europe in 1848, that year has come to be celebrated as one of the most significant in modern European history. Between the time of the novel's action and the time of writing the greater part of Italy had achieved unity and independence, in 1859–60, through the diplomacy of Cavour, the military victories of the combined Piedmontese and French armies, and the extraordinary guerrilla exploits of Garibaldi. The time of the novel is therefore a past that was manifestly continuous with the present – 'my time' in Bakhtin's phrase – especially since, during the period of composition, the war broke out between Austria and Prussia which, rather less heroically, resulted in Venetia being incorporated into the Kingdom of Italy. (Meredith witnessed part of this conflict as a correspondent, but only after the novel was completed.) However, 'the Forty-Eight' was undoubtedly a case in which 'my time' was 'historically significant' enough to qualify for treatment as 'heroic, epic time'. Meredith's letter to Swinburne suggests that he shared Bakhtin's conception of epic time as past and finished, and also that he was retrospectively doubtful about the 'epical' quality that he had insisted on in correspondence during the novel's composition.

I shall begin my discussion of the novel by quoting a passage which, at least in isolation, straightforwardly illustrates the Bakhtinian concept of epic distancing and valorization. I have said that in *Sandra Belloni* the character of Emilia is conceived in a mode of 'heroic and passionate simplicity'. This is true *a fortiori* of the same character in *Vittoria* where, moreover, the mode of characterization is much less intimate (there is nothing in the later novel remotely resembling the hawthorn-blossom incident in *Sandra Belloni*), and she is portrayed to a much greater extent in public scenes and in relation to historically significant events. This is not to say, as we shall see, that she is a straightforwardly 'epic' character, but one extreme of the mode of characterization can be seen in the following passage, where her presence and voice neutralize the hostility of her enemy, Anna von Lenkenstein:

> Countess Alessandra's divine gift, which she could not withhold, though in a misery of apprehension; her grave eyes, which none could accuse of coldness, though they showed no emotion; her simple noble manner that seemed to lift her up among the forces threatening her; these expressions of a superior soul moved Anna under the influence of the incomparable voice to pass over envious contrasts, and feel the voice and the nature were one in that bosom. (*V*, Chapter 45, p. 606)

Every word of this passage enforces the 'epic' elevation, distancing and valorization of Vittoria/Alessandra: the command of emotion, combined with an exemplary wholeness and spontaneity, elevates her to the superhuman status of authentic epic heroes, while the feelings of the focalizer, her enemy – themselves elsewhere portrayed as of a tragic-heroic intensity, being inspired by national feeling and the death of her brother – are shown as changeable and belittled to 'envious'. The whole tendency of this study suggests that this should be identified as stylization, or even a character zone; however, as we shall see, there are reasons why it is difficult to argue for the typical Meredithian dialogic method in this novel.

An epic quality can also be attributed to the novel's opening. *Vittoria* is the only novel of Meredith's to open with a scenic description, of Monte Motterone, where a group of nationalist conspirators meets with Mazzini himself to plan an uprising in Milan. Monte Motterone, 'a towering dome of green', is contrasted with the aspect of the surrounding Alps:

The storm has beaten at them until they have got the aspect of the storm. They take colour from sunlight, and are joyless in colour as in shade. When the lower world is under pushing steam, they wear the look of the revolted sons of Time, fast chained before scornful heaven in an iron peace. Day at last brings vigorous fire; arrows of light pierce the mist-wreaths, the dancing draperies, the floors of vapour.... You behold a burnished realm of mountain and plain beneath the royal sun of Italy. In the foreground it shines hard as the lines of an irradiated Cellini shield. Farther away, over middle ranges that are soft and clear, it melts, confusing the waters with hot rays, and the forests with darkness, to where, wavering in and out of view like flying wings, and shadowed like wings of archangels with rose and with orange and with violet, silver-white Alps are seen. You might take them for mystical streaming torches on the border-ground between vision and fancy. They lean as in a great flight forward upon Lombardy. (1, 1–2)

In isolation this might pass as a typical piece of Meredithian nature-writing, such as we have already seen in *Richard Feverel*. However, the scenic description is imbued with motifs of Italian nationalistic sentiment, and with a peculiar exaltation, as in the comparison of the mountains to chained Titans and the 'mystical streaming torches', that is more suggestive of political excitement than of nature mysticism. The fervid nationalistic sentiment of the group of characters we are about to meet is thus embodied in the very landscape for which, and over which, they are fighting. This is the border of the Kingdom of Piedmont, whose king, Carlo Alberto, is the hero of conservative nationalists, and Lombardy, still part of the Austrian Empire. The leader of the conspirators who are meeting here, Mazzini, is officially exiled from both these territories, and was still an exile from the Kingdom of Italy when the novel was written. He is the hero of the republican nationalists, and will shortly be leader of the short-lived Roman Republic. The second chapter opens with a long and laudatory description of Mazzini which includes these passages:

The eyes were dark as the forest's border is dark; not as night is dark. Under favourable lights their colour was seen to be a deep rich brown, like the chestnut, or more like the hazel-edged sunset brown which lies upon our western rivers in the winter floods,

The Novels of the 1860s 81

when night begins to shadow them.

... The whole visage widened upward from the chin, though not very markedly before it reached the broad-lying brows. The temples were strongly indented by swelling of the forehead above them: and on both sides of the head there ran a pregnant ridge, such as will sometimes lift men a deplorable half inch above the earth we tread. (1, 9–10)

Mazzini's face is described as a landscape: this protagonist in the Italian national struggle, who will later be described by one of his aristocratic countrymen as 'a born intriguer, a lover of blood, mad for the smell of it' (11, 115), is thus authenticated by the narration and removed from the arena of political dialogue to the realm of natural forces, just as the whole national struggle itself is naturalized by the landscape description in Chapter 1.

The scene, then, is emphatically prepared for epic action, and this is further promised when we learn that these conspirators are met to agree on a signal for the uprising in Milan and subsequently throughout Lombardy. There is some rivalry and mutual suspicion among the representatives of the various towns, and some conflict about the advisability of the proposed scheme: the singing of an inflammatory nationalistic aria at La Scala by the untried young *diva*, Vittoria Campa. All conflict appears to be resolved, however, when Vittoria sings the aria with its refrain, 'Italia, Italia shall be free!':

She seized the hearts of those hard and serious men as a wind takes the strong oak-trees, and rocks them on their knotted roots, and leaves them with the song of soaring among their branches. Italy shone about her; the lake, the plains, the peaks, and the shouldering flushed snow-ridges. Carlo Ammiani breathed as one who draws in fire. Grizzled Agostino glittered with suppressed emotion, like a frosted thorn-bush in the sunlight. Ugo Corte had his thick brows down, as a man who is reading iron matter. The Chief alone showed no sign beyond a half lifting of the hand, and a most luminous fixed observation of the fair young woman, from whom power was an emanation, free of effort. (3, 29–30)

The kind of writing I have been discussing, in the opening chapters, promises a kind of narrative that is intermittently fulfilled in the course of the novel. We have seen a description of Vittoria, near the end, that is entirely consistent with this promise. Moreover, this is the only one of Meredith's novels that indulges wholeheartedly in the narration of exciting and violent action, albeit only once, in the superb scene of the duel in the mountain pass between Angelo Guidascarpi and Captain Weisspriess (Chapter 26) – the duel epitomizing the kind of episode that the typical Meredith novel avoids.[54]

However, the first decisive action of the novel is emphatically not of this kind. Monte Motterone is invaded by a group of English characters from *Sandra Belloni*, the friends and relatives of the arch-sentimentalist Wilfrid Pole, including the ideologist of the word with a loophole, Wilfrid's sister Adela. Vittoria, whom the reader familiar with the earlier novel gradually learns to identify with Emilia, overhears their plans to visit Milan, and leaves them a warning note, '*Let none who look for safety go to Milan*' (6, 55). This action is doubly foolish because, as Vittoria knows, Wilfrid is now an officer in the Austrian army and betrothed to an Austrian aristocrat. This note, and subsequent correspondence between Vittoria and Wilfrid, come into the hands of the working-class revolutionary Barto Rizzo, a character who, in the ferocity, ruthlessness, single-mindedness and fearlessness of his devotion to the cause, sometimes represented as madness, is a powerful expression of a fascinated, would-be sympathetic but fearful middle-class response to the idea of popular revolt, uncontrolled by the enlightened aristocracy. Rizzo publicly brands Vittoria a traitress, and it clearly becomes impossible to launch the uprising as planned.

When Rizzo's accusation is brought to Vittoria's notice she says she cannot think what she might have done to arouse suspicion. The reader is left to wonder whether she is stupid or deceitful since, as Meredith boasted in a letter, this novel is different from *Sandra Belloni* and Vittoria is 'no longer tripped and dogged by Philosopher or analyst'.[55]

Jack Lindsay offers a persuasive interpretation of Vittoria's behaviour, as showing that she:

> is still in part the romantic rebel with a cult of spontaneity and absolute virtue.... The vital concrete element in her, with its effort to break through all conventions and grasp only the immediate human reality, inverts itself into a mixture of egoism and helplessness.[56]

However, there is no evidence that the narrator is committed to, or even entertains, such a view of Vittoria. Here is his comment on her state of mind during an interval in the performance of the opera:

> It was harder for her to make a second appearance than it was to make the first, when the shameful suspicion cruelly attached to her had helped to balance her steps with rebellious pride. (20, 230)

This is a standard example of the narrator's voice combining with that of the character: a passage that hovers undecidably between authorial comment and free indirect discourse. Such writing is the staple of dialogic fiction, and we have seen that it is possible to analyse such passages into subtly differentiated but identifiable voices, in ideological dialogue with each other, in *Richard Feverel*, and to a lesser extent in the other novels discussed in this chapter. But such an artistic effect depends on the presence in the novel of what Bakhtin calls 'living heteroglossia':

> Every utterance participates in the 'unitary language' (in its centripetal forces and tendencies) and at the same time partakes of social and historical heteroglossia (the centrifugal, stratifying forces).
> Such is the fleeting language of a day, of an epoch, a social group, a genre, a school and so forth. It is possible to give a concrete and detailed analysis of any utterance, once having exposed it as a contradiction-ridden, tension-filled unity of two embattled tendencies in the life of language.
> The authentic environment of an utterance, the environment in which it lives and takes shape, is dialogized heteroglossia, anonymous and social as language, but simultaneously concrete, filled with specific content and accented as an individual utterance.[57]

Such are the character zones of Sir Austin Feverel, Adrian Harley, the Great Mel, the Countess Louisa and the Pole family. Here, by contrast, are samples of the characters' speech in *Vittoria*. Carlo protests against the plan to use Vittoria's aria as a signal, and proposes an alternative of his own:

'Signorina, there's the danger.... You trust to your good angels once, twice – the third time they fail you! What are you among a host of armed savages? You would be tossed like a weed on the sea. In pity, do not look so scornfully! No, there is no unjust meaning in it; but you despise me for seeing danger. Can nothing persuade you? And, besides,' he addressed the Chief, who alone betrayed no signs of weariness; 'listen, I beg of you. Milan wants no more than a signal. She does not require to be excited. I came charged with several proposals for giving the alarm. Attend, you others! The night of the Fifteenth comes; it is passing like an ordinary night. At twelve a fire-balloon is seen in the sky. Listen, in the name of saints and devils!'

The elderly poet Agostino replies:

'Exactly. I have divined your idea. You have thought, or, to correct the tense, are thinking, which is more hopeful, though it may chance not to seem so meritorious. But, if yours are the ideas of full-blown jackets, bear in mind that our enemies are coated and breeched. It may be creditable to you that your cunning is not the cunning of the serpent; to us it would be more valuable if it were.' (4, 35–6)

Both these speeches are not merely unlike any English that was ever spoken (the demand is not for realism) – they bear no meaningful relation to any of the forces that produce heteroglossia. This is a difficulty that faces a novelist writing a novel with a foreign setting – one that had similarly defeated George Eliot shortly before in *Romola*. To produce the effect of foreign speech the novelist has recourse to unidiomatic expressions ('Attend, you others!'), artificially elevated diction (('it may chance not to seem so meritorious') and expressions that sound like foreign idioms translated ('in the name of saints and devils!'). This is not the kind of discourse that can enter into the ideological dialogue typical of Meredith, or combine meaningfully with the discourse of the narrator.

One of Bakhtin's most important contributions to the theory of the novel is his insistence that 'the human being in the novel is first, foremost and always a speaking human being; the novel requires speaking persons bringing with them their own unique ideological discourse, their own language'.[58] Meredith is a novelist who typically illustrates this maxim *par excellence*. Characters who speak in the manner exemplified by the passages just quoted lack the discursive-ideological substance, the vital substance, of the Bakhtinian or the Meredithian character.

This point will become more clear if we contrast the speech of the one typically Meredithian character in the novel. In the following dialogue Vittoria has divined that Wilfrid requires a scene of sentimental love-play as the price for helping the escape of Angelo Guidascarpi, and swallows her integrity for the cause:

'My best friend! my brother! my noble Wilfrid! my old beloved! help me now, without loss of a minute.'...

'Repeat that – once, only once.... You will repeat it by-and-by? – another time? Trust me to do my utmost. *Old* beloved! What is the meaning of 'old beloved'? One word in explanation. If it means anything, I would die for you! Emilia, do you hear? – die for you! To me you are nothing old or byegone, whatever I may be to you. To me – yes, I will order the carriage – you are the Emilia – listen! listen! Ah! you have shut your ears against me. I am bound in all seeming, but I – you drive me mad: you know your power. Speak one word, that I may feel – that I may be convinced... or not a single word; I will obey you without. I have said that you command my life.' (28, 358)

Throughout this speech a fustian Romantic lover's rhetoric is interwoven with the stern, clipped utterance of the self-suppressing English gentleman. The effect of the whole is calculatedly manipulative. It would be excessive to say that this is precisely the speech of an upwardly mobile bourgeois army officer in the 1840s, but it is broadly identifiable in terms of class and epoch. Moreover, its recurrence would be identifiable and ideologically significant at any point in the narrative, as the speech of Carlo or Agostino could not be.

In his letter to Swinburne Meredith acknowledged that the style of *Vittoria* was 'stiff'.[59] It has none of the variety and dialogic interplay characteristic of his novels. It does, however, boast a remarkable example of another Bakhtinian feature, the 'interpolated genre'. Two and a half chapters are occupied by the detailed summary and extensive pastiche quotation of the opera *Camilla*, in which Vittoria gives her first public performance and at the end of which, stubbornly defying all her friends, she sings the patriotic aria which was to have been the signal for the revolt. A brief extract illustrates the relish with which Meredith parodies the language of Italian opera:

> CAMILLO (*on guard, clasping his wife*).
> ' 'Tis well! I cry, to all we share.
> Yea, life or death, 'tis well! 'tis well!'
> MICHIELLA (*stamps her foot*)
> 'My heart's a vessel tossed on hell!'
> LEONARDO (*aside*)
> 'Not in glad nuptials ends the day.' (21, 247)

There is also an element of parody in the explanation of the elaborate political allegory, in which Count Orso is Austria, Michiella 'Austria's spirit of intrigue', Camillo 'indolent Italy, amorous Italy, Italy aimless' and Camilla 'Young Italy', after Mazzimi's movement. At the same time, the opera is represented both as a serious work of art and as a valid expression of national feeling. What is most interesting, however, is the relationship between the opera's representation of the national movement and the reality of which it forms a part: this is particularly marked in the case of Vittoria's role. The opera has an unusually complicated plot and does portray Italy as divided and corruptible. However, the character of Camilla, sung by Vittoria, is unashamedly ideal, a fact acknowledged in one of the most interesting of the novel's comparatively rare analytical passages:

> The silence of her solitary room coming upon the blaze of light – the colour and clamour of the house, and the strange remembrance of the recent impersonation of an ideal character, smote her with the sense of her having fallen from a mighty eminence, and that she lay in the dust. All those incense-breathing flowers heaped on her table seemed poisonous, and reproached her as a delusion. (20, 231)

Vittoria impersonates an ideal character not only in her portrayal of the role of Camilla, but in her inability to see that she has objectively betrayed the conspiracy, and her stubborn insistence on singing the inflammatory aria despite having been discredited. The contrast between her real situation and the allegorical Camilla may be seen as a hint at the perspective argued for by Jack Lindsay, but it is isolated.

Meredith's use of the opera is historically accurate. Derek Beales writes:

> An air of fantasy hangs over the whole Italian political scene. There is bound to be some unreality associated with a movement of cultural nationalism, consciously creating art and literature for political ends. In this period the impression is enhanced by the significance of the opera and the theatre in public life. It was no doubt true in Italy, as in Spain, that the theatre was the most hopeful medium for liberal propaganda where illiteracy was general. Censorship gave few opportunities for the production of subversive plays in Italy, but there were many demonstrations and riots provoked by the singing of patriotic arias.[60]

Meredith's portrayal of the opera, and of the political intrigues surrounding it, strongly conveys such an 'air of fantasy'. Interestingly, the word fantasy recurs in Beales's discussion of the ideological hero of Meredith's novel: 'Historians, following contemporaries, have scoffed at the fantasies of Mazzini's thought and the unpracticality of his conspiracies.' Beales's own assessment is that Mazzini's contribution derived not from 'the risings he inspired, the societies he formed, or the newspapers and pamphlets he wrote and edited', nor from 'his thought, which now seems... like sublime mysticism and nonsense', but from his personal example and 'significance as a symbol, as Italy incarnate'.[61] The 'fantasy' of Meredith's opera is 'steeped in the sentiment of Young Italy' and its librettist 'put the heart of the creed of his Chief' into Camilla's dying words, 'There is an end to joy: there is no end/To striving' etc. (21, 240 and 252). Moreover, there is a moment at which Carlo wonders how Vittoria can be impressed by the 'airy cloudy language' of the Chief's letter to her (16, 188). And we have seen that, at the opening of the novel, Meredith explicitly portrayed Mazzini as 'Italy incarnate'. It is remarkable how closely the novelist, himself not immune to romanticism, idealism and 'sublime mysticism', anticipated the judgement of a more than usually hard-headed empirical British historian.

Vittoria was the last novel published in a decade during which Meredith strove unavailingly to adapt his art to what he supposed to be the demands of the reading public. The four novels he produced are very different from each other, but they are all characterized by a restraint upon the artistic originality shown in

Richard Feverel, and a largely unproductive conflict between the author's artistic predilection and his orientation to the marketplace. Meredith was to produce one more 'spanking bid for popularity',[62] but this merits a chapter to itself.

3
The Adventures of Harry Richmond

In 1864, with *Sandra Belloni* just completed and *Rhoda Fleming* and *Vittoria* still to be written, Meredith announced among his plans 'an Autobiography. *The Adventures of Richmond Roy, and his friend Contrivance Jack: Being the History of Two Rising Men*: – and to be a spanking bid for popularity on the part of this writer'.[1] Meredith intended this to be another attempt, after the disappointment with *Evan Harrington*, at popular success with the *Once a Week* reading public. An outline of fifteen chapters was submitted to the editor, Samuel Lucas, who was 'charmed...but owing to certain changes going on in relation to O[nce] a W[eek] he has not yet sent word for me to start away'.[2] On the evidence of the surviving outline, *Richmond Roy* was to have been a straightforward regression to the eighteenth-century picaresque model, with adventures loosely hung on the relationship between poverty-stricken gentleman and resourceful rogue-servant, perhaps prompted by Lucas's liking for Smollett.[3] However, Lucas never did 'send word' and when, five years later, Meredith began work on *The Adventures of Harry Richmond* for publication in the *Cornhill Magazine*, it had become a very different work.

In comparison with the novels discussed in Chapter 2, Meredith wrote very little in his letters about *Harry Richmond* during composition. His most substantial comment is in a letter to John Morley: 'As to *Harry Richmond*, I fear I am evolving his personality too closely for the public, but a man must work by the light of his conscience if he's to do anything worth reading.'[4] This is, however, a fairly standard comment by Meredith on his novels, and there are good reasons why, although *Harry Richmond* had changed a great deal from the original *Once a Week* project, he might have expected it to be a popular success.

The choice, unique among Meredith's novels, of a first-person narrator imposes a number of obvious constraints on the stylistic and narratorial tendencies that his readers had found irksome. The style is more straightforward, and even today *Harry Richmond* stands out as the most 'readable' of Meredith's novels. The 'autobiographical' perspective of the first-person narrator limits the possibilities of elliptical and analeptic narrative (Meredith's narrator is much closer to David Copperfield than to Dowell in *The Good Soldier*), and the need to maintain consistency in the narrator's persona excludes intrusive commentary and competing narratorial presences such as the 'Philosopher' in *Sandra Belloni*. Generically, the novel is indebted to the English 'autobiographical' tradition, above all *David Copperfield*, the *Bildungsroman* epitomized of course by *Wilhelm Meister*, and Romance, explicitly represented by the *Arabian Nights*. These generic presences are by no means so obviously stylized, dialogized and subverted as in *Richard Feverel*; nevertheless we shall see that they are not inertly reproduced. As Graham McMaster alleges, most critical commentary on the novel treats generic presences as 'given and unproblematic',[5] a tendency that a dialogic reading must counter. However, in the light of the characteristics so far mentioned, and above all the splendour, humour and vitality of the hero's father, Richmond Roy, compared to whom 'there is no character in the entire century whose mania is so grand or so obscured',[6] it is surprising that *Harry Richmond* was not one of the great Victorian successes. If it had been, we might have had a different, smoother, more orthodox and still read Meredith; almost certainly we would not have had *Beauchamp's Career*, *The Egoist* and *Diana of the Crossways*.

Harry Richmond's development is constructed upon the contrast and conflict between his maternal grandfather, Squire Beltham, one of the richest men in England, and his father, Richmond Roy, who had come to the Beltham home as a singing master, married one daughter and broken the heart of the other, and left his wife who subsequently went mad. Roy is obsessively driven by the belief that he is the legitimate heir of a royal Duke and even, it is strongly hinted, of the throne. He consumes a large proportion of Harry's fortune in pursuing a legal case to establish his birthright, and in cutting a figure in society appropriate to his claims, which demand not only that he appear in society but that he lead it, which briefly he does, to the baffled amusement and admiration of the *beau monde*. Roy is persistently associated with motifs of Romance, and it is in the spirit of Romance that he attempts to engineer the marriage of Harry to Princess Ottilia, the heir of the ruling family of a German Principality. Ottilia, however, is a character from a

Bildungsroman rather than a Romance and, although she loves Harry, she guides him into the more suitable marriage to the English gentlewoman Janet Ilchester, his grandfather's candidate.

Richmond Roy and Squire Beltham are, above all, two powerful, distinctive and opposed voices, an antagonistic dialogue of social heteroglossia, which is rehearsed in the opening chapter and rages throughout the novel (although the antagonists hardly meet), culminating in a tremendous scene in which one silences the other, but at the cost of his own life. In the opening chapter, narrated in the third person, Roy arrives at Riversley, the Beltham home, in the middle of the night, and demands to see his estranged wife. The enraged squire tells him that his daughter has been driven mad by her husband's treatment of her, upon which Roy claims and abducts his young son, Harry.

The following extracts typify Roy's voice in this chapter:

'You now behold who it is, Mr Beltham, that acknowledges to the misfortune of arousing you at an unseemly hour – unbetimes, as our gossips in mother Saxon might say – and with profound regret, sir, though my habit is to take it lightly....

'Permit me first to speak of the cause of my protracted arrival, sir. The ridicule of casting it on the post-boys will strike you, Mr Beltham, as it does me. Nevertheless, I must do it; I have no resource. Owing to a rascal of the genus, incontinent in liquor, I have this night walked seven miles from Ewling. My complaint against him is not on my own account....

'The grounds for my coming at all you will very well understand, and you will applaud me when I declare to you that I come to her penitent; to exculpate myself, certainly, but despising self-justification. I love my wife, Mr Beltham. Yes; hear me out, sir. I can point to my unhappy star, and say, blame that more than me. That star of my birth and most disastrous fortunes should plead on my behalf to you: to my wife at least it will.'
(1, 6–7)

This is a constructed, learned and performed manner of speech. Like the Countess Louisa in *Evan Harrington*, we may suspect Roy of having learned words from the dictionary: certainly he makes a marked choice of latinate, polysyllabic, 'educated' vocabulary. This is combined with an elaborate, periodic sentence-structure to produce a rhetoric that is both periphrastic and dominating. The appeals to Beltham's fellow-feeling as a cultivated gentleman like himself are apparently concessive but in fact coercive, as is the pervasive lightness of tone: this discourse uses 'politeness', and the implied expectation of the same in return, as a weapon. Roy is in control of his discourse; he is not the slave of long words; when he wants to make an emotional effect he deploys the rhetoric of simplicity: 'I love my wife, Mr Beltham.' Despite this tactical simplicity, the whole speech typifies a class discourse that is marked by its difference from and avoidance of common speech. This, however, is also what makes it learnable, 'portable', like the money on which the gentlemanly *milieu* that it represents is based, and exploitable by a charlatan such as Roy, according to one view of him, is.

Squire Beltham's discourse at its most characteristic consists of short, abrupt utterances such as 'What's your business?' and 'You don't cross my threshold while I live', which punctuate the speech just quoted. However, he too is capable of effective extended speech, such as the following, described by Harry as 'the torrent of this tremendous outburst, which was marked by scarce a pause in the delivery':

'Scamp!'

'By no scurrilous epithets from a man I am bound to respect will I be deterred or exasperated.'

'Damned scamp, I say!' The squire having exploded his wrath gave it free way. 'I've stopped my tongue all this while before a scoundrel'd corkscrew the best-bottled temper right or left, go where you will one end o'the world to the other, by God! And here's a scoundrel stinks of villany, and I've proclaimed him 'ware my gates as a common trespasser, and deserves hanging if ever rook did nailed hard and fast to my barn doors! comes here for my daughter, when he got her by stealing her, scenting his carcase, and talking 'bout his birth, singing what not sort o' foreign mewin' stuff, and she found him out a liar and a beast, by God!' (1, 7)

Roy's speech can be vigorously countered only by completely eschewing the model of gentlemanly discourse that it exemplifies. This comes naturally to the squire. His much less elevated vocabulary and unpremeditated sentence-structure do not need illustrating. His speech epitomizes a sociolinguistic structure in which the classes are not clearly separated at such obvious 'linguistic' levels: few of his words, and none of his grammatical structures, are unavailable to the 'commonest' Englishman. The class character of his speech (which is in its way just as clearly marked as that of Roy's) is at the level of what Bakhtin calls 'utterance' and specifically 'addressivity': the use of these words by this speaker addressing this other in this situation. Bakhtin writes:

> Under the conditions of a class structure and especially an aristocratic class structure, one observes an extreme differentiation of speech genres and styles, depending on the title, class, rank, wealth, social importance, and age of the addressee and the relative position of the speaker (or writer).[7]

Roy's exaggerated politeness, expecting and almost coercing a response in kind, is one aristocratic 'speech genre': it implies an equality with the addressee or perhaps, in view of its exaggeration and the gratuitously repeated 'Mr Beltham' (Roy thinks of himself as titled by right) a slight but graciously accented superiority. Beltham's 'speech genre' is equally aristocratic, or at least ruling class. One marker of this is the *freedom* from politeness expressed in the unashamed profanity. Another is the use of the word 'scoundrel', which is not merely a moral judgement but also a social stigma – *OED* perpetuates Johnson's definition, 'A mean rascal, a low petty villain.' Even apart from these details, the unrestrained vernacular vehemence of his denunciation has a meaning that it could not have in the mouth of one of Beltham's tenants: the withholding of such forms of politeness as even a Squire Beltham has at his command expresses a conviction of social as well as moral superiority.

It would be absurd to say that Beltham's class accent, unlike Roy's, is inimitable, since Meredith has imitated it. However, since it has no clearly defined linguistic markers, since it is a matter not of 'language' at the level of grammar and vocabulary but of utterance, since it makes such unrestrained use of vernacular idiom and rural lore, it would be much more difficult for a would-be imitator to know that he was reproducing the Squire's speech and not that of his tenants. It is not 'portable', and is backed up not by money but by property – though, as we shall see, Beltham's property basis is not as transparent in his language as, with his quaint agricultural idioms, it might appear to be.

A countryman whom Harry meets in passing says approvingly of Squire Beltham, 'he rides to hounds, and dines his tenants still, that he does; he's one o'th'old style' (7, 94). This tribute contrasts with Roy's flamboyant patronage of the people at Dipwell, a place with which his connection is obscure, and where he deposits Harry during one of his periods of imprisonment for debt:

> Standing up in the carriage, and holding me by the hand, he addressed them by their names: 'Sweetwinter, I thank you for your attention to my son; and you, Thribble; and you, my man; and you, Baker; Rippengale, and you; and you, Jupp'; as if he knew them personally. It was true he nodded at random. Then he delivered a short speech, and named himself a regular subscriber to their innocent pleasures. He gave them money, and scattered silver coin among the boys and girls. (3, 33)

This contrast between traditional community-based hospitality and the gentleman arbitrarily and impersonally distributing money appears to be straightforwardly to the Squire's credit, and we might suspect an exercise in nostalgia. However, Harry later gives a more sceptically accented version of his grandfather's reputation: 'an Englishman of the kind which is perpetually perishing out of the land' (53, 638). The accent here is subtle and complex, since Harry as narrator is reporting the Squire's reputation among his tenants and servants, and at the same time reproducing his own mean-spirited attitude as a character towards both his grandfather (who has disinherited him) and Janet, who is praising the Squire's generosity. Nevertheless the word 'perpetually' is telling, carrying a suggestion that there is something mythical about this kind of Englishman and the tradition he represents, and even faintly anticipating Raymond Williams's argument about the 'organic community' – 'that it has always gone'.[8] Furthermore, we are reminded more than once that a significant portion of the Squire's vast wealth comes from coal mining, and we don't even need to ask whether the colliers are represented at his hospitable dinners.

Returning to the speech of the two antagonists, we have seen that Roy characterizes Beltham's speech in his own style: 'scurrilous epithets'. In the same chapter Beltham exercises another form of dialogic aggression by mimicking Roy's speech:

'Nor, sir, on your application' – the squire drawled in uncontrollable mimicking contempt of the other's florid forms of speech, ending in his own style, – 'no, you won't.' (1, 9)

When Harry wants to ingratiate himself with his grandfather by 'show[ing] him as much Beltham as I could summon', it is natural that he should do so by adopting a manner of speech: 'Dogs and horses all right, sir?' (19, 223).

It is, however, Roy whose discourse is most marked by commentary, on the part both of Harry and of his grandfather. Harry as a boy is seduced by 'the magical influence of my father's address, a mixture of the ceremonious and the affable such as the people could not withstand' (19, 220); later, when he has come under the refining and educative influence of the Princess Ottilia, he speaks of his father's 'rarely-abandoned seven-league boots of jargon, once so delicious to me' (33, 359). The Squire has a particularly interesting series of epithets for Roy's speech: 'vagabond names', 'like the name of one of those blackguard adventurers' (8, 103; 20, 232: Roy's names – 'Augustus Fitz-George Frederick William Richmond Guelph Roy' – are part of his discourse because he appears to invent and re-invent them, as he invents himself); 'don't talk like a mountebank' (51, 606).

Beltham's epithets may be seen as lending support to the suggestion by Graham McMaster, in one of the few published Bakhtinian studies of Meredith, that Roy is a carnivalesque figure. McMaster points out that 'the pageant, the feast, parade, carnival, masque or Punch and Judy show...are all of them overtly associated with Roy'[9] and argues that he is a figure of the king as clown who, Bakhtin says, is 'elected by all the people and is mocked by all the people. He is abused and beaten when the time of his reign is over.'[10] Just as, in *Evan Harrington*, Louisa is Meredith's surrogate to infiltrate the homes of the aristocracy, so, McMaster suggests, Meredith might be 'compared to the "lower and middle clerics" whom Bakhtin considers to be the channel through which the degrading and renewing powers of the lower strata came to be infused into the upper class world of serious textuality'.[11]

We should, then, work on the assumption that Roy is something more interesting and complex than an absurd impostor, in order to establish what is at stake when Beltham eventually 'exposes' him. Roy is at his most attractive, both to Harry and to the reader, early in the novel when Harry is a child. The reason for this is partly that, as a number of critics have noted, in the early chapters Harry as narrator refrains from hindsight and reproduces the impressions of his younger self.[12] This is also when Roy becomes strongly identified with 'Romance'. The night of Harry's abduction by his father, which is separated off narratorially by the use of the third person, 'stands up' in Harry's memory 'without any clear traces about it or near it, like the brazen castle of romance round which the sea-tide flows' (2, 14), although, as we have seen, the episode has been represented in terms of social heteroglossia. Father and son read the *Arabian Nights* together, generating numerous references throughout the text, and providing an imaginative model by which Harry mediates his experience: 'During this Arabian life, we sat on a carpet that flew to the Continent' (4, 40).

The other main source of the imaginative life fostered in Harry by his father is Shakespeare, and Roy's way of mediating Shakespeare is highly distinctive:

> The scene where Great Will killed the deer, dragging Falstaff all over the park after it by the light of Bardolph's nose, upon which they put an extinguisher if they heard any of the keepers, and so left everybody groping about and catching the wrong person, was the most wonderful mixture of fun and tears. Great Will was extremely youthful, but everybody in the park called him, 'Father William', and when he wanted to know which way the deer had gone, King Lear (or else my memory deceives me) punned, and Lady Macbeth waved a handkerchief for it to be steeped in the blood of the deer; Shylock ordered one pound of the carcase; Hamlet (the fact was impressed on me) offered him a three-legged stool; and a number of kings and knights and ladies lit their torches from Bardolph; and away they flew, distracting the keepers and leaving Will and his troop to the deer. That poor thing died from a different weapon at each recital, though always with a flow of blood and a successful dash of his antlers into Falstaff; and to hear Falstaff bellow! But it was mournful to hear how sorry Great Will was over the animal he had slain. (2, 17)

This is as like Dickens as anything Meredith wrote. The relation to Shakespeare is Dickensian: this Shakespeare is not an aesthetic icon but the protean stuff of popular entertainment and folklore. The *Arabian Nights*, too, is a Romance text available at the popular level.

What might we deduce from this about the meaning of Roy's identification with the Romance genre? Roy's origins are deliberately obscure. He certainly seems to have been the son of an actress, and his father was probably a royal duke. He believes that his parents went through a legitimate form of marriage which *possibly* (Meredith had to be cautious about this topic) makes him the rightful heir to the throne. He is bolstered in pursuing his claim by a mysterious income which he believes to derive from the government but in fact comes from Harry's Aunt Dorothy, who loves him. Nobody believes that his claim stands any chance of being acknowledged, but this does not necessarily mean that there are no grounds for it. Graham McMaster has unearthed a case of a claimant to the throne in 1866, in which the Lord Chief Baron asserted, 'In my opinion it is indecent to go on with an inquiry into such matters unless it is absolutely necessary for the purposes of justice.'[13] The monarchy is established not so much upon legitimacy as on the illusion of legitimacy, and the breaking of the illusion, the substitution of a Richmond Roy (or, in the real-life case, Henry Rives) for Queen Victoria would threaten the institution.

Roy is addicted to Romance because he has constructed himself as a Romance hero, the despised and rejected who at last comes into his true inheritance. This conception of himself, with its heavy emphasis on destiny, is at odds with his real achievement as a self-created man, like the Great Mel in *Evan Harrington*. Mel, however, remembered that he was a tailor. Roy's Shakespearian fantasia, which is free as even his most impressive utterances hardly ever are from humbug, snobbery and pretension, represents a popular cultural level natural to the son of an actress, but a level which his aim in life is to suppress. He is, or could be, a 'rising man' like the heroes of the original 'Richmond Roy' story; he has the genius to be a hero of nineteenth-century individualism, like Julien Sorel. His tragedy is that this genius is devoted to achieving that most inert of statuses, hereditary aristocracy.

Roy's Shakespeare story, as I have said, is very like Dickens. Roy himself is a Dickensian character in the same sense as the Great Mel and Louisa: he is largely the creation of his own discourse. *Harry Richmond*, in general, is the novel in which Meredith seems on most good terms with the great predecessor whom he affected to despise: on the evidence of this novel alone, we can say that his recorded comments on Dickens do not tell the whole truth.

Whereas, in *Evan Harrington*, the relation to Dickens is often uneasy and feebly derivative, here, perhaps because publication in the *Cornhill* rather than *Once a Week* meant that Meredith was not contesting Dickens's own territory, the intertextuality is more productive.

This is most noticeable in the narrative of Harry's schooldays, where Meredith is obviously adapting motifs from *David Copperfield*. Harry hero-worships an older boy, Walter Heriot, just as David idolizes James Steerforth. In both novels there are scenes of confrontation between the idol and an usher or assistant master:

'Silence, Mr Steerforth!' said Mr Mell.

'Silence yourself,' said Steerforth, turning red. 'Whom are you talking to?'

'Sit down,' said Mr Mell.

'Sit down yourself,' said Steerforth, 'and mind your business.' ...

'If you think, Steerforth,' said Mr Mell, 'that I am not acquainted with the power you can establish over any mind here ... you are mistaken.'

'I don't give myself the trouble of thinking at all about you,' said Steerforth coolly; 'so I'm not mistaken, as it happens.'

'And when you make use of your position of favouritism here, sir,' pursued Mr Mell, with his lip trembling very much, 'to insult a gentleman –'

'A what? – where is he?' said Steerforth....

'To insult one who is not fortunate in life, sir, and who never gave you the least offence, and the many reasons for not insulting whom you are old enough and wise enough to understand,' said Mr Mell, with his lip trembling more and more, 'you commit a mean and base action.'

[Mr Creakle enters and demands an explanation of the scene.] Here Steerforth struck in.

'Then he said I was mean, and then he said I was base; and then I called him a beggar. If I had been cool, perhaps I shouldn't have called him a beggar; but I did, and I am ready to take the consequences of it.'

Without considering, perhaps, whether there were any consequences to be taken, I felt quite in a glow at this gallant speech.[14]

'What have you there, Heriot?'

My hero stared. 'Only a family portrait,' he answered, thrusting it safe in his pocket and fixing his gaze on Julia's window.

'Permit me to look at it,' said Mr Boddy.

'Permit me to decline to let you,' said Heriot.

'Look at me, sir, cried Boddy.'

'I prefer to look elsewhere, sir,' replied Heriot, and there was Julia visible at her window.

'I asked you, sir, civilly,' quoth Boddy, 'for permission to look, – I used the word intentionally; I say I asked you for permission...'

'No, you didn't,' Heriot retorted, quite cool; 'inferentially you did; but you did not use the word permission.'...

And you turned upon me impudently...; you concealed what you were carrying...'

'Am carrying,' Heriot corrected his tense....

'Like a rascal detected in an act of felony,' roared Boddy, 'you concealed it, sir...'

'Conceal it, sir.'...

I was standing close by my brave Heriot, rather trembling, studious of his manfulness though I was. His left foot was firmly in advance, as he said, just in the manner to start an usher furious: –

'I concealed it, I conceal it; I was carrying it, I carry it.... I have to assure you respectfully, sir, that family portraits are sacred things with the sons of gentlemen.' (5, 48–9)

Meredith has in effect rewritten the Dickens scene. Heriot's pose is even a mirror-image of Steerforth's in the Phiz illustration. Perhaps surprisingly, his version is lighter in tone, more comic: Mr Boddy is a contemptible cipher, with none of the moral dignity that, in Mr Mell, makes the Dickens scene painful to read. Both scenes, obviously, are representations of 'gentlemanly' insolence and its encouragement by the educational system. Heriot's insolence, however, is more subtly portrayed, and draws more deftly on his social advantages: he is more intelligent than Steerforth, who by comparison is crudely insulting.

The significance of Meredith's rewriting of Dickens goes beyond this particular scene. Steerforth and Heriot both seduce a childhood friend of the hero (this is more evident in the first edition of *Harry Richmond*, where Kiomi is seen dying on the grave of her child).[15] However, while Steerforth is consistently, if not uncritically, portrayed as a Byronic hero, Heriot plainly degenerates into a petty and aimless philanderer, whose condition is, in typical Meredithian fashion, represented by his own discourse, a letter which the narrator Harry ironically reports his earlier self as thinking 'admirably philosophical and coxcombically imitable' (20, 230). Furthermore, the gentlemanly code of Heriot is directly linked to that of Roy (who is responsible for sending Harry to this school). When the schoolmaster loses patience because Harry's school bills have not been paid, Heriot calls him a 'sordid old brute' and says, 'How can he know the habits and feelings of gentlemen?...It's just the way with schoolmasters and tradesmen' (5, 63). Heriot and Harry belong to a group of 'gentlemanly' boys for whom it is a 'title of superiority' to be in debt to 'day-boarders, commercial fellows,' in whom Heriot had 'instilled the sentiment...that gentlemen never failed to wipe out debts in the long run, so it was their interest to make us feel they knew us to be gentlemen' (6, 71). Harry grows out of this version of what is due to a gentleman, but it is Roy's code exactly, and when Harry pays one of his father's creditors Roy accuses him of 'revers[ing] the proper situations of gentleman and tradesman' (47, 549). Squire Beltham on the other hand has a 'punctilious regard for payments' (8, 104).

In a rare second edition of the novel an additional page was added after the title-page with the statement, 'The Story Is Laid on the Foundation of a Young Man's Love for his Father'.[16] This is reminiscent of *Richard Feverel*'s subtitle, 'A History of a Father and Son'. Although the character of Roy is very different from that of Sir Austin Feverel, and his relation to his son is markedly different, there is an important structural similarity. I have argued that Sir Austin aspires to be Richard's *author*, planning his son's life as a *Bildungsroman* or more accurately *Erziehungsroman* (novel of education) on the lines of *Emile*, in which he takes the intrusive and, in Bakhtinian terms, 'transgredient' role of Rousseau's author/narrator/tutor. Roy does not aspire to shape his son's soul in the intrusive manner of Sir Austin, but he does attempt to write the narrative of Harry's life which, inevitably, is an adjunct and extension of his own, part of the 'Romance' of his own self-creation as a hereditary aristocrat. Harry falling in love with a German Princess is a motif perfectly suited to this Romance, and Roy, as he believes, promotes the affair in an increasingly manipulative and mischievous fashion. His mania reaches its extremest point when he compromises Ottilia by luring her to the Isle of

Wight with news of Harry's beating by gipsies, and simultaneously causes the engagement to be announced: 'I pilot you into harbour, and all you can do is just the creaking of the vessel to me. You are in my hands. I pilot you. I have you the husband of the princess within the month' (50, 588).

When Harry and his friend Temple travel on the continent with Roy, Temple remarks that 'there was no feeling we were in a foreign country while he was our companion. We simply enjoyed strange scenes, looking idly out of our windows' (19, 217). This is reminiscent of Bakhtin's account of the chronotope of Greek Romance:

> The world of these romances is large and diverse. But this size and diversity is utterly abstract.... For escape it is important to go to another country; for kidnappers it is important to transport their victim to another country – but which particular country again makes no difference at all. The adventuristic events of the Greek romance have no essential ties with any particular details of individual countries that might figure in the novel, with their social or political structure, with their culture or history.[17]

The opposite extreme of this, in Bakhtin's hierarchy of chronotopes, is the *Bildungsroman* as epitomized above all by *Wilhelm Meister*. In his uncompleted essay on the *Bildungsroman* he did not carry out his promised analysis of *Wilhelm Meister*, but he clearly intended to discuss the novel in the light of his general remarks about time and space in Goethe:

> Goethe's historical vision always relied on a deep, painstaking, and concrete perception of the locality (*Localität*). The creative past must be revealed as necessary and productive under the conditions of a given locality, as a creative humanization of this locality, which transforms a portion of terrestrial space into a place of historical life for people, into a corner of the historical world.[18]

Although it is through his father that Harry is introduced to the court of Eppenwelzen, it is he who experiences it in the spirit of Bakhtin's Goethe. Roy's relationship to the realities of a German principality is epitomized by his bizarre appearance, in one of Meredith's most astonishing scenes, in the guise of a bronze horseman, to satisfy the whim of the Prince's sister. Harry has to learn that loving the heir of a hereditary ruler is a historically hard and specific fate; he learns also that the qualities for which he loves Ottilia are those that make her unlike an English aristocrat: the educated intelligence, candour, courage and freedom from convention that make her fit to be a ruler, and the sense of responsibility that prevents her from deserting this role for the love of a dubiously suitable young Englishman. In a memorable phrase, Ottilia is 'a woman who could only love intelligently' (50, 576). For Roy, on the other hand, she is no more than the prize of the hero of Romance, an adjunct of the destiny that will bring recognition of his birthright – that of an aristocrat whose responsibilities are non-existent, or at best trivial in comparison with those of the ruler of the smallest German state.

Critics are right, then, to discuss the novel in terms of the conflict between Romance and *Bildungsroman*. This discussion, however, tends to be oversimplified. Margaret Tarratt notes that:

> It is more than pure coincidence that the Princess in *Harry Richmond* shares the same name as the heroine of *Elective Affinities*. Like Natalia in *Wilhelm Meister*, the Princess Ottilia is reported a *'schöne Seele'* – the term initially used by Schiller to describe a type of Platonic spiritual beauty, and used also in *Wilhelm Meister* in the diary of Natalia's aunt.[19]

Tarratt does not say why the coincidence of names is significant. The implication is that there is some similarity between the characters, whereas Meredith's Ottilia is strikingly different from Goethe's Ottilie, and any significance in the name is likely to be wholly ironic. *Elective Affinities* (*Die Wahlverwandtschaften*) is a study of the German landed nobility in, as R.J. Hollingsworth says, a state of idleness, the 'worst effect' of which 'is that which it exercises on their emotional lives'.[20] Ottilie falls in love with her aunt's husband, a love which she renounces after accidentally drowning the aunt's baby; she then starves herself to death. She is hardly a woman who 'could only love intelligently.' She bears a closer resemblance to the model of femininity which Harry catches himself half regretting that Ottilia is *not*, when he feels her to be too exalted for him: 'a romantic little lady of semi-celestial rank, exquisitely rash, wilful, desperately enamoured, bearing as many flying hues and peeps of fancy as a love-ballad' (48, 557).

Nor does Ottilia very closely resemble the *'schöne Seele'* (mincingly translated as 'Fair Saint' by Carlyle), the author of the 'Confession' which forms the major 'interpolated genre' in *Wilhelm Meister*. Meredith's use of this phrase in *Harry Richmond* is far from straightforward and typically dialogic. The phrase occurs in a conversation in London society, where Roy has been spreading the rumour of Harry's engagement to Ottilia:

> He summoned me to an introduction to the Countess Szezedy, a merry little Hungarian dame.
> 'So,' said she at once, speaking German, 'you are to marry the romantic head, the Princess Ottilia of Eppenwelzen! I know her well. I have met her in Vienna. Schöne Seele, and bas bleu! It's just those that are won with a duel.' (39, 439)

The exalted phrase of Schiller and Goethe has become a trivial and trivializing conversational tag, equivalent to 'bas bleu'. Note that this speech is supposedly translated from German but 'Schöne Seele' is untranslated, so that it stands out as a fashionable foreign phrase. Meredith shows his understanding of how words become worn down by the degrading environment of fashionable discourse. The Countess Szezedy does not know *Wilhelm Meister* any more than she knows the Princess Ottilia. Her 'romantic head' to be won by a duel is not remotely like the Princess or Goethe's *'schöne Seele'*, and neither are these two very like each other. This degradation of meaning, too, is part of intertextuality.

Goethe's *'schöne Seele'*, the aunt of Wilhelm's eventual wife Natalia, is motivated primarily by religious feeling, and her Confession is described by the narrator as a 'pious Manuscript'. Serious religious feeling is remarkable for its almost complete absence as a motive for Meredith's major characters[21] and Ottilia is no exception. She has been educated by the freethinking and radical Dr Julius von Karsteg, and is preparing to become the ruler of a small state. The *'schöne Seele'* by contrast 'did not feel the smallest inclination or capacity for mingling in public business, or seeking any influence on it'.[22]

Ottilia does bear a resemblance to Goethe's Natalia, though she is considerably more developed, and there is likely to be a direct allusion in Harry's first sight of Ottilia on horseback to Wilhelm's first meeting with his 'fair Amazon' when he is lying wounded by bandits.[23] It is true that another character, in conversation with

Natalia, speaks of 'Deiner schönen hohen Seele',[24] but this is casual compared to the phrase's definitive use with reference to Natalia's aunt. Ottilia and Karsteg exercise an educative function comparable to that of the 'Tower' society gathered around Lothario, and Ottilia even intervenes in Harry's life on one or two occasions without his knowledge – though neither of these functions amounts to the systematic and sinister 'transgredience' of the Tower.

However, while Wilhelm marries Natalia, Ottilia's final influence on Harry's life is to bring about his union with Janet, the partner designed for him all along by his grandfather. As many critics have noted, this part of the novel is unsatisfactory in a number of ways. Perhaps the most disturbing is that as an unintended result of Roy's machinations Ottilia not only loses the man she loves but also marries the crass Prince Hermann, violent German nationalist, proto-Wilhelmite and even proto-Nazi, the representative of a German tradition antithetical to that of the enlightened Dr Karsteg. In Chapter 1 (p. 39) I referred to Spånberg's argument that in the *Bildungsroman* the hero's first love (for example, Marianne in *Wilhelm Meister*) is typically abandoned, sacrificed or outgrown, and that in his treatment of Lucy Meredith resists this convention. In *Harry Richmond* Meredith appears to regress, since there is little doubt that Ottilia is sacrificed, and there is an eloquent silence on her feelings about her marriage.

There is also some awkward plot-contrivance to make Janet available to marry Harry despite his contemptible treatment of her, but we need to place this conclusion in the total context of Harry's relations with women, and his various discourses of sexual attraction. As a youth he is, like a typical Victorian gentleman, attracted to two girls out of his class, the gipsy Kiomi and the miller's daughter Mabel Sweetwinter. Both these girls are seduced by friends of Harry (in the case of Kiomi, this is obscured in the revisions). The friends are probably to be regarded as surrogates for Harry himself, since he later refers to 'stains on me' and the fact that 'a modern man writing his history is fugitive and crepuscular in alluding to them' (48, 558). In both cases our attention is drawn to the style in which he writes about them:

> She had grown a superb savage, proof against weather and compliments. Her face was like an Egyptian sky fronting night. The strong old Eastern blood put ruddy flame for the red colour;

tawny olive edged from the red; rare vivid yellow, all but amber. The light that first looks down upon the fallen sun was her complexion above the brows, and round the cheeks, the neck's nape, the throat, and the firm bosom prompt to lift and sink with the vigour of her speech, as her eyes were to flash and darken.... I write of her in the style consonant to my ideas of her at the time....

She was swept from my amorous mind by Mabel Sweetwinter, the miller's daughter of Dipwell. This was a Saxon beauty in full bud, yellow as mid-may, with the eyes of opening June. Beauty, you will say, is easily painted in that style. But the sort of beauty suits the style, and the well-worn comparisons express the well-known type. Beside Kiomi she was like a rich meadow on the border of the heaths. (23, 261–3)

These descriptions are excellent illustrations of the post-structuralist theme that desire is created by discourse. In these cases moreover the discourse is clearly as much social as sexual: class-ridden and imperialistic. The stylization of these passages is of course signalled by the narrator's own metafictional comments. This is not the case with the following description of Ottilia, which is appropriately more refined:

Her face was like the quiet morning of a winter day when cloud and sun intermix and make an ardent silver, with lights of blue and faint fresh rose; and over them the beautiful fold of her full eyebrow on the eyelid like a bending upper heaven. Those winter mornings are divine. They move on noiselessly. The earth is still, as if awaiting. A wren warbles, and flits through the lank drenched brambles; hill-side opens green; elsewhere is mist, everywhere expectancy. They bear the veiled sun like a sangreal aloft to the wavy marble flooring of stainless cloud. (*HR*, Chapter 33, p. 355)

This is not so plainly an 'already-written' discourse as the previous ones, but there is at least a hint of stylization in the elaborate and formal epic simile and the chivalric strain of 'sangreal'. The point is that a discourse is available to Harry for Ottilia, as for Kiomi and Mabel. With Janet it is otherwise.

For most of the novel Janet is, as Harry says when narrating his twenty-first birthday, 'bald to the heart inhabiting me then' (23,

260). His underestimation of her is a motif running almost throughout the novel. The only significant 'character zone' in the narrator's discourse is, not surprisingly, that of Harry's younger selves, and his ungenerous view of Janet frequently recurs in this character zone, for example:

> Her amiable part appeared to be to let me see how brilliant and gracious the commonplace could be made to look. She kept Heriot at the Grange, against the Squire's remonstrance and her mother's. 'It's to keep him out of harm's way: the women he knows are not of the best kind for him,' she said, with astounding fatuity. (37, 414)

It is not however one of the happiest examples of character zone in Meredith, since the irony becomes increasingly blatant, especially when set against Harry's selfish and insensitive treatment of Janet. What is of most interest in all this is that Harry is unable, for most of the novel, to find a language that adequately represents Janet, and moreover that his aversion to her is frequently expressed as a critique of *her* language:

> We sat hardly less than an hour side by side – I know not how long hand in hand. The end was an extraordinary trembling in the limb abandoned to me. It seized her frame. I would have detained her, but it was plain she suffered both in her heart and her pride. Her voice was under fair command – more than mine was. She counselled me to go to London, at once. 'I would be off to London if I were you, Harry,' – for the purpose of further checking my father's extravagances, – would have been the further wording, which she spared me; and I thanked her, wishing, at the same time, that she would get the habit of using choicer phrases whenever there might, by chance, be a stress of emotion between us. Her trembling, and her 'I'd be off,' came into unpleasant collision in the recollection.' (37, 416)

Janet's trembling is not eloquence enough for Harry; he also requires 'choicer phrases': attraction appears to be possible only when mediated through language. As it happens, the nearest Harry comes to finding a language for Janet is a passage in a chapter which was cut in revision for the 1885 Collected Edition, and which in the first edition came after Chapter 43. Meredith's revisions of his early novels are notoriously careless, and we should not attach too much significance to the removal of this passage:

> Her figure on the lawn, while my old grandfather spoke of her, wore the light of individual character which defined her clearly from other women. She was raising the head of a rose at her arm's length, barely bending her neck to it, nor the line of her back. 'A compassionate thing,' as he who loved her said of her, the act and the attitude combined to symbolize the orderly, simple unpretendingness of her nature. A flower had a flower's place in her regard, and, I knew, a man a man's. She could stoop low to me, – to me this stately girl could bend, and take the shapes and many colours of a cloud running up the wind.[25]

This is an improvement on the earlier, 'glad, frank, unpretending mate, with just enough of understanding to look up to mine' (36, 394), though it still does not do justice to the moral and emotional heroism of Janet. The notable thing about it, in comparison to the language about Kiomi, Mabel and Ottilia, is that it is not at all stylized, and attends closely to its object, with a minimum of metaphorical substitution.

At different stages large portions of the text concerning Harry's relations with both Ottilia and Janet were cut. Several chapters of Harry's second visit to Germany, when the love between him and Ottilia develops, were never published at all,[26] and fifty pages, mostly concerning Harry's relations with Janet, were cut for the Collected Edition.[27] L.T. Hergenhan has argued persuasively that these latter revisions were unfortunate,[28] but it is unlikely that their restoration would answer all critical objections. After twenty years of callous rejection by Harry, Janet becomes engaged to the foolish Marquess of Edbury, just at the moment when Harry finally decides that he loves her. She insists on going through with the marriage, and is rescued from it by an extraordinary sequence of events, 'comically' recapitulating an incident in Harry's childhood, when, the night before the wedding, Edbury follows his long-time mistress, Mabel Sweetwinter, on to the boat of the sternly religious Captain Welch, who takes them off to sea for the good of their souls, whereupon they are all drowned.

This, however, occurs after the true climax of the book, the final and fatal confrontation of Richmond Roy and Squire Beltham, and of their conflicting discourses. This scene is modelled on the popular convention of 'exposure', as of Pecksniff by the elder Martin Chuzzlewit and, most relevantly, Uriah Heep by Micawber. It is, however, a typically modified version. Roy is exposed most importantly to himself, when the Squire reveals to him that the income from 'government', which had been the main basis for his belief that the justice of his claim was tacitly acknowledged, in fact came from the Squire's daughter Dorothy. The exposure of a self-deceiver to himself is of course more tragic than comic, and the contrast is the more poignant for the similarity between Roy and Micawber, another optimist who lives on rhetoric, and whose unlikely triumph comes in just such a scene as this, but as the exposer. It is entirely appropriate that Harry should take his father's part in this scene, with the effect that his grandfather disinherits him. It is a pyrrhic victory for Squire Beltham: although he survives for eight months, it was 'a scene that had afforded him high gratification at the heaviest cost a plain man can pay for his pleasures: it killed him'. But, considering the highly discursive nature of their conflict, Roy's fate is the more significant: 'He collapsed in speech' (53, 632–3). Deprived of (or freed from) the two voices that have shaped his destiny, it is not surprising that Harry should title the ensuing chapter 'I go drifting'.

McMaster asserts that the *Bildungsroman* model 'inevitably forces the novel into an inapt "private" mode, concerned with individual life-choices against a relatively stable given social order'.[29] This conflicts with Bakhtin's view (translated after McMaster's essay was published) that in the *Bildungsroman* 'human emergence ... is no longer man's own private affair. He emerges *along with the world* and he reflects the historical emergence of the world itself.'[30] How does *Harry Richmond* measure up to this criterion? Spånberg writes that 'The squire has his roots in the eighteenth century, Richmond Roy is a representative of the Regency and its equally outmoded attitudes; while Harry, the Victorian modern man, rejects them both as models and stumbles on without any clear sense of direction.'[31] This, however, is a rather inert version of Bakhtin's ideal. The outlook of Harry the narrator is certainly that of a distinctly Victorian kind of Liberalism. In that part of the novel which is most obviously influenced by the *Bildungsroman*, his experience in Germany, he encounters German Culture as Matthew Arnold understood it (in a conversation in which he plays Gulliver to Karsteg's King of Brobdingnag) and is purged of both the inflated chauvinism of his father ('You are a deep reader of English poetry I hope; she adores it, and the English Navy.... the comfort of a volume of Shakespeare to an exiled Englishman' 18, 212–13), and the philistine parochialism of his grandfather ('bidding me bluffly not to be a bookworm and forget I was an Englishman' 30, 321). He also, in a novel written during the Franco-Prussian war and by an author of divided sympathies, encounters in Prince Hermann a virulent example of the new German imperialism:

> Mistress of the Baltic, of the North Sea and the East, as eventually she must be, Germany would claim to take India as a matter of course, and find an outlet for the energies of the most prolific and the toughest of the races of mankind, – the purest, in fact, the only true race. (34, 373)

If Harry Richmond does not seem a very convincing example of Bakhtin's historically significant emergence, it is perhaps partly because these German experiences are not integrated into an engagement with a recognizable contemporary English world: Harry's England consists almost entirely of the 'outmoded' milieux of his grandfather and father. This perhaps also explains why, despite the undoubted intelligence and enlightenment of the narrative persona, Harry the character, at the end, no longer the point of tension between two powerful voices, seems drained of substance. Unlike other Meredithian males (Richard Feverel, Wilfrid Pole, Edward Blancove, and so on), he does not in the end pay the price of his own selfishness and sentimentality. This is paid by others – by Ottilia, condemned to marriage with Prince Hermann, and a whole shipload of people who have to be drowned so that Harry can have Janet. The reader of Meredith should not be surprised that this grotesque 'comedic' resolution is followed by a final reversal, when Harry and his wife arrive at Riversley to find it in flames, and his father (who has accidentally caused it in a final typically flamboyant gesture) presumed dead in the fire. Implicitly, perhaps, Meredith is registering his dissatisfaction with the hero's return to the wife and home waiting for him all along, as the conclusion of a novel of development. (The very grotesqueness of the resolution could, of course, be read as an even more implicit sign of the same dissatisfaction.) Perhaps, recognizing that his hero had not graduated as a true hero of historical emergence,

Meredith felt it necessary to recapitulate the conflict between Roy and Beltham, this time destroying Roy literally and Beltham symbolically.

There are a suspiciously large number of 'perhapses' in the foregoing paragraph. The extravagances of the novel's conclusion, typically disrupting generic security, are a final dialogic insurgence in a novel in which Meredith has, for the most part, subdued his characteristic tendencies. That *Harry Richmond* is to such a considerable degree an artistic success testifies to the flexibility of Meredith's novelistic powers; the fact that despite this artistic success and despite, perhaps more pressingly, the novel having been more commercially successful than its predecessors, Meredith subsequently and consistently returned to the methods he had pioneered in *Richard Feverel*, testifies to the strength of those characteristic tendencies.

4
Beauchamp's Career

Beauchamp's Career is a political novel but one of its most perceptive critics, David Howard, declines to treat it as such, on the grounds that 'In one sense the political reality is never there, or never there nakedly. It is a novel of talk about politics, of conversation which includes politics.' The impression that this is a naive response is immediately dispelled, but at the expense of making Howard's decision to ignore the politics paradoxical: 'This may be merely to say that the novel never forgets it is a novel, never forgets to justify within its fictional world (often very adroitly) the appearance of political statement and judgement.'[1] Meredith, in other words, recognizes that 'political reality' *can* never be 'there nakedly' in a novel (even if that reality is conceived as something that exists at all 'nakedly' outside language). But politics is central to *Beauchamp's Career* because the novel recognizes and exploits the fact that politics *is* language, or was increasingly becoming so in the age of the Second Reform Act.

We can see the advantage of Meredith's method in *Beauchamp's Career* if we compare another novel whose political narrative was prompted (in this case prospectively) by the Second Reform Act, *Felix Holt, the Radical*. Political action is, in Howard's sense, 'there nakedly' in *Felix Holt* when George Eliot embroils her hero in an election riot. Characteristically, Felix intervenes in the riot in order to divert the rioters from murdering the colliery manager, an action which leads to his arrest as a ringleader:

> Felix was perfectly conscious that he was in the midst of a tangled business. But he had chiefly before his imagination the horrors that might come if the mass of wild chaotic desires and impulses around him were not diverted from any further attack on places where they would get in the midst of intoxicating and inflammable materials. It was not a moment in which a spirit like his could calculate the effect of misunderstanding as to himself: nature never makes men who are at once energetically sympathetic and minutely calculating.[2]

The 'tangled business' is figured as something wholly external to Felix and at the same time 'perfectly' present to his consciousness. His perfect consciousness is the antithesis of the 'mass of wild chaotic desires and impulses around him' (the rioters, objectified to the same plane as the 'intoxicating and inflammable materials') and is co-extensive with the perfect consciousness of the narrator, who moves smoothly from this perspective shared with the hero, to panegyric on the hero's character, and authorial generalization or Barthesian *endoxa*. There is throughout the passage no sense of a language that is Felix's and not the narrator's, or of a language other than this one that might represent the rioters differently, or of the possibility of a speaker who might pronounce 'nature never makes men...' sanctimonious nonsense and Felix a hubristic fool. The generally acknowledged failure of the 'nakedly' political part of *Felix Holt* is a failure of language, a failure to recognize the implication of language and politics.

The difference in *Beauchamp's Career* can be seen from the start. It opens with several pages of typically dense and ironic Meredithian prose concerning a panic about a French invasion. This opening is, as much as those of the novels that succeed *Beauchamp*, 'prefatory',[3] but it is considerably less off-putting than the openings of *The Egoist* and *Diana of the Crossways*: it is a masterpiece of ironic prose, comprising a number of elements that establish the dialogic character of the narrator's position:

> When young Nevil Beauchamp was throwing off his midshipman's jacket for a holiday in the garb of peace, we had across Channel a host of dreadful military officers flashing swords at us for some critical observations of ours upon their sovereign, threatening Afric's fires and savagery.... We were unarmed, and the spectacle was distressing. We had done nothing except to speak our minds according to the habit of the free, and such an explosion appeared as irrational and excessive as that of a powder-magazine in reply to nothing more than the light of a spark. (1, 1)

As Margaret Harris says in her Introduction to the novel, the reader is confused as to 'the identity of the ubiquitous incorporative *we* from whom the narration issues'. She nevertheless identifies 'we' as 'the male establishment'.[4] This is certainly one element in the narrative discourse of this part of the novel, but it is infiltrated by another who is the agent of multiple ironies. 'A host of dreadful military officers flashing swords at us' for example combines hints of irony at the expense of both the English and the French – the word 'dreadful' in particular being tonally unstable in the same way as the later 'horrid', on which I shall comment shortly. 'We were unarmed, and the spectacle was distressing' gives us the stoical understatement of the English 'male establishment' without internal irony, but the following sentence, 'We had done nothing except to speak our minds according to habit of the free' carries a note of mock innocence, perhaps veiling boorishly chauvinistic plain-speaking: it echoes Matthew Arnold's sarcastic praise for 'that buoyant ease in holding up one's head, speaking out what is in one's mind, and flinging off all sheepishness and awkwardness' that were supposed to be fostered by English public schools.[5] The following metaphor of the powder-magazine and the spark intensifies this note: it may be 'nothing more than' a spark, but striking it in the presence of a powder-magazine is deliberately provocative.

The invading French troops are imagined wearing 'wide red breeches blown out by Fame, big as her cheeks', a piece of misplaced tatty allegory that ridicules those it pictures, but also by implication those fearing them:

And now those horrid shouts of the legions of Caesar, crying to the inheritor of an invading name [Napoleon III] to lead them against us, as the origin of his title had led the army of Gaul of old gloriously, scared sweet sleep. We saw them in imagination lining the opposite shore; eagle and standard-bearers, and *gallifers*, brandishing their fowls and their banners in a manner to frighten the decorum of the universe. (1, 1–2)

'Horrid' is a beautifully double-voiced word: its association with 'legions of Caesar' permits the already old-fashioned if not archaic use, as synonymous with 'horrible' ('that suggestion/ Whose horrid image doth unfix my hair', *Macbeth*, I, iii), while the already established element of irony in the passage invites the drawing-room associations of the more contemporary sense epitomized by the *OED* examples, 'I should not wear those horrid dresses' (Bulwer Lytton, 1858) and 'The horrid weather has kept me in' (Princess Alice, 1864). This play of the epic or tragic against the trivially social is repeated in 'brandishing their fowls and their banners in a manner to frighten the decorum of the universe' where (in addition to the obviously comic reduction of 'eagles' to 'fowls') the stronger sense of 'decorum' is older if not archaic ('the due decorum and comely beauty of the worlds brave structure', 1635, *OED*) while the current meaning is predominantly social. The clash of codes, registers, contexts, attitudes enfolded in these words (and similarly in 'dreadful' earlier) prefigures the struggles of earnest speech in the kind of social environment Beauchamp inhabits. (Harris comments on Meredith's dramatization of 'the extent to which etiquette operates as a mechanism of social control'.)[6]

The conclusion of the second paragraph can be paralleled by non-fictional texts of Meredith:

> But where were our armed men? where our great artillery? where our proved captains, to resist a sudden sharp trial of the national mettle? Where was the first line of England's defence, her navy? These were questions, and Ministers were called upon to answer them. The Press answered them boldly, with the appalling statement that we had no navy and no army. At the most we could muster a few old ships, a couple of experimental vessels of war, and twenty-five thousand soldiers indifferently weaponed. (1, 2)

> The idea of England with an army at her disposal somewhat less than that of Wurtemberg, not half so well drilled to the tasks of modern warfare, besotted on drugged beer, incapable of marching, badly officered, brainless from the drummer to the Chief – Lord in Heaven! What an idea! Yet people are saying calmly that we may be involved.[7]

The second passage was written during the Franco-Prussian War, shortly before Meredith began work on *Beauchamp's Career*, to Frederick Maxse, the model for Beauchamp. Despite this parallel, and although if ironic at all it is so only by infection, the passage from the novel should be seen as an imitation of Meredith's non-fictional discourse, not direct authorial commentary. I say this not because of any nervous or doctrinaire avoidance of the author, but because, for the reader of the novel, the 'we' who speaks here is not distinct from the ironized 'we' who has spoken earlier and represents, in part, the 'male establishment'. Its function is quite unlike 'nature never makes men...' in *Felix Holt*, and it is a classic example of the dialogic use Meredith makes of his own opinions. As Bakhtin says of Dostoevsky, the author's ideas 'uttered by him in monologic form outside the artistic context of his work (in articles, letters, oral conversations) are merely the prototypes for several of the idea-images in his novels' which 'become thoroughly dialogized and enter the great dialogue of the novel on *completely equal terms* with other idea-images'.[8]

So far Beauchamp himself (who, after the first sentence, is not mentioned until p. 7) has not been implicated in the dialogism. He becomes so, fleetingly, when the narrator states that his partners at balls 'knew not they were lesser Andromedas of his dear Andromeda country' (7). This echoes an earlier sentence: 'What country had anything like our treasures to defend? – countless riches, beautiful women, an inviolate soil!' (3) in which what purports to be a list of separate items is belied by the seemingly transferred epithet 'inviolate', suggesting a subliminal identification of women with the land. The Andromeda analogy which, though belonging to the narrator, characterizes Beauchamp's attitude to women and England, combines the need for protection and threat of violation implicit in the earlier sentence.

This attitude to women is central to the novel and will have a bearing on Beauchamp's relations with Cecilia Halkett. More prominent in this first chapter is the comedy of Nevil's challenge to the French Imperial Guard which is above all a comedy of *language*. When he tried to compose the challenge in French he 'lost sight of himself completely' becoming 'Nevil Beauchamp in moustache and imperial' (9). When he composes in English and translates, the two versions are given to illustrate the complete change of manner that occurs between the languages: 'I take up the glove you have tossed us. I am an Englishman. That will do for a reason' becomes 'J'accepte votre gant. Je suis Anglais. La raison est suffisante.' As the narrator comments, 'imagine French Guardsmen reading it!' (9). The stern, clipped manner of the English gentleman becomes ridiculous when taken out of the language that is its element.

Nevil's education in French has included a familiarity with the neo-classic drama, and we are told that 'he could even relish the Gallic-classic – "Qu'il mourût!" ' (8–9), the elder Horace's words on believing that his son has disgraced himself, the epitome of Corneillian tragic nobility; but Nevil's own effort at a comparable style sounds more like Masquarille, a servant in *Les Précieuses Ridicules*, by Meredith's own favourite Molière, whose speeches are parodies.

The episode ends with Nevil's refusal to make a stylistic alteration on the recommendation of Rosamund Culling, because he has written out the fair copy and would 'rather see it off than have it right' (12), which foreshadows the more painful comedy of his election address.

I have described the passage in Chapter 1 lamenting the poor state of the country's military preparation as an imitation of Meredith's non-fictional discourse, rather than direct authorial intervention. In the fourth chapter, however, we find a passage that it is hard to consider as anything but authorial commentary of the most straightforward and obtrusive kind:

> I am reminded by Mr Romfrey's profound disappointment in the youth, that it will be repeatedly shared by many others: and I am bound to forewarn readers of this history that there is no plot in it. The hero is chargeable with the official disqualification of constantly offending prejudices, never seeking to please; and all the while it is upon him that the narrative hangs. To be a public favourite is his last thought. Beauchampism, as one confronting him calls it, may be said to stand for nearly everything which is the obverse of Byronism, and rarely woos your sympathy, shuns the statuesque pathetic, or any kind of posturing. For Beauchamp will not even look at happiness to mourn its absence; melodious lamentations, demoniacal scorn, are quite alien to him. His faith is in working and fighting. With every inducement to offer himself for a romantic figure, he despises the pomades and curling-irons of modern romance. (4, 38–9)

The narrator continues in this vein for a paragraph of nearly two pages, significantly separated typographically from the narrative; going on, in an echo of the 'Prelude' to *Middlemarch*, to lament that 'indifferent England refused [an epic] to him'.

However, the provenance of this passage, and its relationship with the other discourses that it names and implies, show its function to be more complicated than it seems. Readers of Meredith will be familiar with this kind of testy commentary, but in *Beauchamp's Career* it is rarer than in many of the novels, partly because Meredith cut 'a host of my own reflections'[9] for serial publication in the *Fortnightly Review* and (unlike others) the novel remained in this version for subsequent book publication.

Paradoxically, while so much authorial comment seems to have been cut, this passage was actually inserted during the revision for the *Fortnightly*, apparently at the suggestion of its editor, John Morley, and it gave Meredith considerable difficulty:

> I find I can say better what should be said of Beauchamp in a paragraph at the head of the 4th chapter – I am very shy of prefaces, and by introducing my one or two remarks incidentally I hope to escape from a tone that seems to avoid the apology only by some loftiness – or the reverse. I am afraid it would not be I who could put the intermediate touch. Conception rarely fails me, though ability does, and I can barely conceive of its being done in the proper tone. – I own that you might do it for one of your own works: but for a piece of fiction having a serious aim, and before a public that scorns the serious in fiction, and whose wits are chiefly trained to detect pretension, it is more than commonly difficult.[10]

Meredith's relationship with Morley was at this moment tense and complex. Morley had been, and was again to be, one of his closest friends, but in 1871 he abruptly terminated the friendship in a letter complaining that (in the words of Meredith's reply) Morley felt injured by Meredith's 'manner of speaking... in clashing with [his] "opinions, ideas, and likings,"' and alleged that Meredith was the only friend from whom he 'fail[ed] to get new strength'.[11] The period of composition of *Beauchamp's Career* corresponded more or less exactly with that of his estrangement from Morley, and it was the intercession of friends, to facilitate the publication of the novel, that brought the two men together again. Meredith's letters to Morley at this time are full of the sensitivity, tentativeness and slightly strained good will appropriate to such a situation.

Morley, and to a large extent the review that he edited, was one of the most distinguished representatives of the influential mid-Victorian tradition of rational, optimistic, philosophical radicalism, strongly influenced by John Stuart Mill and to a lesser extent by Comtean Positivism. This was a tradition with which Meredith had considerable sympathy, but it was not one to which he in any simple way *belonged*. For example, he shows in his letters signs of sympathy with Morley's antagonist James Fitzjames Stephen,[12] and the gaiety, spontaneity and genuine intimacy of his friendship with the Tory William Hardman suggests a capacity for detachment from the ethos of the *Fortnightly*.

Clearly the kind (or kinds) of radical discourse associated with the *Fortnightly*, and especially with Morley, must be a presence in *Beauchamp's Career*. It is however, as we shall see, a peculiarly paradoxical and provoking presence. Norman Kelvin sees the relationship with Morley as central to the novel and argues that it was consciously written as 'a repudiation both of the faith in reason Morley adhered to and of the related, even more objectionable belief that art can or ought to be made to serve the ends of political propaganda'.[13] Kelvin rightly draws attention to the last surviving letter that Meredith wrote to Morley before the break:

> [Maxse] advises me in these serious times 'to take to political writing'. I reply that it demands special study. He insists that I have only to give my genuine convictions. I admit the novelty in newspaper writing but urge its insufficiency. 'Not at all', says he. I am to be allowed to produce one volume novels on Questions of the Day. Morley is quoted as being utterly of his opinion. I propose to him an Opera libretto to popularise the Democratic movement and bring our chief personages before the eyes of the nobility. O[dger?] in love with the Princess L[ouise?] meditates the *enlèvement* of the lady that he may breed Radicals from Royalty: delivers idea in ballad...
>
> Fred savagely: 'Good God! How can you spout buffoonery in times like these!'
>
> Pathetic ballad by M[axse] 'In times like these'.[14]

In this same letter Meredith praises Morley's essay on Byron and says, 'if I could write like that I would write more prose' (by which he evidently means non-fiction). The tone of this letter is strikingly different from that of the later ones, not surprisingly if Meredith had come to feel that it was performances such as this that so offended Morley. He not only reports but also re-enacts the 'buffoonery', breaking Maxse's earnestness across the parodied genres. Maxse evidently expected Meredith to write radical equivalents of *Coningsby* whose 'main purpose' was 'to vindicate the just claims of the Tory party to be the popular political confederation of the country'.[15] Contrary to Kelvin's view, however (his study, despite the interesting hints of 'hidden polemic' in this section, is limitingly theme-based) it was not necessary for Meredith consciously to repudiate such views in *Beauchamp's Career*. The manner of the earlier letter to Morley, with its substitution of (deadly serious, and as it turned out offensive) buffoonery for argument, his comment on Morley's 'Byron' essay, and his struggle in writing the 'prefatory' paragraph about Beauchamp, all show that by the very nature of his involvement with language he was doomed to do otherwise. The carnivalesque refusal, in the letter, to be 'serious' has its parallel in the less buffoonish but equally ironic treatment of political discourse in the novel.

To return to our 'authorial' paragraph: if there is, throughout the novel, an element of 'hidden polemic' with Morley, in this paragraph, written with publication by the *Fortnightly* directly in view, it is of a special character. Although it does not reproduce Morley's style his writings are a powerful and immediate presence in it: in the struggle to produce a kind of writing that Morley 'might do... for one of [his] own works', but also in the challenging claim that 'Beauchampism, as one confronting him calls it, may be said to stand for nearly everything which is the obverse of Byronism'. Could the 'one confronting him' be Morley? However that may be, it should be noted that the incongruous bestowal of an 'ism' on Beauchamp is attributed to an anonymous other; also that publication in the *Fortnightly* makes 'Byronism' virtually a reference to Morley's essay, published in the same review four years earlier. Here is what Morley wrote about Byron in that essay, about which Meredith was so complimentary:

> The list of his poems is the catalogue of the elements of the revolutionary spirit. For of what manner is this spirit? Is it not a masterful and impatient yearning after many good things, unsubdued and uninformed either by a just knowledge of the time, and the means which are needed to bring men the fruits of their hope, or by a fit appreciation of orderly and tranquil activity for the common service, as the normal type of the individual life? And this is precisely the temper and the spirit of Byron.[16]

Beauchamp the obverse of this? On the contrary, if not exactly a just description of Beauchamp, it sounds like one of the various Tory verdicts on him, which punctuate the novel, for example that of Blackburn Tuckham: 'he is a very good fellow, I don't doubt... all he wants is emphatically school – school – school' (Chapter 28, p313). The version of Beauchamp (and of the novel) that we are presented with in the 'authorial' paragraph sounds, in fact, more like Morley's ideal of a radical hero than the one we are actually given. The narrator's sarcastic references to 'a romantic figure' and (later in the passage) to setting the hero off 'with scenic effects and contrasts', make a puzzling introduction to a novel among whose triumphs are Nevil's wooing of Renée on a boat at dawn in the Gulf of Venice, his pursuit of Cecilia under sail in the Solent, and his prolonged and terrifying delirium, contracted because of his insistence on visiting a poor and sick supporter. It is true that the promises of such scenes are often not delivered, but certainly 'scenic effects and contrasts' are a significant constituent of the art of *Beauchamp's Career*, while it is largely Nevil's quality as a 'romantic figure' that makes his 'faith... in working and fighting' imaginatively appealing.

As for Byron, there are at least two passages where a Byronic style is a dialogized presence in the narrator's discourse and, while it is true that in both cases the Byronic is associated with Renée, it is not 'objectified' in such a way as to suggest the 'obverse' of Beauchamp. The first, and more subtle, is the description of Renée in Chapter 4, reminiscent of, for example, 'She walks in beauty like the night' and the description of Donna Julia in *Don Juan*:

> Her features had the soft irregularities which run to rarities of beauty, as the ripple rocks the light; mouth, eyes, brows, nostrils, and bloomy cheeks played with one another liquidly; thought flew, tongue followed, and the flash of meaning quivered over them like night-lightning. (5, 43)

This might seem to reinforce Margaret Harris's view that Renée's Venice (and Renée herself) is romantic, picturesque and Byronic, whereas Beauchamp's is Ruskinian and republican.[17] However, Meredith characteristically represents female beauty, not simply as a given feature of the woman, but as an object of masculine sexuality and sensibility. The descriptions of Clara in *The Egoist*, focalized through Willoughby, are notable examples of this, and while this passage is not explicitly focalized through Nevil, it undoubtedly signifies not just how Renée is, but how she appears and appeals to him. Gillian Beer says that Nevil is repeatedly 'tested by being set in Byronic situations and tempted to respond with the swagger and panache and daring which would win him approval in his own class' and that, of course, most of these situations involve Renée.[18] This oversimplifies in the same way as the authorial comment on 'Beauchampism' and 'Byronism' which it sets out to explicate. Here is the second, less subtle evocation of Byronic language, which may well seem to support Beer's opinion, coming as it does in the chapter entitled 'A Trial of Him', in which Nevil overcomes the temptation to elope with Renée:

> That was a quality of godless young heroism not unexhausted in Beauchamp's blood. Reanimated by him, she awakened his imagination of the vagrant splendours of existence and the rebel delights which have their own law and 'nature' for an applauding mother. Radiant Alps rose in his eyes, and the morning born in the night: suns that rose from mountain and valley, over sea and desert, called on all earth to witness their death. The magnificence of the contempt of humanity posed before him superbly satanesque, grand as thunder among the crags: and it was not a sensual cry that summoned him from his pedlar labours, pack on back along the level road, to live and breathe deep, gloriously mated: Renée kindled his romantic spirit, and could strike the feeling into him that to be proud of his possession of her was to conquer the fretful vanity to possess. (40, 458)

The Byronic 'word' is evidently much more 'on display' in this passage than in the earlier one. One might say entirely so if the dialogizing narrator's voice were confined to such derogatory words and phrases as 'contempt of humanity', 'satanesque' and 'fretful vanity'. But there is in the evocation of 'nature' (even within those slightly puritanical inverted commas) and above all the 'Radiant Alps' a note of exultation that any reader of the novels will recognize as authentically Meredithian. It is a note that reminds me by contrast of another passage by Morley on Byron and Romanticism in general:

> That it was presided over by a false conception of nature as a benign and purifying power, while she is in truth a stern force to be tamed and mastered, if society is to hold together, cannot be denied of the revolutionary movement then, any more than it can be denied of its sequels now.[19]

The point of quoting this is that Morley is demonstrably a presence in the narrator's opposition of 'Beauchampism' to 'Byronism' and the passage from Chapter 40 is another where that opposition is in play (satanesque contempt of humanity against 'pedlar labours'). But the presence of the 'Meredithian' exultation (so opposite in spirit to the Morley passage) draws attention to the strained and unconvincing character of the Byronic pastiche at this point: it makes it possible for a reader to think that the appropriate analogies for Nevil's contemplated elopement with Renée are not the tales or life of Byron but those episodes in Meredith's own work where the natural world, and above all the Alpine landscape, are regenerating: the meeting of Diana and Dacier, the union of Clara and Whitford, and the elopements of Weyburn and Aminta, and of Captain Kirby and the Countess Fanny. The looseness of syntax in 'summoned him from his pedlar labours, pack on back along the level road, to live and breathe deep', allowing a 'misreading' rapport of the middle phrase with the last as well as the first, perhaps connives in this thought.

This is not to deny the significance of Nevil's moral conflict, or the nobility of his choice. On the contrary, it is to substitute for a simplified opposition between an implausible 'Beauchampism' and a caricatured 'Byronism' a conflict between competing and honourable principles in Nevil's character, in Meredithian discourse and thought and in the Romanticism towards which he was much more sympathetic than Morley. *Pace* Gillian Beer, the temptations to which Nevil is subjected in his relationship with Renée are not merely 'to respond with the swagger and panache and daring which would win him approval in his own class', but to avert the arranged marriage of a 17-year-old girl with a middle-aged roué, to offer her, when the marriage is accomplished and her husband neglects her, an honourable if lawless love instead of the degrading liaisons to which she is tempted, and to rescue her when she flees to him to escape the horrors of her husband's rekindled 'amour'. Of course, my account is as monologically incomplete as Beer's, and the language in which Meredith renders these internal and external dramas never allows the reader to forget the elements of sentimentality and vanity in Beauchamp's motivation. But the 'temptations' to which he is subjected by Renée take the form, at least in part, of moral imperatives, and are consonant, not with 'satanesque' Byronism, but with some of the most genuinely radical thought of the Romantic period. Beauchamp resembles Shelley more than Byron.[20]

We have still not finished with the relation of *Beauchamp's Career* to *Fortnightly* radicalism. Of all Meredith's novels, it is perhaps the one which most closely approaches Bakhtin's ideal, in which the language of the narrator is interpenetrated by a number of voices, all on the same 'plane', resulting in a kind of discursive model of ideological conflict. We shall be examining some instances of this. The remarkable thing about the novel, given its intimate involvement with the *Fortnightly*, is the absence of any straightforward 'image' of the kind of radical discourse typical of Morley and his associates. Frederick Maxse, of course, was the model for Beauchamp, and he contributed to the *Fortnightly*, and the novel is full of representations of his radical rhetoric. (For example: 'The covert Toryism, the fits of flunkeyism, the cowardice, of the relapsing middle-class, which is now England before mankind, because it fills the sails of the Press, must be exposed' 44, 501.)[21] But Maxse was not typical of the kind of rational, philosophical radicalism the *Fortnightly* centrally stood for: he was a 'firebrand' as Meredith called him, not rational at all, his radicalism was inconsistent (he opposed women's rights) and unstable (he ended his life a Tory).

Where such discourse does make an unambiguous appearance in the novel it is in a startling and provocative form. When Cecilia hears of Everard Romfrey's assault on Dr Shrapnel, she contemplates going to see Nevil, to advise him on how to deal with his uncle. But she cannot and does not even really want to. The passage in which this is explained is a 'hybrid' of the narrator's discourse and Cecilia's character zone:

Why not? Because she was one of the artificial creatures called women (with the accent) who dare not be spontaneous, and cannot act independently if they would continue to be admirable in the world's eye, and who for that object must remain fixed on shelves, like other marketable wares, avoiding motion to avoid shattering or tarnishing. This is their fate, only in degree less inhuman than that of Hellenic and Trojan princesses offered up to the Gods, or pretty slaves to the dealers. Their artificiality is at once their bane and their source of superior pride.

Seymour Austin might have reason for seeking to emancipate them, she thought, and blushed in thought that she could never be learning anything but from her own immediate sensations. (32, 366)

'The accent' refers back to the previous page, where her father tells her, '"Women must not be judging things out of their sphere," with the familiar accent on "women" which proves their inferiority.' Cecilia's free indirect discourse distinctly echoes a passage from Morley's hero, John Stuart Mill:

> What is now called the nature of women is an eminently artificial thing – the result of forced repression in some directions, unnatural stimulation in others. It may be asserted without scruple, that no other class of dependents have had their character so entirely distorted from its natural proportions by their relation with their masters; for, if conquered and slave races have been, in some respects, more forcibly repressed, whatever in them has not been crushed down by an iron heel has generally been let alone, and if left with any liberty of development, it has developed itself according to its own laws; but in the case of women, a hot-house and stove cultivation has always been carried on of some of the capabilities of their nature, for the benefit and pleasure of their masters.[22]

The precise verbal echoes and the identity of general tenor justify regarding the passage from the novel as an 'image' of Mill's discourse. But it is a heavily dialogized image. The calm, rational language of Mill disguises its actual place in the world where, of course, it was engaged in intense ideological struggle or, as Bakhtin puts it, 'The word, directed towards its object, enters a dialogically agitated and tension-filled environment of alien words, value judgements and accents.'[23] Mill's style is cunning and controlled. Consider the way he deploys his rhetoric of 'slaves' and 'hot-house', incorporating it into and as it were subduing it to an objective comparison. In the passage from the novel, by contrast, the rhetoric is nakedly emotional: 'fixed on shelves like other marketable wares, avoiding motion to avoid shattering or tarnishing'. Above all, in Cecilia's free indirect discourse the word 'women' literally encounters the Bakhtinian 'accent' supplied by her father in the immediate dramatic context.

So far there is nothing paradoxical about Meredith's 'image' of Mill's discourse. But this character zone is that of a Tory heiress who, if she has begun to be influenced by the radical ideas of the man she loves, has precisely *not* learned feminism from him. Gillian Beer profoundly comments that Beauchamp 'loses Cecilia finally because he cannot understand that she is growing independently of him through the force of her passionate love for him'.[24] Nevil inspires Cecilia's development but he does not control it or set its limits. In Beer's words, 'All that is most truly radical in Meredith's own apprehension of women is expressed in the psychological portrait of Cecilia's growth and the failure of the relationship between her and Beauchamp.'[25] Only four pages before the passage we are considering, Beauchamp has reflected that 'the bride who would bring him beauty and wealth, and her special gift of tender womanliness, was not yet so thoroughly mastered as to grant her husband his just prevalence with her' (32, 362).

The novel's champion of women's rights is not Beauchamp but Seymour Austin, the enlightened and philosophical Tory, who is one of Nevil's opponents at the election:

> Mr Austin was a firm believer in new and higher destinies for women. He went farther than she could concede the right of human speculation to go.... And he was professedly temperate. He was but for opening avenues to the means of livelihood for them, and leaving it to their strength to conquer the position they might wish to win. His belief that they would do so was the revolutionary sign. (28, 301–2)

This exactly mirrors Mill's liberal ideology:

> What women by nature cannot do, it is quite superfluous to forbid them from doing. What they can do, but not so well as the men who are their competitors, competition suffices to exclude them from; since nobody asks for protective duties and bounties in favour of women; it is only asked that the present bounties and protective duties in favour of men should be recalled.[26]

Seymour Austin is one of a number of brilliantly indivualized Tory voices in the novel, the most attractive and enlightened, but not in any straightforward sense a 'spokesman' or voice of authorial wisdom. Cecilia's trust in him arguably proves misplaced when, after she has been persuaded to give up Beauchamp, he knowingly or otherwise uses her growing attraction to himself, to connive in her entrapment into marriage with Blackburn Tuckham.

Is this procedure of Meredith's perverse, a symptom of pique against Morley? I don't think so. It might help to understand what Meredith is doing, if we look at a sentence chosen, almost at random, from Morley's *On Compromise*, exactly contemporary with *Beauchamp's Career*:

> The right of thinking freely and acting independently, of using our minds without excessive fear of authority, and shaping our lives without unquestioning obedience to custom, is now a finally accepted principle in some sense or other with every school of thought that has the smallest chance of commanding the future.[27]

Morley was genuinely a liberal and pluralist, in no sense a totalitarian, as the thematic content of this sentence makes clear, yet this is unmistakably a discourse that aspires to command the field, to exclude all others, on the ground of its own claimed *in*clusiveness. It does not merely compete with opposing discourses, it denies that they are part of the game, its own principle is 'finally accepted' and no other 'has the smallest chance of commanding the future'. The hubristic blindness of this kind of thinking is, as a matter of history, only too sadly obvious. Moreover, it could not be more remote from novelistic language as practised by Meredith or as theorized by Bakhtin, where the word always has to struggle in a competitive environment of alien words and cannot reach its object without taking these into account. In Meredith's fiction a radical discourse which claimed that it embodied a 'finally accepted principle' could only be an object of satirical scorn. His novel keeps better faith with radical ideas by showing them active but fragmented, leading a healthy but paradoxical existence, showing up in the most unexpected places and keeping dubious company, fighting with enemy ideas and with each other, above all imbued with the passions, anxieties, uncertainties and contradictions of human beings.

In his book on dialogism Michael Holquist writes that novels:

> manifest inter-textuality in their display of the enormous variety of discourses used in different historical periods and by disparate social classes, and in the peculiarly charged effect such a display has on reading in specific social and historical situations. Among the more powerful *inter*-textual effects novels have is the

extra-literary influence they exercise on claims to singularity and authority made by other texts and discourses.[28]

This is an apposite comment on the relation of *Beauchamp's Career* to the radical discourses we have been looking at. But these are not isolated cases. The drama of the novel is to a large extent a drama of conflicting discourses: on nearly every page we find examples of character zones, stylization and pastiche, always with subtly differing accents. There is, in particular, a remarkably varied range of conservative discourses in the novel, and one can find traces, sometimes concentrated, sometimes diffuse, of such diverse influential and/or representative conservative texts as the novels and speeches of Disraeli; Bagehot's *English Constitution*; Fitzjames Stephen's riposte to Mill, *Liberty, Equality, Fraternity*; the *Life and Recollections* of Grantley Berkeley, the model for Everard Romfrey; the epistolary journals of Meredith's friend William Hardman; and Sir George Tomkins Chesney's cautionary tale, 'The Battle of Dorking', which influenced the account of the invasion-scare at the beginning of the novel.

The social medium in which Meredith's hero moves is, for the most part, that of the conservative landed gentry and aristocracy, and the medium in which he literally exists in the novel is largely made up of the language of that class. Meredith shows an intense interest in the varieties of conservative discourse, and its relationship to the 'authorial' discourse is varied and, at times, indefinite.

At one extreme are the wooden reactionaries, such as the old Whig turned Tory, Grancey Lespel, and Cecilia's father, Colonel Halkett. Such a passage as this –

> For power, for no other consideration, those manufacturing rascals have raised Radicalism from its primeval mire – from petty backslum bookseller's shop and public-house back-parlour effluvia of oratory... (20, 204)

– although in Lespel's 'character zone' and compositionally part of the narrative, is as effectively objectified as if it were in quotation marks. Colonel Halkett's language is entirely conservative to the point of being unconscious: it is made up of ideologically charged ready-made phrases such as (with reference to Everard's assault on Shrapnel) 'soundly horsewhipped', 'handsomely flogged' and 'condign punishment' (30, 363–5). All of these are conventional expressions belonging to the lexicon of the horsewhipping class,[29] and 'soundly', in particular, attaches connotations of orthodoxy to the act of violence. Typically his horror at his daughter's developing consciousness is expressed as: 'You've got hold of a language!... a way of speaking!' (37, 422)

The most important reactionary figure in the novel, Everard Romfrey, would not dissent from the language of Lespel and Halkett, and often uses (or is associated with) similar language himself. Again the example (Everard's image of John Bright) is from free indirect discourse:

> One of the half-stifled cotton-spinners, a notorious one, a spouter of rank sedition and hater of aristocracy, a political poacher, managed to make himself heard. (3, 36)

Everard also, like Lespel and Cecil Baskelett, automatically attaches the reactionary insult 'rascal' to radicals (a habit shared by the much more enlightened real-life Tory, William Hardman, the 'model' for Blackburn Tuckham).[30] Everard's language, however, is capable, unlike Lespel's and Halkett's, of entering into the subtlest of dialogic relations. Consider this passage:

> Mr Romfrey considered him to be insatiable for service. Beauchamp, during his absence, had shown himself awake to the affairs of the country once only, in an urgent supplication he had forwarded for all his uncle's influence to be used to get him appointed to the first vacancy in Robert Hall's naval brigade, then forming part of our handful in insurgent India. The fate of that chivalrous Englishman, that born sailor-warrior, that truest of heroes, imperishable in the memory of those who knew him, and in our annals, young though he was when death took him, had wrung from Nevil Beauchamp such a letter of tears as to make Mr Romfrey believe the naval crown of glory his highest ambition. Who on earth could have guessed him to be bothering his head about politics all the while! (13, 125)

The third sentence is highly stylized. The repeated demonstrative, the apposition of slightly varying laudatory terms that has a totalizing effect, the words 'imperishable' and 'annals', all establish a distinct patriotic-funereal rhetoric. This rhetoric, however, is not 'objectified' – it would be rash to judge that the narrator has no part in it, and the structure of the sentence suggests first that it is the narrator's, second that it is Nevil's, and third that it is Everard's, without ever deciding the issue. This is a rhetoric which these three participants in the narrative, often at odds with each other, can share at the appropriate moment and, as it were, sing a solemn trio of lament. 'Chivalrous' is of course a key word in this rhetoric, and in the novel. It is the cornerstone of the ideology that permits Everard to horsewhip Shrapnel for having 'offended' Rosamond; an ideology according to which Nevil acts when, as a boy, he beats Cecil Baskelett for making coarse remarks about Rosamond's doubtful position as Everard's housekeeper. Moreover, as many critics have commented, the chivalric code persists in such characteristic actions of Nevil's as his response to Renée's summons, his insistence that Everard apologize to Shrapnel, his visit to the sick voter, and the final fatal rescue-attempt. Frederick Maxse, interestingly, was fond of appropriating the word 'chivalrous' for radical purposes, describing E.S. Beesly, the Positivist Professor of History at University College London and friend of Karl Marx, as 'one of the ablest and most chivalrous thinkers of the day' and Ernest Jones, former Chartist and first President of the International Working Men's Association, as 'a man actuated by the highest motives and chivalry'.[31] To return to the passage under discussion, it is notable that the dialogic effect I have been analysing is enhanced and contrasted by the 'peeling away' as it were of Everard's character zone, awakened from the harmonious trance of the lament and returned to his typical rough colloquialism, in the final sentence.

Another way in which Everard differs from the 'wooden' reactionaries is his ability to criticize, ridicule and objectify Nevil's language. Bakhtin writes of the simultaneous presence of 'two linguistic consciousnesses... the one being represented and the other doing the representing'.[32] This of course happens all the time in novels, in such techniques as free indirect discourse, but in Meredith, and especially in *Beauchamp's Career*, the process is dramatized; or one might say that it is shifted to a different diegetic level, at which a language is represented by another language which is itself represented. This technique is fundamental to the way political ideas are dramatized in *Beauchamp's Career*, and I shall be describing it in more detail later. Here I shall merely give a couple of examples to show how Everard functions in relation to Nevil's language. The first, the briefest possible, is his mocking corruption of Nevil's catch-word 'humanity' to 'humanitomtity' (4, 45). The second example is more interesting and surprising, since it is before Nevil's discovery of radicalism and the language that Everard criticizes is a recognizable conservative idiom:

> 'We lead them in war,' said he; 'why not in peace? There's a front for peace as well as war, and that's our place rightly. We're pushed aside; why, it seems to me we're treated like old-fashioned ornaments! The fault must be ours....And as for jeering the cotton-spinners, I can't while they've the lead of us. We let them have it! And we have thrice the stake in the country. I don't mean properties and titles.'
> 'Deuce you don't,' said his uncle.
> 'I mean our names, our histories; I mean our duties. As for titles, the way to defend them is to be worthy of them.' (3, 29–30)

This is the Tory idealism of Disraeli's novels:

> The guests at Lord Monmouth's to-day were chiefly Carlists, individuals bearing illustrious names, that animate the page of history, and are indissolubly bound up with the glorious annals of their great country. They are the phantoms of a past, but real Aristocracy; an Aristocracy that was founded on an intelligible principle; which claimed great privileges for great purposes; whose hereditary duties were such, that their possessors were perpetually in the eye of the nation, and who maintained, and, in a certain point of view justified, their pre-eminence by constant illustration.[33]

This is a Tory discourse that, like the closely related chivalric code, persists into Nevil's radical phase – compare 'I say that is no aristocracy, if it does not head the people in virtue – military, political, national: I mean the qualities required by the times for leadership' (28, 310) – and, to his credit, it is one of which Everard contemptuously refuses to avail himself. Here is his response to Nevil's original speech:

> 'Damned fine speech,' remarked Everard. 'Now you get out of that trick of prize-orationing. I call it snuffery, sir; it's all to your own nose! You're talking to me, not to a gallery. "Worthy of them!"... You ought to know better. Property and titles are

worth having, whether you are "worthy of them" or a disgrace to your class. The best way of defending them is to keep a strong fist, and take care you don't draw your fore-foot back more than enough.'

Everard's ability to label Nevil's language, criticize its generic inappropriateness, quote it back at him with an 'accent', and supply a vigorous alternative show him to be far from unconscious like Halkett, and that the most 'medieval' reactionary ideology is not incompatible with sharp intelligence. The 'inter-textual' discourse brought to mind here is not Disraeli but the cool account given by Grantley Berkeley, the 'model' for Everard and like his fictional counterpart a game-law fanatic, of his father's way of dealing with a poacher:

> As an illustration of the readiness with which Lynch law was carried out even in those days, I recollect my father riding along a public path, and meeting a fellow carrying what looked extremely like a well-filled game bag: the former immediately slipped his right foot back out of the stirrup, and kept it in readiness on the flank of his black shooting-mare; then manoeuvring so as to make the offender pass on that side, he launched the toe of his heavy boot against the pit of the man's stomach with such force that the latter went down as if shot. Before he could rise, the exasperated owner of the game had jumped out of his saddle, and begun to search the bag; but was extremely disappointed to find in it nothing but rabbits.[34]

Berkeley's insouciant and on the face of it incongruous use of the idiom of the Wild West is an implicit acknowledgement corresponding to Everard's explicit assertion that 'The same arts that did gain/ A power, must it maintain.'[35]

The other major 'reactionary' character, Cecil Baskelett, is, like Everard, crucially important in the dramatization of political ideas but, unlike all the other characters, he has no identifiable ideological discourse of his own. He has a 'gift', which is specifically a gift of language (and gesture), 'the art of stripping his fellow-man and so posturing him as to make every movement of the comical wretch puppet-like, constrained, stiff, and foolish' (11, 98), but this 'art' is parasitical on the language of others. His main function in the novel, indeed, is to represent the language of others 'with an accent', but unlike Everard he has no discourse of his own to counter with. Significantly, in the 'baiting' of Dr Shrapnel which immediately triggers the horsewhipping, what Shrapnel is provoked by are Cecil's 'perplexingly empty sentences' (30, 346), sustained by nothing but the arrogance of class superiority.

Not all the conservatives in the novel are reactionaries. Blackburn Tuckham's name and origin align him with the industrial north, object of Everard's anachronistic contempt. He is a modern conservative and his discourse can absorb a certain amount of narratorial irony because he represents the dominant power of the age:

> Having won the race and gained the prize, shall we let it slip out of our grasp? Upon this topic his voice descended to tones of priestlike awe: for are we not the envy of the world? Our wealth is countless, fabulous. It may well inspire veneration. And we have won it with our hands, thanks (he implied it so) to our religion. We are rich in money and industry, in those two things only, and the corruption of an energetic industry is constantly threatened by the profusion of wealth giving it employment. This being the case, either your Radicals do not know the first conditions of human nature, or they do; if they do they are traitors, and the Liberals opening the gates to them are fools: and some are knaves.... In a country like ours, open on all sides to the competition of intelligence and strength, with a Press that is the voice of all parties and of every interest; in a country offering to your investments three and a half and more per cent., secure as the firmament! –
>
> He perceived an amazed expression on Miss Halkett's countenance. (26, 285)

Tuckham has none of the geniality or many-sidedness of his model, William Hardman, whose papers are a fascinating study in mid-Victorian Toryism; but his haranguing complacency is offset by the single-mindedness and well-judged restraint of his campaign to win Cecilia, and by the able and energetic way (partly to further his suit) he manages her father's mines. Moreover, he is completely free from the corruption of the outmoded chivalric code which enables Everard to horsewhip Shrapnel: 'he was unreservedly condemnatory of Mr Romfrey' (37, 412). An important point in his favour, especially in Cecilia's eyes, is that he takes her advice to 'listen to Seymour Austin' and is consequently 'much improved, much less overbearing' (ibid.). Admittedly we are merely told this – Tuckham is perhaps the only character in the novel in respect of whom one is tempted to invoke the old 'telling/showing' distinction unfavourably – but it reminds us of the importance of Seymour Austin, the other non-reactionary conservative, whose role in respect of Cecilia's development has already been discussed. Here I need only remind the reader that, in respect of sexual politics, which is arguably the most important politics in the novel, Austin is not only not reactionary but decidedly to the 'left' of the radicals. In the final chapter, apropos of the necessity (lamented by Beauchamp and Shrapnel) for Jenny to be married by a clergyman, we have another passage in which, as in the lament for Robert Hall, three voices are discernible:

> Alas for us! – this our awful baggage in the rear of humanity, these women who have not moved on their own feet one step since the primal mother taught them to suckle, are perpetually pulling us backward on the march. Slaves of custom, forms, shows and superstitions, they are slaves of the priests. (56, 619–20)

Once again the voice of the narrator and those of two characters are simultaneously present, but the internal dynamics of the dialogism are very different: here the narratorial voice is 'representing' and those of the characters, merged together, are 'on display'. Their arrogant blindness is emphasized when compared with Cecilia's anguished self-analysis of her 'enslavement', quoted earlier. The 'conservative' discourses are not confined to the Tories.

The most widely discussed, and most obvious, intertextual presence in *Beauchamp's Career* is that of Carlyle. Comment ranges from John W. Morris's assertion that the novel is 'an astonishing double tribute to Carlyle'[36] to Gary Handwerk's view that 'Carlyle's heroic ideal installs a model of human subjectivity that Meredith is at pains to reject throughout his work.'[37] The most comprehensive view of Carlyle's importance to the novel is the often quoted statement of Gillian Beer:

> Carlyle, then, has a range of conflicting roles within the artistry of the novel: he offers Meredith a parallel for his own problems in persuading an English audience to listen to what he is saying; he focusses the problem of history and fiction which is implicit in

the work as a whole; he is personated in Dr Shrapnel; and, most important, his book *Heroes and Hero-Worship* illuminates Beauchamp intellectually.[38]

Most commentaries have no difficulty with the view that Carlyle is 'personated' (if not ideologically, then at least in style and manner) in Shrapnel, and tend to assume that Carlyle's influence on Beauchamp is assimilated to the Disraelian ideal of the aristocratic leader discussed above.

It will be useful to be quite clear about the character of the one book of Carlyle's explicitly alluded to in the novel, *On Heroes, Hero-Worship and the Heroic in History*, a series of six lectures published in 1841. The topics of the individual lectures are the Hero as Divinity (Odin, whom Carlyle idiosyncratically treats as an historical individual), Prophet (Mahomet), Priest (Luther), Poet (Dante and Shakespeare), Man of Letters (Johnson, Rousseau and Burns), and King (Cromwell and Napoleon). In other words, three of the six lectures deal with religion, two with literature and only one with political leadership; Carlyle has grave reservations about Napoleon, so that Cromwell is the only unambiguous model of the hero as political leader. A second notable point is that several of Carlyle's Heroes (and those whom he tends to write most powerfully about) were despised or reviled at the time of writing. His lecture on Mahomet would still make salutary reading today. Thirdly, not one of Carlyle's heroes was a hereditary aristocrat and several were not even, in Victorian terms, 'well born'. Carlyle exhorts his listeners and readers not so much to emulate the heroes as to acknowledge and 'worship' them. A reasonable conclusion from this is that the book's influence on Beauchamp has less to do with his conception of himself than with his tendency to, as his relatives complain, make an 'idol' of Shrapnel.

An even more important point, and one that is more central to my critical approach, is the universal agreement of critics that, in the words of Lionel Stevenson, 'Carlylean rhetoric is well exemplified'[39] in Shrapnel's discourse, and especially in his letter to Beauchamp, the most important 'interpolated genre' in the novel. Here is part of the passage cited by Stevenson in support of his contention:

> 'Work at the people!... Moveless do they seem to you? Why, so is the earth to the sowing husbandman, and though we cannot forecast a reaping season, we have in history durable testification

that our seasons come in the souls of men, yea, as a planet that
we have set in motion, and faster and faster are we spinning in it,
and firmer and firmer shall we set it to regularity of revolution.
That means life.... Recognize that now we have bare life; at best
for the bulk of men the Saurian lizard's broad back soaking and
roasting in primeval slime; or say, in the so-called teachers of
men, as much of life as pricks the frog in March to stir and yawn,
and up on a flaccid leap that rolls him over some three inches
nearer to the ditchwater besought by his instinct.' (29, 277–8: the
elisions are Cecil Baskelett's comments.)

No one could doubt that this is a parody of Carlyle: the exclamations, archaisms, contorted syntax and grotesque metaphors are all Carlylean.[40] But can this be taken as an 'exemplification' of the style of a writer whom Meredith described as a 'humourist' and one who 'had lightning's power to strike out marvellous pictures and reach to the inmost of men with a phrase'?[41] Shrapnel's style is turgid, buttonholing and completely humourless. Carlyle does often write like this, and he is so little appreciated today that it is not surprising modern critics should think his style 'well exemplified' by a parody of him at his worst. We need to be reminded of Carlyle at his best, of why Victorian readers were inspired by him and compared him with Swift:

For the gowns of learned-serjeants are good: parchment records, fixed forms, and poor terrestrial Justice, with or without horsehair, what sane man will not reverence these? And yet, behold, the man is not sane but insane, who considers these alone as venerable. Oceans of horse-hair, continents of parchment, and learned-serjeant eloquence, were it continued till the learned tongue wore itself small in the indefatigable learned mouth, cannot make unjust just.... Enforce it by never such statuting, three readings, royal assents; blow it to the four winds with all manner of quilted trumpeters and pursuivants, in the rear of them never so many gibbets and hangmen, it will not stand, it cannot stand.... It will continue standing, for its day, for its year, for its century, doing evil all the while; but it has One enemy who is Almighty: dissolution, explosion, and the everlasting Laws of Nature incessantly advance towards it; and the deeper its rooting, more obstinate its continuing, the deeper also and huger will its ruin and overturn be.[42]

When Meredith incorporates pastiche of Carlyle into the narrator's discourse the effect is characteristically humorous and, if he does not achieve the impassioned combination of satirical verve and minatory rhetoric exemplified above, the style is quite different from the windy rhetoric of Shrapnel. The most notorious example is the 'Prelude' of *The Egoist*, but there is another, less extravagant, in the canvassing chapter of *Beauchamp's Career*:

> How if, instead of the solicitation of the thousands by the unit, the meritorious unit were besought by rushing thousands? – as a mound of the plains that is circumvented by floods, and to which the waters cry, Be thou our island. Let it be answered the questioner, with no discourteous adjectives, Thou fool!...
>
> Conceive, for the fleeting instants permitted to such insufferable flights of fancy, our picked men ruling! So despotic an oligarchy as would be there, is not a happy subject of contemplation. It is not too much to say that a domination of the Intellect in England would at once and entirely alter the face of the country.... Criticism, now so helpful to us, would wither to the root: fun would die out of Parliament, and outside of it: we could never laugh at our masters, or command them. (18, 180–1)

What is the function of the Carlylean pastiche here? I suggest that the rueful acknowledgement of the inevitability and even desirability of muddle and compromise is dialogically traversed by a discourse that characteristically deals in absolutes ('cannot make unjust just'), relieving a spirit of rebellion against the acknowledgement. This suspicion will be reinforced if we recognize in this passage a translation into Carlylese of Walter Bagehot's reasoned defence of the *status quo*, and particularly his preference of 'mind coupled with property' to 'pure mind', a discourse as remote from Carlyle's as one might hope to find in the period (and, incidentally, originally published in the *Fortnightly* under G.H. Lewes's editorship):

> Accordingly, the House of Commons, representing only mind coupled with property, is not equal in mind to a legislature chosen for mind only, and whether accompanied by wealth or not. But I do not for a moment wish to see a representation of pure mind; it would be contrary to the main thesis of this essay. I maintain that Parliament ought to embody the public opinion of

the English nation; and, certainly, that opinion is much more fixed by its property than by its mind. The 'too clever by half' people who live in 'Bohemia,' ought to have no more influence in Parliament than they have in England, and they can scarcely have less.[43]

This suggestion is made more plausible by the fact that, within a couple of paragraphs, Meredith's style modulates into something quite close to an imitation, both in manner and substance, of Bagehot's moderate, conservative and 'realistic' appraisal of the Constitution:

> Briefly, then, we have a system, not planned but grown, the outcome and image of our genius, and all are dissatisfied with parts of it; but, as each would preserve his own, the surest guarantee is obtained for the integrity of the whole by a happy adjustment of the energies of opposition. (182)

Such is the character of 'authorial commentary' in Meredith's novels.

I have spoken earlier of the centrality of the 'struggles of earnest speech' and of languages represented by other languages in this novel. Shrapnel's letter is the most important instance of this, but its reception and representation are foreshadowed by numerous episodes earlier in the novel. The first awakening of Nevil's social conscience is narrated as follows:

> Nevil showed that he had gained an acquaintance with the struggles of the neighbouring agricultural poor to live and rear their children. His uncle's table roared at his *enumeration of the sickly little beings, consumptive or bandy-legged, within a radius of five miles of Steynham* (3, 31-2, my italics).

We are not merely told what Nevil said, and that his uncle and his cronies laughed at it. The section in italics, while it semantically reproduces the substance of Nevil's speech, is accented by the voices of the laughing listeners: this is the accent in which they would report Nevil's (at this early stage) charming folly. This is a classic instance of the kind of hybrid discourse that Bakhtin exemplifies with numerous examples from Dostoevsky, Turgenev and Dickens.

Much of the action of the earlier part of the novel is narrated by means of correspondence. This has the effect of backgrounding such actions as Nevil's military exploits which are secondary to the main themes of the novel. However, unlike the epistolary novel, or Meredith's own use of letters in, for example, *Richard Feverel* and *Evan Harrington*, the correspondence is given to us neither whole nor straight, but summarized, excerpted and, most importantly, refracted through the discourse of the fictional reader:

> [Everard] passed with a shrug Nevil's puling outcry for the enemy as well as our own fellows: 'At his steppes again!' And he had to be forgiving when reports came of his nephew's turn for overdoing his duty: 'show-fighting,' as he termed it.
> 'Braggadocioing in deeds is only next bad to mouthing it,' he wrote very rationally. 'Stick to your line. Don't go out of it till you are ordered out. Remember that we want *soldiers* and *sailors*, we don't want *suicides*.' (4, 41)

This not only has the advantages of narrative economy and perspective, but sustains the intense scrutiny of discourse, and particularly Everard's sharp critique of Nevil's language and demeanour, that runs throughout the novel. A more important example comes in the narration of Nevil's campaign to thwart Renée's betrothal, which is handled in similarly indirect and refracted fashion:

> And apparently, according to the wording and emphasis of the letter, it was the mature age of the marquis which made Mr Beauchamp so particularly desirous to stop the projected marriage and take the girl himself. He appealed to his uncle on the subject in a 'really-really' remonstrative tone, quite overwhelming to read. – 'It ought not to be permitted: by all the laws of chivalry, I should write to the girl's father to interdict it: I really am particeps criminis in a sin against nature if I don't!' Mr Romfrey interjected in burlesque of his ridiculous nephew, with collapsing laughter (11, 94–5).

The first sentence is, once again, an instance of hybrid discourse in which the language of Nevil's letter is re-accented by Everard, now with a more severe irony than was called for by mere boyish folly: hence, 'apparently', 'mature age', 'Mr Beauchamp', 'particularly desirous' and, with the intelligent cynicism of the old hunting aristocrat, the plain-speaking of 'take the girl himself', protruding sharply from this ironically mealy-mouthed environment. The double-voicing in this passage is so intense that – possibly as a consequence of an unintended carelessness of construction – a reader cannot decide for certain whether the sentence in quotation marks is Nevil's letter or Everard's burlesque.

These examples are all preliminary to the sequence of discursive battles, culminating in a physical assault, concerning Nevil's candidacy and his attachment to Dr Shrapnel. The narrator announces the candidacy laconically in half a page and gives a bald summary of his electoral Address:

> ultra-Radical: museums to be opened on Sundays; ominous references to the Land question, etc.; no smooth passing mention of Reform, such as the Liberal, become stately, adopts in speaking of property of his, but swinging blows on the heads of many a denounced iniquity. (11, 104)

This is followed by a letter of two pages from Cecil Baskelett to Everard Romfrey which burlesques the candidacy and the Address. (This letter, contrary to my earlier generalization, is given to us 'whole' and 'straight', but this is precisely because it is not a primary discourse: its function is to refract another, Nevil's Address, which is *not* given whole or straight.)

> The electors of Bevisham are summoned, like a town at the sword's point, to yield him their votes. Proclamation is the word. I am your born representative! I have completed my political education on salt water, and I tackle you on the Land question. I am the heir of your votes, gentlemen! – I forgot, and I apologize; he calls them fellow-men. Fraternal, and not so risky. Here at Lespel's we read the thing with shouts. It hangs in the smoking-room....
>
> 'He dashed into the Radical trap exactly two hours after landing. I believe he was on his way to the Halketts at Mount Laurels. A notorious old rascal revolutionist, retired from his licenced business of slaughterer – one of your *gratis* doctors – met him on the high road, and told him he was the man. Up went Nevil's enthusiasm like a bottle rid of the cork. You will see a great deal about faith in the proclamation; "faith in the future," and "my

faith in you." When you become a Radical you have faith in any quantity, just as an alderman gets turtle soup' (105–6).

In so far as *Beauchamp's Career* has a conventional plot, it concerns the rivalry of Nevil and Cecil for Everard's inheritance and the hand of the rich and beautiful heiress, Cecilia Halkett. This 'motivates' the sustained malice of Cecil's role in the novel, but that role, as the ironic reactionary accentor of Nevil's and Shrapnel's utterances, far outweighs his plot-function. It is notable that, in contrast to the previous examples, except for the directly quoted phrases the semantic substance of Nevil's discourse is imperceptible through Cecil's burlesque. Later, when Cecil reads Shrapnel's letter aloud, the words are not literally suppressed but the utterance is obscured by the reader's burlesquing accent, and its reception contrasts markedly with Seymour Austin's rational and moderate response to a silent reading of the same document. Notice also that Nevil's fateful meeting with Shrapnel is first narrated to us in the same burlesque discourse, with the reactionary cliché 'rascal', the sneer at Shrapnel's treating poor people for nothing, and the simile of the champagne cork brilliantly suggesting the natural tendency of Cecil's imagination as well as being a not entirely inappropriate satire on Nevil's enthusiasm.

The display of the Address in Lespel's smoking-room is the occasion for the memorable visit to that room in Chapter 20 by Mrs Lespel (who has 'never once put my head into that room' in her own house for fifteen years, 207) and Cecilia, which provokes Mrs Lespel to say: 'A strange air to breathe, was it not? The less men and women know of one another, the happier for them' (208). This display of profound and institutionalized sexual unease, in a hotbed of opposition to Nevil, links sexual and class politics, all the more effectively for its implied dialogue with Nevil's own prejudices.

Meredith's construction of the novel is such that, to a considerable extent, utterances such as Nevil's Address and their reception motivate the plot. It is as a result of Cecil's letter that Rosamond Culling travels to Bevisham hoping to see Nevil, and is drawn into her fateful meeting with Dr Shrapnel. Rosamond is a key focalizer in the novel, both structurally and ideologically, and it is in her character zone that much of the struggle in the novel is played out. It is in this zone, for example, that we are given the famous evocation of Carlyle's style early in the novel:

a style resembling either early architecture or utter dilapidation, so loose and rough it seemed; a wind-in-the-orchard style, that tumbled down here and there an appreciable fruit with uncouth bluster; sentences without commencements running to abrupt endings and smoke, like waves against a sea-wall, learned dictionary words giving a hand to street-slang, and accents falling on them haphazard, like slant rays from driving clouds; all the pages in a breeze, the whole book producing a kind of electrical agitation in the mind and the joints. This was its effect on the lady. To her the incomprehensible was the abominable, for she had our country's high critical feeling. (2, 22)

This is a brilliant passage, which gives a vivid and recognizable account of Carlyle's style, but accents it throughout with the alarm of a mind which is essentially that of an eighteenth-century gentlewoman. The hints of the Gothic, the images of human structures assaulted by natural forces, the recoil from heteroglossia and stylistic indecorum, even the feeling of bodily invasion make it clear that 'our country's high critical feeling' is inseparable from class exclusiveness, and that Carlyle's very style embodies, to such a mind as Rosamond's, the threat of revolution explicitly made in the passage from *Past and Present* quoted above.

The description of Carlyle's style has a bearing on Rosamond's response to Dr Shrapnel. On arrival in Bevisham she is introduced by a mutual acquaintance to Jenny Denham, Shrapnel's ward, who takes her to Shrapnel's house so that she might meet Nevil there. Her reaction, on this meeting, to Shrapnel's way of speaking and personal manner, sets the fuse that eventually ignites Everard's assault on the old Radical. In response to Rosamond's assertion that Nevil's family have first claim on him, Shrapnel launches into a vehement denunciation of the family:

Sound the conscience, and sink the family! With a clear conscience, it is best to leave the family to its own debates. No man ever did brave work who held counsel with his family. The family view of a man's fit conduct is the weak point of the country. (12, 116)

This is typical of Shrapnel's lack of a sense of audience, both generically and individually. He uses the rhetoric of public speaking when addressing a single person, repeating the word 'family' in four successive sentences, and appears oblivious of the fact that his listener is, effectively, a member of the family in question. Blackburn Tuckham commits the same generic offence when speaking to Cecilia:

> The best education for the people is government. They're beginning to see that in Lancashire at last. I ran down to Lancashire for a couple of days on my landing, and I'm thankful to say Lancashire is preparing to take a step back. Lancashire leads the country. Lancashire men see what this Liberalism has done for the Labour-market. (26, 284)

But this is before he takes lessons from Seymour Austin and, unlike Shrapnel, he is voicing an establishment opinion. Shrapnel, like Tuckham, is a confirmed monologist, and their poor sense of audience is both a social and an intellectual offence, but Tuckham is in no danger of being horsewhipped for addressing a lady like a public meeting. Rosamond reacts to Shrapnel as she does because his conversational manners and signs of harmless eccentricity combine to create an effect of obtrusive ungentlemanliness alien and repulsive to a woman of her background:

> His great feet planted on their heels faced him, suggesting the stocks; his arms hung loose. Full many a hero of the alehouse, anciently amenable to leg-and-foot imprisonment in the grip of the parish, has presented as respectable an air. (12, 122)

This is the posture that Shrapnel adopts to listen to music, after having given Rosamond a lecture on the superiority of the orchestra to the piano and organ, with political parallels:

> 'That is our republic: each one to his work; all in union! There's the motto for us! *Then* you have music, harmony, the highest, fullest, finest! Educate your men to form a band, you shame dexterous trickery and imitation sounds. *Then* for the difference of real instruments from clever shams! Oh, ay, *one* will set your organ going; that is, one in front, with his couple of panting air-pumpers behind – his ministers!' Dr Shrapnel laughed at some undefined mental image, apparently careless of any laughing companionship. '*One* will do it for you, especially if he's born

to it. Born!' A slap of the knee reported what seemed to be an immensely contemptuous sentiment. (121)

Although Rosamond's response to Carlyle portends her feelings and behaviour on this occasion, we should note that Shrapnel's sub-Carlylean rhetoric does not have the same powerful effect on her as the original:

> It was perceptible to her that a species of mad metaphor had been wriggling and tearing its passage through a thorn-bush in his discourse, with the furious urgency of a sheep in a panic; but where the ostensible subject ended and the metaphor commenced, and which was which at the conclusion, she found it difficult to discern – much as the sheep would be when he had left his fleece behind him. She could now have said, 'Silly old man!' (121)

The metaphor, actually, is perfectly sane and thoroughly traditional – a development of the analogy between harmony in music and harmony in the state – but its outlines are obscured for Rosamond by the heavy emphases, exclamations, and general self-addressivity of Shrapnel's utterance, epitomized by his laughter.

Shrapnel, of course, *intends* to be the opposite of discourteous, and he offers her a meal and even a bed for the night, to help her to meet Nevil. But she refuses to enter his house and leaves, agitated by the question 'Whether she had acted quite wisely in not remaining to see Nevil' (123). This partly explains her behaviour in the subsequent encounter with Everard, when she allows him to construe her discomfort in Shrapnel's presence as evidence that he had insulted her. The fact that class prejudice is at the root of the whole horsewhipping episode is subtly conveyed when she fatally weighs words to define Shrapnel's manner:

> 'Was the man uncivil to you, ma'am?' came the emphatic interrogation.
> She asked herself, had Dr Shrapnel been uncivil toward her? And so conscientious was she, that she allowed the question to be debated in her mind for half a minute, answering then, 'No, not uncivil. I cannot exactly explain.... He certainly did not intend to be uncivil. He is only an unpolished, vexatious man; enormously tall.' (13, 128)

This contrasts tellingly with Rosamond's earlier judgement of a 'want of delicacy of perception' in Jenny for similarly weighing words in determining whether Shrapnel was 'eloquent' or 'persuasive' (113). Jenny failed to perceive that a man of Shrapnel's station does not merit subtlety of language, but when it is his behaviour to a lady that is in question, she casts her own importance on the matter.

Rosamond is not egotistical. On the contrary, she is the woman in the novel who most devotedly loves Nevil, with a love that is ambiguously maternal and sexual, and the whole project of her visit to Bevisham is motivated by concern for his interests. The reader is, moreover, aware throughout of the painful aspects of her situation, as Everard's lady-housekeeper, suspected by the prurient of being his mistress. The narrator's tone towards her is invariably sympathetic and the dialogizing of her voice with the narrator's usually – as in the description of Carlyle's style, and of Shrapnel's speech – includes important elements of agreement. Meredith's ability to lay bare the character's motives, especially when they involve social conditioning, without hostility is one of his most outstanding merits.

Rosamond's role as focalizer is important again in the following chapter when, through a window at Steynham, she sees but cannot hear Cecil guying a newspaper article written in praise of Nevil. This episode, in which (for Rosamond and the reader) Cecil's mannerisms completely usurp the written word, is the perfect epitome of his role in the novel:

> He soon had the paper out at a square stretch, and sprightly information for the other two was visible in his crowing throat.... Colonel Halkett wished to peruse the matter with his own eyes, but Cecil could not permit it; he must read it aloud for them, and he suited his action to the sentences. Had Rosamond been accustomed to leading articles which are the composition of men of an imposing vocabulary, she would have recognised and as good as read one in Cecil's gestures as he tilted his lofty stature forward and back, marking his commas and semicolons with flapping of his elbows, and all but doubling his body at his periods. Mr Romfrey had enough of it half-way down the column; his head went sharply to left and right. Cecil's peculiar foppish slicing down of his hand pictured him protesting that there was more and finer of the inimitable stuff to follow. (14, 133–4)

When Rosamond reads the article she is 'quite unable to perceive where the comicality or the impropriety of it lay, for it would have struck her that never were truer things of Nevil Beauchamp better said in the tone befitting them' (134). However, any impression the reader might form that a true and pure utterance has been rescued from malign accentuation is dispelled by a sample of the article itself:

> that illustrious Commander Beauchamp, of our matchless navy, who proved on every field of the last glorious war of this country that the traditional valour of the noble and indomitable blood transmitted to his veins had lost none of its edge and weight since the battle-axes of the Lords de Romfrey, ever to the fore, clove the skulls of our national enemy on the wide and fertile champaigns of France. (135)

This is parody, a rare example in this novel of the brute 'word on display', but there follows an extended account of its author, Timothy Turbot, written in a dialogized pastiche of his voice, which is far from simply parody, just as Turbot himself, despite being an alcoholic Irishman with a fishy name, is far from simple caricature. This passage displays a shrewd assessment of political realities, and of Beauchamp himself, and includes an example of Meredith's distinctive device, the multi-layered representation of language:

> the Radical orator has but two notes, and one is the drawling pathetic, and the other is the ultra-furious; and the effect of the former we liken to the English working man's wife's hob-set queasy brew of well-meant villainy, that she calls by the innocent name of tea; and the latter is to be blown, asks to be blown, and never should be blown without at least seeming to be blown, with an accompaniment of a house on fire. (137–8)

As with Everard's criticism of Nevil's language, one language is represented in another which is itself represented. This is Meredith's original way of conveying the density of political conflict and of social life in general.

The most important and most elaborately represented document is the notorious letter of Dr Shrapnel to Beauchamp. As David Howard says, the letter 'never comes to us straight. It is always introduced or performed by a particular character in a particular dramatic context.... It never speaks for itself.'[44] By far the most powerful of these performances is Cecil's reading to Cecilia, her father and others. This comes about because of the theft of Nevil's greatcoat, containing his papers, which are returned to Steynham, where Everard, in pursuit of his campaign against Nevil's radicalism, purloins the letter. In substance the letter consists of a number of standard democratic, secularist, republican and anti-militarist positions, with a Carlylean section on the English religion of Comfort, a Meredithian passage on Ego, and in conclusion a strikingly conservative argument, addressed *ad hominem* to the lover of Renée, on marriage and the danger of 'rebellion against Society'. Its style is fairly represented by the passage quoted earlier. In appearance it is a 'really abominable scrawl', prompting the narratorial comment that 'The common sentiment of mankind is offended by heterodoxy in mean attire; for there we see the self-convicted villain' (29, 317). Cecil reads the letter 'with ghastly false accentuation, an intermittent sprightliness and depression of tone in the wrong places' (320), 'roaring' passages that have been marked by Nevil, and interjecting comments designed, mainly, to exacerbate the knee-jerk reactionary responses of Cecilia's father. Large sections are omitted, summarized, or represented by selected phrases. The letter is of course parodic, and if presented independently of this context would strain the patience of the reader. However, the fact that it is a private letter read publicly, that it has been stolen, and above all the scene's demonstration of the control of discourse by the wealthy, through the power of burlesque by the emptiest character in the novel, tend to enhance by contrast Shrapnel's earnestness, guilelessness and generosity of spirit. It is as it were the public humiliation of these qualities in the ungainly form of Shrapnel's language that makes the scene peculiarly unpleasant.

The dissemination of the letter has serious consequences in the plot. The motives for Everard's horsewhipping of Shrapnel are multiple, including Shrapnel's defence of a poacher and, most importantly (if only because it is needed to justify the action according to Everard's code), the supposed insult to Rosamond, resuscitated by Cecil's prejudicial account of his own meeting with Shrapnel. However, there can be no doubt that Shrapnel's main offence in Everard's eyes is his influence over Nevil, which the letter has vividly illustrated; and the sentiments of Everard's class are made clear, at the news of the assault, by the reactions of Colonel Halkett – 'The writer of that letter we heard Captain Baskelett read the other day deserves the very worst he gets' – and an otherwise unimportant suitor of Cecilia's: 'Men who write that stuff should be strung up and whipped by the common hangman' (32, 363). Although Everard is the only character who would actually carry out the horsewhipping, the moral responsibility is shared by the conventional members of his class.

After the horsewhipping has taken place, but before the news of it has reached them, Nevil attempts to make Cecilia read part of the letter as a prelude to a proposal of marriage. It is obvious that he wants her to read the section on marriage and society, to reassure her about the reputation he has gained through his relationship with Renée. For her, however, the letter, unappealing in any case, has been irredeemably tainted by the reading:

> A confused recollection of the contents of the letter declaimed at Mount Laurels in Captain Baskelett's absurd sing-song, surged up in her mind revoltingly. She signified a decided negative. Something of a shudder accompanied the expression of it. (356)

So the proposal is baulked, and when they meet again Nevil is obsessed by his campaign to make Everard apologize. The next time he has the opportunity to propose he forces Cecilia instead to accompany him on a visit to Shrapnel's sickbed.

The power of Cecil's representation to prejudice Shrapnel's discourse is underlined by the responses to silent reading of two rational conservatives, Stukely Culbrett – 'If the parsons were men they'd be saying it every Sunday' (36, 397) – and Seymour Austin: 'It would do no harm to our young men to have those letters read publicly and lectured on' (37, 415).

The horsewhipping of Shrapnel by Everard Romfrey is one of the notorious examples of Meredith's avoidance (or, for unsympathetic critics, evasion) of directly narrated action. Purely in terms of narrative effectiveness, it is difficult to see what improvement would be worked on the threatening descent to dry land of Everard carrying his gold-headed whip, followed by the announcement of the result to Cecilia by her father, both scenes taking place on the yachts of the aristocracy, while the story-time of the whipping itself is occupied by Nevil's attempt to make Cecilia listen to Shrapnel's letter. The character who is most affected by the incident – even more, in the long term, than Shrapnel himself – is Nevil, and it is perhaps fitting that the reader, like Nevil, should not have witnessed it.

Shrapnel recovers from the assault, and its most important consequence is Nevil's prolonged campaign for Everard to apologize. Gillian Beer comments:

> Although he is a radical he cannot easily slough off the gentlemanly rituals: in particular, his dogged and disproportionate insistence that his uncle offer Dr Shrapnel a formal apology derives from a dying world of chivalry.[45]

As with his behaviour over Renée, I think that Beer over-emphasizes the class-conditioned character of Nevil's action. It is true that there is a comic and even absurd aspect to Nevil's obsession with the apology, but this is not merely a 'gentlemanly ritual'. Apology is a secularized form of repentance. In the world of gentlemen it is one of the most powerful forms of utterance: in the scarcely passed world of Everard's prime, it would avert a duel. In the context of this novel, where politics is language, the apology represents the recognition of Shrapnel's full and equal humanity – a bestowal of language to counter the proliferation of language that has debased and dehumanized him.

It would be perverse to conclude a discussion of *Beauchamp's Career* without mention of its notorious ending, and in fact the very last words of the novel supply an excellent final example of Meredith's 'authorial' discourse. Married to Jenny and with a son, Beauchamp is abruptly drowned, having saved the life of a poor child, whom Everard Romfrey and Dr Shrapnel, united in grief for the man they both loved, are left looking at:

> This is what we have in exchange for Beauchamp!
> It was not uttered, but it was visible in the blank stare at one another of the two men who loved Beauchamp, after they had examined the insignificant bit of mudbank life remaining in this world in the place of him. (56, 631)

It is characteristic of Victorian novels at least to conclude on a monologic note, usually of epithalamion or, when the hero/ine has died, funeral elegy – the 'In their death they were not divided' of *The Mill on the Floss* or the 'It is a far, far better thing' of *A Tale of*

Two Cities. In the conclusion of *Beauchamp's Career* we have another 'trio' in which, again, the internal dynamics of the constituent voices are different from either of the previous examples. The voices of Everard and Shrapnel are combined, but that of the narrator is neither combined with them, as in the lament for Robert Hall, nor putting them on display, but hesitating between these extremes. As Bakhtin says of Dostoevsky:

> All one-sided seriousness (of life and thought), all one-sided pathos is handed over to the heroes, but the author, who causes them all to collide in the 'great dialogue' of the novel, leaves that dialogue open and puts no finalizing period at the end.[46]

Beauchamp's Career is the most extreme example of Meredith's most characteristic tendency: the multi-layered representation and scrutiny of discourse, in a text that is saturated with images of the competing ideological accents of the day, fleetingly evoked or formally imitated, and orchestrated by the Meredithian narrator. Cecil Baskelett is perhaps the most insidious character in Meredith because he is a kind of anti-type of this narrator, who does malevolently and irresponsibly what, for the narrator and the author, is a matter of the utmost moral and ideological responsibility. But despite all this prominence of 'discourse' and 'language' the effect is not one of depersonalized linguistic play, because for Meredith, as for Bakhtin's Dostoevsky, ideas and discourses 'are combined in an indissoluble unity with images of people'.[47] At the end of the novel what dies and is mourned is not a collection of words but the unique, lived intersection and struggle of ideas and discourses that is a concrete human destiny.

5
The Egoist

With the exception of *Evan Harrington* none of Meredith's earlier novels conforms to the generic requirements of comedy, and in no fewer than four of them – *Richard Feverel, Rhoda Fleming, Harry Richmond* and *Beauchamp's Career* – comedic closure is harshly and suddenly forestalled by the death of a main character. *The Egoist*, however, announces itself in its subtitle as 'A Comedy in Narrative' and is introduced by a 'Prelude' which recapitulates Meredith's 'Essay on Comedy' and informs the reader that the narrative is presided over by the Comic Spirit. As this suggests, *The Egoist* is a much more self-conscious comedy than *Evan Harrington*, and it is also a more devious one.

Nobody dies in *The Egoist* and two couples marry. Moreover, specific generic models are absorbed, played off against each other, and at times parodied. Perhaps the most significant models are the comedies of Molière, particularly those such as *Le Misanthrope, Le Tartuffe* and *L'Avare* which are dominated by a character who embodies a single tyrannical characteristic. Willoughby Patterne is an egoist with the same undeviating consistency as Tartuffe is a hypocrite. As we shall see, however, the fact that *The Egoist* is a novel, and especially a novel by Meredith, means we should be cautious about drawing too simple conclusions from this generic model. The plot and scenic organization also are indebted to neoclassical comedy, especially the dénouement, but again the relationship is not one of simple imitation, and the extreme, parodistic character of the dénouement will play an important part in my argument about the novel's dialogic nature. A secondary, but still important shaping influence is the satirical house-party novel of Peacock. Meredith combines elements of these two genres to achieve a rigorous unity that contrasts markedly with the structure of all his other novels. These spare, classical (and in the case of Peacock slight) models are, however, pressed into the service of a plot that is more reminiscent of the sprawling epistolary novels of Richardson: a young woman's struggles to escape from the clutches of a powerful, predatory man. I have described the plot of *The Egoist* in somewhat melodramatic terms deliberately to emphasize the resemblance to *Pamela*. It is, indeed, in the terms of the 'Prelude', a 'drawing-room' version of *Pamela*, 'where we have no dust of the struggling outer world, no violent crashes' (1), but the more one dwells on the comparison between this story of a young woman struggling to withdraw from an ill-judged engagement, and that one of a young woman struggling to preserve her virtue against a predatory master, the more enlightening it is. Clara's story, one might say, is that of a Pamela who happens to enjoy a more privileged social position. A part of Meredith's achievement is to have adapted to the conventions of social comedy the extensive portrayal of female subjectivity that the epistolary form allowed to Richardson. Female subjectivity and therefore female discourse. One of the most significant features of *Pamela* is that her control of her own telling of the story becomes an issue when Mr B. attempts to steal her letter-journal; in a less obvious way Clara's power of and over discourse is a central issue in *The Egoist*.

The comedic plot has given rise to some scepticism about the novel's feminist credentials. It could be argued that it is an anti-comedy, in that the main plot is concerned not with the making but with the avoidance of a marriage. This certainly gives the novel a somewhat skewed relation to its generic models (including of course *Pamela* in which the heroine eventually marries Mr B.), but it is still the case that the outcome of Clara's escape from Willoughby is her union with Vernon (not, within the pages of the novel, a marriage, but almost certainly to be one). This will be the dominant issue in my discussion of the novel's generic character.

Discourse and genre, then, will be the two main categories of my discussion of *The Egoist*, and I shall focus first on the former, in an attempt to show that, despite the considerations outlined above, it is a less atypical Meredith novel than it might seem.

The comedic rigour of *The Egoist*, and particularly the unvarying conformity of the central character, in Molièrean fashion, to the definition of the title, suggest that, in contrast to Meredith's other novels, we should expect an impermeable boundary between the discourse of the narrator and that of Sir Willoughby Patterne. Something like this might seem to be implied by Meredith's own remark that he put only 'half of me'[1] into it. Close examination of the narrator's discourse, however, shows a different picture. As Judith Wilt has observed, 'The line between Willoughby's interior monologues and the narrator's commentary is very, very thin.'[2] Even in this, his most 'parnassian' novel, the style is not precious and self-regardingly mannered, but vibrant with the echoes of many voices.

As in previous novels the narrator's voice ranges between the 'authorial' and free indirect/direct discourse intensely imbued with the accent of a character (the Bakhtinian 'character zone'), including a variety of pastiches. The 'authorial' voice itself is highly distinctive. Although it is outside the diegesis it is not in a vacuum: it is, as it were, in another scene, at the crossroads of polemic, in intense and continuous dialogue with a variety of addressees, manifested in the turbulent syntax and cramming of rhetorical devices, questions, exclamations, ironically accented *endoxa*, direct appeals to 'you' as addressee. At times the high Meredithian style is a dialogic traffic-jam. This passage concerns Laetitia Dale's youthful devotion to Willoughby:

> The portrait of him at the Hall, in a hat, leaning on his pony, with crossed legs and long flaxen curls over his shoulders, was the image of her soul's most present angel; and, as a man, he had – she did not suppose intentionally – subjected her nature to bow to him; so submissive was she, that it was fuller happiness for her to think him right in all his actions than to imagine the circumstances different. This may appear to resemble the ecstasy of the devotee of Juggernaut. It is a form of the passion inspired by little princes, and we need not marvel that a conservative sex should assist to keep them in their lofty places. What were there otherwise to look up to? We should have no dazzling beacon-lights if they were levelled and treated as clod earth; and it is worth while for here and there a woman to be burnt, so long as women's general adoration of an ideal young man shall be preserved. Purity is our demand of them. They may justly cry for attraction. They cannot have it brighter than in the universal bearing of the eyes of their sisters upon a little prince, one who has the ostensible virtues in his pay, and can practise them without injuring himself to make himself unsightly. Let the races of men be by-and-by astonished at their Gods, if they please. Meantime they had better continue to worship. (3, 22–3)

The reader does not approach this passage untutored, since Willoughby's egoism has already been firmly established in the episode of Lieutenant Patterne's visit and his wooing of Constantia Durham. However, the main thematic burden of the novel is not the parading of a type or humour but – to turn against their author the words of Dorothy Van Ghent's celebrated and astonishingly imperceptive essay – 'insight as to what subtle bonds there might be between Willoughby and society'.[3] This is to a large extent the function of the narrator. In this respect, so early in the novel, the first sentence quoted might seem to do no more than report Laetitia's feelings, without any particular ironic accent: Willoughby might unfortunately be a loathsome egoist, but that need not touch, in principle, the merit of such reverential submission. The tone of the sentence is neutral enough to give at least a mild shock to 'the ecstasy of the devotee of Juggernaut', a phrase that not only exploits Victorian prejudice about oriental religion but also participates in a polemic running throughout Meredith's work, in which he damns contemporary sexual attitudes by matching them with the supposed customs of the East ('Men...have not yet doubled Cape Turk', *DC*, 1, 8). The later hint at suttee also belongs to this polemic. In the third sentence 'little princes' is already a marked phrase, having been used a page earlier in connection with Willoughby's disappointment that Constantia did not 'come to him out of cloistral purity'. However, the slight ideological tug of that phrase is probably, for a contemporary reader, overmatched by the rest of the sentence, which eases itself back as it were against the notorious and convenient complicity of women. The fourth and fifth sentences are a straight-faced pastiche of a conventional defence of feminine submissiveness, with an ironic intervention in the excess of 'here and there a woman to be burnt', with its connotations of witch-hunts and suttee, anticipating a strain of sadistic fantasy in Willoughby. 'Purity is our demand of them', like so much double-voiced language in Meredith, is finely poised between two accents: in the ventriloquized accent, it is the complacent and even pompous assertion of patriarchal values; in the counterbalancing authorial accent, harking back to the account of the wooing of Constantia, it is tense with unspecified consequences: it is followed, as it were, by an intonational row of dots or unstated 'and so', an implied rebound against the 'we' who make the demand. For the reader who hears this accent, some of those consequences are hinted at in the description of the ideal hero as 'one who has the *ostensible* virtues in his pay'. The passage closes with a veiled allusion to another recurring motif of the novel, the allegation that contemporary sexual mores are primitive.

The rhetoric of this passage requires the narrator to be figured as male, and this gendering is more intense elsewhere in the narrative. The whole of Chapter 23 for example, which contains some of the closest analysis of Willoughby's subjectivity, is narrated from an explicitly masculine point of view, and the narrator even goes so far as to say:

> Women have us back to the conditions of primitive man, or they shoot us higher than the topmost star. But it is as we please. Let them tell us what we are to them: for us, they are our back and front of life: the poet's Lesbia, the poet's Beatrice; ours is the choice. (23, 276)

The insistent antithesis of 'we' and 'they' might suggest that, as an early reviewer thought, Meredith is an author of 'men's novels'[4] and female readers can relate to the text only by overhearing it. This is far from the case. The narrator here who leaves it to women, in some other place, to speak for themselves, is by no means the author, and the narrative discourse is replete with passages such as the following:

> The strangeness of men, young and old, the little things (she regarded a grand wine as a little thing) twisting and changeing them, amazed her. And these are they by whom women are abused for variability! (24, 285-6)

> Dr Middleton was offering a second suggestion, but Clara fled, astonished at men as she had never yet been. Why, in a burning world they would be exercising their minds in absurdities! (24, 294)

> Oh, men! men! They astounded the girl; she could not define them to her understanding. Their motives, their tastes, their vanity, their tyranny, and the domino on their vanity, the baldness of their tyranny, clenched her in feminine antagonism to brute power. (33, 398)

These passages are close to what Bakhtin/Voloshinov, in his classic study of reported speech, calls *'substituted direct discourse'*, in which 'the author stands in for his hero, says in his stead what the hero might or should have said, says what the given occasion calls for.... When a complete solidarity in values and intonations exists between the author and his hero... the author's rhetoric and that of the hero begin to overlap'.[5] However, Bakhtin/Voloshinov is here describing a very simple variant of what he calls 'quasi-direct discourse', and we are dealing with a text as dialogically complex as any Bakhtin considered. It is certainly the case that, considered in isolation, these passages conform very closely to the definition of 'substituted direct discourse': not only the thoughts, but also the emotional accents of Clara are reproduced in a narratorial discourse which has no appearance of contradicting them. In isolation, there are only two exceptions to this. In the second passage, Clara is misinterpreting the behaviour of one of the men in question, Vernon, who is attempting to convey to her a coded message in the guise of a pedantic question; but she is right about her father, and about Vernon's *apparent* behaviour. In the first passage the sentence in parentheses is in a different narratorial voice from the rest of the passage. This is a distinctly masculine voice, harmonizing with that of Clara's father (who has reneged on a promise to take her from Patterne Hall because of Willoughby's vintage port) but at the same time under the shadow of a strong ironic accent. This voice in parentheses is a reminder within the passage of what is implicit in the total context: that in a Meredith novel there is no easily definable 'author's rhetoric' to set against that of the character. Thus the strong sense of 'solidarity' with Clara's voice in these passages can only be provisional, and dependent on the reader's final sense of how all the variants of the narrator's voice (most of which are masculine) are organized. We shall be saying more about the various manifestations of Clara's voice later, but at present we must return to these 'masculine' variants.

We have seen that the Meredithian narrator can speak as if in the absence of women, as if in a gentlemen's club. He can also speak of Clara in the tones of a sexually aroused male:

> He placed himself at a corner of the doorway for her to pass him into the house, and doated on her cheek, her ear, and the softly dusky nape of her neck, where this way and that the little lighter-coloured irreclaimable curls running truant from the comb and the knot – curls, half-curls, root-curls, vine-ringlets, wedding-rings, fledgeling feathers, tufts of down, blown wisps – waved

or fell, waved over or up or involutedly, or strayed, loose and downward, in the form of small silken paws, hardly any of them much thicker than a crayon shading, cunninger than long round locks of gold to trick the heart.
Laetitia had nothing to show resembling such beauty. (9, 101)

His offended temper broke away from the image of Clara, revealing her as he had seen her in the morning beside Horace De Craye, distressingly sweet; sweet with the breezy radiance of an English soft-breathing day; sweet with sharpness of young sap. Her eyes, her lips, her fluttering dress that played happy mother across her bosom, giving peeps of the veiled twins; and her laughter, her slim figure, peerless carriage, all her terrible sweetness touched his wound to the smarting quick. (20, 233)

As I said in Chapter 4, Meredith characteristically focalizes descriptions of female beauty through his protagonists, and both of these passages are focalized through Willoughby. But they are by no means instances of Willoughby's 'objectified' character zone. In the first passage quoted the narrator distances himself from Willoughby's response with the word 'doated', and there is an epicurean excess in the descriptive dwelling on detail; but that detail is brought before the reader vividly and alluringly, the excess is indulged in by both narrator and character, the description itself is not accented in such a way as to forestall this, and the reader is not expected to dissent from the comparison with Laetitia.

In the second passage Willoughby's character zone is more dominant, because his jealousy of De Craye plays an important part in it. For much of the novel Willoughby is tormented by the apparent flirtation between Clara and De Craye, who is a predatory male like himself and has been a rival on former occasions. He thus plots the marriage of Clara and Vernon, whom he does not think of as a sexual male, and he evidently thinks the marriage will 'extinguish' Clara's sexuality. In this he is wrong, but the male reader is meant to understand exactly why the thought of marriage between Clara and De Craye is torment to Willoughby. In the passage in question the phrase 'peeps of the veiled twins' is rather sickening in a way that makes one hope, at least, that it belongs to Willoughby, but 'sweet with the breezy radiance of an English soft-breathing day; sweet with sharpness of young sap' is absolutely the Meredithian narrator who, as a sexual male, empathizes with the way this 'sweetness' can be 'terrible' in certain circumstances. Elsewhere De Craye is thought of as 'one whose touch of her would be darts in the blood of the yielder, snakes in his bed: she must be given up to an extinguisher' (39, 474).

Perhaps the crux of the relation between the masculine narrator's discourse and Willoughby's character zone comes when these feelings of tormented jealousy shift into a compensatory fantasy that has a distinctly sadistic quality:

> Ten thousand furies thickened about him at a thought of her lying by the roadside without his having crushed all the bloom out of her which might tempt even the curiosity of the fiend, man. (23, 270)

It would be excessive to say that the narrator is complicit in this feeling; at the same time empathy has gone so far with Willoughby on the way to this, that it cannot be seen as an entirely objectified instance of his character zone. Some trace of the narrator's empathy with his jealousy must remain; and this even has a dialogizing influence on the ensuing passage, his fantasy of a future meeting after he has let her go, which is the most overt parody in the novel:

> Supposing her still youngish, there might be captivating passages between them; as thus, in a style not unfamiliar:
> 'And was it my fault, my poor girl? Am I to blame, that you have passed a lonely unloved youth?'
> 'No, Willoughby; the irreparable error was mine, the blame is mine, mine only. I live to repent it. I do not seek, for I have not deserved, your pardon. Had I it, I should need my own self-esteem to presume to clasp it to a bosom ever unworthy of you.'
> 'I may have been impatient, Clara: we are human!'
> 'Never be it mine to accuse one on whom I laid so heavy a weight of forbearance!'
> 'Still, my old love! – for I am merely quoting history in naming you so – I cannot have been perfectly blameless.'
> 'To me you were, and are.'
> 'Clara!'
> 'Willoughby!'...
> 'Clara! one – one only – one last – one holy kiss!'
> 'If these poor lips, that once were sweet to you....'

The kiss, to continue the language of the imaginative composition of his time, favourite readings in which had inspired Sir Willoughby with a colloquy so pathetic, was imprinted. (270–1)

In isolation, this is as unambiguous an example as one could find of objectified parody, in which the meaning of the character – or of the language represented – is completely subordinated to that of the narrator – or the language representing. The parodied language does not answer back. The parody is not necessarily to be construed as directed at a particular original; nevertheless for Meredith the epitome of this kind of sentimental melodrama was undoubtedly Mrs Henry Wood's *East Lynne*, which he notoriously and unrepentantly rejected as reader for Chapman and Hall before it was published by Bentley in 1861, and which sold 400,000 copies in thirty-five years. Meredith reproached Samuel Lucas for reviewing it favourably, asking, 'Why do you foster this foul taste?'[6] The heroine of *East Lynne* leaves her husband and children for a lover who deserts her, and returns disfigured and disguised as governess to her own children. The culminating scene, in which she is recognized and forgiven by her husband on her deathbed, is a more melodramatic variant of Willoughby's fantasy:

'Archibald!'
She put out her trembling hand. She caught him ere he had drawn quite beyond her reach. He looked at her, he looked round the room, as one does awaking from a dream.
'I could not die without your forgiveness', she murmured, her eyes falling before him as she thought of her past sin. 'Do not turn from me! bear with me a little minute! Only say you forgive me, and I shall die in peace.... I never knew a moment's peace after the mad act I was guilty of in leaving you.... See what it has done for me!' tossing up her grey hair, holding out her attenuated wrists....
'O Archibald, I was mad, I was mad! I could not have done it in anything but madness. Surely you will forget and forgive!'
'I cannot forget, I have already forgiven.... Have you any reproach to cast to me?' he gently said, bending his head a little.
'Reproach to you! To you who must be almost without reproach in the sight of Heaven! you, who were ever loving to me, ever anxious for my welfare! When I think of what you were

and are, and how I requited you, I could sink into the earth with remorse and shame.'[7]

The source of this kind of language and punitive fantasy in one of the best-sellers of the age, written to foster the belief that for a woman adultery is worse than death, makes clear the ideological character of Meredith's parody, which is if anything reinforced by the fact that *East Lynne* was written by a woman complicit with the dominant ideology.

I have described this passage in *The Egoist* as 'objectified parody'. In the total context of the novel, however, the effect is not quite so simple. I have tried to show that there is a continuum from the 'authorial' narrator, via the narrator with the distinct masculine accent, the narrator as the sexual male participating in Willoughby's 'gaze' at Clara and empathizing with his jealousy of De Craye, and finally the compensatory sadistic fantasy in Willoughby's character zone which modulates into this parody. Even here, then, there is the slightest of leakages between the narrator's discourse and that of the character. We might recall the well-known anecdote of Robert Louis Stevenson's, in which a 'young friend of Mr Meredith's' (probably Stevenson himself) complained that Willoughby was a portrait of himself, and the author replied, 'he is all of us'.[8]

Willoughby is not the only character whose inner speech takes the form of a parodied genre:

> Laetitia's bosom swelled upon a mute exclamation, equivalent to: 'Woman! woman! snared ever by the sparkling and frivolous! undiscerning of the faithful, the modest and beneficent!'
>
> In the secret musings of moralists this dramatic rhetoric survives. (32, 391)

Even more notably there are at least two occasions on which Clara's 'secret musings' take the form of novelistic parody. First a sentimental romance of a more genteel and restrained kind than Willoughby's but, like his, articulating a fantasy about the future:

> What would he think? They might never meet, for her to know. Or one day in the Alps they might meet, a middle-aged couple, he famous, she regretful only to have fallen below his lofty standard. 'For, Mr Whitford', says she, very earnestly, 'I did wish at that time, believe me or not, to merit your approbation.'

> The brows of the phantom Vernon whom she conjured up were stern, as she had seen them yesterday in the library. (25, 297)

And, apropos of her disgust at being induced to drink brandy and hot water during her abortive escape attempt, a sententious moral fable:

> And the smell of the glass was odious; it disgraced her. She had an impulse to pocket the spoon for a memento, to show it to her grandchildren for a warning. Even the prelude to the morality to be uttered on the occasion sprang to her lips: 'Here, my dears, is a spoon you would be ashamed to use in your tea-cups, yet it was of more value to me at one period of my life than silver and gold in pointing out,' etc.: the conclusion was hazy, like the conception; she had her idea. (28, 332)

More than most novelists Meredith exemplifies Bakhtin's assertion that 'We speak only in definite speech genres'.[9] In these examples we see the principle extended to inner speech. Later we shall be examining a case in which Clara, speaking with the utmost earnestness, conforms minutely to a very specific speech genre of the period.

Before examining Clara's speech in detail, however, we need to characterize that of Willoughby. Like his generic models in Molière, Willoughby is largely the creation of his own discourse. Like them he is a monologist, in the sense that his word is designed to repel or divert the word of the other. In the most literal sense, he does not enter into dialogue: again and again we see him evading the word of his interlocutor, or even appearing not to hear it:

> 'To have you – to lose you!'
> 'Is it not possible that I may be the first to die?' said Miss Middleton.
> 'And lose you, with the thought that you, lovely as you are...' (6, 58)

However, all utterance strictly speaking is dialogic, in the sense that it speaks to previous utterances of the same words, is oriented towards an addressee who, by thus influencing the utterance, participates in its formation, and conforms to a greater or lesser extent to a variety of speech-genres. Monologism might be described as a specific orientation towards dialogue: a resistance to it; but dialogic relations will assert themselves against the will of the monologist. The death-blow to Willoughby's courtship of Clara is that she finds his discourse monotonous; if the reader also found it monotonous it would be the death-blow to the novel. The reader is, however, better informed than Clara about the total context of Willoughby's utterances, which are moreover laid out for our inspection. We are thus able to see that they are, in fact, tense with involuntary dialogic relations. The following example comes during the scene in which Clara makes her first 'effort after freedom', which Willoughby interprets as jealousy of Laetitia:

'Come, let me allay these...' he soothed her with hand and voice while seeking for his phrase; 'these magnified pin-points. Now, my Clara! on my honour! and when I put it forward in attestation, my honour has the most serious meaning speech can have; ordinarily my word has to suffice for bonds, promises or asseverations: on my honour! not merely is there, my poor child! no ground of suspicion, I assure you, I declare to you, the fact of the case is the very reverse. Now mark me; of her sentiments I cannot pretend to speak; I did not, to my knowledge, originate, I am not responsible for them, and I am, before the law, as we will say, ignorant of them: that is, I have never heard a declaration of them, and I am, therefore, under pain of the stigma of excessive fatuity, bound to be non-cognizant. But as to myself, I can speak for myself, and, on my honour! Clara – to be as direct as possible, even to baldness, and you know I loathe it – I could not. I repeat, *I could not marry Laetitia Dale!* Let me impress it on you. No flatteries – we are all susceptible more or less – no conceivable condition could bring it about; no amount of admiration. She and I are excellent friends; we cannot be more. When you see us together, the natural concord of our minds is of course misleading. She is a woman of genius. I do not conceal, I profess my admiration of her. There are times when, I confess, I require a Laetitia Dale to bring me out, give and take. I am indebted to her for the enjoyment of the duet few know, few can accord with, fewer still are allowed the privilege of playing with a human being. I am indebted, I own, and I feel deep gratitude; I own to a lively friendship for Miss Dale, but if she is displeasing in the sight of my bride by ... by the breadth of an eyelash, then ...' (13, 150–1)

This is a complex and multi-layered utterance. Despite the general consistency ('monotony') and apparent self-addressivity of his speech, Willoughby characteristically speaks only to the moment. He is, paradoxically, constantly re-creating himself in discourse – or, one might put it more extremely, he is constantly re-created by the speech-genres to which he has recourse in order to deal with the demands of the moment. It is thus that he is able in this speech to deny the amorous interest the reader knows he has had in Laetitia, and at the end of the novel to propose to her despite what he has said here (and of course still being engaged to Clara), and the following morning to declare that 'an engagement [is] a solemn bond' (41, 500). One speech-genre of which he makes considerable use, and which is relevant in this instance, is the filibuster. The reader knows that the whole of this speech is irrelevant to the situation, since Clara is not jealous of Laetitia. Whether Willoughby 'sincerely' believes that she is is beside the point; it suits his purpose to believe it and he habitually speaks in a manner in which, as Arnold said of Macaulay's style, it is impossible to be sincere. There is every reason to suppose that he manufactures – more or less consciously – the belief that is convenient to him. This speech is a filibuster because as long as he conducts the conversation on these lines Clara cannot say what he does not want to hear.

Another, even more significant speech-genre which governs the whole utterance, and explicit markers of which frame it, is one that later in the novel Laetitia conveniently names 'fluting', when she reflects that while, on the whole, 'he talked excellently to men... his manner of talking to women went to an excess in the artificial tongue – the tutored tongue of sentimental deference of the towering male: he fluted exceedingly; and she wondered whether it was this which had wrecked him with Miss Middleton' (31, 383).[10] The passage under discussion perfectly exemplifies 'sentimental deference of the towering male' in the way it opens with a patronizing dismissal of Clara's utterance as 'magnified pin-points' and closes with the offer to humour her by dismissing Laetitia.

The ideological character of Willoughby's egoism, one aspect of which is so strongly marked by his 'fluting', is further exemplified when he goes on to speak of his honour and his word, and of the various performatives that are required of him in his daily life. The contrast between the woman's 'magnified pin-points' and the man's 'most serious meaning speech can have' could not be more extreme. Moreover the power-play in Willoughby's language is strongly class- as well as gender-based. 'Honour' can be appealed to only by a gentleman and, more subtly, it is only a powerful man who is 'ordinarily' called upon to supply so many performatives that they require three different names, culminating in a resounding Latinate polysyllable. Furthermore the structure of this part of the speech is very characteristic of Willoughby. He frequently uses lengthy parentheses which give a premeditated, 'public' accent to even the most supposedly intimate speech and make more than the usual demands on the attention of the addressee.

So far it might be said that Willoughby's speech does no more than exemplify the pomposity of the wealthy, patriarchal male. In the middle section, however, the peculiarities of Willoughby's use of language begin to emerge. When he speaks of Laetitia's 'sentiments' a new note enter his speech, of archness, a subdued but nevertheless failed jocularity: 'before the law, as we will say ... under pain of the stigma of excessive fatuity, bound to be non-cognizant'. There is an instability in his tone here, as the relation of addresser to addressee ceases to be simply that of dominant male to submissive female, and takes on a more complex character. The key dialogic element here is Willoughby's knowledge that Laetitia did love him and that he encouraged it or – more accurately, since 'self-knowledge' with Willoughby takes the form of an awareness of potential accusing *others* against whom he needs to defend himself – the presence to him of potential addressees who might bear this knowledge. These addressees might take the form of the 'other' in an interior dialogue, of unspecified actual people not now physically present, of 'the world' which he dreads, or even of Clara if she is better informed than Willoughby hopes she is. His self-defence against these addressees bounces him, as it were, to the extreme declaration, *'I could not marry Laetitia Dale!'* This, in turn, requires him to produce a version of their relationship that explains his obvious satisfaction in Laetitia's company, and which cannot be the true one – that he believes her to be uncritically devoted to him. In response to this demand he produces a series of hackneyed phrases from the lexicon of platonic friendship. The thematically repetitive character of this section of the speech mirrors that of the earlier sections, and is a mark both of the speech's filibustering character and of its tortuous addressivity.

I hope the foregoing analysis shows that, despite the appearance of complacent and monotonous monologue in Willoughby's discourse, his speeches are actually intensely dramatic, and always belong uniquely to the particular situation in which they occur.

I now want to consider Clara's discourse in the novel, to do which is to engage with feminist criticism of it, which in turn will lead us to a consideration of more generic and intertextual questions.

The Egoist has always been acknowledged as a remarkable instance of a feminist (or at least would-be feminist) text by a male Victorian author, but since Kate Millett's critique in *Sexual Politics* this acknowledgement has been complicated by sceptical questioning focused on the fact that, after all, the novel concludes with the heroine's union with a man and implied marriage. This argument has been developed in an article by Carolyn Williams, which takes the important step of making the generic intention of the novel central to the discussion:

> an inherent ambivalence lies at the heart of Meredith's attempted integration of progressive, feminist goals with comedy as a genre; or, in other words, the choice to cast his feminist program of education in the form of a comedy forecloses from the beginning many of its progressive possibilities.... [I]n its dimension as a genre, comedy presses towards a closing affirmation of social stability and order that by definition conserves and recuperates the status quo.[11]

This is the most cogent statement of an argument that will structure my discussion of genre, but I want to defer that discussion until I have attempted to analyse Clara's discourse. I bring Williams's article in here because her case about the novel's ambivalence is centred upon the assertion that Clara is (at least to begin with) inarticulate; that this condemns her to be 'narrated: the narrative's unconscious, the narrative Other, the natural energy caught at its centre'[12] – terms which are of course steeped in the politics of gender – and that despite the admirable and partly realized feminist intentions the male narrator is a participant in the passage of Clara from Willoughby to Vernon in an unbroken patriarchal and dynastic 'Patterne'.

Williams's assertion that Clara is inarticulate is insistent and repeated. It is central to an argument which gathers all the manifestations of her 'naturalness' and 'energy' into a presentation of Meredith as the well-meaning but helpless male colluder/victim of an all too familiar ideology of sexual difference.

As my discussion will show, the text supplies almost no evidence for this version of an 'inarticulate' Clara. On the contrary she is seen as possessing a 'dreadful' power of language and a command of an impressive range of speech-genres; to speak of her as in some special sense 'narrated' is to ignore the large amount of direct and indirect discourse with which she is endowed; and on the occasions when articulateness fails her it is a manifestation not of her naturalness but of her oppression. *The Egoist* is the story not of inarticulate natural female energy but of a civilized, educated and intelligent woman whose articulateness is rendered ineffective.

Early in the novel Vernon reflects on her 'natural wit... as opposed to the paste-sparkle of wit of the town' (5, 47), a phrase that Williams seizes on in support of her argument. This 'natural wit' is described as follows:

> It might be, to a certain degree, her quickness at catching the hue and shade of evanescent conversation. Possibly by remembering the whole of a conversation wherein she had her place, the wit was to be tested. (ibid.)

Clara's wit, in other words, does not take repeatable aphoristic form, like that of Mrs Mountstuart-Jenkinson: it results from the immensely civilized art of 'catching the hue and shade of evanescent conversation'. It is, I need hardly add, dialogic. For example, in a conversation during which Willoughby announces that people who leave his protection are 'extinct' and asks Clara to persuade Vernon to marry Laetitia, she replies: 'Will Mr Whitford offend you to extinction if he declines?' (10, 108). Or, in lighter vein, a conversation with De Craye about a friend of Clara's whom he only vaguely remembers: ' "Will you try her recollection of me?" "It will probably be quite as lively as yours was" ' (25, 307). The command of the difference between the ominous satire of the first example and the playful teasing of the second is not the expression of an inarticulate natural energy.

There is no evidence that Clara's articulateness develops as a result of her struggles to free herself. At a very early stage, when she is still only beginning to feel the necessity to escape, she outmatches Willoughby in line-for-line dialogue:

> 'But does not love shun the world? Two that love must have their substance in isolation.'

'No: they will be eating themselves up'.
'The purer the beauty, the more it will be out of the world'.
'But not opposed'.
'Put it in this way', Willoughby condescended. 'Has experience the same opinion of the world as ignorance?'
'It should have more charity'.
'Does virtue feel at home in the world?'
'Where it should be an example, to my idea'.
'Is the world agreeable to holiness?'
'Then, are you in favour of monasteries?' (7, 75)

Laetitia twice testifies to Clara's 'dreadful power' of expression (16, 191; 48, 603), but it is the real representative of natural energy in the novel, the boy Crossjay, who identifies its dialogic quality: 'And about Miss Dale, when she says a thing, there it is, clear. But Miss Middleton has a lot of meanings' (30, 364).

Clara can also manipulate the tone of a conversation to control a potentially dangerous situation, as when De Craye tries to exploit his awareness of her rift with Willoughby:

The colonel's voice dropped at times to something very like a whisper. He was answered audibly and smoothly. The quick-witted gentleman accepted the correction: but in immediately paying assiduous attentions to Miss Dale, in the approved intriguer's fashion, he showed himself in need of another amounting to a reproof. Clara said: 'We have been consulting, Laetitia, what is to be done to cure Professor Crooklyn of his cold'. De Craye perceived that he had taken a wrong step, and he was mightily surprised that a lesson in intrigue should be read to him of all men. (32, 392)

It is of course not really a 'lesson in intrigue', but even so it would be difficult to find another example in fiction of a teenaged girl outmanoeuvring a 36-year-old man of the world with her command of discourse. A comparison with the scene in *Hard Times* where Sissy Jupe triumphs over James Harthouse with 'child-like ingenuousness'[13] helps to illustrate how *cultivated* Clara's behaviour is in this scene.

There is one remarkable instance of Clara's command of a very precise speech-genre, when she makes her first attempt to persuade Willoughby to release her:

I am penitent for the wrong I have done you. I grieve for you. All the blame is mine. Willoughby, you must release me. Do not let me hear a word of that word; jealousy is unknown to me.... Happy if I could call you a friend and see you with a worthier than I, who might by-and-by call me friend! You have my plighted troth... given in ignorance of my feelings. Reprobate a weak and foolish girl's ignorance. I have thought of it, and I cannot see wickedness, though the blame is great, shameful. You have none. You are without any blame. You will not suffer as I do. You will be generous to me? I have no respect for myself when I beg you to be generous and release me. (15, 175, ellipses in original)

This is not a cry from the heart but a highly stylized utterance, a model of which happens to be recorded in S.M. Ellis's edition of the letter-journals of Meredith's friend, William Hardman. The fiancée of one Mr Harry Chaplin jilted him at the last minute and married Lord Hastings. She wrote to the jilted lover as follows:

To you, whom I have injured more deeply than anyone, I hardly know how to address myself.... Nothing in the world can ever excuse my conduct. I have treated you too infamously, but I sincerely trust the knowledge of my unworthiness will help you to bear the bitter blow I am about to inflict on you. I know I never ought to have accepted you at all.... You must have seen ever since the beginning of our engagement how very little I returned all your devotion to me.... There is no man in the world I have a greater regard and respect for than yourself, but I do not love you in the way a woman ought to love her husband.... And now we are eternally separated for by the time you receive this, I shall be the wife of Lord Hastings. I dare not ask for your forgiveness. I feel I have injured you far too deeply for that. All I can do now is to implore you to go and forget me.... May God bless you, and may you soon find someone far more worthy of becoming your wife than I should ever have been.[14]

Lady Hastings's letter of course is not a cry from the heart either. This genre is so familiar that it must have its origins in fiction, since it is hard to imagine that young ladies were taught to write such letters. In comparing the two examples we find the acknowledgement of injury, self-blame, exculpation of the other, confession of error in having accepted him and wish for a 'worthier' successor to herself. Yet there are differences. We must remember that Lady Hastings is in the situation not of Clara Middleton but of Constantia Durham – who wrote Willoughby a letter that is not recorded but must have resembled this one. Clara's utterance is notably more moderate, particularly in the matter of self-blame, and has a persuasive, not merely an apologetic function. She has the capacity to adapt this essentially written genre both to a different situation and to face-to-face speech.

The occasions on which Clara is rendered inarticulate are not manifestations of her naturalness but the result of specific oppression on the part of her interlocutors, combined with her sensitivity to the dialogic nature of speech. There are one or two minor occasions on which this happens but the most notable are two elaborate dialogic scenes during the prolonged crisis of the plot.

The first of these is a long conversation between Clara and Mrs Mountstuart-Jenkinson, who starts off believing, or affecting to believe, that Clara has been trying to make Willoughby jealous, and silences her with her *grande dame* manner:

'Oh! Mrs Mountstuart, will you listen to me?'
'Presently. Don't threaten me with confidences. Eloquence is a terrible thing in woman. I suspect, my dear, that we both know as much as could be spoken'.
'You hardly suspect the truth, I fear'.
'Let me tell you one thing about jealous men...' (35, 427)

Like Willoughby, Mrs Mountstuart filibusters, going on at length irrelevantly about jealous men, to avoid hearing what Clara has to say. Clara has been softened up by Mrs Mountstuart's kind manner, her earlier criticism of Willoughby's behaviour at her dinner party, and praise of Horace De Craye's wit and good temper – Clara 'was quite at one with her'. Her repeated 'Oh! Mrs Mountstuart' and 'Dear Mrs Mountstuart', which are usually the cue for an interruption, show that she expects a sympathetic listener, and it is this misplaced expectation that makes her – as she is not with Willoughby – vulnerable to silencing. Eventually she succeeds in making Mrs Mountstuart understand that she wishes to break the engagement, to discover that she is speaking to an embodiment of conventional dogma: 'You are just as much bound in honour as if you had the ring on your finger' (431). When she attempts sincerely to convey the paradoxical character of her discovery of the state of her feelings – 'By degrees: unknown to myself; suddenly' – she is met with sarcasm: 'Suddenly and by degrees? I suppose it's useless to ask for a head' (430).

Mrs Mountstuart spends the rest of the conversation consciously or unconsciously (through her 'coarse' emotional understanding, 433) constructing frames for the dialogue which obstruct or distort Clara's speech. For example, she 'already knows' what Clara is saying:

'No love?'
'I have none to give'.
'Dear me! – Yes, yes, but that tone of sorrowful conviction is often a trick, it's not new: and I know that assumption of plain sense to pass off a monstrosity'. (430)

She instructs Clara to explain herself 'in six words', and it is when she attempts to speak in the shadow of this absurd and arbitrary limitation (still handicapped by good will towards her interlocutor) that Clara suffers her most severe collapse of articulateness:

'I came... when I came I was in some doubt. Indeed I speak the truth. I found I could not give him the admiration he has, I dare say, a right to expect. I turned – it surprised me: it surprises me now. But so completely! So that to think of marrying him is...'

Mrs Mountstuart cuts her off to forbid the anticipated simile and says triumphantly, 'Now, by just so much as you have outstripped my limitation of words to you, you show me you are dishonest' (435–6).

Clara's last attempt to speak honestly is in answer to Mrs Mountstuart's question whether there is 'no man living to whom you could willingly give your hand' (436). Clara tries to give a scrupulous account of her feelings for Vernon which Mrs Mountstuart interprets against the evidence ('a beautiful and brave self-denying nature') in the light of her preconception that Clara is attracted to De Craye; she is also only capable of understanding such a confession as an *explanation* of Clara's aversion to Willoughby, and when she discovers that it is not, she says, 'Then you have succeeded in just telling me nothing' (438).

'Nothing' is what Mrs Mountstuart makes of any discourse that falls outside her frame.

The other person who is capable of making Clara inarticulate is her father:

> At one thought of Sir Willoughby, her tongue made ready, and feminine craft was alert to prompt it; but to her father she could imagine herself opposing only dumbness and obstinacy. (15, 171–2)

Her father is for reasons of familial piety what Mrs Mountstuart makes herself by her kind manner: one to whom Clara feels she owes goodwill and sincerity. He is also a fount of misogynistic cliché, so much so that at times he functions as a choric figure, articulating in their most condensed form the prejudices, especially about 'mutability', against which Clara has to contend. Many of his misogynistic utterances take the form of Latin tags, from such canonical authors as Virgil, Cicero and Catullus. In this way Meredith insinuates (part of) the ideological function of classical education. The literally patriarchal authority of the father is continuous with that of the cultural norms. As Dr Middleton says, 'the opinion is universal' that, for example, women have no 'conception of the value of time' (24, 287).

In Chapter 41 Clara, her father and Willoughby participate in a scene that demonstrates Meredith's profound understanding of the dialogic nature of both speech and thought. This scene takes place the morning after Willoughby's failed midnight attempt to persuade Laetitia to marry him, which was overheard by Crossjay. So far Crossjay has told no one his secret, so that Clara is unaware of what has happened and Willoughby, having sworn Laetitia to secrecy, has no reason to suspect that he is about to be exposed. The scene immediately follows an unnarrated encounter between Clara and her father, in which Dr Middleton has vehemently and angrily instructed her to honour her promise to marry Willoughby.

In the earlier part of the scene Clara and Willoughby are tacitly contending over Dr Middleton's presence. Willoughby wants to pin Clara down to a renewal of her commitment in front of her father. 'He understood how he would stand in an instant were Dr Middleton absent. Her father was the tribunal she dreaded, and affairs must be settled and made irrevocable while he was with them' (41, 500). He works hard to exploit Dr Middleton's presence, taking up and repeating the other man's phrase 'a breach of faith' and, as Clara notices, adopting in speech to her a new 'language and tone' which are 'in part addressed to her father' (505). Clara by contrast is unable to speak to the point while her father is in the room:

> Language to express her particular repulsion eluded her. She formed the words, and perceived that they would not stand to bear a breath from her father.... What could she say? he is an Egoist? The epithet has no meaning in such a scene. *Invent!* shrieked the hundred-voiced instinct of dislike within her, and alone with her father, alone with Willoughby, she could have invented some equivalent, to do her heart justice for the injury it sustained in her being unable to name the true and immense objection: but the pair in presence paralyzed her. She dramatized them each springing forward by turns, with crushing rejoinders. The activity of her mind revelled in giving them a tongue, but would not do it for herself. (506)

The passage might have been written to illustrate Bakhtin/Voloshinov's argument that the word is *'the product of the reciprocal relationship between speaker and listener, addresser and addressee....* I give myself verbal shape from another's point of view'.[15] Elsewhere Bakhtin writes of speech which 'literally cringes in the presence or the anticipation of someone else's word, reply, objection'.[16] Clara's 'dramatizing' of the replies of the others is a vivid portrayal of the dynamics of such 'cringing' speech – so extreme in this case that she is unable to speak at all. Moreover, the fact that it is the *combined* presence of Willoughby and her father before which she cringes, together with Willoughby's dialogic exploitation of Middleton's presence, noted earlier, makes this a particularly subtle and complex exemplification of Bakhtin's idea.

As we have seen, Willoughby alone does not have the power to silence Clara. Only the father who literally embodies patriarchal authority and the older woman with the 'decided preference of persons that shone in the sun' (2, 11) can do that. This is a good illustration of the essentially ideological nature of Meredith's theme. In Willoughby's case, it is he whose words are reduced to 'clownish tumult' (15, 176) and a 'shambling, third-rate, sheepish manner' (29, 358) by those of Clara. I shall quote the first of these examples, since it deserves to be known as a classic portrayal of distracted speech. Faced with the necessity of replying to Clara's direct 'petition for a release' Willoughby struggles to say something that will maintain his dignity and 'deal this mad young woman a bitterly compassionate rebuke'. The result is an utterance that is completely off the point, combining a confused sense of the parallel between the indecorum of his situation and the smell of the remnants of breakfast, with a pathetic attempt to impress Clara by recalling his complacently superior letters from America:

> I was at a loss to guess where that most unpleasant effect on the senses came from. They are always 'guessing' through the nose. I mean, the remainder of breakfast here. Perhaps I satirized them too smartly – if you know the letters. When they are not 'calculating'. More offensive than debris of a midnight banquet! An American tour is instructive, though not so romantic. Not so romantic as Italy, I mean. Let us escape. (15, 176)

The transition from the first sentence to the second, from literally guessing about the smell to an allusion to American idiom and twang, is a particularly brilliant illustration of Willoughby's distraction. The confusion leaves it comically uncertain whether it is the breakfast remains or American manners that he considers 'More offensive than debris of a midnight banquet'.

So far, in considering Clara's discourse, we have looked mainly at her 'outer' speech. It goes without saying that, as the heroine of a Meredith novel, she also contributes a great deal of 'inner' speech to the narrative, in both direct and indirect form. An example of her direct inner speech attracted the attention of Freud. In this passage Clara is imagining that her situation would be easier if 'some noble gentleman could see me as I am and not disdain to aid me!' – not as a lover, but a 'comrade'. She compares her situation with that of Constantia Durham, who escaped from Willoughby by eloping with Captain Harry Oxford:

> 'To be able to speak his name and see him awaiting her, must have been relief, a reprieve. She did not waver, she cut the links, she signed herself over. O brave girl! what do you think of me? But I have no Harry Whitford, I am alone....' [T]he sudden consciousness that she had put another name for Oxford, struck her a buffet, drowning her in crimson. (10, 121)

This passage was quoted and discussed by Ernest Jones in a review of *The Psychopathology of Everyday Life* and Freud incorporated this discussion into later editions of the book.[17] Both, however, treat it as simply one among a number of literary representations of slips of the tongue symptomizing unconscious or repressed thoughts; neither draws attention to the fact that Clara's slip occurs in *inner speech* (Jones confuses the issue by calling the passage a 'soliloquy'). She twice makes the same mistake in conversation with Willoughby, but only after this. Bakhtin/Voloshinov's description of inner speech as essentially dialogic casts more light than Jones/Freud on the social character of Clara's most intimate experience: inner speech resembles *'alternating lines of a dialogue'* which are 'joined with one another and alternate with one another not according to the laws of grammar and logic but according to the laws of *evaluative* (emotive) *correspondence, dialogical deployment*, etc.'[18] Thus, between the question addressed to Constantia and the reply ('But I have no Harry Whitford') there is an implicit utterance by Constantia, critical of Clara for not being a 'brave girl'. It is in this dialogic engagement with the imagined Constantia that Clara makes the slip that reveals her unconscious or repressed predilection for Vernon, and this also helps to explain the social phenomenon of the blush. Such overt evidence of inner dialogue is of course not necessary to the Bakhtinian principle: as Bakhtin/Medvedev says, 'Even the inner utterance (interior speech) is social; it is oriented toward a possible audience, toward a possible answer, and it is only in the process of such an orientation that it is able to take shape and form.'[19]

This also applies to the indirect discourse (including free indirect discourse) which is Meredith's more characteristic way of representing inner speech. The outstanding example of this in *The Egoist*, the chapter 'Clara's Meditations', which portrays the turmoil of her mind during the sleepless night after her father's betrayal of her for Willoughby's port, has also attracted distinguished attention, this time from J. Hillis Miller.

Miller acknowledges that this passage 'succeeds... admirably' in creating the 'vivid illusion that there was a person named Clara who went through this experience'[20] and proceeds to deconstruct the 'double assumption' which '[t]hat aspect of realism involving the mimesis in language of states of mind makes', namely 'that there is a prelinguistic self or character, and... that this self in its changes may be expressed, mirrored, or copied without distortion in language'.[21] He quotes extensively from this chapter and from elsewhere in the novel, but his evidence is epitomized by the following passage:

> But the fire of a brain burning high and kindling everything, lit up herself against herself: – Was one so volatile as she a person with a will? – Were they not a multitude of flitting wishes, that she took for a will? – Was she, feather-headed that she was, a person to make a stand on physical pride? – If she could yield her hand without reflection (as she conceived she had done, from incapacity to conceive herself doing it reflectively), was she much better than purchaseable stuff that has nothing to say to the bargain?
>
> Furthermore, said her incandescent reason, she had not suspected such art of cunning in Willoughby. Then might she not be deceived altogether – might she not have misread him?

This leads to her contemplating the possibility that she 'might have the same regard for him as his friends and the world had, provided that he kept at the same distance from her'. But, in a passage omitted by Miller, she revolts from this:

> 'I cannot! I cannot!' she cried aloud; and it struck her that her repulsion was a holy warning. Better be graceless than a loathing wife: better appear inconsistent. Why should she not appear such as she was?' (21, 239–40)

Miller contends that '"Will," "nature," "feelings," "mind," "self," "character" are not names, in this case, for a stable entity or for its faculties. They are, when applied to Clara, figures drawn from an archaic psychology used tropologically to describe what has no proper name' and that '*The Egoist* exposes the inherence of language in character.'[22] So far, one may say, so unsurprising.

However, despite the apparently radical deconstructive scepticism about language seen here, Miller shows an interesting attachment to certain items in Meredith's vocabulary, on which he clearly bestows a more stable signification than to 'will, nature etc'.: '[the name Clara] flits away from any attempt to pin it down'; 'Clara discovers...that not only does she not have a central column of self....She is rather a constant flux, nothing that can be counted on to remain constant. She is the flowing, burning, or blowing of her evanescent moods, whims, wiles, and inconsistencies'; 'she exists, in herself, not as a substantial character, but as a sequence of figures, fleeting, evanescent'; 'The self is revealed to be not something fixed but a multitude of fleeting wishes, feelings, thoughts'; 'What constancy can Clara promise Vernon... if she has no character... if she exists only as a multitude of fleeting and inconsistent wishes?'[23]

This persistent iteration of a particular polarized figure, with evident preference for one pole of the opposition, is remarkable in a piece of deconstructive criticism. In its tendentiousness it is of a piece with Miller's casual apposition of 'the ability of a man or a woman to make promises and keep them' with 'marriage as an institution in which the husband owns his wife'.[24]

The weakness of Miller's analysis, symptomized by these repetitions, is in respect of two features of Clara's meditations which he ignores or fails to see the significance of: their representation in (predominantly) free indirect discourse and their glaringly dialogic character. Miller does recognize the free indirect discourse but does not see its implications for his argument about mimesis. If modern narratologists are correct in their persuasive argument that language can imitate only language, then free indirect discourse is on the boundary of mimesis and diegesis: it is diegetic in the sense that it tells the story (in this case the story of Clara's thoughts), and mimetic only in the sense that it imitates the character's inner speech. It does not, as Miller claims, assume that there is 'a prelinguistic self or character' and so cannot implicitly deconstruct such an assumption.

As regards dialogue, Miller recognizes it only in the sense that he awards all the truth-value to one side of it: he turns it, ideologically speaking, into monologue. For him words such as 'volatile', 'flitting', 'inconsistent' stand for the truth, while 'will' and 'reason' are fictions. I am conscious of the danger of merely substituting one theoretical frame for another, but it does seem to me that Bakhtin's conception of the self as dialogic helps to register the distinctiveness of Meredith's discourse, rather than merely add it to the ever-growing list of self-deconstructing texts:

> The self/other dichotomy in Bakhtin does not, as in Romantic philosophy, emphasize the self alone, a radical subjectivity always in danger of shading off into solipsistic extremes. For the same reason the self, as conceived by Bakhtin, is not a

presence wherein is lodged the ultimate privilege of the real, the source of sovereign intention and guarantor of unified meaning. The Bakhtinian self is never whole, since it can exist only dialogically.[25]

Clara's dialogue is both inwardly and outwardly directed: between versions of the self, or pretenders to the self, and with Whitford, De Craye and others who have accommodated themselves to Willoughby. It could be described, crudely, as a dialogue between the self as will and reason and the self as flitting and volatile. It is the former that asks the questions in the first paragraph, paradoxically, in doing so, negating itself in favour of the other that it despises; and this other asserts itself in the final sentences quoted, including the direct, actually uttered speech. But this is an oversimplification: it would be more adequate to speak of a quadrapartite dialogue, in which each of these versions is split into a favoured and an unfavoured variant: the self as will and reason (with the freedom of choice implicit in those terms)/ as trapped by the consequences of an ignorant choice and an ideologically imposed consistency; as 'featherheaded...purchaseable stuff'/ as free to change and develop. The distinctive dynamic of the dialogue is as follows: 'will and freedom' names the other as the true self but in the act of naming, and of stigmatizing as 'featherheaded', simultaneously stands her ground; this is then reversed, as the other stigmatizes 'will and reason' by naming not her so much as her consequence – 'a loathing wife' – and in so doing redefines her 'self' not as featherheaded but as free to 'appear inconsistent'. Each of these versions of the self is of course evolved in response to external others, specifically Willoughby, Clara's father, Vernon, and so on, or more generally the ideological environment in which Clara is living.

The Bakhtinian 'chain' of language is one of utterances, not of signifiers, and it is held together by responses, not merely difference. To quote Clark and Holquist again:

> The distinctiveness of each response is the specific form of that person's answerability. There is no way for a living organism to avoid answerability, since the very quality that defines whether or not one is alive is the ability to react to the environment, which is a constant responding, or answering, and the total chain of these responses makes up an individual life. This is what

Bakhtin means in saying that there is 'no alibi for being'. How we respond is how we take responsibility for our selves.[26]

Miller's 'only...a multitude of fleeting and inconsistent wishes', abstracted from Clara's dialogue, sounds very like an 'alibi for being'. Clara is not a 'prelinguistic self' but a self in dialogue; this is perfectly consistent with *The Egoist* being (and its feminism based on its being) the story of a woman taking responsibility for herself – that, indeed, is precisely what we see happening in 'Clara's Meditations'. Responsibility includes keeping promises; it also includes questioning the grounds for keeping them, and not making a fetish of it, or one is in danger of becoming Lord Fleetwood in *The Amazing Marriage*, 'the prisoner of his word'. Meredith's world is one in which 'the ability of men and women to make promises and keep them', while problematic, is not equivalent to 'marriage as an institution in which the husband owns his wife'.

Before moving on from language to genre it is necessary to say something about Mrs Mountstuart Jenkinson's celebrated aphorisms. These are of significantly different kinds. In one of his notebooks Meredith wrote:

> A brilliant saying arrests thought: a simple observation instigates it: an idea that fixes the mind to itself cannot be of entire truth: one that leads it forth, altho' it be into the darkness, is the better guide. What we desire to hit is around us, not ahead, and moving with, around us.[27]

This is another indication of the dialogic character of Meredith's attitude to discourse. Most of Mrs Mountstuart's sayings belong to the first category: 'Phoebus Apollo turned fasting friar', 'Here she comes, with a romantic tale on her eyelashes', 'A dainty rogue in porcelain'. Their effect lies in their own internal structure: of opposition, or in the one about Laetitia, substitution of 'eyelashes' for the expected 'lips'. Her most celebrated saying, however, is of a different character: 'You see he has a leg.' This is Meredith's 'simple observation' – not, of course, as simple as it first appears.

The saying inaugurates a narratorial extravaganza that lasts for nearly a whole chapter. It modulates from Mrs Mountstuart's words to a description of her tone – 'just as others utter empty nothings, with never a hint of a stress' – a description of the circulation of the saying among the assembled company on Willoughby's coming of age, and an amplification of its connotations:

> He is everything you have had the goodness to remark, ladies and dear sirs, he talks charmingly, dances divinely, rides with the air of a commander-in-chief, has the most natural grand pose possible without ceasing for a moment to be the young English gentleman he is. Alcibiades, fresh from a Louis XIV[28] perruquier, could not surpass him: whatever you please; I could outdo you in sublime comparisons, were I minded to pelt him. Have you noticed that he has a leg? (2, 12)

There follows an evocation of the English upper classes' persisting 'coy attachment' through 'mournful veneration of the Martyr Charles' to 'the Court of his Merrie Son, where the leg was ribanded with love-knots and reigned'. This passage, in which the narrator himself adopts a coy tone in parody of the social world he is describing, illustrates how the 'leg' insinuates both the class arrogance and the sexual predatoriness of the ideology epitomized in Willoughby. Characters dispute whether the emphasis of the saying should be upon *'see'*, *'he'* or *'leg'*, bringing out a 'slight difference of meaning' with each accent. And, an undercurrent of the whole, possibly not intended by Mrs Mountstuart, there is a hint of the philistinism of a culture whose ideal male despises poetry, and a premonition of the boredom he inflicts on Clara: 'It makes the business of choosing a wife for him superhumanly difficult!' – though Mrs Mountstuart certainly intends *this* in a quite different sense. Her remark truly hits 'around' and leads the mind 'forth, altho' it be into the darkness'.

It will be seen from this, in contrast to my earlier discussion of her, that Mrs Mountstuart fulfils more than one function in the novel. As the older woman complicit in the sustaining of Willoughby's ideological role, she suppresses Clara's speech, yet she also delights in speech, and not only her own. She is a connoisseur of dialogue, distressed when her dinner party is spoilt by a pedantic professor: in a remark that would have appealed to Bakhtin she exclaims, 'As if "in toto" were the language of a dinner-table!' (35, 423). It is *because* she is a connoisseur of dialogue that she is able to suppress it when it suits her to.

We have seen, and shall continue to see, that Meredith's novels are in unremitting dialogue with comedy 'in its dimension as a genre' with its tendency to 'recuperate the status quo'. This dialogue is at its most disruptive in *Richard Feverel*, but persists in the avoidance of closure in *Sandra Belloni*, the wearing out of Dahlia's love for Edward in *Rhoda Fleming*, and the sudden deaths which wrench the conclusions of *Vittoria*, *Harry Richmond* and *Beauchamp's Career*. We shall see further evidence of Meredith's unhappiness with comedy's 'closing affirmation of social stability' in the self-consciousness about the 'Nuptial Chapter' in *Diana of the Crossways*. On the other hand – or, rather, as an explanation of the necessity for this dialogue – comedy as 'a presiding mode or style' is central to Meredith's art.[29] In *The Egoist*, the only novel to be titled a comedy, this dialogue may seem to be in abeyance, or at least to take the special form of agreement, and in the penultimate sentence Meredith's 'Comic Muse' seems reconciled to her traditional generic role when she is portrayed 'Sitting beside' the united lovers, 'grave and sisterly' (50, 626). As we have seen, this reconcilement has implications for a number of feminist readings of the novel. I shall be arguing that the dialogue is by no means in abeyance, only carried on in a more devious manner than hitherto.

In one respect *The Egoist*'s dialogic 'angle' to the conventions of comedy as a genre is obvious. Comedy in this sense deals with courtship and marriage, with lovers' triumph over obstacles, whether in the form of mutual misunderstanding or social prohibition, the most traditional form of the latter being the obstructive fathers. *The Egoist*'s relationship to this traditional comedy plot is decidedly and obviously ironic. The courtship of Willoughby and Clara is completed by the time the latter appears in the novel, the dominant emotion is not sexual attraction but revulsion, the obstructive father's role is to *uphold* the marriage and the dynamic of the plot is the heroine's struggle to escape, in Meredith's superb phrase, 'the tragedy of the embrace' (21, 237). The novel's validation, in this manner, of a woman's sexual aversion to a man, not because of any physical deformity but because of his personality, is one of its strongest claims to approval by feminist critics – and, indeed, this claim has on the whole been conceded.

A further dialogic element is the self-consciousness with which comedic conventions are deployed. In plot-formation comedy shuttles between an unashamed mechanical contrivance, what the Russian Formalists called 'laying bare the device', and a careful naturalization, concealing its own artfulness. The absurdities of many of Shakespeare's comedies – the transfer of Olivia's passion from Viola to Sebastian, the potion in *A Midsummer Night's Dream* – strongly suggest a scepticism about the love-conventions encoded in his plots; Jane Austen by contrast altered the dénouement of *Persuasion*, apparently to make it seem to arise from the lovers' strength of character rather than the contrivance of third parties.[30] On this scale *The Egoist* is much closer to Shakespeare than to Jane Austen. Its dénouement (literally 'unknotting') is brought about by Crossjay lying down to sleep on a sofa under a shawl, having been locked out of his room by Willoughby, and overhearing Willoughby's infamous proposal of marriage to Laetitia. The crudity of this device is perhaps acknowledged in the words of the final chapter, 'So the knot was *cut*' (50, 624, my italics). Such crude devices may often be the recourse of desperation, but that can hardly be so in this case. Willoughby succeeds in swearing Laetitia to silence, but it is hard to believe that she is in honour bound either to make or to keep this promise, Willoughby's behaviour both to her and to Clara being so heinous. Meredith had an easy 'natural' dénouement at hand: to make Laetitia herself the agent of Willoughby's exposure. He chose the other course. In so doing he achieved a number of ends. He consolidated the role of Crossjay as the focus of healthy and generous feeling by resolving the plot through the boy's loyalty to Clara. Because, being a child, Crossjay progressively and indirectly leaks the truth, Meredith is able to achieve the wonderful scenes in Chapters 44 and 45, dialogical extravaganzas which are also a grotesque exaggeration of the conventional *malentendu* of Molièrean comedy, relying on an enormous number of characters speaking inexplicitly and being misunderstood because they falsely assume that their interlocutor already 'knows' what they 'know'.[31] But the most important effect is the superfluity of the plotting itself, the gratuitousness of the contrivance, the flaunting of an artificial means of achieving an end when a more 'natural' one was at hand.

This goes with the overt theatricality of the whole of the novel's final phase. Every critic has noted that these episodes are written as if for the stage – specifically, as if for the kind of comedy in which the development of the plot depends on who is in possession of what information, and which combinations of characters are together on the stage at any time. The *malentendu* effects noted above are obvious examples of this. The chapter-headings come to resemble the scene-divisions of classical French comedy, determined by the characters present, and the final chapter is 'The Curtain Falls'. It goes without saying that the action is carried on by dialogue far more than is usual with Meredith or any other Victorian novelist.

If the function of ideology is to appear natural, then, comedy conspicuously fails in its ideological role here. What then is the point of these 'gratuitous' devices? Are they there, in classic Russian Formalist fashion, as markers of artfulness or rather, in Bakhtin/Medvedev's terms, 'for the sake of something else, a moral value, which against this background stands all the more sharply and vividly precisely as a moral value'?[32] We are not dealing here with a simple case such as the one at issue between Bakhtin/Medvedev and Shklovsky, a story such as Tolstoy's 'Kholstomer' where defamiliarization is used for an obviously satirical purpose. Here the 'moral value' of the defamiliarization, if there is one, is not obvious.

The objection to, or reservation about, *The Egoist* on the part of feminist critics is that for all its enlightenment, in the end Clara is 'passed by one potential husband to another', in 'the line of Patternes, the male line from Willoughby to Vernon'.[33] What were the alternatives for Meredith? He could have left Clara without a sexual partner, or he could have given her sexual fulfilment outside marriage. We do not need to pause long over why the author of *Richard Feverel*, still without a secure popular reputation, should have avoided the latter course. Clara and Vernon do not marry within the pages of the novel and it is as 'lovers' that they 'met between the Swiss and Tyrol Alps over the Lake of Constance' on the final page: this may be a gesture that is relevant to my argument; but there is little reason to suppose that they do not marry, especially as her father is with them. The possibility of the former resolution is, as we shall see, an interesting presence in *Diana of the Crossways*, but it is not seriously considered in *The Egoist*. Although in plot-terms the novel runs comedy backwards, it is still driven by the powerful comedic urge towards self-fulfilment. The name 'Egoist' is not simply a derogatory label for Willoughby; Clara, Vernon and Laetitia all call themselves egoists at some point in the novel (16, 190; 33, 403; 49, 618). John Goode has written a fine study of the term and its immediate history, particularly in Comte, and draws attention to its contemporary biological sense as:

> man's instinct for self-preservation, which Comte defines as nutrition and which is both affirmatively and ironically imaged

in the novel as Crossjay's appetite and Dr Middleton's gastronomic vulnerability, [which] is what has created the society whose finest manifestation is the Comic Spirit.

Willoughby is a *'degenerate* egoist'.[34] Carolyn Williams, in a different essay from the one I have been discussing, sees Willoughby similarly in the context of Darwinian theory as one who, 'seemingly fit,... is... found to be unfit', who given Laetitia's poor health may fail to reproduce, unlike Clara and Vernon.[35] The novel's eventual turn back in the direction of conventional comedy is an affirmation of this 'healthy' egoism.

John Goode argues persuasively that the novel's counter to Willoughby's egoism is not the altruism of Comte and George Eliot, and quotes a passage in which Clara 'encounters the George Eliot solution':[36]

> In this mood she sternly condemned Constantia. 'We must try to do good; we must not be thinking of ourselves; we must make the best of our path in life.' She revolved these infantile precepts with humble earnestness. (9, 95)

The passage in inverted commas qualifies as pastiche, as an image of George Eliot's discourse, so that the phrase 'infantile precepts' is shocking in association with one whom Meredith had described as 'the greatest of female writers'.[37] Specific models for this passage can be found in any of George Eliot's novels, but it is particularly reminiscent of the conversation between Gwendolen and Deronda that runs throughout *Daniel Deronda*: 'I want to be good.... I will try to bear what you think I ought to bear' and 'I have remembered your words – that I may live to be one of the best of women, who make others glad that they were born.'[38]

The Egoist and *Daniel Deronda* have been indirectly linked via their common influence on *The Portrait of a Lady* – Donald D. Stone has made an extensive comparison of Meredith's novel with James's, and Dorothy Van Ghent enlists *The Portrait* in her privative view of *The Egoist*;[39] while F.R. Leavis made a celebrated comparison of George Eliot's novel with James's in *The Great Tradition*. I think there is a case for a more direct comparison, and for examining the possibility that in *The Egoist*, and particularly in the treatment of the relationship between Clara and Vernon, there is an element of 'hidden polemic' with *Daniel Deronda*, which was published just as Meredith was beginning work on his novel.[40]

The differences between the two novels are of course considerable. *Daniel Deronda* is not a comedy, and one of its outstanding merits is its portrayal of how Gwendolen comes to make her disastrous marriage choice – a portrayal which occupies fully a third of the book, and for which there is no equivalent at all in *The Egoist*. There is however a marked correspondence between the central trios of characters, Gwendolen-Grandcourt-Deronda and Clara-Willoughby-Vernon. Grandcourt does not obviously resemble Willoughby, because he uses a minimum of words, but the narrator twice speaks of his 'egoism' – a spelling which the *Saturday* reviewer of *The Egoist* thought novel enough to describe as 'current slang'[41] and whose currency probably derives from George Eliot's interest in Comte, though *OED* gives it a history as long as that of the more familiar 'egotism'. Grandcourt's egoism, like Willoughby's, is portrayed as a disease – 'something like premature age...where impulse is born and dies in a phantasmal world...conspicuous in proportion as the varied susceptibilities of younger years are stripped away' – in contrast to Gwendolen's 'intoxication of youthful egoism'[42] which, though severely chastised, corresponds to the healthy egoism of Clara. Like Clara's, Gwendolen's sexuality is manifested predominantly in negative terms, in the form of revulsion. There is also a significant parallel in the ideological character of Grandcourt's egoism. Like Willoughby he epitomizes the pride of class, wealth and power, tyrannical male dominance and vulgar English chauvinism. Just as Willoughby is considered by his milieu 'the young English gentleman' (2, 12) *par excellence*, so Grandcourt's manners represent 'the extreme type of the national taste'.[43] Deronda, like Vernon, moves in the social world under scrutiny but is not of it; both characters are (or in Deronda's case appears to be, even to himself) disadvantaged cousins of the dominant egoist, both are turned to for support by his bride and supplant him in her affections.

But *Daniel Deronda*, as I have said, is not a comedy, and Gwendolen does not marry Deronda. Indeed Deronda, safely betrothed to Mirah, is indignant at his friend Hans's suggestion that Gwendolen might marry at all: 'Is it absolutely necessary that Mrs Grandcourt should marry again?'[44] Gwendolen is not 'passed on' from Grandcourt to his 'cousin'; at the end of the novel she faces the future with the support only of her family. Few readers, however, will assign this conclusion to George Eliot's credit as a feminist.

Gwendolen is subject to Deronda's influence from the first chapter to the last – the novel's analeptic narrative structure is even designed to ensure this, beginning with his flamboyant and as it turns out uncharacteristic gesture of redeeming her necklace and so discouraging her from further gambling. Her feeling about him is 'something vague and yet mastering'; 'a superstitious dread – due, perhaps, to the coercion he had exercised over her thought'; she longs 'to be judged by Deronda with unmixed admiration'; he becomes 'part of her conscience'; she turns him 'into a priest'; she 'learned to see all her acts through the impression they would make on Deronda'.[45] The word 'submission' is frequently used of her relation to him.[46] In comparison with Deronda, the narrator frequently speaks of Gwendolen not only critically but slightingly: her attempts to imagine his 'ideas' are compared to those of 'a lapdog... framing to itself the motives and adventures of doghood at large'; and at the very end, although she has been through the double remorse of her betrayal of Lydia Glasher and her willing of Grandcourt's death, it is still her 'small life' that is 'for the first time feeling the pressure of a vast mysterious movement' of which Deronda is a part.[47]

Many of these feelings of Gwendolen's are the symptoms of falling in love, but the narrative ensures that they do not issue in any lovemaking, or more intimate knowledge of Deronda that might mitigate her 'submission' to him. Her not marrying him, the avoidance of the comedic resolution, has the reverse of a liberating effect, and Deronda's indignation at the thought of her marrying at all intensifies this.

Vernon Whitford, as I have said, fulfils a similar function to Deronda, but the handling is strikingly different. The relationship between Gwendolen and Deronda is developed through a series of formal conversations which are in some ways the centrepieces of the novel, where, in advising Gwendolen, Deronda articulates the values that inform and structure the novel: the values which, working in Deronda's life through his involvement in Judaism, remove him from her. An important conversation occurs between Clara and Vernon, when she goes to him ostensibly on Willoughby's behalf to persuade him to marry Laetitia, but ends up confessing her wish to be free from her engagement. This conversation, however, is not narrated, and as always when Meredith violates narrative expectation, there is a reason: Vernon's role in supporting and influencing Clara is to be as subdued as possible. The following reflections on this and a subsequent conversation, a hybrid of the narrator's and Clara's voices, are typical of the tone in which Vernon's role is discussed:

> Mr Whitford meant well; he was conscientious, very conscientious. But he was not the hero descending from heaven bright-sworded to smite a woman's fetters off her limbs and deliver her from the yawning mouth-abyss.
> His logical coolness of expostulation with her when she cast aside the silly mission entrusted to her by Sir Willoughby and wept for herself, was unheroic in proportion to its praiseworthiness. He had left it to her to do everything she wished done, stipulating simply that there should be a pause of four and twenty hours for her to consider of it before she proceeded in the attempt to extricate herself. (16, 181)

There is a 'sideward glance'[48] in the tone here, especially of the first paragraph, as if in answer to another version of what his role should be. The most obvious contrast is Harry Oxford: the 'hero descending' is Perseus, who rescued Andromeda from the sea-monster (compare the Andromeda image in *Beauchamp's Career*, p. 115 above) and has already been associated with Oxford (10, 120). The 'sideward glance' is at that desire of Clara's to be rescued like Constantia, which has been manifested by her slips of the tongue. With *Daniel Deronda* in mind, though, another kind of hero, more immediate to Vernon's moral authority and therefore more of a temptation to this novel, can be seen to be exorcized in this dry commentary.

Vernon's discourse, then, is markedly curtailed and subdued in comparison with Deronda's. Nor is he allowed decisively influential action, though he attempts it when he follows Clara to the railway station to prevent her flight. First, Vernon's intervention is stripped of the heroic dimension by being saturated with 'low' associations: the private room in the railway inn, with the portraits of the publican's family 'flat on their canvas as weeds of the botanist's portfolio, although their corpulency was pretty generally insisted on' (27, 321), the 'infamous mixture' of brandy and water that Vernon makes Clara drink (322) and even the necessity of removing her wet boots and stockings. This obtrusion of low contingency has a clear deflationary function, and would be unthinkable in the encounters between Gwendolen and Deronda. Secondly, although Vernon's purpose is achieved, and Clara returns to Patterne Hall, it is by no means straightforwardly the result of his intervention. Her flight is frustrated by a combination of circumstances, of which Vernon's delaying tactic is certainly one, but which also include the simultaneous arrival at the station of de Craye and Mrs Mountstuart-Jenkinson.

There is then a double swerve as it were in *The Egoist*'s relation to comedy as a genre. The reverse plot of Clara's engagement to Willoughby, and the parodic exaggerations of the dénouement, suggest a relation of irony, in the spirit of the generic reverses of *Richard Feverel*. In this way the novel resists comedy's 'closing affirmation of social stability'. But comedy is also the friend of 'man's instinct for self-preservation', including sexual fulfilment, and so the novel swerves back to a traditional closure placed between, to paraphrase Bakhtin, 'generic quotation marks',[49] as it leaves its lovers sitting with the Comic Muse *outside* society, 'between the Swiss and Tyrol Alps over the Lake of Constance' (50, 626), a balancing act as precarious and exhilarating as the novel itself.

6
The Tragic Comedians

The Tragic Comedians is a unique case among Meredith's novels. Although, as we have seen, intertextual elements are important in all of them, this alone is a detailed response to, indeed an alternative version of, a specific other narrative. This other narrative, moreover, purports to be factual, and its relation to Meredith's text is not merely that of a 'source'. In the Prefatory section of the novel Meredith informs us that his characters 'belong to history' and 'breathed the stouter air than fiction's' (1). He goes on to maintain that nothing has been invented, 'because an addition of fictitious incidents could never tell us how she came to do this, he to do that' (2).

This other narrative is *Meine Beziehungen zu Ferdinand Lassalle* by Helene von Racowitza, an account of the author's passionate and ultimately catastrophic love affair with the charismatic leader of the radical German Social Democratic movement. *The Tragic Comedians* stands in a very curious relationship to this text. As we have seen, Meredith does not avail himself of the licence of fiction, even though he changes the names of all the characters. The task he appears to have set himself, and the criterion of success to which he appeals, is a contribution to the understanding of these actual historical personages: an understanding which, of course, the whole enterprise implies and the text explicitly states, is absent from Racowitza's own account: 'Years later she wrote her version of the story, not sparing herself so much as she supposed' (19, 200–1). Yet *The Tragic Comedians* is by no means a work of history or biography. Apart from one essay about Lassalle,[1] Meredith appears to have done no research on the subject: the implication is that he has access to a truer understanding of the events than Racowitza's own, achieved purely by critical reading and his own superior insight.

Critics almost unanimously support this claim, even those who show no sign of having read Racowitza's book: Lionel Stevenson for example writes that *Meine Beziehungen* 'had fascinated him by the author's unintentional revelation of her vanity and shallowness'.[2] For those critics who *have* read *Meine Beziehungen*, the peculiar status of Meredith's text seems to result in confusion. Leonée Ormond claims that 'With the Princess's text in front of him, [Meredith] captures her shallow nature with an objectivity which is occasionally brutal'; despite this, '*The Tragic Comedians* liberates itself from the story which inspired it'.[3] Gillian Beer states that Meredith 'emphasiz[es]...the extent to which [Helene's] false impression of her own character precipitates the tragedy' and gives as her own judgement that in Helene's account 'the whole disaster is seen on a continuous high plane of intensity with herself as martyr'; at the same time, Racowitza's narrative is described as a 'persuasively sympathetic picture...of herself' and Meredith is accused of 'succumbing to his unfortunate tendency to hound characters in order to clarify his moral pattern'.[4]

My own reading of *Meine Beziehungen*, which is handicapped by a limited command of German, suggests that, while Meredith did stay very close to the outlines of the given story, and did not invent new incidents, his narrative is not merely a reinterpretation of Racowitza's but (with one notable exception) a systematic distortion. If this is correct, the book would appear to be damned by Meredith's own suggested criteria. I suspect that most readers would think that, whatever Meredith said, this would be a one-dimensional way of looking at the novel. Equally, however, to treat it as fiction and *Meine Beziehungen* as a mere 'source' like a ladder to be kicked away, would deprive the book of much of its peculiar fascination as well as insult the memories of Racowitza and Lassalle.

Clearly what has to be attempted is a dialogic reading that brings the texts into a more fruitful relationship than the unsatisfactory ones just outlined. However, *The Tragic Comedians* is singularly lacking in the dialogic features that I have been analysing in such novels as *Richard Feverel*, *Beauchamp's Career* and *The Egoist*. The story is told by, for Meredith, an unusually dominant and dogmatic narrator, whose role in offering finalizing judgements is particularly marked in relation to Clotilde, Meredith's version of Helene. There is little if any stylization in the narrative discourse, and although character zones are established by the usual means of free indirect discourse, these are for the most part clearly distinguishable from the word of the narrator. Clotilde, in particular, is for Meredith an exceptionally 'objectified' character. One might go on from this to say that *Meine Beziehungen* itself is objectified: it does not answer back in Meredith's discourse or, in Bakhtin's words, 'exert a counterforce against the author's intentions'.[5] and this suppressed status has been perpetuated by the novel's critics. Yet, in reality, these texts are part of a dialogic series. *Meine Beziehungen* itself was written in the shadow of 'so viele niedrige, ja ehrlos gehässige Angriffe gegen mich gerichtet' [so many base, even disgracefully spiteful attacks directed against me].[6] Much later von Racowitza published another narrative of her relations with Lassalle in her *Autobiography*, in which she commented that since *Meine Beziehungen* much reliable information had been published which had 'done much to dispel the false impressions arising from garbled misstatements',[7] the latter no doubt including *The Tragic Comedians*.

Before comparing Meredith's version with von Racowitza's, I will give an outline of the story that they share. Helene and Lassalle, then in their late teens and late thirties respectively, met at a soirée, after both had been informed by mutual friends of a remarkable resemblance of outlook and temperament. They fell in love immediately but had few opportunities to meet because of the prejudice and ideological hostility of Helene's family, members of the minor German aristocracy. Eventually they arranged that Lassalle would formally ask for her hand but, when Helene mentioned this intention to her mother in advance, her parents' reaction was so violent that she fled to her lover and asked him to take her away – a course that he had earlier pressed on her. Lassalle now insisted on going through with an 'honourable' marriage, with the result that Helene was imprisoned by her family, and bullied and manipulated into writing various messages to the effect that she renounced Lassalle – hoping he would understand that these were forced. During this period neither lover had any reliable knowledge of the other's actions and state of mind, and they lacked sufficient genuine mutual understanding to trust each other. Eventually Lassalle, who had always condemned duelling, challenged Helene's father. The challenge was taken up by Yanko von Racowitza, a young man who devotedly and self-sacrificingly loved Helene. By a grotesque mischance Yanko, who had no experience of weapons and tried to miss, shot Lassalle dead. Subsequently Helene married Yanko, the only blameless person in the story, when he was already dying himself.

A crucial factor in a reader's judgement of Helene/Clotilde's conduct will be one's sense of how quickly and easily she succumbs after her imprisonment. In her own account there is first a period of uncertain duration, but of at least several days,[8] when her father visits her daily to ask her intentions and she always answers that she will marry Lassalle. After this period she is visited by a servant who tells her that Lassalle has left Geneva. There follows 'eine böse, fürchterliche Nacht' [an evil, dreadful night][9] during which she wonders if he has abandoned her. After this she is visited by her brother and sisters who tearfully tell her that if she makes such a dreadful marriage their own prospects will be blighted. These visits are repeated daily: 'das ging tagelang so fort! Sie kamen jeden Tag'.[10] It is after this second unspecified period of days that, under the combined pressure of her doubt of Lassalle and emotional blackmail by her family, she tells her mother that she renounces him.

Meredith's text follows the same basic sequence of events but with a drastically foreshortened effect. The passage of time is again indefinite but at no point is a period of days mentioned. The visits from Clotilde's father are described as a 'tug between rigour and endurance [which] continued for about forty hours' (8, 102); there follows the visit from the servant and the dreadful night, on the morning after which she is visited, as in Racowitza's text, by her sisters and brother. There is, however, no mention of these visits being repeated, or of a period of days before her submission, which seems to happen immediately.

Some foreshortening and condensation is of course necessary and acceptable for artistic purposes, but in this case it is clearly tendentious, and strongly reinforces the Meredithian narrator's case that Helene/Clotilde is culpably weak and 'craven'. Within this narrative sequence there is a further example of tendentiousness. Of the night following the servant's news that Alvan [Lassalle] has left town, Meredith writes:

> She wept through the night. It was one of those nights of the torrents of tears which wash away all save the adamantine within us, if there be aught of that besides the breathing structure. The reason why she wept with so delirious a persistency was, that her nature felt the necessity for draining her of her self-pitifulness, knowing that it nourished the love whereby she was tormented. They do not weep thus who have a heart for the struggle. (8, 103)

Even in isolation this seems a dubious judgement. In Racowitza's text, moreover, there is no mention of weeping: she merely describes it as 'eine böse, fürchterliche Nacht' spent going over the possible meanings of Lassalle's removal. Again, some imaginative licence is available to the novelist even if he wishes to remain in the 'stouter air than fiction's', and it is not unreasonable to imagine that Helene wept. To use this imagined weeping as evidence for an unfavourable judgement of her character is another matter.

The view of Helene/Clotilde as culpably weak-willed, which the narrative distortion just discussed reinforces, is the topic of repeated dogmatic editorializing by the narrator, particularly towards the end of the novel. Gillian Beer's study of the manuscript and proofs shows that much of this editorializing was introduced in late revisions.[11] On two occasions, near the end of the novel, the word 'craven' is used twice on the same page. The related judgement, without which there would have been little point in writing the novel, is that, as the critics cited above assume, Helene was unaware of her culpability and her memoir was self-serving. These judgements come together in this passage, following Alvan's death:

> She could not blame herself, for the intensity of her suffering testified to the bitter realness of her love of the dead man. Her craven's instinct to make a sacrifice of others flew with claws of hatred at her parents. These she offered up, and the spirit presiding in her appears to have accepted them as proper substitutes for her conscience. (18, 197)

That this is a judgement not only of the blighted girl but also of the reflective memoirist is clear in Meredith's concluding observation that 'Years later she wrote her version of the story, not sparing herself so much as she supposed' (19, 200-1). The corresponding passage of *Meine Beziehungen* reads as follows:

> Das einzige, alles Entsetzen in voller Stärke uberlebende Gefühl, war, wie gesagt, der Hass, der tiefe, nie zu überwindende Groll gegen die Eltern – die in ihrem grausamen Egoismus alles Elend verschuldet, und eine ebenso tiefe, dauernde Verachtung gegen mich selbst, gegen meine schmachvolle Willensschwäche.
>
> Dieser auch klage ich mich wieder und wieder an und bekenne mich ihrer unverzeihlich schuldig.

> [The only feeling that survived all the horror in full strength was, as I have said, the hatred, the deep, insuperable resentment

against my parents – who in their cruel egotism were responsible for all the misery, and an equally deep, lasting contempt for myself, for my disgraceful weakness of will.

I accuse myself of this again and again and confess myself unforgivably guilty of it.][12]

Perhaps this is histrionic breastbeating designed to win the reader's sympathy. A subtler reader of German than myself is needed to make this judgement. However, it is notoriously difficult to strike the right note in such matters, and in one respect at least Helene's self-blame is measured and therefore more convincing: she denies that she was in any way guilty in marrying Yanko, 'mein einzigster, uneigennützigster Freund' [my only, most unselfish friend].[13] Moreover, references to her weakness of will occur throughout Racowitza's text.

Helene also confesses the elation that she felt when she heard that Yanko and Lassalle would fight and, as she thought, Yanko would inevitably be killed: 'Ich fühlte nicht einmal Mitleid mit ihm, meinem einzigen Freund; ich sah es eben als nothwendig an; er musste sterben und das konnte mich vielleicht zum Glücke führen!' [I did not even feel pity for him, my only friend; I just regarded it as necessary; he must die and that might perhaps lead me to happiness!][14] It would have been easy for her to hide this unattractive feeling, even from herself.

As for her parents, even a reader of *The Tragic Comedians* who is unacquainted with *Meine Beziehungen* is likely to feel that they fully deserve their daughter's hatred; in her account there is further evidence against them such as the attempt, which Meredith does not use, to marry her to a 40-year-old Sardinian acquaintance when she was 12.[15]

There are numerous other tendentious alterations, some of which I shall describe more briefly. Lassalle was a Jew, and Helene grew up in a virulently anti-semitic environment, though her mother had Jewish ancestry. Before she met him, her interest in him was moderated by the expectation of seeing 'einen ungraziösen, schwarzen, eckigen, kleinen "Jüd"' [an ungraceful, swarthy, awkward little 'Jew']; when she first sees him he is in the company of 'ein kleiner, hässlicher Jude' [an ugly little Jew] who she initially thinks must be Lassalle.[16] These phrases suggest that she had absorbed the conventional anti-semitism of her circle, but there is no sense of special vehemence in her feelings. In *The Tragic*

Comedians, however, 'The Jew was to Clotilde as flesh of swine to the Jew' (2, 11), and Meredith devotes several pages to her prejudice. Helene's phrase 'ein kleiner, hässliger Jude', to describe the man she initially mistakes for Lassalle, becomes:

> The [Jew] was distressingly branded with the slum and gutter signs of the Ahasuerus race. Three hats on his head could not have done it more effectively. The vindictive caricatures of the God Pan, executed by priests of the later religion burning to hunt him out of worship in the semblance of the hairy, hoofy, snouty Evil One, were not more loathsome. She sank on a sofa. That the man? Oh! Jew, and fifty times over Jew! nothing but Jew! (3, 19)

(A sense that the phrase 'hairy, hoofy, snouty Evil One' escapes the boundaries of analogy in which it is ostensibly set is confirmed by the direct use of the phrase 'Satyr-snouty master' to express Victor Radnor's anti-Semitism in *One of Our Conquerors*, 1, 6.)

When Alvan's name is first mentioned to Clotilde, 'professing universal knowledge... she was unwilling to betray her ignorance, and she dimpled her cheek, as one who had often heard the thing said to her before' (1, 9). This directly contradicts *Meine Beziehungen* where, when Baron Korff asks Helene if she knows Lassalle, 'Nein! erwiderte ich unbefangen. Wer ist das?' [No! I replied freely. Who is that?][17]

Lassalle's nickname for Helene, 'golden fox', is changed by Meredith to 'gold-crested serpent', with obvious implications. Helene's image for Lassalle, the eagle, is in *The Tragic Comedians* an image for Clotilde's conception of 'the best of men... the strongest, the great eagle of men' (1, 6), which precedes her meeting with Alvan; this undermines the authenticity of her response to him, by implying that she fits him to a preconception.

One of the most obvious judgements against Lassalle/Alvan is that he is puffed up with patriarchal vanity and has no understanding of women. In *The Tragic Comedians* this judgement is articulated by the narrator (7, 83) and by the Baroness, Meredith's version of the Countess von Hatzfeld, the older woman with whom Lassalle had a long association, dating from his youthful legal defence of her against her husband, and whose hostility to the match provoked Helene's vehement hatred (13, 147). Clotilde, however, thinks that he could not believe her letters of renunciation were sincere because 'it would be to suppose him unacquainted with her, ignorant of the nature of women' (11, 122). This is a straightforward robbery from Helene. When Lassalle writes to the Countess, 'Helene passt als Persönlichkeit so absolut zu mir, wie ich nie eine passende zu finden geglaubt hätte!' ['Helene matches me more perfectly in personality than I had ever believed possible!'] she comments, 'Wie schlecht kannte dieser geniale Mann ein kleinliches Frauenherz!!!' [How poorly this man of genius knew a petty woman-heart!!!][18]

The foregoing is mostly documentation of the relationship between *The Tragic Comedians* and *Meine Beziehungen*. What sense can we make of this relationship and, in particular, how can Bakhtin help us to make sense of it? Bakhtin was intensely hostile to what he called 'The false tendency toward reducing everything to a single consciousness, toward dissolving it in the other's consciousness.'[19] A form of this can be seen in the comments of critics cited above: Helene von Racowitza's consciousness is obliterated in Meredith's, becomes merely an object of his. For Bakhtin, on the contrary:

> The event of the life of the text, that is, its true essence, always develops *on the boundary between two consciousnesses, two subjects*.
> ... This is the meeting of two texts – of the ready-made and the reactive text being created – and, consequently, the meeting of two subjects and two authors.[20]

Allowing Racowitza's text to answer back is to focus on this boundary or meeting, rather than on *The Tragic Comedians* exclusively as master-text. What is at issue is not the truth about Helene's relations with Lassalle, which is unknowable, but the meaning of the meeting between the two consciousnesses.

It is enlightening to consider the novel's position in Meredith's *oeuvre*. It was written between his two most sympathetic portrayals of women struggling for independence: *The Egoist* and *Diana of the Crossways* (*DC*). The lovers of both these women feel betrayed by them, in Diana's case with some reason. They are also sometimes seen by the men in their lives as archetypally feminine. To Dacier Diana is 'instructive in an unprofitable department of knowledge – the tricks of the sex' (*DC*, 35, 399); and even Vernon Whitford thinks of Clara in terms of 'her whims, variations, inconsistencies, wiles' (*E*, 30, 365).

Alvan sees Clotilde in a similar way – 'She had innumerable tricks of indication in these shifty pretty ways of hers, and was full of varying speech to the cunning reader of her' (15, 167) – and in this, at least, Meredith is justified by Helene's account of herself:

> 'Denn' fügte ich hinzu, 'verlangen Sie Alles von mir – nur keine Willensstärke, keine Energie. Bedenken Sie, dass ich *la femme, la plus femme de l'univers* bin, d.h. unberechenbar, *capricieuse – et fille!*'
> 'For,' I added, 'ask anything of me except firmness of will and energy. Remember that I am *la femme la plus femme de l'univers*, that is, unreliable and capricious.'[21]

It is of course a crucial difference between Helene and Meredith's heroines that she accepts and at times appears to relish this identity, though we should remember that it is precisely her lack of 'Willensstärke' for which she condemns herself in her conclusion. Lassalle, correspondingly, appears throughout Racowitza's text as a monster of preening, dominating male vanity: even less than Nevil Beauchamp's does his radicalism touch matters of gender. At times he even sounds like Sir Willoughby Patterne, as when Helene asks him to tell her about his meeting with Bismarck:

> Dieses Kind! 's ist unerhört! mit diesen kleinen Fingern, – denn Du weisst doch, dass es dumm ist, solche kleine Finger zu haben, – mit diesen Elfentatzen greift es frech in meine werthvollsten Geheimnisse, die ich wie Edelsteine im Sicherheitskästchen meines Herzens bewahre, – kramt darin herum, behandelt die koftbaren Juwelen als ihr unbestreitbares Eigenthum, verstreut einige davon, als wäre es Spreu, und verlangt dann die allertheuesten für sich, als Tand, als Schmuck in's Haar! Aber diese naive Frechheit, – ich liebe sie! und darum sollst Du haben, was Du, nichts Schlimmes ahnend, verlangst.

> [This child! – did one ever hear the like? With these little fingers (for you know it is ridiculous to have such little fingers!), with these little elfin paws, she turns over my most precious secrets, that I keep like costly gems in the secret treasury of my heart. She rummages about there, treats these priceless jewels as if they were her own possessions, strews a few of them about as if they were chaff, and then demands the best of all for herself, as

an ornament for her hair! But I adore this naive impudence! Though you had no idea what you were asking for, you shall have it.][22]

Meredith tones this down considerably, reducing the corresponding portion of Alvan's speech to 'Would this ambitious little head know everything?' (7, 79) but the narrator of *The Tragic Comedians* is direct about this aspect of Alvan's character: 'He would have stared like any Philistine at the tale of [women's] capacity to advance to a likeness unto men in their fight with the world' (7, 84). This narrator's final opinion of Alvan is of course much more favourable than the *Egoist* narrator's of Willoughby: there is some passionate and convincing writing about his political convictions and one of *The Tragic Comedians*'s points of superiority to *Meine Beziehungen* is that it gives a much more complete image of its hero. However, although more favourable, this narrator is not *closer* to the character. I have pointed out that the narrator of *The Egoist* is explicitly male and that the relation of his discourse to Willoughby's varies subtly, including important elements of implication of himself as a male with the character's feelings. The narrator of *The Tragic Comedians* is ungendered and more securely extradiegetic. Gillian Beer writes that in this novel 'Meredith never uses general comments as a shield for himself against portraying the painful subtleties of emotion and action', but only in the sense that 'The general is used to remind the reader that he too is involved.'[23] There are no sentences in *The Tragic Comedians* like 'Women have us back to the conditions of primitive man, or they shoot us higher than the topmost star' (*E*, 23, 276). This narrator's comments are more typified by, 'Men and women alike, who renounce their own individuality by cowering thus abjectly under some other before the storm, are in reality abjuring their idea of that other' (8, 93).

Alvan is described as 'not heroic, but hugely man', a 'giant' in whom are 'various giants to be slain' (9, 112). In his next novel Meredith imagines another 'hugely masculine' character, Tom Redworth, but he is one who has slain his giants (*DC*, 42, 473). Alvan is Meredith's only portrayal of unregenerate masculinity towards whom there is a strong balance of authorial sympathy, and his relationship with Clotilde is, in terms of gender characteristics, the most polarized in Meredith's novels. It is for such a subject that he installs his most 'choric', editorializing, ungendered narrator.

This is one distancing device. Is the concept of the 'tragic comedian' itself another? This phrase is applied to both the main protagonists, but it is most elaborately defined in relation to Alvan:

> He was neither fool nor madman, nor man to be adored: his last temptation caught him in the season before he had subdued his blood, and amid the multitudinously simple of this world, stamped him a tragic comedian; that is, a grand pretender, a self-deceiver, one of the lividly ludicrous, whom we cannot laugh at, but must contemplate, to distinguish where their character strikes the note of discord with life; for otherwise, in the reflection of their history, life will seem a thing demoniacally inclined by fits to antic and dive into gulfs. (19, 199–200)

If such a character is a Tragic Comedian, what of Othello, Antony, Coriolanus? All of these have something of the 'lividly ludicrous' about them, but all are tragic. Othello is a particularly pertinent comparison. Gillian Beer has remarked that 'Both heroes are middle-aged men of action, from outside the society of the woman they love, whose public life is made meaningless by the failure of their love.'[24] There are more precise textual parallels. The following is strongly reminiscent of a familiar way of regarding Othello:

> He loved like the desert-bred Eastern, as though his blood had never ceased to be steeped in its fountain Orient; loved barbarously, but with a compelling resolve to control his blood and act and be the civilized man, sober by virtue of his lady's generous aid. (16, 173)

When kicking himself for letting Clotilde go Alvan calls himself, among other 'vulgar epithets', 'dolt' (9, 110), the word that Emilia flings at Othello (V.ii.164); and in his enraged letter of challenge he calls Clotilde, according to his friend von Tresten, 'the name she deserves' (17, 182). This name is never specified, but is obviously 'whore', the word with which Othello brands Desdemona (IV. ii. 87).[25] If Othello qualifies as a tragic hero, so does Lassalle. The marking of him as a 'tragic comedian' is a sign of the authorial relation to this potentially tragic subject which is, I suggest, one of unease: a fear that, for the 'hugely man' with whom he sympathizes, life may indeed be 'a thing demoniacally inclined by fits to antic and dive into gulfs'.[26]

In *The Egoist* Clara 'betrays' a monster of vanity in whom gender lines up ideologically with class, nationality and economic power. Willoughby is a figure otherwise so alien to the authorial consciousness that Meredith can afford a narrator who implicates himself in the character's sexuality. In *Diana of the Crossways* the heroine really does betray her lover, Dacier, who is moreover a more substantial and sympathetic, though more insipid, character than Willoughby. But Dacier is also cold and self-serving; he is emphatically not 'hugely man': this epithet, as we have seen, is reserved for the rational and self-controlled hero, Redworth, who finally wins the heroine. There is nothing even faintly tragic about any of these male protagonists: much to chasten, but nothing to terrify the masculine consciousness.

Moreover, these supposed and actual betrayals are the actions of women in the throes of resisting the sexual, moral and economic dominance of men. Of neither of them would Meredith have written this:

> Men and women alike, who renounce their own individuality by cowering thus abjectly under some other before the storm, are in reality abjuring their idea of that other, and offering themselves up to the genius of Power in whatsoever direction it may chance to be manifested, in whatsoever person. We no sooner shut our eyes than we consent to be prey, we lose the soul of election.
>
> Mark her as she proceeds. For should her hero fail, and she be suffering through his failure and her reliance on him, the blindness of it will seem to her to have been an infinite virtue, anything but her deplorable weakness crouching beneath his show of superhuman strength. (8, 93)

This is the narrator's judgement of Clotilde when, with fatal vanity, Alvan hands her back to her parents, a scene which follows Helene's narrative with exceptional fidelity. It is an inhumanly harsh judgement, and the accompanying prediction, as it applies to Helene, is, as we have seen, a calumny.

Nor would we find, in *The Egoist* or *Diana*, a sentence such as, 'But there was...much more in Alvan than any faint-hearted thing, seeing however keenly, could see' (8, 94). The narrator has unqualified possession of what Bakhtin calls 'transgredience'[27] over the character: a vision that encompasses and exceeds hers.

A woman whose femininity takes the conventional form of weak will and submissiveness fails to remain true to a man whose vanity and politically constructive energy alike make him 'hugely man'. With such a subject, it seems, Meredith has to construct distancing devices: the impersonal narrator, the concept of the 'tragic comedian' and, most seriously, an exaggeration of the woman's guilt. The failure to present a fair or even accurate assessment of Helene's conduct marks, I suggest, the limits of Meredith's feminism.

A further light is cast on this by his treatment of the Baroness, his version of the Countess von Hatzfeld. The Countess does not figure in person in *Meine Beziehungen*. In *The Tragic Comedians* the Baroness plays an important role as commentator on the final stages of the story. She is, unlike Clotilde, genuinely and intelligently interested in and committed to Alvan's political activities, and an authentically liberated woman. She enjoys the respect and obviously not sexually motivated devotion of Alvan's severe friend von Tresten, who despises Clotilde. Meredith describes her ungallantly as 'one of those persons who, after a probationary term in the character of woman, have become men' (13, 145), despite which she is portrayed in an unreservedly favourable light. She is, in short, the antithesis of Clotilde. Her sympathetic and convincing portrayal is to Meredith's credit as a feminist, but such a woman presents no threat to the author who identifies with that which is 'hugely man' in his male characters. The malicious way in which Helene writes about the Countess may partly explain Meredith's hostility. Here is her account of what passed between her and Lassalle when he showed her the Countess's photograph:

'Nun weisst Du, Eure Kassetten-Affaire ist lange her, – so lange, dass ich noch gar nicht auf der Welt war, – damit will ich Dich entschuldigen; den schön ist Deine Gräfin, weiss Gott, nicht.' – Er lachte, gab mir Recht, meinte aber, vor zwanzig Jahren sei sie es noch gewesen: 'sie ist ja sehr alt, denke, sie ist 1805 geboren.' – 'Dann hätte sie sich lieber in Napoleon I verlieben sollen!'

['Now you know, your Cassette Affair was long ago, so long that I was barely in the world, – so I will forgive you it; for, God knows, your Countess isn't beautiful.' – He laughed, said I was right, but that she still had been twenty years ago: 'she is so old, think, she was born in 1805'. – 'Then she should rather have fallen in love with Napoleon I!'][28]

Meredith's version of this scene is notably toned down: Clotilde's comment on the Baroness's appearance is conveyed merely by the drooping of her eyelids and far from laughing Alvan is described as 'colouring' and 'writhing' (7, 70–1). This might be construed as Meredith's implied rebuke for Helene's bad taste in describing herself and Lassalle joking together at the Countess's expense.

The story told in *Meine Beziehungen* is one of operatic extravagance. It is also one that is full of dialogic potential, being essentially a story of failed communication, of messages that mistake their addressees and receivers who misinterpret the intentions of the senders. I have argued that Meredith's narrator largely suppresses dialogue in the Bakhtinian sense, but the novel is at its best on the occasions when it does exploit the dialogic potential of its material. For example, Meredith follows Racowitza when Clotilde, returning Alvan's letters and gifts, appends the word 'Child', 'the gentlest title he had bestowed on her, trusting to the pathos of the world 'child' to tell him that she was enforced and still true' (12, 136). Helene did not know how Lassalle received this message; she only knew that he could not have understood it. Meredith's Alvan interprets it not as the desperate hint of someone whose speech is constrained, but as a free action, and as such it can only seem 'senselessly malign, perhaps flippant, as she could be, he knew' (13, 145).

An even more disastrously misguided message is the letter that Helene wrote, with Lassalle's approval, to the Countess, which drew a reply – much later, when Helene was in captivity and reduced to reliance on the Countess's good will as her final hope – coldly advising her to give up the relationship. Racowitza gives the texts of both these letters and expresses her outrage at such a reply to her 'liebevollen, töchterlichen' [loving, daughterly] message.[29] Meredith summarizes both letters and his judgement of Helene/Clotilde's is, on this occasion, more perceptive than her own:

> To a frigid eye it read as more hypocritical than it really was; for supposing it had to be written, the language of the natural impulse called up to write it was necessarily in request, and that language is easily overdone, so as to be discordant with the situation, while it is, as the writer feels, a fairly true and well-formed expression of the pretty impulse. But wiser is it always that the star in the ascendant should not address the

one waning. Hardly can a word be uttered without grossly wounding. She would not do it to a younger rival; the letter strikes on the recipient's age! She babbles of a friendship: she plays at childish ninny! The display of her ingenuous happiness causes feminine nature's bosom to rise in surges. The declarations of her devotedness to the man waken comparisons with a deeper, a longer-tried suffering. Actually the letter of the rising star assumes personal feeling to have died out of the abandoned luminary, and personal feeling is chafed to its acutest edge by the perusal; contempt also of one who can stupidly simulate such innocence, is roused. (7, 83)

Both thematically and stylistically, in the devastating effect with which it moves between the language and consciousness of the writer and the recipient, this passage is an excellent illustration of Meredith's dialogic intelligence.

On one occasion Meredith had to negotiate between two contradictory accounts of the same incident: a formal interview between Helene, Lassalle's friend Rüstow (Meredith's von Tresten) and the neutral lawyer Dr Hänle (Störchel), at which she was asked if she would meet Lassalle, and she refused. J.M. Ludlow gives an account of this meeting which is based on 'a formal minute of the conversation' drawn up by Hänle shortly afterwards.[30] Given Meredith's generally tendentious treatment of Helene's narrative,[31] one might expect him to adopt this apparently impartial account as the authorized truth. In fact the use he makes of it is much more subtle and interesting. The Ludlow version is the first to be given in Meredith's text, but it is narrated by means of a dialogue between von Tresten and the Baroness:

'How has it gone?' she said.
He replied: 'As I told you. I fancied I gauged the hussy pretty closely.'
'She will not see him?'
'Not she.... It might have been foreseen by everybody concerned in the affair. The girl does not care for him one corner of an eye! She stood up before us cool as at a dancing-lesson, swore she had never committed herself to an oath to him, sneered at him. She positively sneered. Her manner to me assures me without question that if he had stood in my place she would have insulted him.'...

> 'Was she really insolent?'...
> 'She spoke of his vanity....'
> 'Proceed.'
> 'It was more her manner to me, as the one of the two appearing as his friend. She was tolerably civil to Störchel.... she addressed him rather eagerly before we turned on our heels, to tell him she would write to *him*, and let him have her reply in a letter. He will get some coquettish rigmarole.' (17, 179–81)

The details of this are all derived from Ludlow and therefore, ultimately, from Hänle's 'formal minute'. But Meredith desists from giving it as the authorized version, or even telling it via the impartial Störchel. Tresten is Alvan's friend, but not the friend of his love for Clotilde. He is the friend of Alvan's political mission (Rüstow was a former Garibaldino) and of the Baroness. These two have already had one conversation about Clotilde, in the same malevolent tone as this one. The 'formal minute' account of the meeting is, then, narrated through the most prejudiced medium possible, and its effect significantly changed.

Racowitza's version of the meeting is given shortly afterwards, and narrated through Clotilde's retrospective interior monologue. An important factor is that she had earlier been introduced by her father to von Tresten as 'of neither party', but as having 'a profound reverence for the baroness' and convinced of 'the downright impossibility of the marriage' (12, 139–40). Not surprisingly Clotilde considers him 'false' and reacts coldly to him on this first occasion. This fuels his prejudice against her and makes any sympathetic communication between them impossible when he is presented to her a second time in the role of Alvan's friend:

> Two things had helped her to carry out her engagement to submit in this final instance of dutifulness: one was the sight of that hateful rigid face and glacier eye of Tresten; the other was the loophole she left for subsequent insurgency by engaging to write to Count Hollinger's envoy, Dr Störchel.... Here was the friend she required, the external aid, the fresh evasion, the link with Alvan!... She could open her heart to Alvan's true friend – his only true friend. He would instantly discern her unhappy plight. In the presence of his associate she could explain nothing, do nothing but what she had done. He had *frozen* her. She had good reason to know that man for her enemy. (18, 185–6)

The letter to Dr Störchel is written but never received, or even sent. The mild lawyer leaves Geneva early, appalled by Alvan's violent reaction to his report of the interview, and before the letter leaves Clotilde's hands Marko arrives with the news of the challenge. Meredith does not comment on the compatibility or otherwise of these reflections with Tresten's account, and no comment is necessary. Under such a repulsion as she feels, and with the 'loophole' of the letter to Störchel available, she would be likely to behave in a manner compatible with Tresten's account, the effect of which she would not notice or recollect, and which his account would be likely to exaggerate to the point of seeming contradiction.

Meredith's narrative here is penetratively sympathetic, but he does not spare Clotilde. His description of her planned letter to Störchel as a 'loophole' is not the first time that Meredith anticipated this important Bakhtinian concept: 'the retention for oneself of the possibility for altering the ultimate, final meaning of one's own words'.[32] He both used the word and extensively illustrated the concept in *Sandra Belloni*, where an addiction to loopholes is one of the symptoms of the sentimentalism of the Pole family (see Chapter 2, pp. 62 ff). In Clotilde's case the sentimentalism is overt in her grotesque misreading of Störchel, but also more deeply implicit in her seizing on the proposed letter as a means both of deferring the decisive action and of gratifying her revulsion from Tresten. The 'loophole' is a key to her behaviour throughout the period of her captivity, when she formally complies with her parents' demands that she renounce Lassalle, but hopes that it will be obvious from the style or even the handwriting of her notes that they are enforced. Her signature 'Child' when she returns the letters and gifts to Alvan is a notable example.

But Clotilde's loopholes all fail her, and of course it would have been better if she (or Helene) had been braver and stronger. But, unlike the Pole family, she has some excuse for resorting to this device, which is not always sentimental, but may be a necessary resource under extreme pressure: what else but a 'loophole' was the notorious 'equivocation' taught by the Jesuits as a means for Catholics to deceive without lying under torture in the Elizabethan period?

Clotilde is not under torture, but nor is she entirely free, and Meredith's judgement in handling this episode is very fine indeed. If the whole novel had been written in this spirit it would have been a masterpiece. Most commentators have thought it less than that, and various explanations have been offered, ranging from Meredith's poor health to the mere fact of being constrained by a pre-existent narrative. These factors, however, do not account for Meredith's excessive aversion to Helene, the relentlessly unfavourable editorializing and, despite his denial of 'anything invented', his systematic distortion of her narrative. The contrast with his attitudes to the heroines of *The Egoist* and *Diana of the Crossways*, given the parallels between the stories, suggests that *Meine Beziehungen* touched on a weak point of Meredith's feminist sympathies: the dilemma, precisely, of the 'weak' woman whose seductive submission to the 'hugely man' hero masks the capacity to fail him under pressure. Meredith can see – no one better – that the hero invites this failure by encouraging and even insisting on the submission, and most critics have rightly commented that the portrayal of Alvan is well balanced, but for Clotilde even the novel's last words carry an ugly sneer: 'as we are in her debt for some instruction, she may now be suffered to go'.

In 'The Idea of Comedy' Meredith contrasts Congreve's Millamant and Molière's Célimène to 'the pretty idiot, the passive beauty, the adorable bundle of caprices, very feminine, very sympathetic, of romantic and sentimental fiction' and comments that:

> The heroines of Comedy are like women of the world, not necessarily heartless for being clear-sighted....Comedy is an exhibition of their battle with men, and that of men with them: and as the two, however divergent, both look on one object, namely, Life, the gradual similarity of their impressions must bring them to some resemblance. ('IC', 14–15)

Meredith's heroines are not exactly like Millamant and Célimène – as we have seen, the men who love them are capable of seeing them as the opposite stereotype – but, by a combination of intelligence and courage, they draw towards versions of the ideal union suggested here. Helene von Racowitza was, on the evidence, more like a Meredith heroine than either of the extremes posited in the essay, but her story, partly but not entirely by her fault, pointed grimly in the opposite direction: to the life 'demoniacally inclined by fits to antic and dive into gulfs' that threatens when men and women pull apart to their 'hugely' masculine and feminine extremes. It seems that Meredith could not forgive her for that.

7
Diana of the Crossways

Like *The Tragic Comedians* (*TC*), *Diana of the Crossways* draws heavily on the life-story of a real woman of the nineteenth century, but its relationship to its source is very different. In the earlier novel the historical persons are not merely models for the characters: these remain 'real people' who 'belong to history' and 'breathed a stouter air than fiction's' (*TC*, 1–2). The novel offers an alternative analysis and evaluation to that of the real-life protagonist Helene von Racowitza, but it remains, despite the trappings of fiction, committed to those real-life events. *Diana of the Crossways*, by contrast, is prefaced by a statement that its central incident is based on a 'calumny' and that it is to be 'read as a fiction'.

Admittedly this statement appeared only in later editions, at the request of the family of Diana's real-life model.[1] However, it does not violate the spirit of the novel's relationship to its source. On the contrary, the fact that its central incident is based on what Meredith described (if only retrospectively) as a 'calumny' is fundamental to that relationship.

The main sources of the story are two episodes in the life of Mrs Caroline Norton, the witty and beautiful granddaughter of Sheridan. Mrs Norton's husband took a legal action against Lord Melbourne, the Prime Minister, alleging adultery with his wife. Later she became intimate with, and was presumed to be the lover of, Sidney Herbert, a young Cabinet Minister and confidant of Peel. When the story that the Cabinet had agreed to repeal the Corn Laws was leaked to *The Times*, resulting in the resignation of the Government, Mrs Norton was rumoured to have betrayed Herbert's confidence. As a result of her marital experience she became a notable pamphleteer for women's rights, and was largely responsible for the Infant Custody Act of 1838 and some clauses in the Marriage Act of 1857.

Although Penny Boumelha, in the best feminist critique of the novel, rightly comments that the 'story and figure of Diana ... mark the historic shift within English culture, at this period, in the position of at least middle-class women, from the apparently 'private' sphere of the home and domesticity to the public domain of politics',[2] Meredith omits Mrs Norton's legitimate political activity from the story of Diana and focuses, as his central incident, on the 'calumny' of the press-leak. Even before the publication of the novel this story was never more than a scandalous rumour, and in 1895 Henry Reeve, who had been on the staff of *The Times* in 1845, wrote in the *Edinburgh Review* that the information had been given to Delane openly by Lord Aberdeen, Peel's Foreign Secretary.

Given the availability of other versions of the story, and Mrs Norton's authentic political activity, it is provoking that a writer of feminist sympathies should choose to base his novel on what is unmistakably a misogynistic anecdote. It is impossible not to believe that in the forty mid-Victorian years between its first appearance and Meredith's use of it, it was frequently repeated with the explicit statement of or implicit appeal to the moral bitterly drawn by Percy Dacier, Meredith's fictional young Minister: 'the act of folly – the trusting a secret to a woman' (35, 391).[3]

This anecdote is one of the most deeply buried of the numerous other texts that Meredith habitually incorporates, by citation or parody, into his novels. It is important to recognize it as 'another text' in order to avoid the fruitless arguments, that have raged ever since the novel's publication, about the degree of Diana's culpability, the justice of her creator's apparent valuation of her, and whether he cheated by not giving us a direct narration of his heroine's crime. The relationship of Meredith's text to this anecdote is, I will argue, a variant of a kind of discourse that Bakhtin theorized as 'hidden polemic':

> In a hidden polemic the author's discourse is directed toward its own referential object, as is any other discourse, but at the same time every statement about the object is constructed in such a way that, apart from its referential meaning, a polemical blow is struck at the other's discourse on the same theme, at the other's statement about the same object. A word, directed toward its referential object, clashes with another's word within the very object itself. The other's discourse is not itself reproduced, it is merely implied, but the entire structure of speech would be completely different if there were not this reaction to another person's implied words.[4]

Diana's relationship with Dacier, culminating and ending with her betrayal of his secret, occupies approximately the central half of the novel. This may not be one of the more extreme examples of Meredith's 'disturbing angularity of form, persistently dislocating novelistic practice'[5] (compare *Rhoda Fleming*, whose eponymous heroine is absent from the corresponding portion), but it is a case of subtle resistance to the pull of generic expectation. Judging by the comedic resolution that the author permits ultimately (and somewhat grudgingly) to prevail, with the marriage of Diana to Redworth, her involvement with Dacier is a diversion. Redworth is, from the start, the favoured suitor of the narrator and of the structurally and thematically important character Emma Dunstane, Diana's intimate friend. As a diversion from the course of true love the Dacier episode is disproportionately long, given that the coolly objective and quietly ironic portrayal of Dacier himself arouses in the reader neither a strong desire for nor aversion from his union with Diana.

But of course we receive sufficient instructions from the narrator to know that this is not the way to read the novel. The all-composing power of the comedic resolution is parodied when he pretends that his story 'properly closed on the marriage of the heroine Constance and her young Minister of State', and that his remaining readers are 'yet wakeful eccentrics interested in such a person as Diana, to the extent of remaining attentive till the curtain falls' (39, 440–1).

To the 'yet wakeful eccentrics' who are Meredith's implied readers the narrative sequence that culminates in the betrayal of the secret is not a diversion but the heart of the novel. Here the protagonist of the Norton anecdote (who is not the historical Mrs Norton but the 'woman' of the misogynistic proverbs that belong with it) is as it were materialized: the moment of betrayal becomes, not the occasion for a universal cliché, but the focal point of a number of specific pressures in the life of an exposed woman in fashionable London society in the 1840s. As Penny Boumelha says, 'Diana's "betrayal" occurs in the narrative context of... the interrogation of the trope by which "a woman", *this* woman, comes to stand for "woman".'[6]

These can be briefly indicated in plot summary. As a beautiful and precocious teenaged girl, without parents or a settled home, passing from one country-house visit to another, Diana Merrion is subjected to the shock of sexual harassment, most fatally by the husband of her best friend, Sir Lukin Dunstane. Deprived, as she thus feels herself to be, of the protection of her friend's home, she panics and marries the conventional and mean-spirited Augustus Warwick. The marriage is doomed from the start, and a separation is precipitated by Warwick's jealousy of her platonic intimacy with Lord Dannisburgh. The husband loses his court case but the whiff of scandal clings to Diana and, not divorced, she is threatened by demands that she return to him. Already a celebrated wit, she turns to writing for money and becomes a successful novelist and intellectual hostess, giving nightly entertainments to writers, politicians and journalists. Her intimacy with Dacier is cautious and slow-developing, but at one point she agrees to elope with him, only to be called to the bedside of her desperately ill friend. They draw back from this commitment, but their intimacy grows until it entails, once again, the sacrifice of Diana's 'good name'. Increasingly, a motive for her entertainment is to provide Dacier with an influential circle of friends. On the night when Dacier reveals the secret to her she is in debt, unable to write, and piqued because, after her absence nursing Emma, the editor Tonans tells her she has lost touch with public events. When he has told her the news Dacier attempts to exploit her gratitude for his confidence by sexually accosting her. She repels him, but is aroused. This is retrospectively described as a 'state of shivering abjection' (38, 426).

A more obviously disruptive and typically Meredithian instance of narrative unconventionality is the manner in which the betrayal is narrated. The text does not witness the transaction between Diana and Tonans but waits in the ante-room of his office with her maid, Danvers. The story-time of the transaction is covered by Danvers's reflections on the masculine atmosphere of the newspaper office:

> This was not a place for compliments. Men passed her, hither and yonder, cursorily noticing the presence of a woman. She lost, very strangely to her, the sense of her sex and became an object – a disregarded object. Things of more importance were about. Her feminine self-esteem was troubled; all idea of attractiveness expired. Here was manifestly a spot where women had dropped from the secondary to the cancelled stage of their extraordinary career in a world either blowing them aloft like soap-bubbles or quietly shelving them as supernumeraries. (32, 374)

There is in this passage a mixture of overt and hidden polemic. The overt polemic requires little comment, except that it derives an added piquancy from the use of Danvers as focalizer. Elsewhere in the novel Danvers is portrayed in the manner Meredith customarily uses with servants and (with the partial exception of *Rhoda Fleming*) lower-class characters generally: a kind of arch condescension. Here there is no ironic angle between her perceptions and the narrator's. What she feels (it is implied) is what any woman – indeed, what a particularly acute and sensitive woman – would feel in this environment. It is what we can imagine Diana feeling,[7] except that she is not available to feel it, being distracted by the fortuitous 'importance' of the news she has for Tonans. Our attention is shifting to the hidden polemic, which has to do with the very substitution of this passage for Diana's encounter with Tonans. Instead of witnessing the 'woman' of the anecdote committing her crime, we are made to feel the contempt for women in the heart of the masculine establishment, where men are unconcerned with sexual conquest or social graces, and a woman is not just an object but a 'disregarded object'. In other words, as usual, Meredith's narrative indirection is itself polemical, implicitly rebuffing those readers who would judge Diana's action without reference to her position in society.

This is not to say that we are asked to judge Diana a creature without responsibility, a passive victim of circumstances. My plot summary suggests that vanity is an element in her motivation, and one of the narrator's most authorial utterances insists on the necessarily guilty character of the 'flecked heroine of Reality' in contrast to the 'true heroine of Romance', Constance Asper: 'not always the same; not impeccable; not an ignorant-innocent, nor a guileless' (35, 399). A certain unease in the role of authoritative commentator is perhaps revealed by Meredith's use of negatives to characterize Diana. Appropriately, the case is more effectively put in dialogue, between Diana and Emma:

> 'If I took it honestly, I should be dumb, soon dust. The moment we begin to speak, the guilty creature is running for cover. She could not otherwise exist. I am sensible of evasion when I open my lips.'
> 'But Tony [Emma's pet name for Diana] has told me all'.
> 'I think I have. But if you excuse my conduct, I am certain I have not.'

'Dear girl, accounting for it is not the same as excusing.'
'Who can account for it! I was caught in a whirl.' (38, 428)

The dialogue profoundly implies that neither the protagonist nor the sympathetically involved observer can tell the truth, because of the limitations of their subject-positions. But the angle between them, as it were, gestures towards it. The impossibility of sincerity, in the sense of an exact correspondence between words and subjective experience, is a recurrent thought in Meredith, which I shall be further examining later in this chapter.

But for Dacier, the man who has apparently loved and understood Diana, her crime is unforgivable, and he punishes her in the most effective way, by immediately marrying her antithesis, the 'true heroine of Romance', Constance Asper. To understand this apparent paradox we have to trace one of Meredith's most subtle exercises in the development of character through double-voiced discourse. Shortly after the introduction of Dacier into the novel, we read of his attitude to Constance, to whom he is 'half engaged':

> Her transparency displayed to him all the common virtues, and a serene possession of the inestimable and eminent one outweighing all; but charm, wit, ardour, intercommunicative quickness, and kindling beauty, airy grace, were qualities that a man, it seemed, had to look for in women spotted by a doubt of their having the chief and priceless. (16, 178)

Reading this sentence is a typically dynamic experience. It is, of course, focalized through Dacier, and the first clause suggests a matter-of-fact disenchantment with Constance that runs parallel to the narrator's valuation, and sufficiently explains his reluctance to commit himself to this highly advantageous marriage. With the second clause, however, a gap seems to open up between character and narrator. It is not at this stage certain what the 'inestimable and eminent one outweighing all' is, and so the ideological slant of the passage is uncertain, but this exaggerated emphasis on a single virtue is incompatible with the narrator's values, on the evidence so far. This suspicion that the first two clauses are double-voiced is confirmed by the rest of the sentence, where it is implied that this virtue is the one that Diana reputedly lacks. In the course of the dialogized sentence the reader can recognize Diana by the list of her attributes, deduce that the unnamed virtue is 'purity', establish that Constance is the antithesis of Diana (an important thematic strain), that Dacier is influenced by the conventional male valuation of purity, that the narrator is at an ironic distance from him in this respect, and that his attraction to Diana will be a cause not only of emotional but also of ideological conflict.[8]

That passage occurs when Dacier's attraction to Diana is incipient. The next is a postscript to the episode in which he follows her to France to make his first proposition, which she kindly but firmly rejects:

> They parted as the plainest of sincere good friends, each at heart respecting the other for the repression of that which their hearts craved; any word of which might have carried them headlong, bound together on a Mazeppa-race, with scandal for the hounding wolves, and social ruin for the rocks and torrents.[9]
>
> Dacier was the thankfuller, the most admiring of the two; at the same time the least satisfied. He saw the abyss she had aided him in escaping; and it was refreshful to look abroad after his desperate impulse. Prominent as he stood before the world, he could not think without a shudder of behaving like a young frenetic of the passion. Those whose aim is at the leadership of the English people know, that however truly based the charges of hypocrisy, soundness of moral fibre runs through the country and is the national integrity, which may condone old sins for present service, but will not have present sins to flout it. He was in tune with the English character. (22, 255)

The first paragraph speaks identically of Diana and Dacier, so it may be taken as the direct voice of the narrator, who pays Dacier the compliment of speaking of him literally 'in the same breath' as his heroine. At the beginning of the second paragraph Dacier is distinguished by the greater intensity and conflict of his feelings: a distinction which tends to raise him still higher as a sympathetic protagonist. The complications occur in the final two sentences. Can the statement that 'soundness of moral fibre runs throughout the country' be single-voiced in a novel that represents conventional sexual morality in the figure of Lady Wathin? This assertion is represented as what every aspiring politician 'knows', and as far as the practical consequences are concerned – that a politician cannot afford a flagrant breach of conventional morality – we are not invited to question it; but the politician is also required to 'know' that conventional morality is 'soundness of moral fibre', and the statement in question sounds more like the public utterance of a politician than the language of Meredith's narrator. The double-voicedness is intensified in the final sentence quoted and, like much of the language associated with Dacier, its precise accent waits on the further development of his character.

Three chapters later Dacier has persuaded Diana to elope with him, under various pressures, including a threatened action by her husband to make her return to him. The lovers arrange to meet at the railway station and while waiting for her Dacier reflects on the woman he is risking his career for:

> He was sure of her, sure of her courage. Tony and recreancy could not go together.... She had brains and ardour, she had grace and sweetness, a playful petulancy enlivening our atmosphere, and withal a refinement, a distinction, not to be classed; and justly might she dislike being classed. Her humour was a perennial refreshment, a running well, that caught all the colours of light; her wit studded the heavens of the recollection of her. In his heart he felt that it was a stepping down for the brilliant woman to give him her hand; a condescension and an act of valour. She who always led or prompted when they conversed, had now in her generosity abandoned the lead and herself to him, and she deserved his utmost honouring. (26, 288)

Here, though Dacier perhaps places more emphasis on Diana's more obviously alluring characteristics, and we are reminded that 'his critical taste was rather for the white statue that gave no warmth', it would be an excess of refinement to distinguish his voice from the narrator's. Nevertheless, the two voices are in principle separate because Dacier's is that of a character in a dramatic situation, and subject to change. In this case the irony of his concurrence with the narrator's voice becomes apparent almost immediately, when he has to cope with Diana's failure to turn up:

> The sole consolation he has is to revile the sex. Women! women! Whom have they not made a fool of! His uncle [Lord Dannisburgh] as much as any – and professing to know them. Him also! the man proud of escaping their wiles. 'For this woman...!' he went on saying after he had lost sight of her in her sex's trickeries. The nearest he could get to her was to conceive that the

arrant coquette was now laughing at her utter subjugation and befooling of the man popularly supposed invincible. If it were known of him! The idea of his being a puppet fixed for derision was madly distempering. He had only to ask the affirmative of Constance Asper tomorrow! A vision of his determining to do it, somewhat comforted him. (26, 289–90)

Dacier's reaction to his disappointment is strikingly reminiscent of Sir Willoughby Patterne – the resort to misogynistic cliché, the fear of public ridicule, and the thought of avenging himself by going to another woman all have their equivalents in Willoughby's much more prolonged humiliation at the hands of Clara. The same narratorial technique as in the previous passage – free indirect speech – produces an effect that is, in dialogic terms, at the opposite pole. Here Dacier's language is virtually, in Bakhtin's word, 'objectified':

> Objectified discourse is likewise directed exclusively toward its object, but is at the same time the object of someone else's intention, the author's.... Discourse that has become an object is, as it were, itself unaware of the fact, like the person who goes about his business unaware that he is being watched.[10]

But this is not predictable, like the *voltes-face* of a character such as Parson Adams, nor does it, as with Parson Adams, cancel the truth of his previous utterance. What it does is to dialogize that utterance, separating the character's fragile hold on it from the narrator's more secure one.

The reader, it should be said, does not at this point know why Diana has let Dacier down, only that she has been peremptorily summoned by Redworth. The reader is, therefore, to a limited extent put to the test him/herself. When Dacier discovers that she was diverted by Emma's critical illness his previous opinion of her is not only restored but intensified. It should also be said that, however unworthy, in the light of the truth, his reaction at the station might appear to be, Diana proves to be capable of – in terms of the 'brute facts' by which Dacier's rejection of her is 'justified' (35, 392) – a much more serious betrayal than the failure to keep an assignation. His reaction here – the resort to misogyny and the thought of turning to Constance – proves to be a rehearsal for that greater trial of his loyalty.

The effect of the 'hybrid' discourse associated with Dacier is that the character is open, his development not predictable. He shares something of the freedom of the author/narrator's discourse, and the 'dialogue' in the passages I have been discussing could be described as a struggle between this and the more 'objectified' discourse associated with his class, gender, political ambition and temperamental affinity with Constance Asper. His development is not predictable in the text, but it is inevitable in terms of the novel's hidden polemic with its source anecdote: he becomes, in effect, the bearer of the anecdote, the man whose life is an embodiment of its ideological meaning. The result, for Dacier, is a catastrophic decline into objectified discourse – he becomes a 'word on display':[11]

> The angelical beauty of a virgin mind and person captivated him, by contrast. His natural taste was to admire it, shunning the lures and tangles of the women on high seas, notably the married; who, by the way, contrive to ensnare us through wonderment at a cleverness caught from their traffic with the masculine world: often – if we did but know! – a parrot-repetition of the last male visitor's remarks. But that which the fair maiden speaks, though it may be simple, is her own.
>
> She too is her own: or vowed but to one. She is on all sides impressive in purity. The world worships her as its perfect pearl: and we are brought refreshfully to acknowledge that the world is right. (35, 394)

Here the narrator's discourse is confined to the words spoken *about* Dacier. The free direct discourse is entirely objectified: the intentions of the character and the narrator are opposite. The content of the passage is particularly interesting, because it is *about* dialogism. We have seen that, as a 'brute fact', it is true that Diana borrows the words of the men she gathers around her: on one occasion she repeats the words of 'the last male visitor' Redworth, about the Corn Laws, for Dacier's benefit (29, 342). Such assimilation is a mark of her participation ('traffic', which in Dacier's use has connotations of prostitution) in the masculine world of ideas and affairs. The 'simple' but 'her own' word of Constance, on the other hand, is the mark of her exclusion from any world in which ideas are shared and exchanged: to that world she is, as Danvers felt in the newpaper office, 'cancelled'.

Dacier shrank into objectified discourse once before, when he was disappointed at the railway station, and recovered. This time, however, there is no way back. He sinks into the hell of a full-scale objectified parody. Constance shows him a sketch she has made of his house:

'The look of the place pleases you?'
'Oh! yes; the pines behind it; the sweet little village church; even the appearance of the rustics; – it is all impressively old English. I suppose you are very seldom there?'
'Does it look like a home to you?'
'No place more!'
'I feel the loneliness.'
'Where I live I feel no loneliness!'
'You have heavenly messengers near you.'
'They do not always come.'
'Would you consent to make the place less lonely to me?'
Her bosom rose. In deference to her maidenly understanding, she gazed inquiringly.
'If you love it!' said he.
'The place?' she said, looking soft at the possessor.
'Constance!'
'Is it true?'
'As you yourself. Could it be other than true? This hand is mine?'
'Oh! Percy.' (35, 397)

When Meredith describes Constance as 'the true heroine of Romance' he is not so much criticizing her character as acknowledging that she is a representation of a literary image. On her infrequent appearances in the novel she is entirely consistent with this image, inhabiting, as it were, the enclave of another novel within this one. By participating in this dialogue Dacier enters this other novel, never to return.

I have described Dacier's retreat into objectified discourse as 'catastrophic' for the character. Is it also catastrophic for the novel? David Howard memorably described Meredith as 'the most irritating novelist of the nineteenth century'.[12] Irritated readers will find grosser examples than Dacier's disappearance into parody, but it is a case that challenges admiration. The main theme of this chapter is polemic, and particularly the 'hidden polemic' that structures the novel. Often, though not always, Meredith's irritating behaviour is related to his polemical activity. But polemic in Meredith is almost never of the kind that George Eliot indulged in when she hijacked the character Felix Holt for the faintly ventriloquized monologic authorial discourse of 'An Address to Working Men'. Gillian Beer simplifies when she writes that Meredith 'is obliged to blacken Dacier in order to excuse Diana'.[13] One might say rather that the complex and open character, Dacier, of Meredith's novel disappears and is supplanted by the hero of the misogynistic anecdote who, the author implies, belongs in the kind of novel parodied by the dialogue with Constance. This is more than a petty authorial punishment of the character. Meredith's parody of other novelistic discourses invariably has an ideological edge; one might say that Dacier's entry into this 'other novel' is an entry into a conventional, conservative and misogynistic set of beliefs convenient for his political advancement: he is entrapped in this 'novel' as a man becomes entrapped in such a set.

There are many instances of ostensibly more straightforward polemic in the novel, many of them directly or indirectly in Diana's voice. An example is the following account of her thoughts during the 'Conflict of the Night' after Redworth arrives at the Crossways with the mission of persuading her to stay and face her husband's accusations:

> A woman's brutallest tussle with the world was upon her. She was in the arena of the savage claws, flung there by the man who of all others should have protected her from them. And what had she done to deserve it? She listened to the advocate pleading her case; she primed him to admit the charges, to say the worst, in contempt of legal prudence, and thereby expose her transparent honesty. The very things awakening a mad suspicion proved her innocence. But was she this utterly simple person? Oh, no! She was the Diana of the pride in her power of fencing with evil – by no means of the order of those ninny young women who realize the popular conception of the purely innocent. She had fenced and kept her guard. Of this it was her angry glory to have the knowledge. But she had been compelled to fence. Such are men in the world of facts, that when a woman steps out of her domestic tangle to assert, because it is a tangle, her rights to partial independence, they sight her for their prey, or at least they complacently suppose her accessible. (10, 116)

In some ways this chapter is equivalent to the 'Clara's Meditations' chapter of *The Egoist*: both use extensive free indirect discourse to convey the intense and conflictual night-thoughts of the heroine. Diana's thoughts, however, take much more the form of outwardly directed polemic than Clara's: her inner life is represented in a public discourse. At one level, precisely that at which private experience can properly be simplified and stiffened into public polemic, the narrator is in agreement with this discourse. But if that were the only level at which Diana's experience could be read she would be as much a pattern heroine as Constance Asper. However, at another level, the sentient level at which private experience is unruly and unpredictable, the narrator is almost never wholly in agreement with his heroine. Diana's status as the most articulate of Meredith's heroines produces a paradox: the narrator consistently defends her articulacy against those who would silence women, but is aware that the more articulate a character is, the more her discourse raises the questions of sincerity that I have already touched on. In the case under consideration Diana is arguing herself into a bid for 'freedom' – the odious paradox of the law being that if exonerated she remains Warwick's wife – but her conception of freedom is based on the delusion that 'she was a contemplative, simply speculative political spirit, impersonal albeit a woman' (15, 167). It is the freedom to be sexually *hors de combat*.

Diana is articulate over a large range of genres, from the inner discourse that we have just examined to published poems and novels. Discourse is brought into question in all Meredith's novels but *Diana of the Crossways* and *Beauchamp's Career* are the ones in which this is most thematically explicit. It is the theme of the notorious first chapter which, as Gayla S. McGlamery says, 'introduces the multi-voiced or dialogic methodology utilized in the rest of the novel'.[14] In this chapter we are introduced to a number of diarists who, we do not realize at this stage, are not to be characters in the novel but have a purely discursive existence. These diarists are subjected to criticism: one is dismissed as writing in the style of 'our literary market'; another's 'unadorned harsh substantive statements' have more than a page devoted to them; a third is described as 'a gossip presenting an image of perpetual chatter' (1, 4–6).

These diarists quote the sayings of Diana. Like Sir Austin Feverel and Mrs Mountstuart Jenkinson she is an aphorist, and one specific way in which the chapter introduces the novel's dialogic method is that the narrator's polemic on behalf of women's speech is combined with a critique of these particular utterances of his heroine:

> though the wit of a woman may be terse, quite spontaneous, as this lady's assuredly was here and there, she is apt to spin it out of a museful mind, at her toilette, or by the lonely fire, and sometimes it is imitative; admirers should beware of holding it up to the withering glare of print. (1, 9)

Several pages follow in which a number of these sayings are quoted and subjected to ponderous critical commentary and exegesis – we come to recognize this narrator as the 'philosopher' of *Sandra Belloni*. Diana's distinction of mind is conveyed not by these aphorisms or even by the set conversations over which she presides (as in Chapter 28), but rather by her conduct of real dialogic situations, particularly the 'fencing' to which she has to resort in dialogue with Dacier, for example when he follows her to Caen:

> 'Your happiness, I hope, is the chief thought in such a case,' he said.
> 'I am sure you would consider it.'
> 'I can't quite forget my own.'
> 'You compliment an ambitious hostess.'
> Dacier glanced across the pastures. 'What was it that tempted you to this place?'
> 'A poet would say it looks like a figure in the shroud. It has no features; it has a sort of grandeur belonging to death. I heard of it as the place where I might be certain of not meeting an acquaintance.'
> 'And I am the intruder.'
> 'An hour or two will not give you that title.'
> 'Am I to count the minutes by my watch?'
> 'By the sun. We will supply you an omelette and piquette, and send you back sobered and friarly to Caen for Paris at sunset.' (22, 250–1)

However, this fencing has nothing to do with sincerity: indeed, it testifies to the very conditions that make sincerity impossible for Diana. When the narrator's discourse touches directly on this question, it does so in a way that brings the very nature of sincerity into question. 'The letter had every outward show of sincereness in expression, and was endowed to wear that appearance by the writer's impulse to protest with so resolute a vigour as to delude herself' (18, 205): if the appearance of 'sincereness in expression' may be the mark of self-delusion, how can we recognize genuine sincerity, even in ourselves? 'Between sincerity and a suspicion so cloaked and dull that she did not feel it to be the opposite of candour, she fancied she was passionless' (19, 214): again, the 'cloak' is internal; can we be insincere if we believe we are sincere?

Not surprisingly the same question runs through Diana's most ambitious form of discourse, her novels. About the first of these we know almost nothing. Judging by the title of the second, *The Princess Egeria*, it is a fantasy projection of herself as the nymph or goddess who advised the Roman king Numa; several critics have noted that Diana evades the fact that this mythical relationship was also sexual. The hero of *The Young Minister of State* is modelled on Percy Dacier, and the novel is written in complete ignorance of the author's feelings towards Dacier, while in the fourth, *The Cantatrice*, she is able to mock Redworth's calculating turn of mind because she assumes that his outward appearance corresponds to the inner reality, and she has no inkling of his feelings for her. Significantly the most detailed statement of theme is given for her fifth novel, *The Man of Two Minds*, which gives her the most difficulty, and which remains unfinished:

> He is courting, but he is burdened with the task of tasks. He has an ideal of womanhood and of the union of couples: a delicacy extreme as his attachment: and he must induce the lady to school herself to his ideal, not allowing her to suspect him less devoted to her person; while she, an exacting idol, will drink any quantity of idealization as long as he starts it from a full acceptance of her acknowledged qualities. (30, 360)

This, unlike its predecessors, reads like the scenario of a Meredith novel. Gillian Beer reads this passage as 'an unconscious commentary on her own view of her relationship with Dacier'.[15] I would see it rather as the dramatization of her inner conflict: her half-awareness of the delusiveness and intractability of her self-idealization. These two interpretations are not mutually exclusive, since the relationship with Dacier and the idealization of herself are mutually necessary. After the frustrated elopement a year passes before they meet again and the following conversation takes place (Dacier is the first speaker):

> 'I have felt with you: you are the wiser. But, admitting that, surely we can meet. I may see you?'
> 'My house has not been shut.'
> 'I respected the house. I distrusted myself.'
> 'What restores your confidence?'
> 'The strength I draw from you.'
> ... [T]hose last words of Percy's renewed her pride in him by suddenly building a firm faith in herself. Noblest of lovers! she thought, and brooded on the little that had been spoken, the much conveyed, for a proof of perfect truthfulness. (27, 318)

It is not surprising that Dacier's behaviour to her when he tells her the secret, and her response, should make her feel 'a dethroned woman' (32, 370). This word is used by Donald D. Stone to describe Meredithian motifs that are ostensibly very different, 'exposing an authoritarian figure through laughter':

> The pompous Shagpat is shaved (which removes his source of power); the princely Willoughby is brought down from his pedestal and exposed to the scrutiny of his fiancée Clara and to the 'world' surrounding Patterne Hall; Victor Radnor, the financial and would-be political leader, is laid low. Such figures resemble the monarch of carnival celebration; first puffed up, then dethroned, stripped, humiliated.[16]

Stone is of course alluding to *Rabelais and His World*, where Bakhtin pays considerable attention to the carnival custom of crowning and uncrowning a 'king'. What is of most interest is Bakhtin's metaphorical extension of this idea to the relation between consciousness and what he calls 'the material bodily lower stratum' which, he claims, 'liberates objects from the snares of false seriousness, from illusions and sublimations inspired by fear'. This extends to the most degraded of objects, the anal 'swab', concerning which he quotes Rabelais:

> Do not believe the old women here when they prattle that the felicity of the heroes and demigods in the Elysian fields lies in their asphodel or ambrosia or nectar. On the contrary,

they are happy, to my mind, because they swab their rumps with a goose.

Bakhtin comments: 'The material bodily lower stratum is productive. It gives birth, thus assuring mankind's immortality. All obsolete and vain illusions die in it, and the real future comes to life.'[17] It might seem a long way from anal swabs to Diana Warwick, but we should note that, as well as 'dethroned', several other words in the passage from Stone, such as 'pedestal', 'exposed' and 'stripped' occur prominently in this novel, and that the preoccupation with faeces is the provocative extreme of Bakhtin's concept of the 'material bodily lower stratum' which of course includes sexuality. Diana is haunted by the suspicion that the 'poetic ecstasy' of the Alpine encounter with Dacier from which their intimacy dated had 'not been of origin divine', had 'sprung from other than spiritual founts... from the reddened sources she was compelled to conceal' (24, 276).

We see then that Diana habitually presses discourse into the service of averting this uncrowning or dethronement, keeping her trapped in the 'illusions and sublimations inspired by fear'. Significantly she cannot speak of it even to Emma, her intimate friend:

> Little by little her story was related – her version of the story: for not even as woman to woman, friend to great-hearted friend, pure soul to soul, could Diana tell of the state of shivering abjection in which Dacier had left her on the fatal night; of the many causes conducing to it, and of the chief. That was an unutterable secret, bound by all the laws of feminine civilization not to be betrayed. (38, 426)[18]

When in the final chapter Diana submits to Redworth's embrace the experience 'was not like being seated on a throne' (43, 483): at last dethroning has a Bakhtinian positiveness. To see how Meredith arrives at this conclusion we have to deal with another example of polemic, this time the characteristic Meredithian polemic with the genre in which he is working – specifically, the dominant generic force exerted on the Victorian novel by comedy. I have already, in Chapter 5, discussed the arguments of some feminist critics that Meredith's feminism is compromised by what he calls the 'nuptial' conclusion, and have argued that a dialogic awareness of this issue is perceptible in *The Egoist*'s relationship to its own generic conventions. A similar awareness is more overt in *Diana of the Crossways*.

One of Meredith's ploys in *The Egoist* is to make Vernon Whitford much more recessive than any of his previous important male characters. In *Diana* by contrast he chooses, particularly at the end of the novel, to make his hero Redworth a much more vehemently and stereotypically masculine figure. In the last few pages he is described as 'hugely masculine' (42, 473), a 'stormy man' (43, 487) with eyes 'tolerably hawkish in their male glitter' (43, 483). As, with Emma's backing, his proposal looms at her, Diana feels 'her dreams of freedom, her visions of romance, drowning' (43, 475), 'She was not enamoured' (43, 487) and after accepting him 'She was dominated, physically and morally, submissively too' (43, 488). Whereas Vernon Whitford was an unworldly scholar and would-be journalist, Redworth is a successful capitalist, Member of Parliament and prospective Irish Secretary who compares his favoured Irish policy to the management of a horse (3, 41–2). He has also, over a period of years, shown himself to be unselfishly and practically devoted to Diana's interests, and has the backing of the nearly always reliable character Emma Dunstane, to whom he exhibits 'the true beauty of masculine character' (8, 93).

Meredith is determined, in the closing chapters, to emphasize Redworth's virility and represent the force that overcomes Diana's reluctance as specifically erotic. In order to offset the predominant sense of restraint in Redworth's character Meredith gives us this dialogue between Sir Lukin Dunstane and one of his London cronies, motivated by a false rumour that Redworth is to marry Mary Paynham:

> 'He'll make a deuced good husband to any woman – if it's true,' said Sir Lukin.... 'He's a cool-blooded old boy, and likes women for their intellects.'
>
> Colonel Launay hummed in meditative emphasis. He stared at vacancy with a tranced eye, and turning a similar gaze on Sir Lukin, as if through him, burst out: 'Oh, by George, I say, what a hugging that woman'll get!'
>
> The cocking of ears and queries of Sir Lukin put him to the test of his right to the remark; for it sounded of occult acquaintance with interesting subterranean facts; and there was a communication, in brief syllables and the dot language, crudely masculine. (41, 463–4)

In this ambience there can be little doubt that 'hugging' is a metonymic and phonetic substitution (by character or narrator) for 'fucking', and this usage gives a certain colouring to the description of Redworth's embrace of Diana, after his successful proposal, as a 'hug', especially since her sensations are conveyed in language that we have come to associate with conventional novelistic representation of female orgasm: 'a big storm-wave caught her from shore and whirled her to mid-sea, out of every sensibility but the swimming one of her loss of self in the man' (43, 483).

As we have seen, throughout the novel Meredith has been at pains to suggest that Diana's belief that she is sexually passionless is a delusion, brought on by the trauma of her premarital experiences and the revulsion of her marriage to Warwick. We have also seen that this is not a secret that the narrator shares with the reader over the character's head, but a suspicion – or more – that is present to Diana's consciousness at crucial times in the plot. One very important, though necessarily only half-articulate, thematic element in the novel is the *'demi-vierge'* condition of the married woman separated from her husband. The woman who has scandalized the Lady Wathin world by her friendships with Lord Dannisburgh and Dacier is precisely the one whose social status forces sexual repression on her, and the sexual repression is one of the elements motivating her erratic behaviour, particularly her betrayal of Dacier's secret.

The story is narrated in a way that does not exactly refuse, but dialogizes the comedic closure of Diana's marriage. The final chapter is self-consciously titled 'Nuptial Chapter', and the one before it 'The Penultimate: Showing a Final Struggle for Liberty and Run into Harness'. This ironic hint that Diana is engaged in a struggle with the generic demands of the novel she inhabits has, in fact, been made explicit in a well-known passage two chapters earlier:

> The woman of flesh refuses pliancy when we want it of her, and will not, until it is her good pleasure, be bent to the development called a climax, as the puppet-woman, mother of Fiction and darling of the multitude! ever amiably does, at a hint of the Nuptial Chapter. (40, 448)

Judith Wilt comments on this in a passage that exemplifies how Meredith brings out Bakhtinian concepts in critics who have not even read Bakhtin – in this case, 'hidden polemic':

The civilized reader whom Meredith has raised from 'the multitude' by this kind of rhetoric, the one who has identified with Diana in her quest for freedom, will not rush to the Nuptial Chapter either, and many readers of the novel have taken Meredith to mean that the Nuptial Chapter itself...is inconsistent with Diana's character, and that therefore the ending of the novel is a betrayal of his own principles.[19]

The 'rhetoric' is that of the Philosopher in *Sandra Belloni*, the antagonist of Dame Gossip in *The Amazing Marriage*, and the didactic commentator of the first chapter of *Diana*. Wilt's suggestion that, in effect, Meredith is engaging in a hidden polemic with the ideal reader of this rhetoric is subtle and persuasive. Her conclusion, however, returns us to a disappointingly monologic author:

> He means to say that he has read through the layers of Diana's very modern and freedom-loving character with all the insight and clarity of which he is capable finally to discern that she wants a Nuptial Chapter, that it is in fact her chosen ending.[20]

This conception of the author is, in essence, that of the Edwardians. It is a Meredith who will not come back today – certainly not one who will recommend himself to feminist readers.

An alternative view of Meredith's use of self-referential devices is that the fictional choices available to him do not allow a conclusion that is 'consistent with Diana's character' – or rather, since he actually makes quite a good job of motivating the marriage – a conclusion that will be all-composing. There is no reason, for example, to suppose that we are to interpret the phrase 'loss of self in the man' as a final achievement of true femininity, or as anything but a highly problematic condition of Diana's sexual fulfilment.

Another highly relevant feature of the conclusion – indeed of the whole novel – is the prominence of Diana's friendship with Emma. The two women 'often talked of the possibility of a classic friendship between women, the alliance of a mutual devotedness men choose to doubt of' (7, 87), and the novel keeps faith with this possibility. The final scene is between, not Diana and Redworth, but Diana and Emma, and although the last words hint that Diana is pregnant, the function of the scene is not one of choric subordination to the marriage. If it does not supplant the marriage as the concluding action, it balances it, maintains the one element that has been constant in Diana's life throughout the book, and provides some reassurance that the marriage has not been entirely a 'loss of self in the man'. As Janet Murray writes, it is a 'striking example of Meredith's deeply felt feminism that he conceived of the intellectual and emotional relationship between the two women as primary'.[21]

At the climax of the novel's plot, when Diana collapses into a suicidal stupor after the break with Dacier, it is Emma who shares with her the love-scene that begins to restore her to life. It would be impossible for Redworth, or any male character, to play this role. It is difficult to quote from this scene without making it seem like the parodic love-scene of Dacier and Constance:

> 'It is Emmy,' said the voice.
> Emma's heart sprang to heaven on a rush of thanks.
> 'My Tony,' she breathed softly.
> She hung for a further proof of like in the motionless body.
> 'Tony!' she said.
> The answer was at her hand, a thread-like return of her clasp.
> 'It is Emmy come to stay with you, never to leave you.' (36, 409–10)

Sentimentality, however, is a feature not just of local style but of structural function. This scene, which may seem sentimental in isolation, plays against stresses and reservations in the friendship of Diana and Emma, which it does not cancel. The most important of these is Diana's evasion, for a long time, of Emma's invitations, as a result of Sir Lukin's advances to her. At the conclusion of the novel Emma plays an active role in promoting Redworth's suit, a role which includes a blistering and not entirely fair attack on Diana's behaviour to Redworth.

Throughout the novel Emma plays an important narrative role as the channel – and to some extent the excuse – for Meredith's use of summary in narrating some of the most important events. Without the friendship the story would not be told. The crisis in Diana's marriage, for example, is narrated entirely indirectly, through Emma, Lukin and Redworth. Emma's condition as an invalid and the use of her as focalizer, picking up hints from Diana's letters, motivates the indirect method. Emma's sources of information are complemented by the gossip that Lukin picks up in London – the narrative thus embodies, in a sense, these particular versions of the masculine and feminine worlds, and dramatizes the marriage of the sick woman confined to the country and the errant husband cruising the London demi-monde.

This use of Emma as focalizer, which is sustained at intervals throughout the novel, with the fact that Emma is Diana's shrewd and intelligent critic as well as devoted friend, means that the friendship is not just an element in the story but part of the narrative discourse, which we have to traverse in order to see Diana at all.

The critical method that I have adopted has one serious danger: the concept of dialogism, particularly when extended to include a 'dialogical' relationship to the genre in which the author is working, can be used to justify anything the author does, and neutralize critical discrimination. Having concentrated, in this chapter, on justifying two major features of the novel that have attracted adverse comment – Diana's betrayal of Dacier and her marriage to Redworth – I will redress the balance, in conclusion, by considering another example of Meredith's 'disturbing angularity of form'.

Many readers, not surprisingly, have been startled by Meredith's treatment of Diana's first marriage, and particularly of her husband, Augustus Warwick. In narratological terms, Warwick is banished from the level of *scene*, and confined to *summary*, and reference to him is invariably focalized through another, usually hostile, character. The first reference to him is in Chapter 1, where the first phase of the story, dealing with her marriage, friendship with Lord Dannisburgh and the court case, is narrated in a proleptic and refracted fashion, by quotation from the 'diarists'. One such diarist is cited as reporting a scene when Warwick publicly mocked Diana's 'silvery laugh' by exclaiming, 'yang – yang – yang!' (1, 7). Extraordinarily, this is almost the only instance of Warwick's direct speech. The nearest approach elsewhere is embedded in Diana's speech, in dialogue with Emma: 'I "rendered" him ridiculous – I had caught a trick of "using men's phrases"' (14, 157). Here, evidently, Warwick's words are 'on display', selected and objectified by Diana's self-justifying discourse. Apart from these meagre citations the most vivid impressions of Warwick come through the words of others. Diana's own first words about him, that he is a 'gentlemanly official', are never signifantly modified. Later he is more pungently characterized through the indirect discourse of Sir Lukin: 'as there was no resemblance between [Diana and himself], there must, he deduced, be a difference in their capacity for enduring the perpetual company of a prig, a stick, a petrified poser' (13, 142). Lukin is a character whose words, direct or indirect, are almost always at a sharp angle to the narrator's, and his reflections on Diana's marriage are invariably given an ironic twist by an implicit reminder that the marriage is his fault. But the epithets applied to Warwick, although clearly part of Lukin's 'character zone' and lexically in 'intonational quotation marks',[22] convey a judgement that the narrator shows no sign of dissenting from. The meeting of Emma Dunstane, the most reliable focalizer in the novel, with Warwick is narrated thus: 'He appeared. Lady Dunstane's first impression of him recurred on his departure' (6, 70) – surely one of the most remarkable disappearing-acts in the art of narrative. More favourable views of Warwick come exclusively from Lady Wathin, herself a satirically objectified character whose approval is tantamount to authorial condemnation.

Restriction to summary, and to focalization through other characters, is not necessarily a damaging procedure. Indeed, Warwick shares this treatment with his 'rival', Lord Dannisburgh. But Meredith, when he wants to be, is a master of indirect narration, and Dannisbugh is a triumph of this mode of characterization. Entirely by summary, implication and the words of others an impression emerges of a worldly, intelligent, civilized, 'pagan' aristocrat of pre-Victorian stamp, a serious if slightly cynical politician, a man accustomed to the conquest of women who, in his declining years, has possibly surprised himself by the delight he finds in a chaste *amitié amoureuse* with the brilliant young Mrs Warwick. No doubt readers are deprived of pleasures that a 'scenic' portrayal of Dannisburgh would have provided, but such a portrayal would not necessarily have resulted in a more 'rounded' characterization and, by using the summary method, Meredith succeeds brilliantly in conveying the required impression with the utmost economy of means.

Economy is clearly a factor in Meredith's treatment of Warwick, too, but in this case there is a heavy price to be paid. After the separation Warwick falls ill and there is a campaign, led by Lady Wathin, to persuade or force Diana to return to him and nurse him. Diana refuses, with the backing of Emma and implicitly of the narrator. Warwick dies. A reader might wish to give a considered assent to this harsh rejection of a woman's duty as traditionally understood, but the relentlessly two-dimensional and 'objectified' portrayal of Warwick blocks such an assent. Duty to such a 'character' cannot be a moral issue, and a reader may suspect that it is too convenient for the author that it should not be.

When reading of Dannisburgh one is not tempted to make invidious comparisons with such classic portrayals of worldly aristocrats as Stendhal's Count Mosca and Lampedusa's Prince Salini. Thinking about Warwick, however, I cannot help being reminded of George Eliot's famous buttonholing of the reader in favour of Mr Casaubon or, even more relevantly, of the portrayal of that other 'gentlemanly official', Alexey Karenin. I repeat that this is not because the scenic method of characterization is invariably superior to summary, but because of the adequacy of the characterization to its function in the narrative. (In fact, I do not think that George Eliot satisfactorily handles the moral issues raised in Dorothea's marriage to Casaubon, but this is not because of any inadequacy in the portrayal of Casaubon.[23]) These comparisons suggest a possible motivation, additional to the compositional one, and perhaps not entirely conscious, for the widely felt weakness in the treatment of Warwick. I have suggested that possibly, in *The Egoist*, Meredith is engaged in a hidden polemic with *Daniel Deronda*, and there is perhaps in *Diana* a comparable, but less felicitous, response to *Middlemarch* and to George Eliot's treatment of female duty generally. If it were at all plausible that Meredith could have read *Anna Karenina* by 1885, I would suggest a similar response to Tolstoy's novel, whose story has much closer parallels with *Diana* than any of George Eliot's. *Middlemarch* and *Anna Karenina* are distinguished by their remarkably intimate and sympathetic but unsentimental and unsparing portrayals of repulsive husbands. Casaubon and Karenin, as subjects, have the same status as their wives. The result, a late-nineteenth-century novelist of feminist leanings might despairingly reflect, is that Dorothea resolves to bind herself to her husband's abominably egotistical posthumous wishes (only to be saved by his conveniently timed death) and Anna kills herself.

If any of this had consciously gone through the mind of such a scrupulous novelist as Meredith, it is unlikely that he would have adopted the crude solution of squeezing Warwick out. However, such comparisons do raise the problematic thought that, when the sexes are not equal in reality, their even-handed treatment in fiction may be to the detriment of women.

While this may interestingly contextualize such a gross deformity as the treatment of Warwick, it does not justify it. Some recent commentators on Bakhtin have noticed similarities to D.H. Lawrence's ideas about the novel in such essays as 'Morality and the Novel', and it is as well to be reminded that a novelist may use dialogical methods and still, in Lawrence's words, 'put his thumb in the scale, to pull down the balance to his own predilection'. 'That', says Lawrence, 'is immorality.'[24]

If the treatment of Warwick is a polemical excess, it should not overshadow the polemical triumphs of the novel, which are all of a dialogical and artistic nature: the hidden polemic with the source anecdote, the passage of Dacier from participation in the narrator's discourse to objectified parody, the championing and critique of Diana's discourse, and the generic dialogism of the conclusion. It is by these means that Meredith achieves what has intrigued, perturbed and delighted the 'wakeful eccentrics' at whom he aims: a committed feminist novel that keeps faith with the irregularity and undecidability of life.

8
The Final Phase

In contrast to the opening of *The Egoist*, which promises 'human nature in the drawing-room of civilized men and women, where we have no dust of the struggling outer world', *One of Our Conquerors* opens with five chapters set in the streets of London, and its first sentence deposits its hero literally in the mud of the pavement on London Bridge.

Meredith was not, of course, trying to write a naturalistic novel, but this impression of London, agitated and contemporary, under a grotesque, polluted and turbulent sky, is unlike anything else in his work. *One of Our Conquerors* is his only truly contemporary novel, his most metropolitan and bourgeois novel, challenged only by *Sandra Belloni* in its unusual lack of interest in the titled and landed aristocracy, and his most tragic novel. Those readers who reach the end of this self-confessedly 'trying piece of work'[1] will attest that it is authentically and desolatingly tragic. Yet Meredith's handling of a tragic story is, predictably, not devoid of parodically deflating allusions to tragic conventions: that first sentence gives us the 'conqueror' hero, at the height of his fortunes and hubristically contemplating further triumphs, literally falling by slipping on a piece of orange peel.

This initiatory episode exemplifies, in its sharpest form, a process of enfolding and transferring significance, almost approaching the allegorical, that is distinctive to this novel. Victor Radnor, the genial financier, condescendingly benevolent to the working class, is helped to his feet by one of them who leaves muddy marks on his waistcoat. Victor exclaims, in a would-be jocular way, 'Oh, confound the fellow!' and an altercation ensues, which culminates in the man retorting, 'none of your dam punctilio' (1, 1–3). The outlandish word, the alien and hostile word about whose discursive origins Meredith typically has his hero speculate ('was it a London cockney crow-word of the day, or a word that had stuck in the fellow's head from the perusal of his pot-house newspaper columns?' 1, 4), combines extraordinarily with the physical sensation of the fall to unsettle Victor in a way that prefigures and subsumes the narrative. 'The recollection of the word *punctilio* shot a throb of pain to the spot where his mishap had rendered him susceptible' (3). Throughout the novel he recurrently places two fingers on this spot at the back of his head, which is never unambiguously said to have been physically injured – the word 'punctilio' *is* the injury.

It is at this moment that he first grasps at an 'idea' that he believes he once possessed, and which haunts him in conjunction with the 'punctilio bump' to the end of the story (which is his madness and death): 'A short run or attempt at running after the idea, ended in pain to his head near the spot where the haunting word punctilio caught at any excuse for clamouring' (9–10). We are never led to believe that this 'idea' is anything more than a vague notion of benevolent capitalism, and Victor's terrible nemesis comes at a political meeting where he is proposing himself as a Member of Parliament, with political ideas no more coherent than they are here.

We can begin to see how the incorporation of the alien word, like a discursive 'foreign object' in the body, driving out Victor's paternalistic idea, epitomizes the workman's angry rejection of benevolence on Victor's terms, and exemplifies the enfolding of the narrative.

The early chapters that follow, which are by contemporary standards an extreme example of free indirect discourse, appear randomly to follow Victor's thoughts and movements, but can on analysis be seen as a brilliantly controlled summation; the writing passes between the public and the private, intimate feeling and ideological discourse, the individual(ist) walking in the street and the turbulent cityscape through which he walks, constituting a poem of the social in fractured, multi-planed polyphony. The following extract is typical of the way Victor's inner speech, unmarked by inverted commas to allow a free transition between direct, indirect and authorial discourse, is used to manage these passages. We also see in it an example of the Bakhtinian principle, noted earlier in *The Egoist* but much extended in this novel, that 'inner speech' resembles 'inner dialogue' and 'is oriented toward a possible audience':[2]

> Yes, well, and if a tumble distorts our ideas of life, and an odd word engrosses our speculations, we *are* poor creatures, he addressed another friend, from whom he stood constitutionally

in dissent, naming him Colney; and under pressure of the name, reviving old wrangles between them upon man's present achievements and his probable destinies: especially upon England's grandeur, vitality, stability, her intelligent appreciation of her place in the universe; not to speak of the historic dignity of London City. (1, 5-6)

With striking rapidity the text takes a plunge from this conventional patriotic rhetoric into what Bryan Cheyette calls 'the semitic discourse at the heart of this racially differentiating "Englishness"':[3]

> the ghastly vision of the Jew Dominant in London City, over England, over Europe, America, the world (a picture drawn in literary sepia by Colney: with our poor hangneck population uncertain about making a bell-rope of the forelock to the Satyr-snouty master; and the Norman Lord de Warenne handing him for a lump sum son and daughter, both to be Hebraized in their different ways), fastened on the most mercurial of patriotic men, and gave him a whole-length plunge into despondency. (1, 6)

Gillian Beer comments that 'Meredith appears, disconcertingly, to be implicated' in this gross anti-semitism, but that this is a 'trap for his contemporary readers, inviting them to relax upon a stream of narrative composed of their prejudices and then gradually revealing the gap between such values and the values of his work' – a trap into which '[f]ew modern readers are likely to fall'.[4] For Cheyette, however, it is Meredith himself who imagines 'a Hebraized dystopian city' and 'Many popular novels followed Meredith and constructed a future world ruled over by a "Jewish aristocracy".'[5]

It is particularly important, in cases such as this, not to fall back on lazy assertions of dialogism and stylization. A marked anti-semitism occurred, much earlier, in the sentimentally valorized direct speech of Emilia in *Sandra Belloni*. Richard L. Newby has attributed to Meredith certain anti-semitic passages in *The Ipswich Journal*, but on purely impressionistic evidence.[6] In his next novel, *Lord Ormont and his Aminta*, there is an unracialized portrayal of a Jew, the lawyer Arthur Abner, who discusses anti-semitism with the hero; and, of course, in *The Tragic Comedians* the hero himself is

Jewish, his portrayal racialized only to a minor and favourable degree, and the heroine's anti-semitism vehemently satirized.

Perhaps of more relevance than the comparatively isolated instances of Jewish characters and 'semitic discourse' in his writing is the fact that Meredith undoubtedly participated enthusiastically and uncritically in the racial thinking of the time, not in his case usually with reference to Jews but more commonly to Celts and Saxons, especially in *Diana of the Crossways*: we shall be seeing an example of this from *The Amazing Marriage* later in this chapter. We should also remember that one of the most strikingly 'Bakhtinian' characteristics of Meredith's novelistic practice, exemplified in the opening of *Beauchamp's Career*, is that, as Bakhtin says of Dostoevsky, ideas 'uttered by him in monologic form outside the artistic context of his work' are 'combined [in his novels] in an indissoluble unity with images of people', that it is 'absolutely impermissible to ascribe to these ideas the finalizing function of authorial ideas in a monologic novel' – one must 'investigate the *function* of ideas in Dostoevsky's polyphonic world'.[7] Let us then investigate the function of the anti-semitic discourse in *One of Our Conquerors*, to do which is to investigate its context.

First, we should note that, unlike *Lord Ormont and his Aminta*, there are no Jewish characters in *One of Our Conquerors* and that the anti-semitic discourse is confined to the first few pages, where it is certainly closely associated, if not 'combined in an indissoluble unity' with the image of Victor. It emerges, we have seen, as a kind of reaction to Victor's patriotic rhetoric, and this juxtaposition is repeated a few pages later:

> But is the Jew of the usury gold becoming our despot-king of Commerce?
> In that case...we bid ourselves remember the sons of whom we are; instead of revelling in the fruits of Commerce, we shoot scornfully past those blazing bellied windows of the aromatic dinners, and beyond Thames, away to the fishermen's deeps, Old England's native element, where the strenuous ancestry of a race yet and ever manful at the stress of trial are heard around and aloft whistling us back to the splendid strain of muscle, and spray fringes cloud, and strong heart rides the briny scoops and hillocks, and Death and Man are at grip for the haul.
> There we find our nationality, our poetry, no Hebrew competing. (1, 8–9)

Meredith had a weakness for this kind of muscular patriotic rhetoric, verging on the homoerotic, which here has eerie echoes of the exaggeratedly Anglo-Saxon diction of some of Hopkins's less successful poems, such as 'Harry Ploughman', which Meredith could not have read. It is however legitimate here to speak of stylization or even pastiche. For one thing, the passage is immediately followed by the sardonic comment, 'We do; or there at least we left it. Whether to recover it when wanted, is not so certain', where the deflation is as much in the contrastingly down-to-earth diction as in the sentiment.

Another justification for reading the patriotic rhetoric in this way is precisely its relation to the anti-semitic discourse, and the significance this has for Victor. For Victor of course is not a seafarer but a financier; it is only the discourse of 'race' that distinguishes him from the dreaded 'Jew'. One of Cheyette's most compelling arguments is that the 'fearful recognition of "the Jew" within the writer resulted in a semitic discourse which attempted to irrevocably banish or contain this confusing "other". The closer the "self" identified, however unconsciously, with the semitic "other", the more vehement the rejection of this unwelcome double.'[8] It is not necessary to clear Meredith of all 'implication' in this discourse to argue that its function is as much diagnostic as symptomatic. The 'semitic' and 'Anglo-Saxon' discourses are bound to each other as polarized extremities. To the extent to which we can attach them to the character, to his subjectivity and objective situation, their ideological function is revealed.

That function, we might say, is related to the instability of Victor's conception of himself, and so we see another instance of the enfolding and summating character of his initial fall. There are also strong historical resonances here. Meredith was not Balzac, and did not centre his story on Victor's financial dealings, but the text is sprinkled with references to the instability of the financial world: early in the novel Victor's friend Simeon Fenellan says 'An unstable London's no world's market-place' (3, 21) and later the narrator describes London as 'a City issuing out of hospital' (12, 128). Jack Lindsay claims that 'Behind *One of Our Conquerors* lies the financial crisis of 1890',[9] which Meredith's friend H.M. Hyndman analysed from a Marxist perspective in his *Commercial Crises of the Nineteenth Century* (1892). Lindsay's specific claim is a bit unlikely, since the novel was well under way by the end of 1889, but Meredith's portrayal of the underlying instability of a financial 'conqueror' could be seen as a prescient if displaced analysis of the mood of the financial world immediately prior to the crisis. Hyndman writes of the standing in 1889 of Messrs. Baring, Bros. & Co., whose unwise enterprises precipitated the crisis, and of the City's admiration for its head, Lord Revelstoke, and the 'feeling of satisfaction throughout the country that a purely English house should stand so high at a time when German Jews held the leading place in nearly every great continental city' but who accepted 'some of the worst financial enterprises that any third-rate firm of adventurers ever tried to foist upon the public' and 'allowed himself to be completely bamboozled by an American adventurer'.[10] This is further ground for arguing that Meredith is not merely 'constructing' but is representing and analysing the construction of the discourse of 'the Jew'.

I said that the portrayal of Victor's instability is 'displaced', but it might be more accurate to speak of an effect of interpenetration between the public points of reference I have just been discussing, with their necessary ideological discourses, and the 'private' realm in which predominantly we see Victor, and in which the narrative is mainly located. In Gayla S. McGlamery's words, 'In *One of Our Conquerors* the political is also the personal; the two intertwine and conflate, and ultimately are indistinguishable.'[11] The *hubris* to which Victor's fall is a comic and proleptic allusion is not directly concerned with his business dealings but a matter of private life – or, more accurately, the point precisely at which private life is inescapably public. He has built a grandiose country house, secretly from his family, and he is about to reveal it to them. But he is not legally married to the mother of his daughter. Twenty years earlier he married, for money, a much older woman, whom he deserted with her beautiful young companion, Nataly. There has been no divorce, but Victor lives with Nataly, whom he devotedly loves, as man and wife to all but their closest friends. The price of the forbearance of 'Mrs Burman' (as she is called throughout the novel, though her legal name of course is Mrs Radnor) is that Victor and Nataly should live quietly. But the 'conqueror' cannot tolerate this, and twice already he has tried to set up as a country gentleman, and been forced to give up because of strategic revelations emanating from his legal wife. To Victor this behaviour is insane vengefulness, and because the reader's view of Mrs Burman is focalized entirely through him, it is possible to be persuaded by the often hysterical rhetoric of his inner discourse, and mistake it for the author's, especially when it incorporates claims on behalf of natural feeling quite consistent with the views of an author whose later novels repeatedly justify the breaking of the marriage tie in certain circumstances. Meredith's method leaves it to the reader to reflect that a little tact and discretion are a small price to pay to soothe the *amour-propre* of a wife deserted in the late nineteenth century. Not to reflect this, however, is to underestimate the magnitude of Victor's *hubris*. The building of 'Lakelands', and Victor's obsessive determination to settle there, elicit a series of threats from Mrs Burman, and a consequent stress that brings about first an estrangement between Victor and Nataly and eventually her death from a heart attack (ironically hours before Mrs Burman herself dies) with Victor's ensuing madness and his own death.

The fall, and Victor's reflections arising from it, are followed by another episode which further exemplifies Meredith's bravura narrative method. Victor meets his friend Simeon Fenellan and asks him, '"Anything doing in the City?"... The reply was deferred until they had reached the pavement, when Mr Fenellan said: "I'll tell you", and looked a dubious preface, to his friend's thinking' (2, 15). They take lunch together and the topic is, apparently, resumed:

> 'Come!' said Mr Radnor.
> The appeal was understood.
> 'Nothing very particular. I came to the City to look at a warehouse they want to mount double guard on. Your idea of the fireman's night-patrol and wires has done wonders for the office'.
> 'I guarantee the City if all my directions are followed'.
> Mr Fenellan's remark, that he had nothing very particular to tell, reduced it to the mere touch upon a vexatious matter, which one has to endure in the ears at times; but it may be postponed. So Mr Radnor encouraged him to talk of an Insurance Office investment. (3, 21)

This is incomprehensible at a first reading. Victor's original question related not to business matters but to Mrs Burman, who has heard of the Lakelands project and plans to thwart it. The narrative mimics Victor's repression of this troublesome knowledge by cloaking it in the evasions of the conversation and even of his consciousness, so deferring the reader's understanding. The last paragraph quoted is typical of the way the reader's grasp of the situation is weakened and distorted by Victor's characteristic repression – Mrs Burman's power to disrupt his life is far more than something to be endured 'in the ears', but its 'postponement' disables the first-time reader from making this judgement.

This episode also typifies the interpenetration of the public and private. Donald R. Swanson has remarked that:

> Victor's 'aim' disregards the needs of those for whom he is responsible: Nataly and Nesta – just as England's quest for commercial power is unrelated to the real needs and wishes of her people.[12]

Such a substitution (necessary to the non-Balzacian novelist whose theme is 'the malady afflicting England')[13] is only possible, can only escape a bald and arbitrary-seeming allegory, by such narrative techniques as we have seen, which enlist the strategies of consciousness of the hero where the connection is vital and dynamic. Another example can be seen, in this same conversation, when the word 'punctilio' erupts in Victor's consciousness again. This is the conclusion of a Horatian rhapsody of rural retreat, by means of which Victor idealizes his Lakelands project:

> 'And the two dear souls on their own estate, Fenellan! And their poultry, cows, cream. And a certain influence one has in the country socially. I make my stand on a home – not empty punctilio.'
>
> Mr Fenellan repeated, in a pause, 'Punctilio,' and not emphatically.
>
> 'Don't bawl the word,' said Mr Radnor, at the drum of whose ears it rang and sang. (3, 24)

We are here in territory where Freud and Bakhtin meet – the social character of the unconscious. Victor's use of 'punctilio' is not exactly, like Clara Middleton's 'Harry Whitford' (see Chapter 5, p. 172), a Freudian slip, but it is a word over which he does not have conscious control, and which appears to have an independent life in his mind. We have seen that it is emphatically the word of another, that Victor thinks of as a 'cockney crow-word' or a word from 'pothouse newspaper columns'. Its uncontrolled eruption into his speech is in effect the eruption of his antagonist, now internalized. Its eruption into this particular discourse of 'home', 'dear souls' and rural retreat signifies an unwelcome connection between that incident, in which his attempted jocular condescension was exposed as class-antagonism, and his family-feeling, which he uses to disguise a craving for self-display and exclusivity (Nataly's desire for 'poultry, cows, cream' would be satisfied by a cottage, and she hates the idea of Lakelands). Once again, the apparently trivial incident of the fall enfolds some of the key meanings of the text.

The connection between the ideology by which Victor lives his public life, and his ideas of 'home', has been established shortly before in the conversation when Fenellan cites a German friend as saying that English 'individualismus' is 'another name for selfishness... an individualism of all of a pattern, as when a mob cuts its lucky, each fellow his own way' and Victor, returning to the obsessive Lakelands theme, says, 'we don't court neighbours at all – perhaps the elect.... You see, that was my intention – to be independent of neighbouring society' (3, 22–3).

The opening movement of the novel culminates in a chapter that makes characteristic use of an 'interpolated genre', in this case a 'Poem, or Dramatic Satire, once famous, THE RAJAH IN LONDON (London, Limbo and Sons, 1889)' (5, 36). This permits an abrupt shift of style, mode and focalization, as we are given the Rajah's view of the city, which merges into the narrative of Victor's walk home. 'Behind his courteousness, [the Rajah] is an antagonistic observer of his conquerors' (41): thus the discourse of imperialism is attached to Victor's eponymous title. It is in this chapter that we are given the turbulent portrayal of London, unique in Meredith:

> In April, the month of piled and hurried cloud, it is a Rape of the Sabines overhead from all quarters, either one of the winds brawnily larcenous; and London, smoking royally to the open skies, builds images of a dusty epic fray for possession of the portly dames. There is immensity, swinging motion, collision, dusky richness of colouring, to the sight; and to the mind idea. London presents it. If we can allow ourselves a moment for not inquireing scrupulously (you will do it by inhaling the aroma of the ripe kitchen hour), here is a noble harmony of heaven and the earth of the works of man, speaking a grander tongue than barren sea or wood or wilderness. Just a moment; it goes; as,

when a well-tuned barrel-organ in a street has drawn us to recollections of the Opera or Italy, another harshly crashes, and the postman knocks at doors, and perchance a costermonger cries his mash of fruit, a beggar-woman wails her hymn. For the pinched are here, the dinnerless, the weedy, the gutter-growths, the forces repressing them. That grand tongue of the giant City inspires none human to Bardic eulogy while we let those discords be.... For this London, this England, Europe, world, but especially this London, is rather a thing for hospital operations than for poetic rhapsody. (5, 39–40)

This is one of the most remarkable passages in Meredith, an instance where his fractured and contorted style is triumphantly justified as the mediation of a dissident vision. What is remarkable is not so much the direct invocation of the lives of the poor and destitute, the gesture towards naturalism, though this is almost unique in Meredith, but the metaphorical extravaganza with which it begins and ends. It ends with a metaphor that anticipates the opening lines of 'Prufrock' to which, indeed, it may have contributed, if Gillian Beer is right in speculating that Eliot 'had read this novel, with its scenes of the City workers streaming across London Bridge, its constant allusions to Wagner and particularly to *Tristan and Isolde*'.[14] The comparison of the clouds to the Rape of the Sabines, though initially suggested no doubt by baroque painting, and conducted in a facetious tone, is profoundly disruptive of the 'epic' description that it seems designed jocularly to reinforce. 'Brawnily larcenous' insists on the actuality of rape, while the image of 'London, smoking royally to the open skies', lodged between this phrase and 'dusty epic fray for possession of the portly dames' implies a more than merely picturesque significance. It might not be gratuitous, in view of the immediate proximity of the Rajah, to recall that the Rape of the Sabines was a fiction of the conquest of a native people by a future imperial power, a 'dusty epic fray for possession' that seems directly relevant to 'London, smoking royally' – or at least would do so to the Rajah. Even the connection with painting is not merely innocent or picturesque, since the reference recurs a few pages later, in another extraordinary image – 'The figures of the hurtled fair ones in sky were wreathing Nelson's cocked hat when Victor... emerged from the tideway to cross the square, having thoughts upon Art' which are thoughts about the possession of works of art, his purchases of pictures having been 'his unhappiest ventures' and 'A real Raphael in your house' being 'aristocracy to the roof-tree' (42).

I have focused almost entirely on the first five chapters of *One of Our Conquerors* because they are a concentrated and sustained example of a method of narration that Meredith has here brought to the furthest point that it reaches in his work. The rest of the novel is consistent with this, though it does not always sustain this level of artistry (the best parallel to the opening can be found in the variations rung on the corporative voice of the visitors to the opening of Lakelands in Chapter 23). Thematically, the obvious sacrifice I have made is in relation to the strong feminist element centred on Victor's daughter Nesta and her friendship with a 'fallen woman'. However, this is such a recurrent thematic element in Meredith's later work, and so prominent elsewhere in this study, that I have felt justified in passing over it in favour of the more distinctive aspects of this most unsusual and resistant of Meredith's novels.

However 'trying', *One of Our Conquerors* has been treated with respect by modern critics. Its successor, by contrast, has had almost no friends, and Barbara Hardy's dismissal is characteristic: '*Lord Ormont and his Aminta*... shows [Meredith] at his most sentimental, and... the famous artificiality serves the interests of the sentimentality.'[15]

This novel can most superficially be seen as the culmination of a sequence of Meredithian approaches to the theme of female liberation from patriarchal marriage: Clara Middleton extricates herself, with enormous difficulty, from betrothal to an epitome of the vices of the English gentleman; Diana Warwick leaves her much more shadowily portrayed and apparently equally repellent husband but is prevented, by a series of plot-devices, from entering another sexual relationship until after his death; Aminta Farrell leaves Lord Ormont and lives, with the narrator's obvious approval, in an adulterous relationship with Matey Weyburn until her husband's death.

I have argued in my chapters on *The Egoist* and *Diana of the Crossways* that those novels owe much of their characteristic astringency to being in a relationship of ironic resistance to prevailing novelistic conventions, both of form and of reticence – conventions that Meredith had so fatally flouted in *Richard Feverel*. But *Lord Ormont and his Aminta* was written in the decade of 'New Woman' fiction, of *The Woman Who Did* and *The Awakening*, and Meredith can bring his lovers together in a scene more sexually suggestive even than the notorious 'Enchantress' chapter of *Feverel*:

'Matey, I'm for a dive.'
He went after the ball of silver and bubbles, and they came up together. There is no history of events below the surface. (27, 324)

However, this freedom permits a slackening of the generic tension and dialogism that is such an important aspect of the ideological form of Meredith's best novels. For the first time since *Evan Harrington*, there is a straightforward resolution of the most classically New Comedic kind – the triumph of youth and love over age and social barriers, with the establishment of a new, international and democratic social order (Matey and Aminta's school) in place of the old imperialistic order epitomized by Ormont. It is true that Ormont's death in the novel's concluding lines has a certain poignancy, as that of one who had at last generously forborne to take revenge on the adulterous couple; but it does not, like that of Richmond Roy, cast a shadow over the comedic resolution, which is only confirmed and made less transgressive by the implication that Matey and Aminta will now marry.

The novel has had one champion in Graham McMaster, who finds in the most obvious weakness of the plot – the failure adequately to motivate the behaviour of Lord Ormont that alienates his wife – a key to its ideological orientation. Ormont is an elderly war hero who marries, privately and abroad, a young middle-class girl who hero-worships him. He is in disgrace with the colonial authorities and the bourgeois press for exercising 'a too prompt military hand' (2, 20) in India, and the reader is given to understand that it is resentment at this treatment which motivates him to keep his young wife out of society and encourage the belief that she is his mistress. McMaster argues from this weakness of realistic motivation that the plot is actually motivated by 'a political [anti-imperialistic] discourse that it gives rise to, allows to be articulated'; 'by this period the necessity of the (Indian) Empire had become an almost undiscussable dogma.... This is why the problems of Empire are transferred to the marriage plot.' He acknowledges that this might be 'rephrased adversarially by saying that the novel is a thin allegory' but argues that 'this would be to assume that because the realistic novel was hegemonic at this period, every exemplar had perforce to reproduce its typical rhetoric' and that Meredith 'repudiated realistic techniques because these had...become compromised by being too thoroughly at the service of the "metropolitan" culture'.[16]

I cite McMaster's argument (which also contains some penetrating observations about Henry James's hostility to the novel) because it gives a version of the novel that is more interesting than most accounts, consistent with the general radicalism of Meredith's later fiction and in particular with his habitual association of female emancipation with other ideological issues. As an interpretation of the novel, I think it is convincing. If I still think that it is a 'thin allegory' this is not because of any nostalgia for realism. *Lord Ormont* is hardly the first of Meredith's novels to 'repudiate realistic techniques': the motivation of characters such as Sir Austin Feverel and Sir Willoughby Patterne can only be understood intertextually – Sir Austin's prolonged refusal to see Richard after his marriage and Willoughby's proposal to Laetitia while he is still engaged to Clara are no more realistically motivated than Lord Ormont's treatment of Aminta.

I have myself used the word 'allegorical' to decribe what I have called the 'process of enfolding and transferring significance' in *One of Our Conquerors*. In that novel there is no realistic portrayal of Victor's financial dealings: the story is entirely transposed, as it were, to the key of private life. What saves it from being a thin – or, to use a better metaphor, a *stiff* – allegory is the mercurial narrative discourse which, with its constant movement into and out of Victor's consciouness, and between the private and the public, the intimate and the ideological, materializes the continuities between these realms.

Lord Ormont is not without its dialogical *tours de force*. The whole of the opening chapter, which introduces us to the novel's hero and heroine Matey Weyburn and Aminta Farrell as schoolboy and schoolgirl, is written in a kind of adult version of schoolboy slang, as if by an 'old boy' reminiscing. It is in this voice, and through the hero-worship of the schoolchildren, that we are first introduced to Lord Ormont's exploits. This voice, for all its apparent naive charm, is extremely reactionary, and effectively illustrates how imperialistic assumptions are written into the vernacular of school life. Another brilliantly accomplished character zone is that of Lord Ormont's sister, Lady Charlotte Eglett, whose language (in both formal dialogue and free indirect discourse) always rings true with a complex note made up of aristocratic toughness, love of home and family, class prejudice, honesty, fairness and, in relation to the handsome young Weyburn, sexual wistfulness: she is an outstanding example of a character who by no means represents the novel's values, but whose word is 'as fully weighted as the author's word'.[17] There is a considerable amount of free indirect discourse attributed to the three main characters, but none has as rich or powerful a voice as Lady Charlotte, and in particular Lord Ormont, in whose inner discourse the 'allegorical' transference of the imperialistic theme to the marriage plot must take place, is not remotely comparable, as a vehicle for such a transference, to Victor Radnor. Ormont's behaviour qualifies him to be one of Meredith's unforgettable monsters but such characters – Willoughby Patterne, Richmond Roy, the Countess Louisa, Victor himself – are triumphs of discourse and it is by this criterion, not that of an irrelevant realism, that the novel fails.

Lord Ormont and His Aminta was written within the period of composition of Meredith's last published novel, *The Amazing Marriage*, which he had begun as long ago as 1879. This, together with the parallels between the central relationships of the two novels, relationships which in Susan Morgan's words are 'so bizarre as to be surreal',[18] may partly account for the comparative insipidity of *Lord Ormont*, as if some of its energy leaked into the other novel. The (*pace* McMaster) 'thin allegory' of Ormont's treatment of Aminta is set into a novel that does not otherwise extravagantly breach the norms of realism, whereas *The Amazing Marriage* draws freely and self-consciously on a variety of fictional modes. Moreover, for this novel's monstrous husband, Lord Fleetwood, Meredith achieves an inner discourse which, though more blatant and rigid than Victor Radnor's, makes him a more compelling figure than Ormont.

The variety of modes is most immediately apparent in the use – much more extensively and successfully than in *Sandra Belloni* – of double narration. This narrative device is based on a fiction that a number of critics rightly consider an additional narrative level or subplot.[19] The first chapter is headed 'Enter Dame Gossip as Chorus'. It may not occur to a first-time reader that this is literally the name of a narrator until the beginning of Chapter 3, where she says, 'I have still time before me, according to the terms of my agreement with the person to whom I have, I fear foolishly, entrusted the letters and documents' (25). At the end of this chapter she breaks off (or is broken off) in mid-sentence and another narrative voice takes over. This second voice, commonly referred to by critics as the Novelist, narrates most of the novel, with some interruptions from Dame Gossip, who is literally given the last as well as the first word.

Both these narrative voices are varied and dialogic, and there is some stylistic overlap between them. Dame Gossip is female and uneducated, and her narrative is oral in manner. The Novelist is male and educated, and his narrative is decidedly 'written'. These differences are enough to suggest that their relationship is a hierarchical one. The Novelist, not being named, is implicitly closer to the author, and he controls the 'authorial' space of the chapter-headings, where he names and comments on Dame Gossip. Their relationship is emphatically *not* like the image of artistic co-operation that with unconscious satire Dame Gossip herself offers, of a painting in which an artist who can paint people but not animals, and one who can paint animals but not people, 'combine without bickering' (3, 26).

This narrative method is not merely a formal device, nor is its significance confined to this text. Gillian Beer considers that 'There is...no final authority to whom we may turn for our reading of events',[20] a view which I agree we must accept, but in accepting we must recognize the stress, polemical imbalance and weight of Meredith's history as a novelist at work in the conflict. Beer is right to say that the Novelist is 'not wholly to be identified with Meredith',[21] but Meredith was not merely falling into lazy shorthand when he wrote to Stevenson, 'Dame Gossip pulls one way and I another'.[22] Dame Gossip, who favours lively action and distrusts explanation and analysis, represents those demands of the reading public against which Meredith had struggled throughout his career, and with which we have seen him negotiating during the serialization of *Evan Harrington*. He began writing *The Amazing Marriage* before the period of his late celebrity, and even during that period, when he was completing the novel, he invariably adopted the attitude of the neglected and misunderstood novelist. When *The Amazing Marriage* was serialized in Scribner's magazine Meredith still had to submit to cuts, and his son telegraphed to the publishers, on the novelist's behalf, asking that this be done, 'cutting reflections, retaining story'[23] – a final triumph of Dame Gossip which cannot have escaped Meredith's ironic awareness. In using this narrator he invited an old enemy into his tent.

Beer's view is contested by Robert M. DeGraff on the grounds that Dame Gossip's narrative is unreliable, she narrates only a small proportion of the novel, she is addicted to low genres ('delight in the melodramataic and sentimental') and the norms of the Novelist are those of Meredith's other writings.[24] His argument, which appeals to 'accuracy', 'truth' and 'facts', unintentionally highlights an aspect of the fictionality of *The Amazing Marriage* which distinguishes it from all Meredith's earlier novels (if not from *The Shaving of Shagpat*) and has a crucial bearing on the presence of Meredith's antagonist within the narrative discourse.

To put it simply, the question in *The Amazing Marriage* is not the representation of 'facts' but the generation of narrative. The nature of the 'treaty' between the narrators is obscure, but a crucial part of it is that she has handed over to him 'the letters and documents of a story' (3, 25). Some of these 'documents' resemble the orthodox materials of biography, and are directly quoted by the Novelist: these include the letters of the heroine's sister-in-law, Henrietta, and the journal of Gower Woodseer, a 'Scholar Gipsy' figure modelled on Stevenson. Dame Gossip's materials also, however, include street-ballads and the reports of rumour, and the Novelist's relation to this material is decidedly uneasy. Dame Gossip represents the generative forces of narrative, and the Novelist attempts to select, filter and censor the materials that she provides. There is more 'story' than the Novelist is willing to authenticate: within the text, he is the arbiter of Dame Gossip's 'reliability', but if we agree with Gillian Beer that 'The reader becomes the arbitrator',[25] the narrative is blurred at the edges.

A prominent example of such unauthenticated story is the episode in which, on the basis of ballad and oral tradition, Dame Gossip tells of the heroine, Carinthia, chasing her estranged husband, Lord Fleetwood, along Piccadilly at a time when she was supposed to be resident in Wales. The Novelist disdainfully rejects the story as 'an impossible one. Carinthia had not the means to travel: she was moneyless' (28, 289–90). The incident is certainly unlikely, but it is obviously not literally impossible. We base our judgement in such matters not on general probability but on the norms of likelihood that have been established within the text. What kind of story is *The Amazing Marriage*?

The following outline of the story is uncontested by the novelistic narrator. A young married Countess elopes to the Austrian mountains with a sea-captain more than forty years her senior. Here their children are brought up remote from civilization, though this is significantly modified in the case of their son, Chillon John, when he is sent to school in England. When the children are on the threshold of adulthood their parents die within a week of each other of broken hearts, the mother because of the separation from her son and fear that he has heard scandalous gossip about her, and the father because of her death. The brother and sister leave their mountain home, he in pursuit of the woman he loves, and arrive at a fashionable resort where, at the first social occasion of her life, and on first meeting, Carinthia receives a proposal of marriage from the richest man in England, Lord Fleetwood. She accepts, and although he subsequently regrets his rashness, he is obsessively the 'prisoner of his word' and goes through with the marriage. However, immediately after the wedding he treats his wife with contempt, taking her to a bare-knuckle boxing match and abandoning her at an inn to which he returns at night through a window, for an unrepeated consummation of the marriage. Abandoned and pregnant from this single consummation she lives for a time at a servant's home in Whitechapel, from which she ventures once to protect her husband against a hostile crowd in Vauxhall Gardens and later in Wales, where her husband witnesses her saving a child from a rabid dog, and whence she is ceremonially escorted to his seat in Kent by a body of Welsh 'cavaliers'. Gradually her love for him dies, while his for her perversely grows, until it is she who rejects him. She follows her brother to Spain as a nurse in support of the Carlist cause, her husband becomes a Catholic recluse and dies, and she marries a widowed friend whose dying wife had bequeathed him to her.

By ordinary standards of probability this story is absurd. Not only numerous incidental episodes, but also most of the essential 'kernels' of the story, are highly unlikely. A part of the novelistic narrator's role is to 'naturalize' parts of the story, particularly those parts stemming from the perverse behaviour of Lord Fleetwood. However, this can only be a partial enterprise, and many elements in the story, such as the deaths of Carinthia's parents, her pregnancy, her refuge among the poor and her adventure in Spain clearly derive from non-realistic fictional models. In the case of her pregnancy the Novelist even exaggerates the sense of unrealism by acknowledging only obscurely and retrospectively that the marriage had been consummated. Most of Meredith's novels contain some such elements, but none in such profusion. In this context, there is no inherent unlikelihood in contested episodes such as Carinthia's pursuit of Fleetwood in Piccadilly, and the Novelist's norms are not necessarily canonical.

The ground contested by Dame Gossip and the Novelist is termed 'romance'. For her:

> as it is good for those to tell who intend preserving their taste for romance and hate anatomical lectures, we never can come to the exact motives of any extraordinary piece of conduct on the part of man or woman. (13, 140)

He mocks:

> her endless ejaculations over the mystery of Life, the inscrutability of character, – in a plain world, in the midst of such readable people! To preserve Romance (we exchange a sky for a ceiling if we let it go), we must be inside the heads of our people as well as the hearts. (20, 209)

A strong point on her side, which he denies but does not argue against, is that his method leads to Meredith's *bête noire*, Naturalism:

> Things were so: narrate them, and let readers do their reflections for themselves, she says, denouncing our conscientious method as the direct road downward to the dreadful modern appeal to the senses and assault on them for testimony to the veracity of everything described. (35, 367)

Her method, moreover, is not merely that of rumour and popular balladry. The main narrative is a variant of the story of patient Griselda – albeit one in which Griselda loses her patience – and in the Clerk's Tale Chaucer makes no more attempt to analyse the behaviour of his monstrous husband than she does:

> But ther been folk of swich condicion
> That whan they have a certein purpos take,
> They kan nat stynte of hire entencion,
> But, right as they were bounden to a stake,
> They wol nat of that firste purpos slake.[26]

We should not too readily take for granted that the analytic approach of the Novelist represents a sophisticated and enlightened understanding of human behaviour. Consider the following retort to the Dame's ejaculation that 'Young men are mysteries!':

> In fine, he was a millionaire nobleman, owning to a considerable infusion of Welsh blood in the composition of him. Now, to the Cymry and to the pure Kelt, the past is at their elbows continually. The past of their lives has lost neither face nor voice behind the shroud; nor are the passions of the flesh, nor is the animate soul, wanting to it. Other races forfeit infancy, forfeit youth and manhood with their progression to the wisdom age may bestow. These have each stage always alive, quick at a word, a scent, a sound, to conjure up scenes, in spirit and in flame. (Chapter 28, 296)

Meredith's race-psychology is perhaps, from a late twentieth-century point of view, his most dated characteristic, though it takes comparatively inoffensive forms. A modern reader is likely to feel that the Novelist does not cast any more light on Fleetwood's motivation than the Dame at this point.

When the Novelist attempts to account for Fleetwood's 'conversion' to Carinthia, he produces a rare example in Meredith of apparently unironic inflated writing. The incident that prompts this passage is her rescue of the child from a rabid dog, and her preparedness to save the child's life by cauterizing the bite. Defensively, in a fatuous attempt to preserve some of his failing sense of superiority, he asks, 'Will she take the world's polish a little?':

> But his was not the surface nature which can put a question of the sort and pass it. As soon as it had been formed, a vision of the elemental creature calling him husband smote to shivers the shell we walk on, and caught him down among the lower forces, up amid the higher; an infernal and a celestial contest for the extinction of the one or the other of them, if it was not for their union. She wrestled with him where the darknesses roll their snake-eyed torrents over between jagged horns of the netherworld. She stood him in the white ray of the primal vital heat, to bear unwithering beside her the test of light. They flew, they chased, battled, embraced, disjoined, adventured apart, brought back the

count of their deeds, compared them, – and name the one crushed! (33, 345)

This does not mean, of course, that the Novelist has nothing to offer in response to the Dame's reductive mystification; it means, rather, that we should not necessarily take the opposition between them on the terms proposed. As always, and whatever he says about himself, the Meredithian narrator is primarily a master not of analysis but of discourse. I have said that both narrators are dialogic, but Dame Gossip is primarily so only in the weak sense that she *quotes* the voices that constitute her dialogue. In the first chapter, for example, she makes prolific use of the Meredithian technique of quoting fictional texts: a ballad of Countess Fanny and Captain Kirby, a song about them, a song from a popular stage melodrama, Kirby's *Maxims for Men* and Nymney's *Letters and Correspondence*.

The Novelist's narrative, on the other hand, is characterized by the familiar profuse Meredithian use of free indirect and direct discourse, combining a variety of individual and collective speech-idioms at differing degrees of dialogic angle to 'his' own voice. One *tour de force* of this kind is the account of the boxing match in Chapter 16, much of which is narrated in the colloquial, jargon-laden voice of a connoisseur. But the most prominent and significant dialogized voice is that of Fleetwood himself. There is an excellent analysis in Gillian Beer's book of one such passage, from Chapter 17, in which there is 'no grammatical or syntactical distinction between the narrator's commentary and the character's thoughts'.[27] What I wish particularly to emphasize is that such passages illustrate not merely the fluid interchange between the narrator and the character's *thoughts* but his *discourse*: Fleetwood is the extreme development of a type of Meredithian character earlier represented by Richard Feverel, Wilfred Pole and Harry Richmond, whose inner world is markedly a world of discourse, who is constantly representing himself to himself, in the shadow of the narrator's ironic presence:

He was the prisoner of his word; – rather like the donkeys known as married men: rather more honourable than most of them. He had to be present at the ball at the Schloss and behold his loathed Henrietta, suffer torture of chains to the rack, by reason of his having promised the bitter coquette he would be there. So hellish did the misery seem to him, that he was relieved by the prospect of lying a whole day long in loneliness with the sunshine of the woods, occasionally conjuring up the antidote face of the wood-sprite [Carinthia, whom he has just seen for the first time perched on a dangerously projecting tree] before he was to undergo it. But, as he was not by nature a dreamer, only dreamed of the luxury of being one, he soon looked back with loathing on a notion of relief to come from the state of ruminating animal, and jumped and shook off another of men's delusions...; already he regarded his recent subservience to the conceited and tripped peripatetic philosopher [Woodseer] as among the ignominies he had cast away on his road to a general contempt; which is the position of a supreme elevation for particularly sensitive young men. (11, 122–3)

The passage negotiates between free indirect discourse, more or less ironized, and direct authorial comment, in a way that is very familiar to readers of Meredith. Still more distinctive is the double accent of the first sentence, which prophesies the consequence of Fleetwood's proposal to Carinthia: in it can be detected both the blunt judgement of the narrator and the rather more self-admiring accent of Fleetwood himself, which is magnified in the remainder of the sentence. To be 'the prisoner of his word' is to fetishize an aristocratic code much as Sir Willoughby Patterne does, though with a less crass self-interest:

He was renowned and unrivalled as the man of stainless honour: the one living man of his word. He had never broken it – never would. There was his distinction among the herd. In that, a man is princely above princes. The nobility of Edward Russett, Earl of Fleetwood, surpasses the nobility of common nobles. (15, 153)

But this sense of superiority, which he projects both to himself and to others, is no more than a dandification of moral obligation, putting on the same level a trivial social commitment and a proposal of marriage. A similar dandification is perceptible in phrases such as 'rather more honourable than most of them' and 'another of men's delusions': these are characteristic examples of the discourse by which Fleetwood represents himself to himself.

It is perhaps significant that it is through language that Carinthia is first represented to Fleetwood. He reads in Gower Woodseer's note-book the phrases:

A beautiful Gorgon – a haggard Venus.... A panting look.... A look of beaten flame: a look of one who has run and at last beholds.... From minute to minute she is the rock that loses the sun at night and reddens in the morning', [and exclaims], 'Just to know there is a woman like her, is an antidote.... I only want to hear she lives, she is in the world.... I should think her sacred.' (8, 78–9)

The blindness of Fleetwood's logocentrism is ironically revealed when, having constructed an ideal person on the basis of Woodseer's highly figurative language, he says, 'talk of her, pray; without comparisons. I detest them' (80).

Fleetwood first sees Carinthia in a scene which, as A.H. Able and Judith Ann Sage have noted, Meredith has borrowed from Peacock.[28] As Fleetwood finds Carinthia seated on a 'sturdy, blunted and twisted little rock-fostered forest tree pushing horizontally for growth about thirty feet above the lower ground' (11, 121), in *Crotchet Castle* the medievally inclined Mr Chainmail sees Susannah Touchandgo lying on a 'gnarled and twisted oak... over the abyss'.[29] Susannah's behaviour has an explicit literary source in her reading of Rousseau, and although Mr Chainmail has been prepared for this sight not by descriptions of Susannah but by previous glimpses of her, he has encoded these in literary images as 'his lady of the lake, his enchantress of the ruined castle'.[30] Meredith's scene, in other words, has at least two generations of literary ancestry though, as Judith Ann Sage points out, he obscured the debt to Peacock by deleting from manuscript a long descriptive passage in which it is even more marked.

Fleetwood's response to the sight of Carinthia is that 'he longed to tell Woodseer that he had seen a sort of Carinthia' – this being of course, for him at this stage, the name of a collection of tropes in Woodseer's notebook. When, the same evening, he offers marriage to Carinthia, the 'person' to whom he is proposing has an almost entirely discursive existence. And the discourse in question is, crucially, not her own: after their marriage he hates her phrase, 'my husband', and what he calls her 'baby English' (15, 156).

The way that Fleetwood's response to Carinthia is prepared for, even generated, by language – the language of another – recalls the more obviously ironic episode in *Richard Feverel*, where Richard dicovers, through a conversation with Ralph Morton, that his cousin Clare is 'a charming creature', and falls in love with the next 'charming creature' that he meets, who happens to be not Clare but

Lucy (see Chapter 1, p. 29). We may also recall, in *Harry Richmond*, that the hero's attraction to Kiomi, Mabel and even Ottilia is mediated through various stylized discourses of female beauty, but that his eventual mate Janet is for most of the novel 'bald to the heart inhabiting me' because he cannot find a language to describe her, and dislikes her manner of speech (see Chapter 3, pp. 104–7). In *The Amazing Marriage* the stylized images of female beauty are mainly supplied by Gower Woodseer, a character whose development is counterpointed with Fleetwood's, and who is initially fascinated by Fleetwood's young stepmother Livia:

> To leave her was to have her as a moon in the heavens and to think of her creatively. A swarm of images rushed about and away, took lustre and shade. She was a miracle of greyness, her eyes translucently grey, a dark-haired queen of the twilights; and his heart sprang into his brain to picture the novel beauty; language became a flushed Bacchanal in a ring of dancing similes....
>
> Woodseer sat for a certain time over his note-book. He closed it with a thrilling conceit of the right thing written down; such as entomologists feel when they have pinned down the rare insect. But what is butterfly or beetle compared with the chiselled sentences carved out of air to constitute us part owner of the breathing image of an adored fair woman? We repeat them, and the act of repeating them makes her close on ours, by virtue of the eagle thought in the stamped gold of the lines. (9, 96–7; 10, 103–4)

By giving this appropriative discourse to the sentimentally valorized Woodseer, the affectionate portrait of his friend Stevenson, rather than to Fleetwood, and by implicating the narrator in it in a way familiar from *The Egoist*,[31] Meredith makes Fleetwood less of an exceptional monster, but an extreme representation of the syndrome of masculinity, language and sexuality that has been a major theme throughout his work. The full title of Chapter 8, in which these characters meet, is 'Of the encounter of two strange young men and their consorting: in which the male reader is requested to bear in mind what wild creature he was in his youth, while the female should marvel credulously.'

By the time Fleetwood sees Carinthia again on their wedding day the intoxication of Woodseer's phrases about her has worn off and, like Harry Richmond with Janet, he can find no language for her:

> she had beauty – of its kind. Or splendour or grandeur, was the term for it. But it bore no name. None of her qualities – if they were qualities – had a name. She stood with a dignity that the word did not express. (17, 178)

It is, moreover, the re-accentuation of her phrase 'my husband', in his memory of it on her lips when he returned to consummate the marriage, that epitomizes his later, belated desire for her.

There are many notes on which a study of Meredith's novels might end, but this is as appropriate as any. The master stylist is above all a master of the representation of style, whose creative genius is inseparable from an acute critical awareness of the ideological character of language and a remarkable capacity to combine discourses in the mutually illuminating ways that Bakhtin termed 'dialogic'. This ideological awareness extends to class, money and nationality, but is most persistently active in matters of gender, where, as the 'we' who attempt to own women by describing them in the above-quoted passage illustrates, the 'dialogic imagination' is a case of not forgetting that he is always himself implicated in the discourse he is criticizing.

Notes

Introduction

1. Oscar Wilde, 'The Decay of Lying', 1891, *Complete Works of Oscar Wilde*, London and Glasgow, Collins, 1966, p. 976.
2. Virginia Woolf, *The Second Common Reader*, 1932, Harmondsworth, Penguin, 1944, p. 174.
3. David Howard, '*Rhoda Fleming*: Meredith in the Margin', Ian Fletcher (ed.), *Meredith Now: Some Critical Essays*, London, Routledge, 1971, p. 131.
4. Gillian Beer, *Meredith: A Change of Masks*, London, Athlone Press, 1970, p. v.
5. M.M. Bakhtin, 'Discourse in the Novel', *The Dialogic Imagination: Four Essays*, ed. Michael Holquist, tr. Caryl Emerson and Michael Holquist, Austin, University of Texas, 1981, p. 276.
6. For Bakhtinian critiques of Saussure see M.M. Bakhtin, 'The Problem of Speech Genres', *Speech Genres and Other Late Essays*, ed. Caryl Emerson and Michael Holquist, tr. Vern W. McGee, Austin, University of Texas, 1986, pp. 60–102, and V.N. Voloshinov, *Marxism and the Philosophy of Language*, tr. Ladislav Matejka and I.R. Titunik, Cambridge, Mass. and London, Harvard University Press, 1986, pp. 58–61.
7. See Gary Saul Morson and Caryl Emerson, *Mikhail Bakhtin: Creation of a Prosaics*, Stanford, Calif., Stanford University Press, 1990.
8. 'Discourse in the Novel', *The Dialogic Imagination*, p. 298.
9. Donald D. Stone draws attention to Bakhtin's use of the word 'chaos' to describe the effect of Dostoevsky's world: 'Meredith and Bakhtin: Polyphony and Bildung', *Studies in English Literature*, vol. 28 no. 4, 1988, p. 695.
10. 'Discourse in the Novel', *The Dialogic Imagination*, p. 300.
11. Ibid., p. 298.
12. Mikhail Bakhtin, *Problems of Dostoevsky's Poetics*, ed. and tr. Caryl Emerson, Minneapolis, University of Minnesota, 1984, p. 82 (Bakhtin's italics).
13. E.g. 'To say that a writer has a style in this sense of idiosyncrasy is by no means necessarily to praise him. The individuality of Meredith's style is undeniable; there is a growing body of opinion that it was not a good one.' J. Middleton Murry, *The Problem of Style*, Oxford University Press, 1922, p. 5.
14. Margaret Conrow, 'Coming to Terms with George Meredith's Fiction', in George Goodin (ed.), *The English Novel in the Nineteenth Century*, University of Illinois, 1972, pp. 194–5.

15. George Meredith, *The Shaving of Shagpat: An Arabian Entertainment*, London, Chapman and Hall, 1856, p. v.
16. Jacob Korg, 'Expressive Styles in *The Ordeal of Richard Feverel*', *Nineteenth Century Fiction*, vol. 27 no. 3, December 1972, p. 253.
17. Donald David Stone, *Novelists in a Changing World: Meredith, James and the Transformation of English Fiction in the 1880s*, Cambridge, Mass., Harvard University Press, 1972, p. 127 n.
18. *Meredith: A Change of Masks*, p. 95.
19. E.M. Forster, *Aspects of the Novel*, London, Arnold, 1927, p. 122.
20. Richard Stang, *The Theory of the Novel in England 1850–1870*, London, Routledge, 1959, pp. 127–32.
21. *Meredith: A Change of Masks*, p. 103.
22. *Mikhail Bakhtin: Creation of a Prosaics*, pp. 290–1.
23. Allon White, *The Uses of Obscurity: The Fiction of Early Modernism*, London, Routledge, 1981, p. 173 n. 32.
24. M.M. Bakhtin, 'Forms of Time and of the Chronotope in the Novel', *The Dialogic Imagination*, p. 252. What Bakhtin explicitly states here is that relations between *chronotopes* ('the intrinsic connectedness of temporal and spatial relationships that are artistically expressed in literature', ibid., p. 84) are dialogical, and the chronotope 'defines genre and generic distinctions' (ibid., p. 85).
25. Unlike the other terms that Bakhtin developed for his theory of novelistic discourse, 'polyphony' is a concept that he discusses only in relation to Dostoevsky and his influence, in *Problems of Dostoevsky's Poetics* and the incomplete essays and notes written when he revised that book, collected in *Speech Genres and Other Late Essays*. However, Donald D. Stone is surely right in describing the Meredithian protagonist, like the Dostoevskian, as 'freed from authorial control, but poised among the historical tensions that lie outside the novel but are expressed in it' ('Meredith and Bakhtin: Polyphony and Bildung', p. 697.)
26. *Marxism and the Philosophy of Language*, p. 41. I shall several times be citing this book and *The Formal Method in Literary Scholarship* by P.N. Medvedev as examples of Bakhtinian thought. Since the 1970s some scholars have argued that these texts, and some others published under the name of V.N. Voloshinov, were largely written by Bakhtin. This is a highly complex controversy among Bakhtin scholars on which I am not competent to judge. However, no one denies that the texts form, together with Bakhtin's undisputed writings, a closely interconnected body of thought by what is often termed 'the Bakhtin School'. It is in this spirit that I cite these texts, and follow the convention of referring to their authors as 'Bakhtin/Voloshinov' and 'Bakhtin/Medvedev'.
27. Henry James, letter to Edmund Gosse, 15 October 1912, Leon Edel (ed.), *Letters of Henry James*, vol. 4, Cambridge, Mass. and London, Belknap Press, 1984, p. 631. James's immediately preceding judgement is less often quoted: 'The fantastic and the mannered in him were as nothing to the intimately sane and straight.'

28. C.L. Cline (ed.), *Letters of George Meredith*, Oxford, Clarendon Press, 1970, 7 December [1870], vol. 1, p. 432.
29. L.G. Hergenhan, 'The Reception of George Meredith's Early Novels', *Nineteenth Century Fiction*, vol. 19 no. 2, September 1964, p. 214 and n., citing Q.D. Leavis, *Fiction and the Reading Public*, London, Chatto and Windus, 1932, p. 169. Leavis, however, makes no reference to Meredith.
30. Peter Keating, *The Haunted Study: A Social History of the English Novel, 1875–1914*, London, Secker, 1989.
31. David Howard, '*Rhoda Fleming*: Meredith in the Margin', *Meredith Now*, p. 131.
32. *Problems of Dostoevsky's Poetics*, p. 208.
33. Lionel Stevenson, *The Ordeal of George Meredith*, London, Peter Owen, 1954, p. 8.
34. Judith Wilt, *The Readable People of George Meredith*, New Jersey, Princeton University Press, 1975, p. 76.
35. *The Dialogic Imagination*, p. 427.
36. Mikhail Bakhtin, *Rabelais and His World*, tr. Hélène Iswolsky, Bloomington, Indiana University Press, 1984, p. 201.
37. Ibid., p. 197.
38. See Donald D. Stone, 'Meredith and Bakhtin: Polyphony and Bildung' and Graham McMaster, '*Harry Richmond*: Meredith's Unwritten Attack on Victorian Legitimacy', *POETICA*, 24, November 1986, pp. 64–85.
39. See Gary Saul Morson and Caryl Emerson, *Mikhail Bakhtin: Creation of a Prosaics*, for an extended and informed critique of the carnivalesque as expounded in *Rabelais and His World*.
40. Julia Kristeva, 'Word, Dialogue and Novel', *Desire in Language: A Semiotic Approach to Literature and Art*, tr. Thomas Gora, Alice Jardine and Leon S. Roudiez, Oxford, Basil Blackwell, 1980, p. 66.
41. Roland Barthes, 'From Work to Text', *Image–Music–Text*, ed. and tr. Stephen Heath, London, Fontana, 1977, p. 160.
42. 'The Problem of the Text', *Speech Genres and Other Late Essays*, p. 107.
43. *Marxism and the Philosophy of Language*, p. 26 (Bakhtin/Voloshinov's italics).
44. 'Discourse in the Novel', *The Dialogic Imagination*, p. 272.
45. *Problems of Dostoevsky's Poetics*, p. 96 (Bakhtin's italics).

1 The Ordeal of Richard Feverel

1. *Saturday Review*, viii, 9 July 1959; *Critical Heritage*, p. 75.
2. *The Critic*, xix, 2 July 1959; *Critical Heritage*, p. 66.
3. *Letters*, vol. 1, p. 39 [7 July 1959], to Samuel Lucas.
4. Samuel Lucas, *The Times*, 14 October 1859. *Critical Heritage*, p. 82.
5. Justin McCarthy, 'Novels with a Purpose', *Westminster Review*, xxvi, July 1864; *Critical Heritage*, p. 127.
6. J.B. Priestley, *George Meredith*, London, Macmillan, 1926, p. 160.

Notes   257

7. John W. Morris, 'Inherent Principles of Order in *Richard Feverel*', *PMLA*, 78, 1963, p. 334.
8. Virginia Woolf, *The Second Common Reader*, 1932, Harmondsworth, Penguin, 1944, p. 174.
9. Gillian Beer, *Meredith: A Change of Masks*, p. 16.
10. Sven-Johan Spånberg, *The Ordeal of Richard Feverel and the Traditions of Realism*, Uppsala University, 1974, pp. 68, 75.
11. *Meredith: A Change of Masks*, p. 21.
12. Jacob Korg, 'Expressive Styles in *The Ordeal of Richard Feverel*', p. 260.
13. Donald D. Stone, 'Meredith and Bakhtin: Polyphony and Bildung', p. 696, citing *The Dialogic Imagination*, p. 329.
14. 'Discourse in the Novel', *The Dialogic Imagination*, p. 322.
15. The first four chapters of the first edition were, rather carelessly, cut to one by Meredith for the edition of 1878. These changes, and others including a whole excised chapter between Chapters 18 and 19 of the revised version, are documented in the *Bibliography and Various Readings* volume of the Memorial Edition (1911). The first edition has been reprinted by Modern Library College Editions (1950), Introduction by Lionel Stevenson, and Holt, Rinehart and Winston, Inc. (1964), Introduction by Charles J. Hill.
16. 'Discourse in the Novel', *The Dialogic Imagination*, pp. 316, 320.
17. Frank D. Curtin, 'Adrian Harley: The Limits of Meredith's Comedy', *Nineteenth Century Fiction*, 7, 1953, p. 276.
18. Judith Wilt, another critic who has recognized the dialogic character of Meredith's fiction, has referred to Adrian's 'tonal identification with the narrator' and remarked that 'Meredith senses in himself the same mental temptations and tendencies that Adrian surrendered to, and badly needs to separate himself from them' (*The Readable People of George Meredith*, pp. 102n., 108). Wilt also rightly points out that Adrian does not, as Curtin says, define the limits of Meredith's comedy but rather those of what Meredith called 'satire' (ibid., pp. 105–6n.).
19. Jacob Korg comments on voices 'associated with' Adrian and Sir Austin: op. cit., pp. 261–2.
20. *Problems of Dostoevsky's Poetics*, p. 95. Original italics.
21. Sven-Johan Spånberg, 'The Theme of Sexuality in *The Ordeal of Richard Feverel*', *Studia Neophilologica*, xlvi, 1974, p. 208.
22. Allon White, *The Uses of Obscurity: The Fiction of Early Modernism*, p. 27. White borrows the term 'legitimation crisis' from Jurgen Habermas: see his *Legitimation Crisis*, tr. Thomas McCarthy, Boston, Mass., Beacon Press, 1975; and William Outhwaite, *Habermas: A Critical Introduction*, Cambridge, Polity Press, 1994, pp. 63–7.
23. Phyllis Bartlett, 'Richard Feverel, Knight-Errant', *Bulletin of the New York Public Library*, vol. 63 no. 7, July 1959, pp. 329–40.
24. *Problems of Dostoevsky's Poetics*, p. 59.
25. Gary Saul Morson and Caryl Emerson, *Mikhail Bakhtin: Creation of a Prosaics*, p. 330.
26. See, for example, Shlomith Rimmon-Kenan, *Narrative Fiction: Contemporary Poetics*, London and New York, Routledge, 1983, pp. 109ff.

27. Peter Cominos, 'Late-Victorian Respectability and the Social System', *International Review of Social History*, 8 (1963), p. 35; quoted Sven-Johan Spånberg, 'The Theme of Sexuality in *The Ordeal of Richard Feverel*', p. 203. According to Spånberg sexuality was primarily 'a sociological and physiological issue' for the Victorians.
28. Richard C. Stevenson, 'The Spirit of Critical Intelligence in *Richard Feverel*', J.H. Buckley (ed.), *The Worlds of Victorian Fiction*, Boston, Mass., and London, Harvard University Press, 1975, pp. 211–12.
29. *Bibliography and Various Readings*, p. 33.
30. 'Discourse in the Novel', *The Dialogic Imagination*, p. 362.
31. Christopher Morris, in an early post-structuralist analysis of the novel, argued that in *Richard Feverel* desire is seen to be created by discourse, but surprisingly does not cite this obvious and crucial instance; Christopher Morris, 'Richard Feverel and the Fictional Lineage of Desire', *ELH*, 42, 1975, pp. 242–57.
32. Bakhtin on the 'love idyll' in 'Forms of Time and of the Chronotope in the Novel', *The Dialogic Imagination*, p. 226.
33. Ibid., p. 84.
34. Ibid., p. 101.
35. 'The *Bildungsroman* and its Significance in the History of Realism (Toward a Historical Typology of the Novel)', *Speech Genres and Other Late Essays*, p. 23. Bakhtin's italics.
36. 'Forms of Time and of the Chronotope in the Novel', *The Dialogic Imagination*, p. 252.
37. Susanne Howe, *Wilhelm Meister and his English Kinsmen*, New York, Columbia University Press, 1930. Howe also discussed *Evan Harrington* and *Beauchamp's Career* but, surprisingly, not *Harry Richmond*, which perhaps shows the most direct Goethean influence of all Meredith's novels.
38. J.H. Buckley, *Season of Youth: The Bildungsroman from Dickens to Golding*, Boston, Mass., Harvard University Press, 1974, Chapter 3.
39. Nikki Lee Manos, 'The Ordeal of Richard Feverel: Bildungsroman or Anti-Bildungsroman?' *Victorian Newsletter*, 70, Fall 1986, pp. 18–24.
40. *The Ordeal of Richard Feverel and the Traditions of Realism*, p. 31.
41. This is discussed in greater detail in Spånberg's article, 'The Theme of Sexuality in *The Ordeal of Richard Feverel*'. Spånberg's demonstration that Sir Austin's horror of sexual precocity was by no means unique, and his account of the character as an analysis of the deformations of the model Victorian gentleman, illustrates one of the most important ways in which current ideological discourse is present in the novel.
42. *The Ordeal of Richard Feverel and the Traditions of Realism*, pp. 31–32.
43. Mikhail Bakhtin, 'Author and Hero in Aesthetic Activity,', Michael Holquist and Vadim Liapunov (eds), *Art and Answerability*, tr. Vadim Liapunov, Austin, University of Texas Press, 1990, p. 12.
44. Ibid., p. 191.
45. Ibid., p. 15.
46. Jean-Jacques Rousseau, *Emile or Education*, tr. Barbara Foxey, London, Everyman's Library, Dent, 1911, p. 18. My italics.

47. Ibid., pp. 298–9. My italics.
48. *The Ordeal of Richard Feverel and the Traditions of Realism*, p. 70.
49. Ibid., p. 52.
50. For an instance of Rousseau sounding like Sir Austin, consider: 'I return to my system, and I say, when the critical age approaches, present to young people spectacles which restrain rather than excite them.... Remove them from great cities.... Choose carefully their company, their occupations, and their pleasures' (*Emile*, p. 192). And of Sir Austin sounding like Rousseau: 'he caught intelligible signs of the beneficent order of the universe, from a heart newly confirmed in its grasp of the principle of human goodness, as manifested in the dear child who had just left him; confirmed in its belief in the ultimate victory of good within us, without which nature has neither music nor meaning, and is rock, stone, tree, and nothing more' (10, 82).
51. *Bibliography and Various Readings*, p. 38. This passage, excised in revision, is the only occasion on which the stages of the System are formally laid out, but several of them are of course mentioned in the surviving text. Spånberg points out close similarities to the five stages of Emile's development (*The Ordeal of Richard Feverel and the Traditions of Realism*, p. 34).
52. Mikhail Bakhtin, 'From the Prehistory of Novelistic Discourse', *The Dialogic Imagination*, p. 44.
53. Viscountess Milner, 'Talks with George Meredith', *National Review*, cxxxi (1948), p. 456; cited Gillian Beer and Margaret Harris (eds), *The Notebooks of George Meredith*, Salzburg, Institut für Anglistik und Amerikanistik, Universität Salzburg, 1983, p. 146.
54. *Letters*, vol. 2, p. 910, 16 March 1888, to Mrs J.B. Gilman.
55. *Letters*, vol. 3, p. 1478, 10 February 1903, to Mrs Alice Meynell.
56. *Meredith: A Change of Masks*, p. 20.
57. Ibid., p. 19.
58. S.M. Ellis (ed.), *A Mid-Victorian Pepys: the Letters and Memoirs of Sir William Hardman, M.A, F.R.G.S.*, Cecil Palmer, London, 1923, p. 133.
59. *Meredith: A Change of Masks*, p. 20.
60. For example, 'A brilliant saying arrests thought' (*The Notebooks of George Meredith*, p. 50); 'A maker of Proverbs – what is he but a narrow mind the mouthpiece of a narrower?' (Sir Austin's 'old Notebook', 44, 536).
61. *Problems of Dostoevsky's Poetics*, p. 96.
62. *Letters*, vol. 2, p. 910, 16 March 1888, to Mrs J.B. Gilman.
63. 'Forms of Time and of the Chronotope in the Novel', *The Dialogic Imagination*, p. 85.
64. *The Ordeal of Richard Feverel and the Traditions of Realism*, p. 65
65. 'The *Bildungsroman* and its Significance in the History of Realism', *Speech Genres and Other Late Essays*, p. 12.
66. Ibid., p. 16.
67. Spånberg discusses the influence of French realism, especially Stendhal, on Meredith, in *The Ordeal of Richard Feverel and the Traditions of Realism*, pp. 75–84.

68. For a discussion of *ORF* as a refutation of Carlyle's alleged distortion of Goethean *Bildung* and 'the anti-*Bildung* forces in nineteenth-century England' see Nikki Lee Manos, *op. cit.*
69. Thomas Carlyle, *Sartor Resartus*, ed. Kerry McSweeney and Peter Sabor, Oxford University Press, World's Classics, 1987, pp. 117–18.
70. Ibid., p. 118.
71. Ibid., 'Introduction', p. xxii.
72. *Problems of Dostoevsky's Poetics*, p. 108.
73. Ibid., p. 117.

2 The Novels of the 1860s

1. Samuel Lucas, *The Times*, Friday, 14 October 1859; *Critical Heritage*, p. 84.
2. Ibid., p. 82.
3. John Sutherland, *The Longman Companion to Victorian Fiction*, London, Longman, 1988, p. 676.
4. *Letters*, vol. 1, p. 49, 20 December 1859, to Samuel Lucas.
5. Ibid., p. 52, [?5 January 1860], to Samuel Lucas.
6. Ibid., p. 57, [?9 February 1860], to Samuel Lucas.
7. *The Ordeal of George Meredith*, p. 76.
8. *Letters*, vol. 1, p. 57, [9 February 1860], to Samuel Lucas. For a detailed account of the serialization of *Evan Harrington*, see Royal A. Gettmann, 'Serialization and *Evan Harrington*', *PMLA*, 64, 1949, pp. 963–975.
9. It is noteworthy, however, that Lucas followed *Evan Harrington* with another 'sensation' novel, Shirley Brooks's *The Silver Cord*, and that unlike Meredith's novel this quickly went into a second edition (see L.T. Hergenhan, 'The Reception of George Meredith's Early Novels', *Nineteenth Century Fiction*, vol. 19, no. 2, September 1964, p. 226 and n.).
10. *Letters*, vol. 1, p. 36 [*ante* 27 April 1859], to Tom Taylor.
11. Ibid., p. 330 [February–March 1866], to Algernon Swinburne.
12. Ibid., p. 419, 15 June [1870], to William Hardman.
13. Edward Clodd, *Memories*, London, Watts and Co., 1926, p. 156.
14. *Letters*, vol. 1, p. 216, 14 July 1863; p. 219, 19 July 1863; p. 233, 13 November 1863.
15. Jean-Jacques Rousseau, *Emile*, p. 162.
16. Natalie Cole Michta, 'The Legitimate Self in George Meredith's *Evan Harrington*', *Studies in the Novel*, vol. 21, no. 1, 1989, p. 46.
17. J.M.S. Tompkins, 'On Re-reading *Evan Harrington*', *Meredith Now*, pp. 114–29.
18. *Problems of Dostoevsky's Poetics*, p. 92.
19. *The Ordeal of George Meredith*, p. 82.
20. 'Forms of Time and of the Chronotope in the Novel', *The Dialogic Imagination*, pp. 86 ff.
21. *Problems of Dostoevsky's Poetics*, p. 196.

22. V.S. Pritchett sees Louisa as a Dickensian character of this kind: 'Meredith is carrying the Dickensian soliloquist a step further – towards his relation to social pressures and the lure of a romantic idealism, poor but observable. Quick, wounded and critical, Meredith was capable of a psychological extension of the genuine Dickensian character', *George Meredith and English Comedy*, London, Chatto and Windus, 1970, p. 78.
23. Peter Bailey, *Leisure and Class in Victorian England: Rational Recreation and the Contest for Control, 1830–1885*, London, Routledge; Toronto and Buffalo, University of Toronto Press, 1978, p. 74.
24. Margaret Tarratt, ' "Snips", "Snobs" and the "True Gentleman" in *Evan Harrington*', *Meredith Now*, p. 108.
25. 'Forms of Time and of the Chronotope in the Novel', *The Dialogic Imagination*, pp. 125–6.
26. Donald D. Stone, *Novelists in a Changing World: Meredith, James, and the Transformation of English Fiction in the 1880s*, Cambridge, Mass., Harvard University Press, 1972, p. 103.
27. L.G. Hergenhan, 'The Reception of George Meredith's Early Novels', pp. 225–6.
28. *Letters*, vol. 1, p. 70, November [1860], to D.G. Rossetti.
29. A selection of phrases from the letters of the period gives a flavour of the complex drama of composition: 'I am getting temporarily tired of my *Emilia*' (April 1861, p. 75); 'anxious to finish' (July 1861, p. 93); 'untouched for months' (November 1861, p. 116); 'done lots of' (May 1862, p. 143); 'goes slowly forward, for the reason that I have rewritten it' (June 1862, p. 149); 'remodelled the whole – making the background more agreeable and richer comedy' (June 1862, p. 152); 'A dreadful hitch' (August 1862, p. 156); 'I hope to finish this dreadful work in six weeks' (January 1863, p. 185); 'overwhelmed with disgust' (March 1863, p. 195); 'must also rewrite two "frolic" chapters' (October 1863, p. 232); 'I have never so cut about created thing' (December 1863, p. 239). All from *Letters*, vol. 1.
30. *Letters*, vol. 1, p. 248, [?11 or 18 March 1864], to Frederick Maxse.
31. *Problems of Dostoevsky's Poetics*, p. 233.
32. The other examples of foreign speech in the novel are strikingly different. Mr Pericles, the Greek musical connoisseur, Mrs Chump, the amorous Irish widow and Emilia's father are given conventional markers of linguistic deviance and incompetence, which are both irritating and offensive. As Leech and Short say of so-called eye-dialect, 'it is its non-standardness that strikes us, not the supposed phonetic reality behind it' (Geoffrey N. Leech and Michael H. Short, *Style in Fiction: A Linguistic Introduction to English Fictional Prose*, London and New York, Longman, 1981, p. 168). However, the grotesque effect of the representation of their speech, in contrast to the cultivated speech of the Poles, has an ironic function, since Mr Pericles is the guarantor (both for the Poles and for the reader) of Emilia's musical genius, and Mrs Chump holds the key to the financial complications which threaten the collapse of the fortune on which the Poles' cultivation is built.

33. *The Readable People of George Meredith*, pp. 117–18.
34. Perhaps the most interesting example of this polemic (not involving the philosopher) is the narrator's defiant assertion that understanding his character's behaviour is essential, which includes the following parenthesis: '(though I need not be told what odium frowns on such a pretension to excess of cleverness)' (13, 110–11). Perhaps the most wounding review Meredith received was that of *Modern Love and Other Poems* by R.H. Hutton in *The Spectator* during the composition of *SB* (xxxv, 24 May 1862, *Critical Heritage*, pp. 92–6), which, being anonymous, provoked Meredith to a remark, revealing of his private misogyny at this period, about 'criticisms from whipsters or women' (see *The Ordeal of George Meredith*, pp. 112ff). Hutton uses the word clever three times in the first page, including the extremely wounding phrase, 'a clever man, without literary genius, taste, or judgement'. The word continued to be a staple of Meredith's reviewers, and one wonders how they would have managed without this word, which invariably connotes disapproval without having any unfavourable denotative content. None of the OED definitions specifies a note of disapproval, but such a note is present in all the 19th century illustrations (by Austen, Carlyle, Lamb and Kingsley) of definition 3: 'possessing skill or talent; able to use hand or brain readily and effectively; dexterous, skilful; adroit'.
35. See Robert Graves, *The White Goddess*, New York, Farrar, Strauss and Giroux, 1966, p. 176.
36. *Letters*, vol. 1, p. 250 [26 March 1864], to Frederick Maxse.
37. Ibid., p. 290 18 October 1864, and p. 291 [24 October 1864], both to William Hardman.
38. Ibid., p. 295 [21 November 1864], to Augustus Jessopp.
39. Ibid., p. 302, 30 January [1865], to Augustus Jessopp.
40. Ibid., p. 303; p. 305 [February 1985], to Frederick Maxse.
41. J.C. Jeaffreson, *Athenaeum*, no. 1981, 14 October 1865, *Critical Heritage*, p. 137.
42. David Howard, '*Rhoda Fleming*: Meredith in the Margin', *Meredith Now*, p. 140.
43. J.C. Jeaffreson, op. cit., p. 138.
44. See Jeanne Fahnestock, 'Bigamy: The Rise and Fall of a Convention', *Nineteenth Century Fiction*, vol. 36, no. 1, June 1981 pp. 47–71: 'The peak years of the fashion are 1862, 1863, 1864, and 1865. By a very conservative estimate, twelve novels with bigamy as a plot element appeared in 1862, twelve in 1863, thirteen in 1864, and sixteen in 1865.... In 1866 the number dropped sharply to six. Perhaps the fashion peaked the week of 3 December 1864 when three of the four novels reviewed in the *Athenaeum* had plots constructed around bigamy' (pp. 55–6). Fahnestock does not refer to *Rhoda Fleming*. Interestingly, Thomas Hardy employed a variant of bigamy as a device for resolution in *Desperate Remedies*, the novel that he wrote under the influence of Meredith's advice, in 1869, to pay more attention to plot.

45. David Howard, op. cit., p. 131. The final paragraph, telling of the last seven years of Dahlia's life, from which the phrases 'among the ashes' and 'In truth, she sat among the clouds' are quoted, was inserted in the revised edition in 1885 (see *Bibliography and Various Readings*, p. 169).
46. *Problems of Dostoevsky's Poetics*, p. 185.
47. 'Discourse in the Novel', *The Dialogic Imagination*, p. 364.
48. David Howard, op. cit., p. 135.
49. *Letters*, vol. 1, pp. 322–3, [December 28, 1865], to Frederick A. Maxse.
50. Ibid., p. 302, 30 January [1865], to Augustus Jessopp.
51. Ibid., p. 354, 2 March 1867, to Algernon C. Swinburne.
52. 'Epic and Novel', *The Dialogic Imagination*, pp. 13, 14, 18.
53. Ibid., pp. 22–3, 27–8.
54. Duels in Meredith usually either take place but are not narrated (*Richard Feverel, Beauchamp's Career, The Tragic Comedians, Lord Ormont and his Aminta*) or are averted (*Evan Harrington, Diana of the Crossways*). The duel in *Harry Richmond* (HR) is narrated, but in an ironic and deprecatory tone (HR, 32, 340–2). Perhaps significantly, the duel in *Vittoria* is highly unorthodox, since Guidascarpi is armed only with a dagger, and Weisspriess loses because he cannot fight with pride or honour when he has such an advantage.
55. *Letters*, vol. 1, p. 264, 6 June [1864], to Augustus Jessopp.
56. Jack Lindsay, *George Meredith, his life and work*, London, Bodley Head, 1956, p. 168.
57. 'Discourse in the Novel', *The Dialogic Imagination*, p. 272.
58. Ibid., p. 332.
59. *Letters*, vol. 1, p. 354, 2 March 1867.
60. Derek Beales, *The Risorgimento and the Unification of Italy*, London, George Allen and Unwin; New York, Barnes and Noble, 1971, p. 46.
61. Ibid, pp. 58, 57.
62. *Letters*, vol. 1, p. 255, 18 May 1864, to Augustus Jessopp.

3 The Adventures of Harry Richmond

1. *Letters*, vol. 1, p. 255, 18 May 1864, p. 255, to Augustus Jessopp.
2. Ibid., p. 275 [13 July 1864], to William Hardman.
3. *The Notebooks of George Meredith*, pp. 96–100. The outline is discussed in some detail by Richard B. Hudson, 'Meredith's Autobiography and "The Adventures of Harry Richmond"', *Nineteenth Century Fiction*, vol. 9, 1954–5, pp. 38–49.
4. *Letters*, vol. 1, p. 415, 27 January 1870, to John Morley.
5. Graham McMaster, '*Harry Richmond*: Meredith's Unwritten Attack on Victorian Legitimacy', *POETICA: An International Journal of Literary-Linguistic Studies*, 24, November 1986, p. 66.
6. Ibid., p. 67.
7. Mikhail Bakhtin, 'The Problem of Speech Genres', *Speech Genres and Other Late Essays*, p. 96.

8. Raymond Williams, *Culture and Society 1780–1850*, 1958, Harmondsworth, Middlesex, Penguin, 1963, p. 253.
9. McMaster, op. cit., p. 71.
10. Mikhail Bakhtin, *Rabelais and His World*, p. 197, quoted McMaster, op. cit., p. 71.
11. McMaster, op. cit., p. 73.
12. cf. Gillian Beer, *Meredith: A Change of Masks*, p. 51; Renate Muendel, *George Meredith*, Boston, Mass., Twayne, 1986, p. 85.
13. McMaster, op. cit., p. 69.
14. Charles Dickens, *David Copperfield*, 1849–50, London, Nelson, n.d., Chapter 7, pp. 101–3.
15. *Bibliography and Various Readings*, p. 220. Heriot also dies in this version, so that the whole story conforms more to the melodramatic-moralistic model represented by the Steerforth-Little Em'ly story.
16. Sven-Johan Spånberg (ed.), *The Adventures of Harry Richmond: The Unpublished Parts*, Uppsala, Acta Universitatis Upsaliensis, 1990, p. 25.
17. 'Forms of Time and of the Chronotope in the Novel', *The Dialogic Imagination*, p. 100.
18. 'The *Bildungsroman* and Its Significance in the History of Realism (Toward a Historical Typology of the Novel)', *Speech Genres and Other Late Essays*, p. 34.
19. Margaret Tarratt, 'The *Adventures of Harry Richmond* – Bildungsroman and Historical Novel', *Meredith Now*, p. 170.
20. R.J. Hollingdale, 'Introduction' to Johann Wolfgang von Goethe, *Elective Affinities*, tr. R.J. Hollingdale, Harmondsworth, Penguin, 1971, pp. 15–16.
21. *Rhoda Fleming* is an exception that proves the rule, since her religious feeling is clearly portrayed unsympathetically.
22. Thomas Carlyle, *Wilhelm Meister's Apprenticeship and Travels*, translated from the German of Goethe, vol. 1, *The Works of Thomas Carlyle*, Centenary Edition, vol. XXIII, London, Chapman and Hall, 1899, Book 6, p. 430.
23. Ibid., Book 4, Chapter 6, pp. 262 ff.
24. J.W. von Goethe, *Wilhelm Meisters Lehrjahre: Goethes Werke*, Band VII, Hamburg, Christian Wegner Verlag, 1950, p. 532; translated, 'thy fair lofty soul', Carlyle, op. cit., vol. 2, p. 112.
25. *Bibliography and Various Readings*, pp. 179–80.
26. See Sven-Johan Spånberg, *Harry Richmond: the Unpublished Parts*.
27. See *Bibliography and Various Readings*, pp. 170–220.
28. L.T. Hergenhan, 'Meredith's Revisions of *Harry Richmond*', *Review of English Studies*, new series, vol. 14, no. 53, 1963, pp. 24–32.
29. McMaster, op. cit., p. 66.
30. 'The *Bildungsroman* and its Significance in the History of Realism', *Speech Genres and Other Late Essays*, p. 23, Bakhtin's italics.
31. Spånberg, op. cit., p. 21.

4 Beauchamp's Career

1. David Howard, 'George Meredith: "Delicate" and "Epical" Fiction', in John Lucas (ed.) *Literature and Politics in the Nineteenth Century*, London, Methuen, 1971, p. 160.
2. George Eliot, *Felix Holt, the Radical* (1866), Standard Edition, Edinburgh and London, Blackwood, vol. II, pp. 122–3. For a more extended comparison of *Beauchamp's Career* and *Felix Holt*, see Mohammad Shaheen, *George Meredith: A Reappraisal of the Novels* (London: Macmillan, 1981), pp. 57–63.
3. See Gayla S. McGlamery, 'The Dialogic Meredith: Prefaces to the Novels of the 1880s', Ph.D. dissertation, Ann Arbor, Mich., 1984.
4. Margaret Harris, 'Introduction' to *Beauchamp's Career*, World's Classics paperback edition, Oxford University Press, 1988, p. xviii.
5. Matthew Arnold, *Culture and Anarchy* (1869), Cambridge: Cambridge University Press, 1932, p. 9.
6. Harris, op. cit., p. xxiv.
7. *Letters*, vol. 1, p. 425, Tuesday, 26 July 1870, to Frederick Maxse.
8. *Problems of Dostoevsky's Poetics*, p. 92.
9. *Letters*, vol. 1, p. 484, 22 May 1874, to John Morley.
10. *Letters*, vol. 1, pp. 486–7, 23 July 1874, to John Morley.
11. *Letters*, vol. 1, p. 443, 23 March 1871, to John Morley.
12. See *Letters*, vol. 1, pp. 474–5, 1 January 1873, to Frederick Greenwood, the conservative editor of the *Pall Mall Gazette*: 'Fitzjames Stephen's articles are fine outhitting and have judicial good sense.' Morley complained to Frederic Harrison of an unnamed 'very sensible man' who wrote to him praising Stephen in similar terms: 'How splendidly masculine! What noble common sense!' (Edwin Mallard Everett, *The Party of Humanity: The Fortnightly Review and its Contributors 1865–1874*, New York, Russell and Russell, 1939, p. 286). Stephen's complaint in his Dedication against 'the commonplaces and the vein of sentiment' in the press might be a presence in Cecilia's silent criticism of Nevil for 'allowing himself to appear moved by his own commonplace utterances' (33, 376). An example of Stephen's 'fine outhitting' might be his lampoon of Mill addressing a pimp: 'Without offence to your better judgement, dear sir...' set beside his own preferred style: 'You dirty rascal...', *Liberty, Equality, Fraternity*, 1873–4, Cambridge, Cambridge University Press, 1973, pp. 137–8). This is crude use of heteroglossia but may have appealed to Meredith as relief from Morley's manner exemplified in the extract from *On Compromise* quoted below.
13. Norman Kelvin, *A Troubled Eden: Nature and Society in the Works of George Meredith*, Edinburgh and London, Oliver and Boyd, 1961, p. 87.
14. *Letters*, vol. 1, p. 432, 7 December [1870], to John Morley.
15. Benjamin Disraeli, 'Preface to the Fifth Edition' (1849) of *Coningsby* (first publ. 1844), London, Longman's Green, 1923, p. vii. Arnold Kettle rightly remarks that 'Meredith is very conscious – as conscious as Disraeli – of "forces" in the historical sense. But he tackles

the problem of their representation in concrete terms on a far more serious artistic level than Disraeli had any conception of', *Meredith Now*, p. 191.
16. John Morley, 'Byron' (first publ. *Fortnightly Review*, 1870), *Critical Miscellanies*, London, Macmillan, 1886, vol. 1, p. 227.
17. Margaret Harris, op. cit., p. xxi.
18. *Meredith: A Change of Masks*, p. 82.
19. Morley, op. cit., p. 226. The original *Fortnightly* text reads 'crushed' for 'mastered'.
20. Donald D. Stone points out that the translation of Plato that occupies Beauchamp at the end of the novel, and of course his death by drowning, link him with Shelley (*The Romantic Impulse in Victorian Fiction*, Cambridge, Mass., Harvard University Press, 1980, pp. 314–15). The death could perhaps be seen as combining those of Shelley and Byron: drowning in a heroic and arguably radical cause.
21. Compare with this, and with Beauchamp's thoughts about the press and starting a radical paper generally, Maxse's *The Causes of Social Revolt* (London, Longman's, Green, Reader and Dyer, 1872), pp. 32–44. Like Beauchamp, Maxse thinks there 'is no comparison between the power of the weekly and the daily press' (p. 42), but unlike Beauchamp he dismisses the notion of a 'daily Radical organ' as 'impracticable' (pp. 42–3). Among the papers that Maxse thought 'have probably done more than any others to create distrust and hatred between classes', and that he accused of 'deal[ing] in cynical sneers at all earnest thought' (p. 42n.) was the *Pall Mall Gazette*, for which a few years earlier Meredith was writing 'almost every week' (*Letters*, vol. 1, p. 375), and with whose editor, Frederick Greenwood, he was on friendly terms (see note 15). Maxse however distinguishes between the political and the literary articles of the *PMG*.
22. John Stuart Mill, 'The Subjection of Women', 1869, *On Liberty, Representative Government, The Subjection of Women*, London, Oxford University Press (World's Classics), 1912, pp. 451–2. According to Morley, he took 'The Subjection of Women' when it was first published to Meredith who 'could not be torn from it all day'. John Morley, *Recollections*, London, Macmillan, 1917, vol. 1, p. 47; quoted James S. Stone, *George Meredith's Politics*, Port Credit, Ontario, P.D. Meany, 1986, p. 48. For Meredith's admiration of Mill, see *Letters*, vol. 1, p. 139 and p. 408. Both these letters are to Maxse.
23. 'Discourse in the Novel', *The Dialogic Imagination*, p. 276. Compare, however, 'The very words necessary to express the task I have undertaken, show how arduous it is.... The difficulty is that which exists in all cases in which there is a mass of feeling to be contended against' ('The Subjection of Women', p. 427).
24. *Meredith: A Change of Masks*, p. 88.
25. Ibid., p. 89.
26. 'The Subjection of Women', p. 458.
27. John Morley, *On Compromise*, 1874, London, Macmillan, 1886, p. 1.
28. Michael Holquist, *Dialogism: Bakhtin and His World*, London, Routledge, New Accents, 1990, p. 88.

29. cf. *OED*: 'I will fulfil your errand, and horsewhip him soundly' (Bulwer Lytton, 1829); 'You take pains to whip me so handsomely' (Shirley, 1628); 'He had been brought to condign punishment as a traitor' (Macaulay, 1848).
30. 'The Conservatives support Governor Eyre, and Bright and his rascally crew are assailing him right and left', S.M. Ellis (ed.), *The Hardman Papers. A Further Selection (1865–1868) from the Letters and Memoirs of Sir William Hardman*, London, Constable, 1930, p. 85.
31. Frederick Maxse, *A Plea for Intervention*, London, E. Truelove, 1871, p. 8; *Our Political Duty*, London, Metchim and Son, 1869, p. 43.
32. 'Discourse in the Novel', *The Dialogic Imagination*, p. 359.
33. *Coningsby*, Book 6, Chapter 2, p. 311.
34. The Hon. Grantley F.Berkeley, *My Life and Recollections*, London, Hurst and Blackett, 1865, vol. 1, p. 26. Incidentally, during Grantley Berkeley's childhood the 'janitor' of Berkeley Castle was a former surgeon of his father's regiment called Shrapnell (ibid., p. 22).
35. Andrew Marvell, 'An Horatian Ode upon Cromwell's Return from Ireland'.
36. John W. Morris, '*Beauchamp's Career*: Meredith's Acknowledgement of his Debt to Carlyle', Richard B. Davis and John L. Lievsay (eds), *Studies in Honour of John C.Hodges and Alvin Thacker*, Knoxville, University of Tennessee Press, 1961, p. 106.
37. Gary Handwerk, 'On Heroes and their Demise: Critical Liberalism in *Beauchamp's Career*', *Studies in English Literature*, vol. 27 no. 4, Autumn 1987, p. 665.
38. *Meredith: A Change of Masks*, p. 81.
39. Lionel Stevenson, 'Carlyle and Meredith', in John Clubbe (ed.), *Carlyle and his Contemporaries, Essays in Honor of Charles Richard Sanders*, Durham, North Carolina, Duke University Press, 1976, p. 276.
40. Margaret Harris has compared Shrapnel's letter with one by an actual radical Southampton doctor, Edwin Hearne, who according to notes by Maxse was the model for Shrapnel. In the extracts quoted by Harris there is no trace of Carlylean influence in Hearne's style, which is quiet and rational. Since Shrapnel's idiosyncratic use of language virtually *is* the character, it seems reasonable to say that he is Meredith's invention. Margaret Harris, 'The Epistle of Dr Shrapnel to Commander Beauchamp in Meredith's *Beauchamp's Career*', *Notes and Queries NS* vol. 29 no. 4, pp. 317–20.
41. *Letters*, vol. 1, p. 327 [15 January 1866], to Frederick Maxse; vol. 2, p. 661, 23 May 1882, to André Raffalovich. Meredith was critical of the imitation of Carlyle by other writers, for example his friend Cotter Morison in his *Life of St Bernard*: 'Originally the work was strongly impregnated with this Carlylese element, but happily Morison had the good sense to be guided by Meredith, to whom he submitted it, and expunged the greater part of it.' S.M. Ellis (ed.), *A Mid-Victorian Pepys: The Letters and Memoirs of Sir William Hardman, MA, FRGS*, London, Cecil Palmer, 1923, p. 249.
42. Thomas Carlyle, *Past and Present*, Book 1, Chapter 2, Centenary Edition, London, Chapman and Hall, vol. 10, 1899, pp. 10–11.

43. Walter Bagehot, 'The English Constitution', 1867, in Norman St John Stevas (ed.), *The Collected Works of Walter Bagehot*, London, The Economist, 1974, vol. 5, p. 314.
44. David Howard, 'George Meredith: "Delicate" and "Epical" Fiction', p. 160.
45. *Meredith: A Change of Masks*, pp. 103–4.
46. *Problems of Dostoevsky's Poetics*, p. 165.
47. Ibid., p. 92.

5 The Egoist

1. *Letters*, vol. 2, p. 569, 16 April 1879, to Robert Louis Stevenson. Meredith appears to have had little enthusiasm for the novel at the time of writing: in a letter a few weeks later he says, 'I finished a 3 volume work rapidly, and as it comes mainly from the head and has nothing to kindle imagination, I thirsted to be rid of it soon after conception' (*Letters*, vol. 2, p. 572, 30 May 1879, to G.W. Foote). In later life, however, perhaps in response to critical acclaim, he seems to have been more inclined to emphasize its merits: 'The Egoist comes nearer than the other books to the proper degree of roundness and finish' (*Letters*, vol. 3, p. 1578, 9 November 1906, to Dr H.R.D. Anders).
2. *The Readable People of George Meredith*, p. 175.
3. Dorothy Van Ghent, *The English Novel: Form and Function*, New York, Rinehart & Co., 1953, p. 189. Van Ghent thought there was no such insight in the novel.
4. *Saturday Review*, viii, 9 July 1859; *Critical Heritage*, p. 74.
5. V.N. Voloshinov, *Marxism and the Philosophy of Language*, p. 138.
6. *Letters*, vol. 1, p. 131 [post 25 January 25, 1862], to Samuel Lucas.
7. Mrs Henry Wood, *East Lynne*, 1861, London, Nelson, n.d., Part 3, Chapter 23, pp. 488–9.
8. J.A. Hammerton, *George Meredith in Anecdote and Criticism*, London, Grant Richards, 1909, p. 222.
9. 'The Problem of Speech Genres', *Speech Genres and Other Late Essays*, p. 78.
10. *OED* does not give a definition of 'flute' in this sense, though it does cite Meredith (*ORF*) for a more conventional sense.
11. Carolyn Williams, 'Unbroken Patterns: Gender, Culture and Voice in *The Egoist*', *Browning Institute Studies*, vol. 13, 1985, p. 48.
12. Ibid., p. 58.
13. Charles Dickens, *Hard Times*, ed. Paul Schlicke, Oxford and New York, World's Classics, Oxford University Press, 1989, Book 3, Chapter 2, p. 307.
14. S.M. Ellis (ed.), *The Hardman Papers: A Further Selection (1865–1868) from the Letters and Memoirs of Sir William Hardman* London, Constable, 1930, pp. 247–8 (Ellis's hiatuses). A familar fictional variant is Little Em'ly's letter to Ham in *David Copperfield*, which has 'you, that I have wronged so much, that never can forgive me' and 'some good

girl, that will be...worthy of you' (*David Copperfield*, Chapter 31, p. 474). This is a variant, however, because Em'l'y has left to be Steerforth's mistress, which demands more melodrama and the assertion that she is suffering.

15. *Marxism and the Philosophy of Language*, p. 86. Original italics.
16. *Problems of Dostoevsky's Poetics*, p. 196.
17. Ernest Jones, 'The Psychopathology of Everyday Life', *American Journal of Psychology*, vol. 22 no. 4, October 1911, pp. 477–527 (pp496–7); Sigmund Freud, *The Standard Edition of the Complete Works of Sigmund Freud*, vol. 6, *The Psychopathology of Everyday Life*, London, Hogarth Press and Institute of Psycho-analysis, 1960, pp. 98–100.
18. *Marxism and the Philosophy of Language*, p. 38. Original italics.
19. M.M. Bakhtin/P.N. Medvedev, *The Formal Method in Literary Scholarship*, tr. Albert J. Wehrle, Cambridge, Mass. and London, Harvard University Press, 1985, p. 126.
20. J. Hillis Miller, *Ariadne's Thread: Story Lines*, New Haven, Conn. and London, Yale University Press, 1992, p. 108.
21. Ibid., p. 110.
22. Ibid., pp. 110, 119.
23. Ibid., pp. 110, 113, 114, 125.
24. Ibid., p. 124.
25. Katerina Clark and Michael Holquist, *Mikhail Bakhtin*, Cambridge, Mass. and London, Belknap Press, 1984, p. 65.
26. Ibid., p. 67.
27. Gillian Beer and Margaret Harris (eds), *The Notebooks of George Meredith*, Salzburg, Institut für Anglistik und Amerikanistik, 1983, p. 50.
28. Margaret Harris's emendation for 'Louis IV', 'an evident slip in the manuscript repeated in printed versions', Margaret Harris (ed.), *The Egoist*, World's Classics, Oxford University Press, 1992, p. xxii.
29. For all the foregoing quotations in this paragraph, see Carolyn Williams, op. cit., p. 48.
30. See D.W. Harding, Introduction to *Persuasion*, Harmondsworth, Penguin, 1965, pp. 23–6.
31. For example: 'My daughter *has* refused him, sir?' 'Temporarily it would appear that she has declined the proposal.' 'He was at liberty?...he could honourably...?' 'His best friend and nearest relative is your guarantee.' (44, 557). 'She has refused him!' 'Who?' 'She has!' 'She? – Sir Willoughby?' 'Refused! – declines the honour.' 'Oh! never! No, that carries the incredible beyond romance! But is he perfectly at...?' 'Quite, it seems.' (45, 563). The relevant passage in Bakhtin is in his late essay 'The Problem of the Text', in which he writes of the situation 'widely used in comedy' of 'a dialogue between two deaf people, where the real dialogic contact is understood but where there is no kind of semantic contact between the rejoinders....Here the viewpoint of a *third* person is revealed in the dialogue (one who does not participate in the dialogue, but *understands* it)' (*Speech Genres and Other Late Essays*, p. 125).

Here Bakhtin describes the conventional situation. Meredith exaggerates it to the point at which it is extremely difficult, if not impossible, for the reader to maintain this viewpoint of the understanding third person.

32. *The Formal Method in Literary Scholarship*, p. 60.
33. Carolyn Williams, op. cit., pp. 66, 65. Regarding Williams's point about the family, it is not clear whether Vernon is related to Willoughby through the male line and therefore a member of the 'family of Patternes'. Willoughby's argument that he has an interest in Crossjay being educated as a gentleman because the boy bears his name, not Vernon's, may suggest that Vernon does not belong to the Patterne family, but is not conclusive. Willoughby had a 'cousin Grace Whitford' who married when he was fourteen (44, 550): unless she was Vernon's sister, this suggests that Vernon is related to Willoughby through his own father who, if Vernon and Willoughby are first cousins, must be the brother of Willoughby's mother, not his father. More to the point, if Patterne is not merely a family name but an ideological symbol, as Williams rightly suggests – 'the family Patterne, and the pattern of male dominance' (p65) – Vernon is an outsider to this ideology: not 'the English gentleman wherever he went' but 'a new kind of thing, nondescript, p. roduced in England of late, and not likely to come to much good himself, or do much good to the country' (4, 25).
34. John Goode, 'The Egoist: Anatomy or Striptease?' *Meredith Now*, p. 209.
35. Carolyn Williams, 'Natural Selection and Narrative Form in *The Egoist*', *Victorian Studies*, vol. 27 no. 1, Autumn 1983, p. 55.
36. John Goode, op. cit., p. 221.
37. *Letters*, vol. 1, p. 296, ?end of November 1864, to Miss Jennett Humphreys.
38. George Eliot, *Daniel Deronda* (1876) Standard Edition, Edinburgh and London, William Blackwood and Sons, n.d., Chapter 65, vol. 3, p. 342; Chapter 70, vol. 3, p. 407.
39. Donald D. Stone, *Novelists in a Changing World*; Dorothy Van Ghent, op. cit.
40. Elizabeth A. Daniels refers briefly to the relationship between *Daniel Deronda* and *The Egoist* in her essay, 'A Meredithian Glance at Gwendolen Harleth', G. Haight and R. Van Arsdel (eds), *George Eliot: A Centenary Tribute*, Totowa, New Jersey, Barnes and Noble, 1982, pp. 28–37; Daniels, however, finds nothing problematic in the relationship of Gwendolen and Deronda.
41. *Saturday Review*, xlviii, 15 November 1879; *Critical Heritage*, p. 220. George Eliot had earlier used 'egoism' in *Middlemarch*, 1871–2, Standard Edition, Edinburgh and London, William Blackwood and Sons, n.d., Chapter 27, vol. 1, p. 403.
42. *Daniel Deronda*, Chapter 28, vol. 2, pp. 62–3; Chapter 31, vol. 2, p. 117.
43. Ibid., Chapter 35, vol. 2, p. 209.
44. Ibid., Chapter 69, vol. 3, p. 392.

Notes

45. Ibid., Chapter 24, vol. 1, pp. 415–16; Chapter 29, vol. 2, p. 78; Chapter 29, vol. 2, p. 81; Chapter 35, vol. 2, p. 210; Chapter 35, vol. 2, p. 234; Chapter 54, vol. 3, p. 195.
46. e.g., Chapter 36, vol. 2, p. 255; Chapter 44, vol. 3, p. 4.
47. Ibid., Chapter 44, vol. 3, p. 3; Chapter 69, vol. 3, p. 399.
48. *Problems of Dostoevsky's Poetics*, p. 199.
49. Compare Bakhtin's phrase, 'intonational quotation marks', 'From the Prehistory of Novelistic Discourse', *The Dialogic Imagination*, p. 44.

6 The Tragic Comedians

1. J.M. Ludlow, 'Ferdinand Lassalle, the German Social-Democrat', *Fortnightly Review*, new series vol. 5, 1869, pp. 419–53.
2. *The Ordeal of George Meredith*, p. 238.
3. Leonée Ormond, '*The Tragic Comedians*: Meredith's Use of Image Patterns', *Meredith Now*, pp. 233, 236.
4. Gillian Beer, 'Meredith's Revisions of *The Tragic Comedians*', *Review of English Studies*, vol. 14 no. 3, 1963, pp. 35, 42, 36.
5. *Problems of Dostoevsky's Poetics*, p. 198. Bakhtin is here describing certain kinds of parodic discourse, but a similar principle can be applied to the relationship between the texts I am discussing.
6. Helene von Racowitza, *Meine Beziehungen zu Ferdinand Lassalle*, Breslau und Leipzig, Schottlaender, 1880, p. 1.
7. Helene von Racowitza, *An Autobiography*, tr. Cecil Mar, London, Constable, 1910, p. 67.
8. 'Wie die Tage fortschritten, wunderte ich mich freilich ein wenig, so gar keine Nachricht von Lassalle zu erhalten' [Naturally, as the days passed, I wondered why I had no news of Lassalle], *Meine Beziehungen*, p. 146.
9. *Meine Beziehungen*, p. 149.
10. Ibid., p. 150.
11. Beer, op. cit.
12. *Meine Beziehungen*, p. 186.
13. Ibid., p. 187.
14. Ibid., pp. 181–2.
15. Ibid., pp. 9ff.
16. Ibid., pp. 32, 36.
17. Ibid., p. 28.
18. Ibid., p. 122.
19. 'From Notes Made in 1970–71', *Speech Genres and Other Late Essays*, p. 141.
20. 'The Problem of the Text', *Speech Genres and Other Late Essays*, pp. 106–7 (Bakhtin's italics).
21. *Meine Beziehungen*, p. 84; this is one of a number of passages that are directly transcribed in the *Autobiography*, from which I give the translation, p. 102, though this lacks the additional note of gallic affectation in 'fille'.

22. *Meine Beziehungen*, pp. 111–12; tr. *Autobiography*, p. 122. Several critics have commented on the resemblance between Alvan and Willoughby, for example: Gillian Beer, 'Meredith's Idea of Comedy: 1876–1880', *Nineteenth Century Fiction*, vol. 20, 1965, p. 172; Gayla S. McGlamery, 'The Dialogic Meredith: Prefaces to the Novels of the 1880s', Ph.D., Ann Arbor, Mich. 1984, pp. 72–3.
23. Beer, 'Meredith's Revisions of *The Tragic Comedians*', pp. 43–4.
24. Ibid., p. 41n.
25. However, both the word 'dolt' and the implied 'whore' derive from Ludlow, who quotes Lassalle to the Countess von Hatzfeld, 'what crushed him far more, perhaps, than the loss of the girl, was his own doltishness' (op. cit., p. 445); and writes that Lassalle wrote to Helene's father 'in disgraceful terms of his daughter as an abandoned ——' (pp. 450–1).
26. Donald D. Stone comments suggestively on Meredith's possible identification with Alvan in *Novelists in a Changing World*, pp. 140–1.
27. See Chapter 1, pp. 32–5 for a discussion of this term, which is borrowed from Bakhtin's early work, 'Author and Hero in Aesthetic Activity'.
28. *Meine Beziehungen*, p. 101. The 'Cassette Affair' was the theft of a deed box that had been given by the Countess's husband to his mistress. Although Lassalle successfully defended himself at trial, this episode remained a serious blot on his reputation.
29. For Racowitza's account of the correspondence, and her feelings on receiving the Countess's letter, see *Meine Beziehungen*, pp. 160ff.
30. 'Ferdinand Lassalle, the German Social-Democrat', p. 450.
31. Her account is in *Meine Beziehungen*, pp. 175ff.
32. *Problems of Dostoevsky's Poetics*, p. 233.

7 Diana of the Crossways

1. Lionel Stevenson, *The Ordeal of George Meredith*, p. 260.
2. Penny Boumelha, '"The Rattling of her Discourse and the Flapping of her Dress": Meredith Writing the "Women of the Future"', in Susan Sellars and Linda Hutcheon (eds), *Feminist Criticism: Theory and Practice*, Toronto, University of Toronto Press, 1991, p. 198.
3. For Mrs Norton and the scandal of the newspaper story see Jane Gray Perkins, *The Life of Mrs Norton*, London, Murray, 1909, pp. 197–9, and A.A.W. Ramsay, 'The Crisis in the Cabinet, 1845', *Cornhill Magazine*, vol. 160, 1939, pp. 188–201.
4. *Problems of Dostoevsky's Poetics*, p. 195.
5. Joseph Moses, *The Novelist as Comedian: George Meredith and the Ironic Sensibility*, New York, Schocken, 1983, p. 8.
6. Boumelha, op. cit., p. 199.
7. Significantly, more than one critic has mistaken the subject of this passage for Diana: see Boumelha, op. cit., p. 200; Jenni Calder, 'Cash and the Sex Nexus', *Tennessee Studies in Literature*, vol. 27, 1984, p. 42.

8. Bakhtin's theoretical account of a sentence such as this is as follows: 'A character in a novel always has...a zone of his own, his own sphere of influence on the authorial context surrounding him, a sphere that extends – and often quite far – beyond the boundaries of the direct discourse allotted to him. The area occupied by an important character's voice must in any event be broader than his direct and "actual" words. This zone surrounding the important characters of the novel is stylistically profoundly idiosyncratic: the most varied hybrid constructions hold sway in it, and it is always, to one degree or another, dialogized; inside this area a dialogue is played out between the author and his characters – not a dramatic dialogue broken up into statement-and-response, but that special type of novelistic dialogue that realizes itself within the boundaries of constructions that externally resemble monologues.' 'Discourse in the Novel', *The Dialogic Imagination*, p. 320.
9. Mazeppa was a Cossack hetman, or military commander, who in his youth was tied to a horse and let loose on the steppe by the outraged husband of a Polish lady. He was the hero of a poem by Byron. A comment by a waggoner in *EH* suggests that this image was familiar in popular culture and had burlesque connotations: 'Warn't he like that Myzepper chap, I see at the circus, bound athert gray mare!' (*EH*, 10, 121).
10. *Problems of Dostoevsky's Poetics*, p. 189.
11. 'Discourse in the Novel', *The Dialogic Imagination*, p. 322.
12. '*Rhoda Fleming*: Meredith in the Margin', *Meredith Now*, p. 131.
13. *Meredith: A Change of Masks*, p. 163.
14. Gayla S. McGlamery, 'The Dialogic Meredith: Prefaces to the Novels of the 1880s', Ph.D., Ann Arbor, Mich., 1984, p. 94.
15. *Meredith: A Change of Masks*, p. 161.
16. 'Meredith and Bakhtin: Polyphony and Bildung', p. 702.
17. *Rabelais and His World*, pp. 376, 378.
18. Reluctance to build even more on verbal parallels between Meredith and modern theorists relegates to a footnote the observation that Julia Kristeva's concept in *Powers of Horror* of 'abjection', the revulsion from the transgression of bodily boundaries – and therefore from 'the lower bodily statum' itself – deriving from fear of the maternal body has been seen by a number of commentators as a dark variant of Bakhtin's carnivalesque 'grotesque body'. For discussion of this parallel I am indebted to a forthcoming study of Bakhtin by Sue Vice.
19. *The Readable People of George Meredith*, pp. 70–1.
20. Ibid., p. 74.
21. Janet Horowitz Murray, *Courtship and the English Novel: Feminist Readings in the Fiction of George Meredith*, Harvard Dissertations in English and American Literature, New York, Garland, 1987 (dissertation originally submitted 1974), p. 170. Murray's study includes an excellent analysis of the climactic scene with Dacier, pp. 149ff.
22. 'From the Prehistory of Novelistic Discourse', *The Dialogic Imagination*, p. 44.

23. See my *George Eliot: Her Beliefs and Her Art*, London, Elek and Pittsburgh University Press, 1975, pp. 161ff.
24. D.H. Lawrence, *Phoenix*, London, Heinemann, 1936, p. 528.

8 The Final Phase

1. *Letters*, vol. 3, p. 1573, 15 October 1906, to John H. Hutchinson.
2. *Marxism and the Philosophy of Language*, p. 38; *The Formal Method in Literary Scholarship*, p. 126.
3. Bryan Cheyette, *Constructions of 'the Jew' in English literature and Society: Racial representations, 1875–1945*, Cambridge University Press, 1993, p. 171.
4. Gillian Beer, '*One of Our Conquerors*: Language and Music', *Meredith Now*, p. 270.
5. Cheyette, op. cit., pp. 6, 99.
6. Richard L. Newby, 'George Meredith and the *Ipswich Journal*', *Ball State University Forum*, vol. 27, Part 1, 1987, pp. 37–43. The quality of Newby's evidence is exemplified by the following: 'This anti-Jewish diatribe is a prolonged jeer, and Meredith "enjoyed jeering at people"' (p41).
7. *Problems of Dostoevsky's Poetics*, p. 92.
8. Cheyette, op. cit., p. 272.
9. Jack Lindsay, *George Meredith: His Life and Work*, London, Bodley Head, 1956, p. 298.
10. H.M. Hyndman, *Commercial Crises of the Nineteenth Century*, 1892, London, National Council of Labour Colleges, 1932, pp. 156–7.
11. Gayla S. McGlamery, '"The Malady Afflicting England": *One of Our Conquerors* as Cautionary Tale', *Nineteenth Century Literature*, vol. 46 no.3, December. 1991, p. 329.
12. Donald R. Swanson, *Three Conquerors: Character and Method in the Mature Works of George Meredith*, The Hague and Paris, Mouton, 1969, p. 104.
13. See note 1.
14. *Meredith Now*, p. 277.
15. Barbara Hardy, '*Lord Ormont and his Aminta* and *The Amazing Marriage*', *Meredith Now*, p. 296.
16. Graham McMaster, 'All for Love: the Imperial Moment in *Lord Ormont and his Aminta*', *Shiron*, vol. 30, 1991, pp. 37, 43, 37.
17. *Problems of Dostoevsky's Poetics*, p. 7.
18. Susan Morgan, 'Dumbly a Poet: Lost Harmonies in Meredith's Later Fiction', *Huntingdon Library Quarterly*, vol. 47 no.2, 1984, p. 116. This phrase refers to all of Meredith's last four novels, but most obviously fits the marriages in these two.
19. See, in particular, Judith Wilt, *The Readable People of George Meredith*, pp. 210–40, for the most substantial and possibly the best extant discussion of the novel.
20. Gillian Beer, *Meredith: A Change of Masks*, p. 172.
21. Ibid.

22. *Letters*, vol. 3, p. 1153, 25 January 1894, to R.L. Stevenson.
23. Lionel Stevenson, *The Ordeal of George Meredith*, p. 316.
24. Robert M. DeGraff, 'The Double Narrator in *The Amazing Marriage*', *The Victorian Newsletter*, 49, Spring 1976, pp. 24–6.
25. Gillian Beer, *loc. cit.*
26. Geoffrey Chaucer, 'The Clerk's Tale', ll.701–5, in F.N. Robinson (ed.), *The Complete Works of Geoffrey Chaucer*, London, Oxford University Press, 1957, p. 109.
27. *Meredith: A Change of Masks*, pp. 175–6.
28. A.H. Able, *George Meredith and Thomas Love Peacock: A Study in Literary Influence*, 1933, New York, Phaeton Press, 1970, p. 100; Judith Ann Sage, 'George Meredith and Thomas Love Peacock: A Note on Literary Influence', *English Language Notes*, no.4, June 1967, pp. 279–83.
29. Thomas Love Peacock, *Three Novels*, Nelson, London, 1940: *Crotchet Castle* (first published 1831), Chapter 14, p. 287.
30. Ibid., p. 288.
31. It was Stevenson who wrote about the 'young friend of Meredith's' who complained that Willoughby was a portrait of himself, to which Meredith replied, 'No, my dear fellow; he is all of us'. Stevenson added that 'I am like the young friend of the anecdote – I think Willoughby an unmanly but a very serviceable exposure of myself.' J.A. Hammerton, *George Meredith in Anecdote and Criticism*, London, Grant Richards, 1909, p. 222.

Bibliography

The edition of Meredith's novels cited is the Standard Edition (London: Constable, 1914–20).

Able, A.H., *George Meredith and Thomas Love Peacock: A Study in Literary Influence*, 1933, New York, Phaeton Press, 1970
Arnold, Matthew, *Culture and Anarchy*, 1869, Cambridge University Press, 1932
Bagehot, Walter, 'The English Constitution', 1867, in Norman St John Stevas (ed.), *The Collected Works of Walter Bagehot*, London, The Economist, 1974, vol. 5
Bailey, Peter, *Leisure and Class in Victorian England: Rational Recreation and the Contest for Control, 1830–1885*, London, Routledge; Toronto and Buffalo, University of Toronto Press, 1978
Bakhtin, M.M., *Art and Answerability*, ed. Michael Holquist and Vadim Liapunov, tr. Vadim Liapunov, Austin, University of Texas, 1990
Bakhtin, M.M., *The Dialogic Imagination: Four Essays*, ed. Michael Holquist, tr. Caryl Emerson and Michael Holquist, Austin, University of Texas, 1981
Bakhtin, Mikhail, *Problems of Dostoevsky's Poetics*, ed. and tr. Caryl Emerson, Minneapolis, University of Minnesota, 1984
Bakhtin, Mikhail, *Rabelais and His World*, tr. Helene Iswolsky, 1968, Bloomington, Indiana University Press, 1984
Bakhtin, M.M., *Speech Genres and Other Late Essays*, ed. Caryl Emerson and Michael Holquist, tr. Vern W. McGee, Austin, University of Texas, 1986
Bakhtin, M.M./Medvedev, P.N., *The Formal Method in Literary Scholarship*, tr. Albert J. Wehrle, Cambridge, Mass. and London, Harvard University Press, 1985
Barthes, Roland, *Image–Music–Text*, ed. and tr. Stephen Heath, London, Fontana, 1977
Bartlett, Phyllis, 'Richard Feverel, Knight-Errant', *Bulletin of the New York Public Library*, vol. 63 no. 7, July 1959, pp. 329–40.
Beales, Derek, *The Risorgimento and the Unification of Italy*, London, George Allen and Unwin; New York, Barnes and Noble, 1971
Beer, Gillian, 'Meredith's Revisions of *The Tragic Comedians*', *Review of English Studies*, vol. 14 no. 3, 1963, pp. 33–53
Beer, Gillian, 'Meredith's Idea of Comedy: 1876–1880', *Nineteenth Century Fiction*, vol. 20, 1965, pp. 165–76
Beer, Gillian, *Meredith: A Change of Masks*, London, Athlone Press, 1970

Beer, Gillian and Harris, Margaret (eds), *The Notebooks of George Meredith*, Salzburg, Institut für Anglistik und Amerikanistik, Universität Salzburg, 1983
Berkeley, The Hon. Grantley F., *My Life and Recollections*, London, Hurst and Blackett, 1865
Boumelha, Penny, ' "The Rattling of her Discourse and the Flapping of her Dress": Meredith Writing the "Women of the Future" ', in Susan Sellars and Linda Hutcheon (eds), *Feminist Criticism: Theory and Practice*, Toronto, University of Toronto Press, 1991, pp. 197–208
Buckley, J.H., *Season of Youth: The Bildungsroman from Dickens to Golding*, Boston, Mass., Harvard University Press, 1974
Calder, Jenni, 'Cash and the Sex Nexus', *Tennessee Studies in Literature*, vol. 27, 1984, pp. 40–53.
Carlyle, Thomas, *Past and Present*, 1843, Centenary Edition vol. 10, Chapman and Hall, 1899
Carlyle, Thomas, *Sartor Resartus*, 1833–4, ed. Kerry McSweeney and Peter Sabor, World's Classics, Oxford University Press, 1987
Carlyle, Thomas, *On Heroes, Hero-Worship, and the Heroic in History*, 1841, Centenary Edition vol. 5, London, Chapman and Hall, 1901
Cheyette, Bryan, *Constructions of 'the Jew' in English Literature and Society: Racial Representations, 1875–1945*, Cambridge University Press, 1993
Clark, Katerina and Holquist, Michael, *Mikhail Bakhtin*, Cambridge, Mass. and London, Belknap Press, 1984
Clines, C.L. (ed.), *The Letters of George Meredith*, 3 vols, Oxford, Clarendon Press, 1970
Clodd, Edward, *Memories*, London, Watts and Co., 1926
Conrow, Margaret, 'Coming to Terms with George Meredith's Fiction', in George Gooding (ed.), *The English Novel in the Nineteenth Century: Essays on the Literary Mediation of Human Values*, Urbana, University of Illinois Press, 1972, pp. 176–95
Curtin, Frank D. 'Adrian Harley: The Limits of Meredith's Comedy', *Nineteenth Century Fiction*, 7, 1953, pp. 272–82
Daniels, Elizabeth A., 'A Meredithian Glance at Gwendolen Harleth', in G. Haight and R. Van Arsdel (eds), *George Eliot: A Centenary Tribute*, Totowa, New Jersey, Barnes and Noble, 1982, pp. 28–37
DeGraff, Robert M., 'The Double Narrator in *The Amazing Marriage*', *The Victorian Newsletter*, 49, Spring 1976, pp. 24–6.
Dickens, Charles, *David Copperfield*, 1849–50, London, Nelson, n.d.
Dickens, Charles, *Hard Times*, 1854, ed. Paul Schlicke, Oxford and New York, World's Classics, Oxford University Press, 1989
Disraeli, Benjamin, *Coningsby*, 1844, London, Longman's Green, 1923
Eliot, George, *Felix Holt, the Radical*, 1866, Standard Edition, Edinburgh and London, Willam Blackwood and Sons, n.d.
Eliot, George, *Middlemarch*, 1871–2, Standard Edition, Edinburgh and London, William Blackwood and Sons, n.d.
Eliot, George, *Daniel Deronda*, 1876, Standard Edition, Edinburgh and London, William Blackwood and Sons, n.d.
Ellis, S.M. (ed.), *A Mid-Victorian Pepys: The Letters and Memoirs of Sir William Hardman, M.A, F.R.G.S.*, Cecil Palmer, London, 1923

Ellis, S.M. (ed.), *The Hardman Papers: A Further Selection (1865–1868) from the Letters and Memoirs of Sir William Hardman*, London, Constable, 1930

Everett, Edwin Mallard, *The Party of Humanity: The Fortnightly Review and its Contributors 1865–1874*, New York, Russell and Russell, 1939, p. 286

Fahnestock, Jeanne, 'Bigamy: The Rise and Fall of a Convention', *Nineteenth Century Fiction*, vol. 36 no. 1, June 1981, pp. 47–71

Fletcher, Ian (ed.), *Meredith Now: Some Critical Essays*, London, Routledge, 1971

Forster, E.M., *Aspects of the Novel*, London, Arnold, 1927

Freud, Sigmund, *The Psychopathology of Everyday Life*, 1904, *The Standard Edition of the Complete Works of Sigmund Freud*, vol. 6, London, Hogarth Press and Institute of Psycho-analysis, 1960

Gettmann, Royal A., 'Serialization and *Evan Harrington*', *PMLA*, 64, 1949, pp. 963–75

Goethe, Johann Wolfgang von, *Elective Affinities*, 1809, tr. R.J. Hollingdale, Harmondsworth, Penguin, 1971

Goethe, Johann Wolfgang von, *Wilhelm Meister's Apprenticeship and Travels*, 1796–1829, tr. Thomas Carlyle, *The Works of Thomas Carlyle*, Centenary Edition, vol. XXIII–XXIV, London, Chapman and Hall, 1899

Graves, Robert, *The White Goddess*, New York, Farrar, Strauss and Giroux, 1966

Hammerton, J.A. (ed.), *George Meredith in Anecdote and Criticism*, London, Grant Richards, 1909

Handwerk, Gary, 'On Heroes and their Demise: Critical Liberalism in *Beauchamp's Career*', *Studies in English Literature*, vol. 27 no. 4, Autumn 1987, pp. 663–81

Harding, D.W., Introduction to Jane Austen, *Persuasion*, Harmondsworth, Penguin, 1965

Harris, Margaret, 'The Epistle of Dr Shrapnel to Commander Beauchamp in Meredith's *Beauchamp's Career*', *Notes and Queries* new series, vol. 29 no. 4, August 1982, pp. 317–20

Harris, Margaret, 'Introduction' to *Beauchamp's Career*, World's Classics, Oxford University Press, 1988

Hergenhan, L.T., 'Meredith's Revisions of *Harry Richmond*', *Review of English Studies*, new series, vol. 14 no. 53, 1963, pp. 24–32

Hergenhan, L.T., 'The Reception of George Meredith's Early Novels', *Nineteenth Century Fiction*, vol. 19 no. 2, September 1964, pp. 213–35

Holquist, Michael, *Dialogism: Bakhtin and his World*, London, Routledge, New Accents, 1990

Howard, David, 'George Meredith: "Delicate" and "Epical" Fiction', in John Lucas (ed.), *Literature and Politics in the Nineteenth Century*, London, Methuen, 1971, pp. 131–71

Howe, Susanne, *Wilhelm Meister and his English Kinsmen*, New York, Columbia University Press, 1930

Hudson, Richard B., 'Meredith's Autobiography and "The Adventures of Harry Richmond"', *Nineteenth Century Fiction*, vol. 9, 1954–5, pp. 38–49

Hyndman, H.M., *Commercial Crises of the Nineteenth Century*, 1892, London, National Council of Labour Colleges, 1932

Johnson, Diane, *Lesser Lives: The True History of the First Mrs Meredith and Other Lesser Lives*, London, Heinemann, 1973
Jones, Ernest, 'The Psychopathology of Everyday Life', *American Journal of Psychology*, vol. 22 no. 4, October 1911, pp. 477–527
Keating, Peter, *The Haunted Study: A Social History of the English Novel, 1875–1914*, London, Secker, 1989
Kelvin, Norman, *A Troubled Eden: Nature and Society in the Works of George Meredith*, Edinburgh and London, Oliver and Boyd, 1961
Korg, Jacob, 'Expressive Styles in *The Ordeal of Richard Feverel*', *Nineteenth Century Fiction*, vol. 27 no. 3, December 1972, pp. 253–67
Kristeva, Julia, *Desire in Language: A Semiotic Approach to Literature and Art*, tr. Thomas Gora, Alice Jardine and Leon S. Roudiez, Oxford, Basil Blackwell, 1980
Lawrence, D.H., *Phoenix*, London, Heinemann, 1936
Leech, Geoffrey N. and Short, Michael H., *Style in Fiction: A Linguistic Introduction to English Fictional Prose*, London and New York, Longman, 1981
Lindsay, Jack, *George Meredith, His Life and Work*, London, Bodley Head, 1956
Ludlow, J.M., 'Ferdinand Lassalle, the German Social-Democrat', *Fortnightly Review*, new series, vol. 5, 1869, pp. 419–53
Manos, Nikki Lee, 'The Ordeal of Richard Feverel: Bildungsroman or Anti-Bildungsroman?', *Victorian Newsletter*, 70, Fall 1986, pp. 18–24
Maxse, Frederick, *Our Political Duty*, London, Metchim and Son, 1869
Maxse, Frederick, *A Plea for Intervention*, London, E. Truelove, 1871
Maxse, Frederick, *The Causes of Social Revolt*, London, Longman's, Green, Reader and Dyer, 1872
McGlamery, Gayla S., 'The Dialogic Meredith: Prefaces to the Novels of the 1880s', Ph.D. dissertation, Ann Arbor, Mich., 1984
McGlamery, Gayla S., '"The Malady Afflicting England": *One of Our Conquerors* as Cautionary Tale"', *Nineteenth Century Literature*, vol. 46 no. 3, December 1991, pp. 327–50
McMaster, Graham, '*Harry Richmond*: Meredith's Unwritten Attack on Victorian Legitimacy', *POETICA: An International Journal of Literary-Linguistic Studies*, 24, November 1986, pp. 64–85
McMaster, Graham, 'All for Love: the Imperial Moment in *Lord Ormont and his Aminta*', *Shiron*, vol. 30, 1991, p. 35–55
Michta, Natalie Cole, 'The Legitimate Self in George Meredith's *Evan Harrington*', *Studies in the Novel*, vol. 21 no. 1, 1989, pp. 41–59
Mill, John Stuart, 'The Subjection of Women', 1869, *On Liberty, Representative Government, The Subjection of Women*, London, World's Classics, Oxford University Press, 1912
Miller, J. Hillis, *Ariadne's Thread: Story Lines*, New Haven, Conn. and London, Yale University Press, 1992
Millett, Kate, *Sexual Politics*, London, Hart-Davis, 1971
Morgan, Susan, 'Dumbly a Poet: Lost Harmonies in Meredith's Later Fiction', *Huntingdon Library Quarterly*, vol. 47 no. 2, 1984, pp. 113–28
Morley, John, *On Compromise*, 1874, London, Macmillan, 1886
Morley, John, *Critical Miscellanies*, vol. 1, London, Macmillan, 1886

Morris, Christopher, 'Richard Feverel and the Fictional Lineage of Desire', *ELH*, 42, 1975, pp. 242–55

Morris, John W., '*Beauchamp's Career*: Meredith's Acknowledgement of His Debt to Carlyle', Richard B. Davis and John L. Lievsay (eds), *Studies in Honour of John C. Hodges and Alvin Thacker*, special number of *Tennessee Studies in Literature*, Knoxville, University of Tennessee Press, 1961, pp. 101–8

Morris, John W., 'Inherent Principles of Order in *Richard Feverel*', *PMLA*, 78, 1963, pp. 333–40

Morson, Gary Saul and Emerson, Caryl, *Mikhail Bakhtin: Creation of a Prosaics*, Stanford, Calif., Stanford University Press, 1990

Moses, Joseph, *The Novelist as Comedian: George Meredith and the Ironic Sensibility*, New York, Schocken, 1983

Muendel, Renate, *George Meredith*, Boston, Mass., Twayne, 1986

Murray, Janet Horowitz, *Courtship and the English Novel: Feminist Readings in the Fiction of Meredith*. Harvard Dissertations in American and English Literature, New York, Garland, 1987.

Murry, J. Middleton, *The Problem of Style*, Oxford, Oxford University Press, 1922

Newby, Richard L., 'George Meredith and the *Ipswich Journal*', *Ball State University Forum*, vol. 27, Part 1, 1987, pp. 37–43

Peacock, Thomas Love, *Three Novels*, Nelson, London, 1940

Perkins, Jane Gray, *The Life of Mrs Norton*, London, Murray, 1909

Priestley, J.B., *George Meredith*, London, Macmillan, 1926

Pritchett, V.S., *George Meredith and English Comedy*, London, Chatto and Windus, 1970

Racowitza, Helene von, *Meine Beziehungen zu Ferdinand Lassalle*, Breslau und Leipzig, Schottlaender, 1880

Racowitza, Helene von, *An Autobiography*, tr. Cecil Mar, London, Constable, 1910

Ramsay, A.A.W., 'The Crisis in the Cabinet, 1845', *Cornhill Magazine*, vol. 160, 1939, pp. 188–201.

Rimmon-Kenan, Shlomith, *Narrative Fiction: Contemporary Poetics*, London and New York, Routledge, 1983

Rousseau, Jean-Jacques, *Emile or Education*, 1762, tr. Barbara Foxey, London, Everyman's Library, Dent, 1911

Sage, Judith Ann, 'George Meredith and Thomas Love Peacock: A Note on Literary Influence', *English Language Notes*, no. 4, June 1967, pp. 279–83

Shaheen, Mohammad, *George Meredith: A Reappraisal of the Novels*, London, Macmillan, 1981.

Spånberg, Sven-Johan, *The Ordeal of Richard Feverel and the Traditions of Realism*, Uppsala University, 1974

Spånberg, Sven-Johan, 'The Theme of Sexuality in *The Ordeal of Richard Feverel*', *Studia Neophilologica*, xlvi, 1974, p. 208.

Spånberg, Sven-Johan (ed.), *The Adventures of Harry Richmond: The Unpublished Parts*, Uppsala, Acta Universitatis Upsaliensis, 1990

Stang, Richard, *The Theory of the Novel in England 1850–1870*, London, Routledge, 1959

Stephen, Fitzjames, *Liberty, Equality, Fraternity*, 1873–74, Cambridge University Press, 1973
Stevenson, Lionel, *The Ordeal of George Meredith*, London, Peter Owen, 1954
Stevenson, Lionel, 'Carlyle and Meredith', John Clubbe, (ed.), *Carlyle and his Contemporaries, Essays in Honor of Charles Richard Sanders*, Durham, North Carolina, Duke University Press, 1976, pp. 257–79.
Stevenson, Richard C., 'The Spirit of Critical Intelligence in *Richard Feverel*', in J.H. Buckley (ed.), *The Worlds of Victorian Fiction*, Boston, Mass., and London, Harvard University Press, 1975, pp. 211–12.
Stone, Donald D., *Novelists in a Changing World: Meredith, James, and the Transformation of English Fiction in the 1880s*, Cambridge, Mass., Harvard University Press, 1972
Stone, Donald D., *The Romantic Impulse in Victorian Fiction*, Cambridge, Mass., Harvard University Press, 1980
Stone, Donald D., 'Meredith and Bakhtin: Polyphony and Bildung', *Studies in English Literature*, vol. 28 no. 4, Autumn 1988, pp. 693–712
Stone, James S., *George Meredith's Politics*, Port Credit, Ontario, P.D. Meany, 1986
Sutherland, John, *The Longman Companion to Victorian Fiction*, London, Longman, 1988
Swanson, Donald R., *Three Conquerors: Character and Method in the Mature Works of George Meredith*, The Hague and Paris, Mouton, 1969
Van Ghent, Dorothy, *The English Novel: Form and Function*, New York, Rinehart & Co., 1953
Voloshinov, V.N., *Marxism and the Philosophy of Language*, tr. Ladislav Matejka and I.R. Titunik, Cambridge, Mass. and London, Harvard University Press, 1986
White, Allon, *The Uses of Obscurity: The Fiction of Early Modernism*, London, Routledge, 1981
Wilde, Oscar, *Complete Works of Oscar Wilde*, London and Glasgow, Collins, 1966
Williams, Carolyn, 'Natural Selection and Narrative Form in *The Egoist*', *Victorian Studies*, vol. 27 no. 1, Autumn 1983, pp. 53–79
Williams, Carolyn, 'Unbroken Patternes: Gender, Culture and Voice in *The Egoist*', *Browning Institute Studies*, vol. 13, 1985, pp. 45–70.
Williams, Ioan (ed.), *Meredith: The Critical Heritage*, London, Routledge; New York, Barnes and Noble, 1971
Williams, Raymond, *Culture and Society 1780–1850*, 1958, Harmondsworth, Penguin, 1963
Wilt, Judith, *The Readable People of George Meredith*, New Jersey, Princeton University Press, 1975
Wood, Mrs Henry, *East Lynne*, 1861, London, Nelson, n.d.
Woolf, Virginia, *The Second Common Reader*, 1932, Harmondsworth, Penguin, 1944

Index

The index includes a number of Bakhtinian concepts. However, some such concepts, such as 'dialogism' and 'discourse', are so pervasive that indexing would be pointless. Substantial discussions of novels are indicated in **bold**.

Able, A.H. 251
Alice, Princess 113
All the Year Round 47–8, 54
anti-semitism 192–3, 232–5
Arabian Nights 90, 96
Arnold, Matthew 108, 113, 162
Austen, Jane 180

Bagehot, Walter 127, 136–7
Bailey, Peter 57
Bakhtin, Mikhail 2, 5–7, 9–12, 14–15, 18–19, 28–37, 39, **44–6**, 53–4, 58, 62–3, 75, 77–8, 84–5, 95, 100–1, 108, 115, 123, 124, 126, 129, 137, 149, 152, 154–5, 160, 171, 173, 175–8, 181, 188–9, 194, 203, 206, 213, 220–1, 223, 231, 233, 237, 243, 253, 269–70, 271, 273
Balzac, Honoré de 41, 234, 237
Barthes, Roland 11–12, 16, 112
Bartlett, Phyllis 19
Beales, Derek 87
Beer, Gillian 1, 3, 4, 14, 18, 36, 120–2, 125, 133–4, 148, 188, 191, 216, 219, 232, 239, 244–5, 249, 264, 272
Beesly, E.S. 129
Berkeley, Grantley 127, 131
Bildungsroman 5, 30–4, 39–46, 90, 91, 100–4, 108
Boumelha, Penny 205–7, 272
Bright, John 128
Brooks, Shirley 260
Buchanan, Robert 49
Buckley, J.H. 31
Bulwer Lytton, Edward 113, 267

Byron, Lord 100, 118–22, 266, 273

Calder, Jenni 272
Carlo Alberto, King 80
Carlyle, Thomas 42–4, 51, 57, 103, 133–6, 140–4, 146, 267
carnival 10–11, 45–6, 95, 119, 220–1
Cavour, Camilio di 78
character zone 6, 15–17, 19–25, 51–3, 65, 106, 123–4, 127–9, 140–1, 152, 154–7, 210–14, 242–3
Chaucer, Geoffrey 247
Chesney, Sir George Tomkins 127
Cheyette, Bryan 232, 234
chronotope 30–1, 39, 53, 255
Clark, Katerina 175–7
Clodd, Edward 49
Collins, Wilkie 47–9
Comedy (*see also* New Comedy) 46, 53–4, 60, 61–3, 109, 150–1, 178–81, 186, 197, 207, 223–4
Cominos, Peter 23
Comte, Auguste 117, 181–3
Congreve, William 204
Conrow, Margaret 2
Corneille, Pierre 115
Cornhill Magazine 89, 98
Curtin, Frank D. 16

Daniels, Elizabeth A. 270
DeGraff, Robert M. 245
Dickens, Charles 1, 4, 47–9, 53–4, 57, 59, 90, 96–9, 108, 136, 147–8, 166, 261, 268–9
Disraeli, Benjamin 127, 130–1, 134, 265–6

Dostoevsky, Fyodor 9, 12, 18–19, 36, 115, 136, 149, 233, 255
Duff Gordon family 50

Eliot, George 1, 4, 9, 73, 84, 111, 114, 116, 148, 182–6, 216, 228
Eliot, T.S. 239
Emerson, Caryl 2, 4, 10, 19
epic 77–82, 116
Erziehungsroman 27–8, 30–4, 37, 100
Everett, Edwin Mallett 265

Fahnestock, Jeanne 262
feminism 5, 124–5, 133, 164, 177, 181, 184, 199, 204, 205–6, 225, 228–9, 240
Fielding, Henry 53, 213
Forster, E.M. 4
Fortnightly Review 116–23, 136
Franco-Prussian war 109, 114
Freud, Sigmund 172, 237
Frye, Northrop 37

Garibaldi, Giuseppe 78, 202
Gettmann, Royal A. 260
Gissing, George 74
Goethe, Johann Wolfgang von 21, 31, 33, 39, 42, 46, 90, 101–4, 260
Goode, John 181–2
Graves, Robert 262
Greek Romance 30
Greenwood, Frederick 265, 266

Habermas, Jurgen 257
Handwerk, Gary 33
Harding, D.W. 269
Hardman, William 36, 117–18, 127, 128, 167, 267
Hardy, Barbara 240
Hardy, Thomas 1, 4, 29, 37, 262
Harris, Margaret 112, 114, 120, 267, 269
Hastings, Lady 167–8
Hatzfeld, Countess von 193–4, 199–200
Herbert, Sidney 205
Hergenhan, L.G. 8, 107, 260

heteroglossia 2–3, 5, 9, 12, 30, 84, 91–3, 96, 127–8
hidden polemic/sideward glance 9, 118–19, 163, 185, 206, 209, 214, 216, 209, 214, 216, 223–4
Hollingsworth, R.J. 102
Holquist, Michael 10, 126, 175–7
Household Words 47, 49
Hopkins, G.M. 234
Howard, David 1, 8, 71–3, 76, 111, 145–6, 215
Howe, Susanne 31
Hudson, Richard B. 263
Hutton, R.H. 262
Hyndman, H.M. 234–5

imperialism 239, 241, 243
interpolated genres 7, 85, 217–18, 238, 249
intertextuality 11–12, 14, 21, 25–46, 53–4, 73–6, 90–1, 96–108, 111–30, 133–7, 141–4, 150–2, 158–60, 167–8, 179–80, 182–204, 205–6, 223–4, 234, 240–1
Ipswich Journal 8, 232

James, Henry 1, 7, 60, 255
Jeaffreson, J.C. 71–2, 76
Johnson, Diane 18
Johnson, Samuel 59, 93
Jones, Ernest (Chartist) 129
Jones, Ernest (Freudian) 173
Joyce, James 4, 14

Keating, Peter 8
Keats, John, 29
Kelvin, Norman 118
Kettle, Arnold 265–6
Kingsley, Charles 26
Korg, Jacob 3, 14, 18
Kristeva, Julia 11, 273

Lampedusa, Giuseppe di 228
Lassalle, Ferdinand 187–204, 272
Lawrence, D.H. 4, 229
Leavis, F.R. 182
Leavis, Q.D. 8
Leech, Geoffrey N. 261

Lever, Charles 47
Lindsay, Jack 82, 86, 234
loophole (word with a) 62–7, 82, 203
Lucas, Samuel 13, 47–9, 89, 158, 260
Ludlow, J.M. 272

Manos, Nikki Lee 31, 260
Mansfield, Katherine, 4
Marvell, Andrew 131
Maxse, Frederick 7, 77, 114, 118, 123, 129, 266
Mazzini, Giuseppe 79–81, 86–7
McCarthy, Justin 13
McGlamery, Gayla S. 217, 235, 265, 272
McMaster, Graham 90, 95, 97, 108, 241–3
McSweeney, Kerry 44
Medvedev, P.N. 173, 181, 255
Melbourne, Lord 205
menippean satire 46
Meredith, Arthur 19
Meredith, George
  The Adventures of Harry Richmond 4, 5, 49, 53, **89–110**, 150, 179, 241, 243, 249, 252–3, 258, 263
  The Amazing Marriage 8, 9, 40, 66, 122, 177, 224, 233, **243–53**
  Beauchamp's Career 6–8, 13, 36, 44, 53, 75, 90, **111–49**, 150, 179, 188, 195, 217, 233, 258, 263
  Diana of the Crossways 5, 8, 11, 36, 74, 75, 90, 112, 122, 153, 179, 181, 194, 196, 198, 204, **205–29**, 233, 240, 263
  The Egoist 5, 7, 13, 26, 74, 75, 90, 112, 120, 122, 136, **150–86**, 188, 194–6, 198, 204, 213, 217, 220, 222, 228, 230, 231, 237, 240, 242, 243, 250, 252
  Emilia in England, see *Sandra Belloni*
  Evan Harrington 8, **47–61**, 64, 83, 91, 95, 97, 98, 138, 150, 241, 243, 244, 258, 263, 273

'The Idea of Comedy and the Uses of the Comic Spirit' 150, 204
Lord Ormont and His Aminta 26, 122, 232–3, **240–3**, 263
One of Our Conquerors 4, 8, 9, 26, 193, 220, **230–40**, 243
The Ordeal of Richard Feverel 1, 3, 5, 7, 8, **13–46**, 47–54, 75, 83, 88, 90, 100, 109, 110, 138, 150, 179, 181, 186, 188, 240–1, 242, 249, 251–2, 263
Rhoda Fleming 8, 40, **70–6**, 77, 89, 109, 150, 179, 207, 209, 264
Sandra Belloni (Emilia in England) 9, 26, 53, **60–70**, 71, 76, 79, 82, 83, 89, 109, 179, 203, 218, 224, 230, 232, 243, 249
The Shaving of Shagpat 3, 220, 245
The Tragic Comedians **187–204**, 205, 232–3, 263
Vittoria 26, 40, 71, **76–88**, 89
Meredith, Mary 18–19
Michta, Natalie Cole 51
Mill, John Stuart 7, 44, 117, 124–5, 127, 265, 266
Miller, J. Hillis 173–7
Millett, Kate 5, 164
modernism 1
Molière 5, 26, 115, 150–1, 160–1, 180, 204
monologism 2, 17–18, 122, 142, 148, 160
Moravian Brethren 9
Morgan, Susan 253
Morison, Cotter 267
Morley, John 89, 116–22, 124, 126, 265, 266
Morris, Christopher 258
Morris, John W. 13–14, 40, 133
Morson, Gary Saul 2, 4, 19
Moses, Joseph 272
Mudie's Circulating Library 8, 13, 47, 49, 66
Muendel, Renata 264
Murray, Janet Horowitz 225, 273
Murry, John Middleton 254

naturalism   230, 247
Newby, Richard L.   232, 274
New Comedy   5, 14, 30, 37, 39–40, 241
New Criticism   13–14
Norton, Caroline   5, 205–6

objectified discourse/word on display   21, 127, 158, 213–15, 226–8
Once a Week   47–9, 89, 98
ordeal, novel of   40
Ormond, Leonée   188

Pall Mall Gazette   265, 266
parody, *see* stylization
pastiche, *see* stylization
Peacock, Thomas Love   150, 251
Peel, Sir Robert   205
Perkins, Jane Gray   272
polyphony   5, 231, 233, 255
Priestley, J.B.   13
Pritchett, V.S.   261

Rabelais, François   10–11, 220–1
Racowitza, Helene von   187–204, 205, 272
Racowitza, Yanko von   189, 192
Ramsay, A.A.W.   272
Reade, Charles   47
Reform Act, Second,   111
Richardson, Samuel   5, 150–1
Rimmon-Kenan, Shlomith   257
Risorgimento   77–87
Romance (*see also* Greek Romance)   90–1, 96–7, 100–2, 209–10, 247
Romanticism   44, 121–2, 175
Rossetti, D.G.   60
Rousseau, Jean-Jacques   21, 28, 31–4, 39, 51, 100, 259
Ruskin, John   120
Russian Formalism   179, 181
Rüstow, Colonel von   201–2

Sabor, Peter   44
Sage, Judith Ann   251
Saussure, Ferdinand de   2, 10
Schiller, Friedrich   103

sentimentalism/sentimentality   45, 61–70, 109, 225
Shaheen, Mohammad,   265
Shakespeare, William   21, 28–9, 34, 40, 49, 57, 96–7, 113, 179–80, 197
Shelley, Percy Bysshe   122, 266
Shklovsky, Viktor   181
Short, Michael H.   261
sideward glance (word with a) *see* hidden polemic
Smollett, Tobias   47, 53, 89
Spånberg, Sven-Johan   14, 18, 31–3, 39, 104, 108, 258, 259
speech genres   160, 162, 165–8
Stang, Richard   4
Stendhal   41, 97, 228, 259
Stephen, James Fitzjames   117, 127, 265
Stevenson, Lionel   48, 134, 187–8
Stevenson, Richard G.   26
Stevenson, Robert L.   159, 244, 245, 252, 275
Stone, Donald D.   3, 14, 59–60, 182, 220, 255, 266, 272
Stone, James S.   266
Stubbs, Patricia   5
stylization/parody/pastiche   3, 10, 14, 16, 25–30, 42–6, 51–2, 74, 86, 104–5, 112–14, 118, 120–30, 134–7, 145–6, 150, 152–3, 157–60, 178, 215–16, 230, 234
Sutherland, John   48
Swanson, Donald R.   237
Swift, Jonathan   51, 108, 135
Swinburne, Algernon   77, 78

Tarratt, Margaret   57, 102
Tolstoy, Leo   181, 228
Tompkins, J.M.S.   51
transgredience   32–5, 100

Van Ghent, Dorothy   153, 182
Vice, Sue   273
Voloshinov, V.N.   6, 12, 154–5, 171, 173, 255

White, Allon   5, 18, 35
Wilde, Oscar   1–2, 4

Williams, Carolyn 5, 164, 181–2
Williams, Raymond 94
Wilt, Judith 9, 66, 151–2, 257, 274
Wood, Mrs Henry 74, 158–9

Woolf, Virginia 1, 4, 14
word on display *see* objectified discourse

OHIO UNIVERSITY LIBRARY
Please return this book as soon as you have finished with it. In order to avoid a fine it must be returned by the latest date stamped below. All books are subject to recall after weeks or immediately if